"You're Going to Love This Kid!"

"You're Going to Love This Kid!"

TEACHING STUDENTS WITH AUTISM IN THE INCLUSIVE CLASSROOM

by

Paula Kluth, Ph.D.
Syracuse University

with invited contributors

Jessica Kingsley *Publishers*
London

Jessica Kingsley Publishers
116 Pentonville Road
London N1 9JB
England

www.jkp.com

First published in the United States of America by
Paul H. Brookes Publishing Co., Inc.
Post Office Box 10624
Baltimore, Maryland 21285-0624

www.brookespublishing.com

Typeset by Auburn Associates, Inc.
Baltimore, Maryland.
Manufactured in the United States of America
by Sheridan Press, Springfield, Virginia.

Most of the individuals described herein are composites
or fictional accounts based on actual experiences. Individuals' names
have been changed and identifying details have been altered
to protect their confidentiality.

Cover illustration by Barbara Moran. Ms. Moran is a graphic artist,
presenter, self-advocate, advocate for people with disabilities,
and a person with autism. Her art work has been displayed across
the country. She is currently working on her autobiography.
Her unique and captivating drawings can be purchased on
http://www.karlwilliams.com/moran.htm.

Permission to reprint the following is gratefully acknowledged:

Excerpt from THE DIVING BELL AND THE BUTTERFLY by
Jean-Dominique Bauby, copyright © 1997 by Editions Robert Laffont,
S.A., Paris. Used by permission of Alfred A. Knopf, a division of Random House, Inc.

Excerpt from TEACHER by Sylvia Ashton Warner, copyright © 1963
by Sylvia Ashton Warner. Reprinted with the permission of Simon & Schuster.

Excerpt from THE BOY WHO WOULD BE A HELICOPTER reprinted
by permission of the publisher from THE BOY WHO WOULD BE A
HELICOPTER by Vivan Gussin Paley, pp. 57–58, Cambridge, Mass.: Harvard
University Press, Copyright © 1990 by the President and Fellows of Harvard College.

Excerpt from SCHOOLING WITHOUT LABELS: PARENTS, EDUCATORS,
AND INCLUSIVE EDUCATION, by Douglas Biklen. Reprinted by permission of
Temple University Press. © 1992 by Temple University. All Rights Reserved.

British Library Cataloguing-in-Publication Data are available from the British Library

Kluth, P.
"You're going to love this kid!": teaching students with autism in the inclusive classroom
ISBN 1-84310-175-0

Contents

About the Authors

Paula Kluth, Ph.D., is Assistant Professor in the Department of Teaching and Leadership at Syracuse University in Syracuse, New York. Dr. Kluth has a master's degree in educational policy from the Harvard Graduate School of Education and a doctoral degree in special education from the University of Wisconsin. She is a former special educator who has served as a classroom teacher and inclusion facilitator. She has taught in and engages in research in both elementary and secondary schools. Her professional and research interests center on differentiating instruction and on including students with significant disabilities in inclusive classrooms.

with

Christi Kasa-Hendrickson, Ph.D., is Assistant Professor at the University of Northern Iowa in Cedar Falls in the Department of Special Education. Dr. Kasa-Hendrickson received her doctoral degree from Syracuse University in Syracuse, New York. She is a former elementary school teacher who has focused her career on inclusive education.

Eileen Yoshina, M.Ed., a writer and educator, is currently teaching writing at the South Puget Sound Community College in Olympia, Washington, and is working on her first novel for young adults. Ms. Yoshina holds a master's of education in human development and psychology from Harvard University. A former elementary school general education teacher, Ms. Yoshina has taught in inclusive schools and believes in using an inclusive and social justice orientation in her teaching and educational writing.

Foreword

Paula Kluth is probably the best person around to write a book about how to support autistic children in public schools. She knows the first three rules of education as well as anybody I can think of.

Rule number one is to listen before you talk. And by listen, I don't just mean pretend to listen, but really listen as if you are ready to be told an important secret. The second rule is to love your students. And by love I don't mean like a mom or a pet owner; I mean the love between two people who need each other to make their way through the hard times and the easy times together. The third rule is that there are no rules. And that doesn't mean that nothing really matters; it means that people matter too much to try to make rules about what they need.

So, welcome to this wonderful book. By the time you finish it, you will know what a blessing you might become for a child who has the good luck to meet you.

Eugene Marcus
Syracuse, New York

Author's note: *Eugene Marcus is a man with autism who believes in his own rights and those of others with and without disabilities. He is a product of Syracuse's inclusive school system. He is co-teaching undergraduate courses at Syracuse University, where he also serves as an associate of the Facilitated Communication Institute. Mr. Marcus has written numerous articles and has conducted research on his own means of communication, facilitated communication. He lectures frequently on communication, inclusive schooling, autism, and the rights of people with disabilities.*

Preface

On the morning of my first day of teaching, I was told I would be working with a 6-year-old student with autism named Jacob. I was given dozens of files to review. I marveled at the stacks of reports, evaluations, observations, clinical assessments, work samples, and standardized test results. I couldn't believe a child so small could have so many "credentials." As I reviewed the files my feelings changed from stunned to overwhelmed to terrified. Jacob's paperwork was filled with information about his inability to be a student or a learner. The documents detailed his challenging behaviors, skill deficits, and communication problems. I was dazed—I was scarcely 22 years old, I had only recently graduated from my teacher preparation program, and I remembered little from the one or two lectures I had attended on autism.

Before I could complain to my colleagues or sneak out the back door of the building, I heard my name on the loudspeaker and was beckoned to the school office. I grudgingly made my way down the hallway only to be met halfway by a grinning and extremely animated school administrator. Dr. Patrick Schwarz seized me by the shoulders and said, "So, you're going to be Jacob's teacher. That's fantastic. You're going to LOVE this kid!"

This inspirational leader could not have been more accurate in his assessment of Jacob or the future I would have with this young student. In the next few years, Dr. Schwarz, the school principal, my general education colleagues, Jacob, and the other students in the school all collaborated to create an inclusive environment and experience in the first-grade classroom. The first few weeks of school were a challenge, but the school community worked together to create success for this young man. Administrators shifted classroom schedules to accommodate Jacob's need for a recess break early in the day; students worked to learn Jacob's communication system; teachers created materials and invented lessons that intrigued and engaged their new student; Jacob's family shared their expertise and gave suggestions for making him comfortable in his new school, and Jacob worked daily to meet new friends, learn classroom routines, and participate in lessons.

Though Jacob did not speak, occasionally struggled with challenging behaviors, and needed a wide range of adaptations to engage in curriculum and instruction, he was soon participating and succeeding in all aspects of school life. Through this energetic, precocious, and unique 6-year-old, I learned how to be a teacher—not just of students with autism—but of all learners with and without disabilities in the inclusive classroom.

An important piece of this story is obviously the role of my former administrator, Dr. Patrick Schwarz. His positive attitude and encouraging behaviors influenced my impression of Jacob; inspired me to learn about students in holistic ways; and prompted me to study more about autism, behavior supports, skill instruction, communication needs, and curriculum development.

Unfortunately, the perspective and attitude offered by Dr. Schwarz seems to be rare. The dominant paradigm in educating students with autism has been and continues to be based on deficits, labels, and a positivist tradition. This paradigm was verified by the information in Jacob's files and is exemplified in much of the educational literature, college textbooks, and popular media sources that introduce pre-service teachers to autism (Cowley, 2000; Hallahan & Kauffman, 1994; Leaf & McEachin, 1999; Lovaas, 1981; Maurice, Green, & Luce 1996; Scheuermann & Webber, 2001).

I believe Jacob's story is an appropriate way to illustrate an alternative approach to educating students with autism. Dr. Schwarz's approach to educating Jacob was based on a positive, individualized, and inclusive ideology instead of based only on student needs, failures, and struggles. This anecdote portrays the possibilities that exist when educators see students as part of the school community, view inclusive schooling as a possibility for all learners, and understand "inclusion" as something that can be pursued every day for every student instead of something that is appropriate for some and not others.

This book provides concrete examples of how to plan lessons, engineer a safe and comfortable classroom, provide communication opportunities, and understand and support challenging behaviors. Drawing on classroom and school observations, as well as my own experience as an elementary and high school teacher, I explore pragmatic ways of making schools safe, challenging, and accessible for students with autism spectrum disorders. The chapters are designed to highlight how any student with autism spectrum disorders can be supported to participate in academic instruction, school routines, and social activities.

The book consists of 12 chapters. Each chapter is concerned with a different school issue/structure (e.g., lesson planning, collaboration) and provides concrete examples of how learners with autism can be supported in inclusive schools and classrooms.

Chapter 1 outlines definitions of autism and attempts to illustrate how autism is experienced by individuals with the labels of autism, Asperger's syndrome, and other related labels.

Chapter 2 begins with a description of inclusive schooling and provides information about how teachers and school leaders can work toward inclusive education in both elementary and secondary schools. This chapter also outlines the federal laws related to special education.

The role of the teacher is reviewed in Chapter 3. This chapter explores some of the values and beliefs that support the development and sustenance of inclusive schools.

Chapter 4, co-authored with Eileen Yoshina, features voices of families of students with autism and gives ideas for partnering with mothers, fathers, siblings, and other family members in respectful and meaningful ways.

In Chapter 5, I share specific strategies helpful in the creation of a positive, safe, and comfortable educational environment. Ideas for arranging and organizing classrooms are provided as well as information related to controlling and adjusting classroom lighting, sounds, temperature, and smells.

Chapter 6 contains ideas for building classroom community and supporting the development of social relationships of all students in the inclusive classroom. This chapter also details some of the specific relationship-related struggles encountered by individuals with autism.

Supporting a student's communication is critical; if a teacher in an inclusive classroom wants to develop better curriculum and instruction for a student, find more effective and sensitive ways to address his or her behavior, or learn more about his or her social needs, the teacher needs to be able to bring out that student's "voice." Chapter 7 illustrates different ways student communication can be bolstered and supported in the inclusive classroom. Different types of augmentative and alternative communication are also described in this chapter.

Although students with autism are increasingly being educated in general education classrooms, they are often excluded from rich and meaningful literacy experiences such as reading and writing stories, book clubs, acting and performing, journaling, and whole-class and small-group discussions. In Chapter 8, I explore why students with autism may not be receiving the literacy instruction they need or deserve and explore several different ways educators might promote literacy development for students with autism.

The focus of Chapter 9 is behavior. In this chapter, behavior is explored from an alternative perspective. Instead of examining how to stop or treat behaviors, I present behavior as something that must be understood in context and interpreted carefully. Positive ways to support a range of behaviors are provided throughout the chapter.

Chapter 10 contains tools and structures to assist educators in planning lessons appropriate both for students with autism and related disabilities and for all learners in inclusive classrooms. A step-by-step process is provided for teaching a wide range of learners in diverse schools.

Chapter 11, "Teaching Strategies," is co-authored with Christi Kasa-Hendrickson, a professor of education and a former elementary classroom teacher. This chapter is a collection of classroom-tested ideas that can be used either with all students in the classroom, for a handful of students, or for any individual student who needs something extra or something different in classroom materials, daily instruction, or in curriculum.

Chapter 12 is focused on collaboration and teaming. Teachers truly committed to an inclusive schooling agenda need the expertise and support of others; this chapter gives these educators suggestions for working with all team members and tips for structuring the collaborative classroom.

I believe this book is unique in that most texts related to teaching students with autism

- Do not include information or ideas useful for today's diverse, inclusive classrooms
- View autism and autism spectrum disorders from a medical model and/or a deficit perspective; that is, most books focus on diagnosis and the limitations of the disability
- Treat communication, behavior, and learning problems as things that "belong" to students instead of as issues that must be understood in context and within relationships
- Lack perspectives, ideas, and suggestions from individuals with autism and autism spectrum disorders and their families

"You're Going To Love This Kid" alternatively

- Focuses exclusively on inclusive schooling
- Views inclusion as both an ideology and a pedagogy
- Proposes sensitive new ways to see and understand students with autism
- Stresses how students with autism can participate in the curriculum and instruction in the inclusive classroom if appropriately and creatively supported
- Includes frameworks, approaches, and strategies useful for teachers, administrators, and other school personnel (e.g., therapists, counselors, volunteers)
- Features the voices of those with autism and autism spectrum disorders

As I speak with colleagues in schools and universities, many seasoned veterans of both secondary and primary classrooms understand how to include students with learning disabilities, cognitive disabilities, emotional disabilities, and physical disabilities in general education classrooms, but they remain puzzled as to how to support and teach students with autism in these same environments and learning experiences. This book is written for this audience—those committed to inclusive schooling and looking for answers.

REFERENCES

Cowley, G. (2000, July 23). Understanding Autism. *Newsweek.*

Hallahan, D., & Kauffman, J. (1994). *Exceptional children: Introduction to special education.* Boston: Allyn & Bacon.

Leaf, R., McEachin, J., Harsh, J.D., & Boehm, M. (1999). *A work in progress: Behavior management strategies and a curriculum for intensive behavioral treatment of autism.* New York: DRL Press.

Lovaas, O.I. (1981). *Teaching developmentally disabled children: The ME book.* Austin, TX: PRO-ED.

Maurice, C., Green, G., & Luce, S.C. (1996). *Behavioral intervention for young children with autism: A manual for parents and professionals.* Austin, TX: PRO-ED.

Scheuermann, B., & Webber, J. (2001). *Autism: Teaching does make a difference.* Florence, KY: Wadsworth Publishing.

Acknowledgments

Many people helped to shape and write this book. I am indebted, first and foremost, to all of the students with whom I work, but especially to Jason, Andrew, Franklin, Paul, Caleb, Kelsey, Michael, and their families. You were the first to teach me about autism.

Many other friends and colleagues with the label of autism have helped me to think critically about dis/ability, including Mark Van Boxtel, Barb Moran, Jamie Burke, Jon Micheal, Christie Sauer, Roy Bedward, Sean Sokler, and Hesham Khater. The families of individuals with autism have also been incredibly generous with their time and energy; their stories and teachings have been invaluable.

I would like to thank the administrators, teachers, paraprofessionals, and staff of Kruse Education Center in Orland Park, Illinois. The teachers at Kruse taught me how to teach and crafted many of the strategies shared in this book. I am especially grateful for the support of Barbara Schaffer and Peg Sheehan during my first year of teaching. Thanks also go to Dr. Patrick Schwarz, who first told me "You are going to LOVE this kid!" My colleagues at Stoner Prairie Elementary School in Verona, Wisconsin, also taught me a great deal about supporting diverse learners. Special thanks go to my second-grade team and specifically to Erin DiPerna.

Several mentors have shaped my thinking about autism and inclusive schooling. My work is based on the ideas and writings of Dr. Lou Brown and Dr. Alice Udvari-Solner. My thinking about autism has also been shaped by Sue Rubin, Eugene Marcus, Dr. Anne Donnellan, Dr. Douglas Biklen, and Dr. Mayer Shevin. I am grateful for their guidance and mentorship and for engaging in work that has made such a positive impact in the fields of autism, curriculum and instruction, educational policy, special education, and disability studies. These acknowledgments would not be complete without mentioning the hard work and innovation of the students at Syracuse University. So much of this material comes from my experiences teaching future educators; I am grateful to my students for asking great questions and for working as change agents in public schools every day.

I am indebted to the friends who read pieces of this manuscript and gave thoughtful feedback: Kelly Chandler, Tracy Knight, Gail Gibson (Kelly's mom), Matt Grant, Kathy Kurowski, Lori and Bernie Micheal, Janna Woods, Sally Young, Nancy Rice, Christi Kasa-Hendrickson, and Eileen Yoshina. Each one of you gave something unique and important to this project.

My mother, Mary, read and lived this book for many months; she offered helpful feedback, gave loving encouragement, and asked smart and thoughtful questions about the project for more than a year. My sister, Victoria, has been encouraging me to write this book for nearly 10 years. I thank her for her faith in this project and in me. I am also grateful to Todd for great program management, wonderful technical support, and incredible grace and wisdom.

Kind thanks go to Barry Prizant for reviewing this work more than once and giving such insightful feedback. And last but not least, I am grateful to those at Paul

H. Brookes Publishing Co. for the time and care that they invested in this project. Thank you to Melissa Behm, Rebecca Lazo, Elaine Niefeld, Jessica Reighard, Lisa Yurwit, Leslie Eckard, Rebecca Torres, and Amy Kopperude—you have all been incredibly supportive and patient. Special gratitude goes out to former Brookes editor Lisa Benson, who brought me the idea for this book and convinced me to write it.

To all of those individuals with autism who have written autobiographical works and shared their experiences—without your thoughts and ideas, this text and others like it would not be possible.

*To Franklin Wilson, a gifted and patient teacher,
and to Pat Wilson, my teacher's teacher*

CHAPTER 1

Defining Autism

Autistic children don't deserve to be molded into someone
they are not. They deserve to learn and grow, and feel comfortable
about themselves. Their worlds can expand to include new experiences, and
they can become teachers, opening others to their viewpoints. (O'Neill, 1997, p. 1)

A teacher recently called me to ask a question about a new student in her eighth-grade classroom. The teacher wanted to know more about the student, who had been diagnosed as having autism[1], and wanted the other students to feel comfortable with their new classmate. For these reasons, the teacher asked me if I thought it would be a good idea to have the social worker do a classroom presentation on autism or to have the student's parents come in and answer questions about disabilities. I asked her if the student had a reliable way to communicate. The teacher told me that, yes, the student could speak and was actually quite verbal and engaging. Then I asked the teacher about the student's needs and ideas. Specifically I wanted to know if the student with autism wanted the social worker or her parents to visit the classroom. The teacher answered, "I don't know, I didn't ask her."

Too often, teachers forget to tap into the most important resource of all: students with autism and their families. Sonny, one of my former colleagues, learned this lesson when he was told that he would have a student with autism in his third-grade classroom. For weeks he called me on the telephone, pestering me to send him a textbook about autism. I resisted, fearing that he would have one of two responses. He would either 1) see the medical/technical definitions and fear he was "not qualified" to teach a student with autism or 2) read the text and declare himself quite ready to serve as an expert on the topic. Neither of these outcomes, I reasoned, would be good news for Ronnie, his new student.

Before I could figure out how to appease Sonny, he called to tell me that Ronnie's family had invited him to dinner. The apprehensive teacher accepted the invitation and spent 3 hours in the family home getting to know Ronnie. When Sonny came back to school the next day, he was feeling more confident about being Ronnie's teacher. He told me all about Ronnie's ability to use a complex communication system (a series of signs and gestures), his ability to play complicated video games, and his interest in building card houses.

---

[1]I generally use the words "autism" or "autism spectrum" throughout this book when referring to students with any label related to autism; all of the information, suggestions, ideas, and recommendations also apply to students with Asperger's syndrome, PDD-NOS, and the other disabilities I have highlighted in this chapter.

In getting to know Ronnie as an individual, my colleague was practicing what Kliewer and Biklen called *local understanding*, which is "a radically deep, intimate knowledge of another human being" (2001, p. 4). The intimacy of the relationship, these researchers claimed, is important because "it allows those in positions of relative authority or power to see in idiosyncratic behavior demonstrations of understanding that are otherwise dismissed or disregarded by more distant observers" (p. 4). This means that getting to know Ronnie in a personal way and seeing him as an individual helped Sonny generate effective supports. It also helped the teacher serve as an advocate for Ronnie. When the technology teacher suggested that instruction using computers would be too difficult for Ronnie, Sonny objected, citing the student's video game prowess as an example of his abilities in problem-solving, fine motor control, and complex thinking. The technology teacher agreed to include Ronnie in the lessons and was pleasantly surprised when Sonny and Ronnie proved him wrong.

WHAT IS AUTISM?

One of the first questions a teacher wants answered when he or she learns that a student with autism is coming into the classroom is "What is autism?" Autism is a difficult term to define because the disability is complex and no two individuals with the label of autism experience it in the same way. Although many people with the label of autism have much in common, they tend to have more differences than commonalities. For example, some individuals with autism appear to welcome touch, while others find it painful. Some students crave interaction and social situations, while others need more space and time alone. Some are extremely talkative, while others cannot use speech reliably. It is critical to remember that students with autism vary widely in experiences, skills, abilities, interests, characteristics, gifts, talents, and needs. If you know one person with autism, you know ONE person with autism. For these reasons, I offer several descriptions of autism and many interpretations of the disability from different perspectives.

What the Experts Say

I begin with the most important and useful definitions of autism—those that come from people with autism, experts who experience the disability every day, who know what it feels like to have a disability label, and who struggle with societal notions of normalcy:

Autism isn't something a person *has*, or a "shell" that a person is trapped inside. There's no normal child hidden behind the autism. Autism is a way of being. It is pervasive: It colors every experience, every sensation, perception, thought, emotion, and encounter, every aspect of existence. It is not possible to separate the autism from the person—and if it were possible, the person you'd have left would not be the same person you started with. (Sinclair, 1993, p. 1)

We live in a country where image is kind of a reality more real than reality. My main answer to that is: I don't need surgery to make me real any more than a beautiful woman "really" needs her eyelids sewn back. The fact that I think I do and she thinks she does is more fairy tale than real. Eagerness to be like others didn't make Pinocchio real—it turned him into a donkey! And eagerness by parents to cure autism or retardation or compulsiveness will not drive great distances toward the final solution to the actual problem. Because the person who believes "I will be real when I am normal," will always be *almost* a person, but will never make it all the way. (Marcus, 1998, p. 2)

Autism means having to watch how I feel every second that I am awake. Autism means having challenges when I leave the room fearing that others will say unkind things about me to other people. Autism means being dateless on weekends as well as constant loneliness, only watching TV on Saturday night. Autism means not being able to fit in on social peer relations. However, autism, in my case, means that I have a calendar memory for birthdays, being articulate and having skills. I, all in all, would rather be autistic than normal. (Ronan, as cited in Gillingham, 1995, p. 90)

Some aspects of autism may be good or bad depending only on how they are perceived. For example, hyperfocussing is a problem if you're hyperfocusing on your feet and miss the traffic light change. On the other hand, hyperfocusing is a great skill for working on intensive projects. This trait is particularly well suited to freelancers and computer work.

I would never argue that autism is all good or merely a difference. I do find that my autism is disabling. However, that doesn't mean that it is all bad or that I want to be cured. I may not be altogether happy with who I am, but that doesn't mean I want to be someone else. (Molton, 2000)

One foot in and one foot out
　is what Asperger's is all about
Sometimes I think why me;
　other times I think it's the best way to be
A little different from the rest
　makes you think you're second best
Nobody quite understanding
　a hard life which is very demanding.
I look like any other child
　but little things just make me wild. (Royal, as cited in Attwood, 1998, p. 42)

I believe Autism is a marvelous occurrence of nature, not a tragic example of the human mind gone wrong. In many cases, Autism can also be a kind of genius undiscovered. (O'Neill, 1999, p. 14)

One of the most notable aspects of the definitions put forward by people with autism is the fact that so many individuals across subgroups and labels define autism by the gifts it brings them. This is not to say that everyone who experiences autism always experiences it as something positive. In fact, many individuals with autism describe it as something very difficult and painful at times. I highlight the positive spin that some put on their definitions, however, to show the discrepancies that often occur among traditional ways of viewing autism and the ways of knowing employed by people with the label of autism. Consider a few more ways in which some individuals with autism and Asperger's syndrome describe the gifts associated with their "dis/ability":

I like being different. I prefer having AS to being normal. I don't have the foggiest idea exactly what it is I like about AS. I think that people with AS see things differently. I also think they see them more clearly. (Hall, 2001, p. 15)

We can describe a situation like no one else. We can tell you what intangibles feel like and secret flavors taste like. We can describe for you, in unbelievable depth, the intricate details of our favorite obsessions. (Willey, 2001, p. 29)

Glancing at the ground as I walked along, I noticed some movement at my feet and saw the last exit moments of a cicada crawling out of a hole in the ground. I watched this creature transform before my eyes from a dull brownish-green bug into a beautiful bright green and gold, singing creation. The process took only one and a half hours. I have since heard that people thought my standing in the heat for one and a half hours to watch an insect was a crazy thing to do. I think it is they who are crazy. By choosing not to stand and watch, they missed out on sharing an experience that was so beautiful and exhilarating. (Lawson, 1998, p. 115)

The Medical Model

As of 2003, when this book was published, no biological markers were associated with autism; therefore, the categories and descriptions provided have been constructed and culturally reproduced based on the judgment and opinion of scholars, researchers, and the medical community. Put more succinctly, the following definitions or labels "represent efforts to classify and think about the problems developing children may encounter" (Contract Consultants, IAC, 1977, p. 8) but they are limited in that they can give us little information about individual learners and their needs. A student's label should never drive curriculum, instruction, assessment, and supports. Any learner's educational program should be based on his or her individual characteristics and abilities. A disability label can, however, give teachers a starting point for learning about a student's needs.

Autism Spectrum Disorders

Autism is often referred to as a *spectrum disorder*—that is, a disorder in which symptoms can occur in many varieties and with varying degrees of intensity. Autism, first described in the 1940s by American psychiatrist Leo Kanner, is the third most common developmental disability behind mental retardation and cerebral palsy. Some sources report that autism affects 2–7 of every 10,000 children (see Fombonne, 1999). A 1996 study by the Centers for Disease Control and Prevention, however, indicated that the rate could be as high as 2–3 in every 1,000 children in some parts of the country.

Autism typically appears before a child reaches the age of 3, although it is not always diagnosed until the child is age 4 or older, if ever. It is four to five times more likely in boys than in girls (Powers, 1989).

Autism has traditionally been defined by terms outlined in medical literature. According to the *Diagnostic and Statistical Manual of Mental Disorders-Fourth Edition-Text Revision* (DSM-IV-TR) (American Psychological Association, 2000), a reference book designed to provide guidelines for the diagnosis and classification of mental disorders, individuals with autism have "delayed or abnormal functioning" in at least one of the following areas:

- Social interaction
- Communication
- Patterns of behavior (e.g., restricted, repetitive, stereotyped), interests, and activities

Table 1.1 provides more details of the DSM-IV-TR diagnostic criteria for autism.

Asperger's Syndrome Asperger's syndrome is a label given to some learners who fall within the autistic spectrum. Students labeled with Asperger's syndrome typically experience communication differences, struggle with change and transitions, and have intense and absorbing areas of interest. These students often exhibit excellent rote memory skills (e.g., figures, facts, dates). Many also

Table 1.1. DSM-IV-TR definition of autism

A. A total of six (or more) items from (1), (2), and (3), with at least two from (1), and one each from (2) and (3):

  (1) qualitative impairment in social interaction, as manifested by at least two of the following:
    (a) marked impairment in the use of multiple nonverbal behaviors, such as eye-to-eye gaze, facial expression, body postures, and gestures to regulate social interaction
    (b) failure to develop peer relationships appropriate to developmental level
    (c) a lack of spontaneous seeking to share enjoyment, interests, or achievements with other people (e.g., by a lack of showing, bringing, or pointing out objects of interest)
    (d) lack of social or emotional reciprocity

  (2) qualitative impairments in communication as manifested by at least one of the following:
    (a) delay in, or total lack of, the development of spoken language (not accompanied by an attempt to compensate through alternative modes of communication such as gesture or mime)
    (b) in individuals with adequate speech, marked impairment in the ability to initiate or sustain a conversation with others
    (c) stereotyped and repetitive use of language or idiosyncratic language
    (d) lack of varied, spontaneous make-believe play or social imitative play appropriate to developmental level

  (3) restricted, repetitive, and stereotyped patterns of behavior, interests, and activities as manifested by at least one of the following:
    (a) encompassing preoccupation with one or more stereotyped and restricted patterns of interest that is abnormal either in intensity or focus
    (b) apparently inflexible adherence to specific, nonfunctional routines or rituals
    (c) stereotyped and repetitive motor mannerisms (e.g., hand or finger flapping or twisting, or complex whole-body movements)
    (d) persistent preoccupation with parts of objects

B. Delays or abnormal functioning in at least one of the following areas, with onset prior to age 3 years: (1) social interaction, (2) language as used in social communication, or (3) symbolic or imaginative play.

C. The disturbance is not better accounted for by Rett's Disorder or Childhood Disintegrative Disorder.

have exceptional interest and ability in math and science. Students who are labeled with Asperger's syndrome may go undiagnosed for years and may be seen by others as simply quirky or eccentric. Table 1.2 provides more details of the DSM-IV-TR diagnostic criteria for Asperger's syndrome.

Although Asperger's syndrome was once seen as a disability or label distinct and separate from autism, it is now understood as a variant of autism, although it has its own diagnostic criteria. Some characterize Asperger's syndrome as mild autism, but this characterization of "mild" may not take into account the complexities of looking typical but having other types of misunderstood differences. Luke Jackson (2002), in his wonderfully informative book *Freaks, Geeks, and Asperger Syndrome: A User Guide to Adolescence*, challenged the notion of "mild autism":

> AS [Asperger's syndrome] is usually described as a mild form of autism but, believe me, though the good outweighs the bad there are some bits that most certainly are not mild. AS people reading this, do you feel as if you only have a "mild"problem when you are having one of those days where you feel as if you may well be from another planet? (p. 21)

Kalen Molton appears to agree with Jackson. She has shared that some of the ways in which others have discounted the significance of her Asperger's syndrome have caused her great stress:

Table 1.2. DSM-IV-TR definition of Asperger's syndrome

A. Qualitative impairment in social interaction, as manifested by at least two of the following:

   (1) marked impairment in the use of multiple nonverbal behaviors such as eye-to-eye gaze, facial expression, body postures, and gestures to regulate social interaction

   (2) failure to develop peer relationships appropriate to developmental level

   (3) a lack of spontaneous seeking to share enjoyment, interests, or achievements with other people (e.g., by a lack of showing, bringing, or pointing out objects of interest to other people)

   (4) lack of social or emotional reciprocity

B. Restricted, repetitive, and stereotyped patterns of behavior, interests, and activities, as manifested by at least one of the following:

   (1) encompassing preoccupation with one or more stereotyped and restricted patterns of interest that is abnormal either in intensity or focus

   (2) apparently inflexible adherence to specific, nonfunctional routines or rituals

   (3) stereotyped and repetitive motor mannerisms (e.g., hand or finger flapping or twisting, or complex whole-body movements)

   (4) persistent preoccupation with parts of objects

C. The disturbance causes clinically significant impairment in social, occupational, or other important areas of functioning.

D. There is no clinically significant general delay in language (e.g., single words used by age 2 years, communicative phrases used by age 3 years).

E. There is no clinically significant delay in cognitive development or in the development of age-appropriate self-help skills, adaptive behavior (other than in social interaction), and curiosity about the environment in childhood.

F. Criteria are not met for another specific Pervasive Developmental Disorder or Schizophrenia.

No matter how high functioning we are, a great deal of effort is going into coping. Some people have called Asperger syndrome "nerd disorder" as a way of minimizing it. There is a fine line between "normal but odd" and "very high functioning autistic." My personal opinion is that the line is where the traits become disabling. I have a very good "guest mode" where I can appear quite normal; however, being forced to sustain guest mode for an extended period can, and has, led to a serious breakdown. My ability to behave near normally at times has led others to believe that I can do it all the time and if I don't then I am lazy, unmotivated, manipulative, and deliberately annoying. No one expects a tightrope walker to do it all the time. (2000)

Other Disability Labels Related to Autism A few other labels in addition to autism and Asperger's syndrome are given to people who have "autistic-like" characteristics. Sometimes students do not meet the DSM-IV-TR criteria, but they do have learning, communication, behavioral, or other differences and need supports similar to those experienced by students with the labels of autism and Asperger's syndrome. These learners have other labels such as pervasive developmental disorder-not otherwise specified (PDD-NOS) and childhood disintegrative disorder.

Students with Rett syndrome, Williams syndrome, fragile X syndrome, and Landau-Kleffner syndrome also share characteristics with students with autism. Students with these diagnoses may have some of the same needs as those with the label of autism and may benefit from the strategies and ideas shared in this book.

Diagnosis and Labeling: Important Considerations

Diagnostic labels such as autism, Asperger's syndrome, and PDD-NOS can be very helpful; they can provide individuals with disabilities, families, educators, and researchers with a common language and framework and connect people to resources, information, funding, and services. In addition, labels can provide a starting point for educators in terms of making connections and having conversations. An overreliance on these labels, however, can serve as a barrier to understanding students as individuals and can lead teachers and others to believe that disability categories are static, meaningful, and well understood when in fact they are none of these things. Great caution should be exercised in assigning and using labels.

Because labels are subject to change at any time and because they are in many ways experimental, some families and professionals have started to use the broader term *autism spectrum* as a way of including all of the labels that are connected to autism. Although this label has many of the same problems as others, it may help educators move away from understanding autism, Asperger's syndrome, PDD-NOS, and other labels as distinct and separate disability areas. The more that is uncovered about autism, the more unclear the distinctions among types of autism become. Because we are learning new facts about the autism spectrum every day, at this point we can only be sure of three things: 1) we have very little information on this disability; we *don't* know more than we *do* know (Anne Donnellan, personal communication, May 2, 2002); 2) we will have new definitions, terminology, understandings, and conceptual knowledge in the near future; and 3) many of the things we feel we understand will prove to be wrong. For these reasons, it is important to be aware of some of the cautions or problems associated with defining autism and labeling students.

Consider: (How Much) Does a Particular Diagnosis Matter? Some debate exists as to the usefulness of differentiating one "type" of autism from another. For example, some question the usefulness of using the label Asperger's syndrome instead of autism. Some professionals insist that using the "right" label is crucial in understanding student needs and characteristics and in giving students appropriate supports. Labeling, however, is tricky business. Because autism, Asperger's syndrome, and PDD-NOS cannot be diagnosed by any definitive medical tests, labels are assigned based on questionnaires, rating scales, psychological tests, and other instruments and tools. This means that there is a large degree of judgment and bias in diagnosing and labeling; the process is very subjective.

I have heard stories of families going from one professional to the next looking for clarification on their child's label: Is it autism? Is it Asperger's syndrome? Is it something else? One mother asked me to visit her daughter and then proceeded to ask me if I thought she had autism or Asperger's syndrome. I told her that diagnosing and testing children wasn't something I normally did as an educator, but I asked her to tell me what she thought about her daughter's label. As we ended the conversation, I asked her only one question: "What would you do differently tomorrow if you called this autism instead of Asperger's syndrome?"

Diagnosis does not necessarily provide families, teachers, or other professionals with useful information about what needs or abilities the student has or how to teach him or her most effectively. If a student has behavioral, communication, or sensory differences, he or she will still have these same characteristics after diagnosis. Furthermore, having a diagnosis of autism or PDD-NOS or Asperger's syndrome does not predict the particular difficulties that an individual will have or give families or teachers much information about that individual's prognosis or potential.

What Do We Learn from Assessments?

In many cases, assumptions are made about students based on their performance on diagnostic tests. Use of testing tools is a problem for many students with autism for a variety of reasons. Some students have difficulty manipulating materials, communicating, or responding to directions in typical ways. For example, a student with autism may be asked to "draw a triangle" as part of an assessment. The student may know what a triangle is but be unable to draw it; in this situation, the test will not reveal what the child *knows*; the assessor will learn only that the student cannot *draw a triangle on command*. Likewise, a child being assessed might be asked to examine pictures of four animals and choose the picture of the horse. Again, if the child knows which picture is the horse but has no reliable pointing response, she will "fail" that item. Because many students with autism struggle with motor control, these learners will be unable to perform on these tests, and, in many cases, they will be seen as lazy, slow, or even as having mental retardation.

When I was a student teacher in a high school, I was asked to accompany Caleb, a teenage boy with autism, to an evaluation. As part of the testing, Caleb was given a diagnostic test. The instrument used was a nonverbal, multiple-choice test designed to evaluate the hearing vocabulary or receptive knowledge of vocabulary. The test required students to study four pictures at a time and answer increasingly difficult questions about the pictures. Early questions in the test asked students only to identify a picture (e.g., "Which one is the horse?"). Subsequent questions tapped into higher order thinking and required the test taker to know about properties, qualities, or uses of the items/things pictured (e.g., "Which one eats grass?"). Caleb didn't make it to the complex, higher order questions. He got most of the items in the first five questions wrong because he failed to point at anything, and, in response to the next two questions, he stabbed at "incorrect" pictures. During the entire assessment, Caleb wiggled in his seat, moved out of his chair several times, and placed his cheek against the testing pictures twice. It was difficult to tell if he was uncomfortable, excited, confused, or unable to perform the task expected of him. On the last test item, the examiner asked Caleb to show her "the light bulb." He was being asked to choose from four pictures (horse, dollhouse, umbrella, light bulb). Caleb put his face close to the pictures again, perhaps in an attempt to see them better (the student also had low vision). Then he grabbed the table lamp in front of him and shook it wildly. The examiner took the lamp from Caleb and gently asked him to continue with the test. Again she asked him, "Show me the light bulb," and again Caleb grabbed and shook the lamp.

I suggested to the examiner that Caleb might be showing her "the light" in the only way he could. She agreed that he might be using the lamp to show his understanding, but she explained that she could not know for sure. She did note his response in the testing materials, but Caleb received a very low score on the test. Although that examiner saw Caleb's ability, the next person who reads his test scores will only see a number.

Assessment is also problematic in that the professionals assessing the students sometimes do not know the student well and therefore do not understand the student's communication abilities or needs. Consider the story of Wendy Robinson, who took her son to the doctor's office for an assessment only to be questioned and ultimately insulted by a professional assessing her son:

Our next referral was to a doctor who was attached to the pediatric unit on a part-time basis to assess problems similar to Grant's. She asked me lots of questions and gave Grant simple tests to do. He failed miserably at most things. He was not in the mood today to perform in his usual contrary way. She asked me if he held his hands in the air when I removed his clothes before bath or bed.

"Yes," I replied.

"Are you sure?" she retorted. "I can't believe he does that." (1999, p. 21)

Of course, many professionals are conscientious and understand the need to collaborate closely with other professionals and families, but even the most sensitive educators should reflect on what types of values, beliefs, and expectations they are bringing to an assessment. Everyone involved in the process should be committed to a team approach that is student and family centered. Furthermore, students should be assessed using a range of authentic tools including observations across environments; interviews with family members; and, if possible, interviews with the student.

Where Do Most Definitions of Autism Come From?

In her insightful text, *Autism: A New Understanding*, Gail Gillingham challenged the ways in which most definitions of autism have been constructed. The primary flaw in most definitions, she contends, is the lack of "direct experience" that has informed descriptions of autism. Comparing the definition of depression with that of autism, Gillingham pointed out that only the former seems to have been informed by the perspectives of individuals experiencing the condition or disability:

> When we look at the criteria for depression, we find it includes symptoms such as recurrent thoughts of death, markedly diminished interest or pleasure in all activities, and feelings of worthlessness. The criterion for Social Phobia includes the symptoms of a marked and persistent fear of social situations, the recognition that this fear is excessive and irrational and that exposure to the feared situation provokes anxiety. None of these symptoms can be determined without taking the actual experience of the person who is diagnosed into account.
>
> This does not happen with autism, Asperger's syndrome, or PDD-NOS. There is no mention at all of the actual experience of autism in the DSM-IV. Instead, individuals rely completely on their own observations to diagnose the condition. Do we see an impairment in communication? Do we experience an impairment in social interaction? The repetitive and stereotypic behaviors are observed and measured directly from our viewpoint. No one has taken the time or effort to include anything from the actual experience of the autistics. I assume this is because we do not believe that they are capable of sharing anything useful. However, if the direct experience of those who are diagnosed with depression or social phobia is considered valuable information, why are we not accessing the same from those who have autism? I expect that this lack of input from direct experience invalidates the whole process of diagnosis. It would be fascinating for me to see how autistic people would choose to rewrite this section of the DSM-IV. I am certain it would not look the same if they had the opportunity to add their comments. (2000, p. 169)

Indeed, the DSM-IV-TR and other standard definitions of autism appear to communicate not only an "outsider" perspective but also one that is too heavily focused on deficits. In reading most definitions of autism, one learns only what a person cannot do and little about possible strengths or abilities. The language used in definitions and diagnosis is problematic for another reason. Leary and Hill (1996) pointed out that this diagnostic language is often filled with assumptions that can be incorrect or even damaging. For the purpose of diagnosis, behaviors are often described with phrases such as "prefers to," "failure to," or "unusual interest in" without specifying what particular symptoms may lead to that impression.

As Leary and Hill indicated, how can an observer (especially one who does not have an intimate knowledge of the child) know if a child "prefers" to play alone. Perhaps the child prefers to play with his sister but is playing alone because the sister is wearing a lotion or cologne that bothers his sensory system. Or perhaps he is playing alone because he is not sure how to "enter" the game she is playing with neighbor children. Language commonly used in diagnostic testing and reporting should be questioned for these reasons.

Liane Holliday Willey, a woman with Asperger's syndrome who disagrees with the ways in which she is often characterized, proposed more sensitive and hopeful way to see individuals with autism spectrum labels:

According to the most potent educational, medical and psychological policy makers in the world, Asperger's syndrome is a disability. I only accept the term "disability" because it is the password that opens the doors to the support and intervention services we Aspies [people with Asperger's syndrome] need if we are to meet our potential. If it was practical, I would wish the word away, at least when it is used in a sentence with AS. The word comes with too many negative images. Picture—powerless, incompetent, weak, helpless, pathetic, useless, and incapable. Think—hopeless and doomed. I will not buy into the notion that AS is a dead-end diagnosis. I like to say Aspies are not defective but that we are simply different; differently able, if you will. Yes, we have learning inefficiencies, but never are we without the ability to learn, grow, cope and progress. Pushed further, I would assert we Aspies are fine like we are, or at least we would be if only society would learn to be more accepting and empathetic toward the atypical. (2001, pp. 138–139)

COMMON CHARACTERISTICS OF INDIVIDUALS WITH AUTISM

Although no two students with autism look, behave, communicate, or learn in the same way, students with autism do share some general characteristics. Some of the most significant characteristics are shared in this section.

Movement Differences

Movement differences describe symptoms involving both excessive, atypical movement and the loss of typical movement. Movement differences involve difficulties with starting, executing, and switching movements. These difficulties may impede postures, actions, speech, thoughts, perceptions, emotions, and memories (Donnellan & Leary, 1995; Leary & Hill, 1996). Individuals with movement differences may walk with an uneven gait, engage in excessive movements (e.g., rocking, hand flapping, pacing), produce speech that is unintentional, stutter, or struggle to make transitions from room to room or situation to situation.

Many individuals with autism experience these movement problems constantly. Although many people without autism struggle to combine thoughts and movements, engage in excessive pencil-tapping or nail biting, get lost in repetitive or obsessive thoughts, or sing the same tune repeatedly without realizing it, they are seldom significantly affected by these experiences.

A movement difference can cause difficulties with the dynamics of movement such as in starting, executing (e.g., speed, control, target, rate), continuing, stopping, combining, or switching movements. The complexity of disturbed movements may range from simple to those affecting overall levels of activity and behavior. Many individuals who experience movement disturbance report differences in internal mental processes such a perception, changes in attention, consciousness, motivation, and emotion.

Different ways of moving can be incredibly frustrating for the people who experience them and confusing for those who observe them. According to Donnellan and Leary, atypical movements often mask the competence of individuals who exhibit them and may have an impact on a person's ability to communicate and relate to others. For example, "delay in responding or inability to regulate movements may affect the ability to turn attention from one event to another in a timely fashion, or use conventional signs of communication" (1995, p. 42). In many cases, these movement differences are assumed by observers to be symptoms of mental retardation (Donnellan & Leary, 1995).

Understanding and recognizing movement differences can help teachers to better support students and to prevent them from making false and damaging assumptions about learners with autism. For instance, a teacher who is unaware of a student's movement problems might assume that a student who is gazing up at the ceiling or pacing in the back of the room is not attending to a lecture. A teacher who is aware of the student's movement differences, however, may not jump to such a conclusion. A friend of mine, Christie, will stand up, screech, and run around the room when she gets together with family. Because the family has become familiar with Christie's movement differences and because Christie has been able to explain some of her behavior to her family, they do not assume she is asocial or unable to understand the family's conversations. Instead, they assume that Christie is interested in being part of the group and include her in every way they can. Seeing movement in this context can prevent teachers from making uninformed interpretations of other people's motives and intent. Consider, for example, how some people with autism describe their movement differences:

I never really know when sounds are coming out of my mouth or when my arms need to move or when my legs need to run and jump. I also have a hard time controlling my thoughts when someone is not helping me focus. You see my mind is very active and thoughts jump around like popcorn being popped. I have very interesting thoughts. It's just that they keep firing off so fast that it's hard to stop them unless someone helps to focus my attention on something. You can imagine how hard it is to get anything done with a roller coaster mind without any clear destination.

My eyes are unable to move up and down and left to right at will without me moving my head in the directions I'm facing. I can see things really well from the corner of my eyes. When I look at someone facing me sometimes I see three eyes instead of two, and it looks scary [sic] so I avoid directly looking at people sometimes. This makes it hard for people to know whether I'm paying attention. (Fihe, 2000, p. 1)

How to conduct my self when the body is constantly trying to find some stability? By this I mean to say that some times I felt that my body was made of just my head while sometimes I felt that it was made of just my legs. It was very difficult to feel the complete body when I was not doing anything. (Mukhopadhyay, 2000, p. 73)

At school I was more direct in how I expressed my irritation and scorn, getting flushed, giggling uncontrollably, running around the room and biting my hand. (Blackman, 2001, p. 127)

Stereotypical movements aren't things I decide to do for a reason; they're things that happen by themselves when I'm not paying attention to my body. (Cessaroni & Garber, as cited in Donnellan & Leary, 1995, p. 53)

Constantly asking questions was another of my annoying fixations, and I'd ask the same question and wait with pleasure for the same answer—over and over again. If a particular topic intrigued me, I zeroed in on that subject and talked it into the ground. (Grandin, 1996a, p. 35)

Sometimes I am just not able to contain my actions and myself. Ninety percent of an autistic person's efforts while in public are spent trying to avoid inappropriate behaviors that "normal" people seem to be able to easily suppress. One place where I had a terrible time trying to sit still and not make noise was in the small theater watching the play *The Diviners*.

    I didn't have a terrible time at the play, quite the contrary. In fact, I loved this play. Deep into the drama, I relaxed my guard and was soon a noisy, rocking back and forth in my seat, spectator. Good things don't often cause this reaction, so we might say that the Ian Weatherbee behavior-o-meter registered a four-star reading for *The Diviners* and its excellent cast. (Weatherbee, 1999, p. 2)

But I am not hurting anyone when I scream
and I need to do it so much to get my balance
perhaps one day I won't need it but now I am sure it
is still important. (Sellin, 1995, p. 216)

    Clearly, examining the concept of movement differences can bring new understanding to the struggles, abilities, and perhaps the gifts of people with a range of disabilities.

Sensory Differences

People with autism tend to have unusual sensory experiences. Jared Blackburn, a man with autism, described how these sensory differences can cause discomfort and frustration:

One common effect of these heightened senses is that autistic people are vulnerable to sensory overload with continued low-level bombardment. This may also result from too much emotional or social stimulation. Autistic people may become overloaded in situations that would not bother (or might even entertain) a normal person. When overloaded, autistic people have trouble concentrating, may feel tired or confused, and some may experience physical pain. Too much overload may lead to tantrums or emotional outburst. Another result of too much overload may be "shutdown," in which the person loses some or all of the person's normal functioning. Shutdown may feel different to different people, but is extremely unpleasant. (1997)

    A student's sense of hearing, touch, smell, sight, or taste may be more sensitive or less sensitive than is typical. In other cases, students may have difficulty interpreting a sense. It is not uncommon for a person with autism to avoid being touched, for example. Some students may be able to tolerate only some types of touch. One of my students, for instance, could not tolerate being touched, even in a gentle way. If I brushed his hand or tried to guide him somewhere by lightly grasping his shoulder, he screamed as if in pain. If, instead, I gave him a firm handshake or slapped him on the back, he appeared unaffected.

The hearing of individuals with autism is also often affected. Students may be bothered by sounds that teachers cannot even detect, as Tyler Fihe, a young man with autism, reported:

I hear things that many people can't hear. For example, I can be in one room of the house and hear what my mother is saying on the telephone even when she has the door shut. There are also certain sounds that are painful to listen to like the microwave, the telephone ring, lawnmowers, leaf blowers, the blender, babies crying, vacuum cleaners, and my mom's VW vanagon when it just starts up. (Fihe, 2000)

As Fihe pointed out, a range of noises and sounds may cause a person with autism anxiety, including those that may seem benign to the average person. For instance, a student might be completely distressed by the sound of a crayon moving across a tablet or frightened by the hissing of a radiator. Many people with autism also have trouble understanding conversation or verbal directions because they have trouble processing sound.

Vision can also be affected. Students may be sensitive to certain types of light, colors, or patterns. As one individual with autism described, visual sensitivity may not only have a negative impact on the person's sensory system but can also cause the individual to become fearful or anxious:

It may be because things that I see do not always make the right impression that I am frightened of so many things that can be seen: people, particularly their faces, very bright lights, crowds, things moving suddenly. Large machines and buildings that are unfamiliar, unfamiliar places, my own shadow, the dark, bridges, rivers, canals, streams, and the sea. (Jolliffe et al., as cited in Attwood, 1998, p. 137)

Teachers should watch to see if a student seems bothered by things she sees in the classroom (e.g., a certain poster, a bulletin board). Even the color of the walls in the classroom can bother a student's sensory system.

Students with autism may also have a heightened or otherwise different sense of smell. The individual with autism may find some smells unbearable and others pleasant, helpful, or calming. For instance, one of my former students avoided any teacher who wore perfume but loved to smell the hair of a fellow student who used a fruity-smelling shampoo. (See Chapter 5 for more information on sensory differences.)

Communication Differences

Many students with autism have communication differences that affect speech and language and many use few or no spoken words. For students who do speak, their speech may have unusual qualities. For instance, a student may have unusual speech intonation or use repetitive speech (echoing the words of others). Furthermore, conversational timing and rhythm may be difficult for someone with autism to learn or use. Students might also struggle with using language. Some students, for instance, have difficulties using pronouns or learning the rules of conversation. Others may find figurative language (e.g., jokes, metaphors) hard to decipher.

Students may have difficulties with expressive or receptive communication. That is, they may have trouble sharing thoughts and ideas or struggle to understand what they hear or see. Many students experience difficulties with both receptive and expressive communication.

Students are increasingly finding communication success through the use of various teaching strategies and technologies, including facilitated typing and writing, picture exchange communication systems, and augmentative and alternative communication devices (see Biklen, 1990; Bondy & Frost, 2002; Crossley, 1997; Mirenda, 1999). These technologies, interestingly, are not only giving students access to words, but in many cases are also changing the ways educators, families, and researchers think about the communication and abilities of students with autism. As more students are able to tap into reliable communication and share their stories, individuals without autism are also beginning to change the ways in which they understand autism. (See Chapter 7 for more information on communication.)

Socialization and Interaction Differences

A common stereotype is that students with autism are not interested in social relationships. Although some individuals with autism do report that they need time alone or find some social situations are challenging, some of these same individuals also claim that they crave social interaction and friendship. That is, it is possible for a person with autism to both struggle with and want relationships. In fact, some individuals with autism claim that being with people is not challenging but the "things" that accompany being with people make building friendships difficult. For instance, my friend Mary Kathleen loves to be with her friends but has a hard time figuring out the rules of conversation; therefore, she finds parties very stressful and unpleasant. Another friend, Theola, values the one-to-one relationships she has with her sisters, nieces, and nephews, but cannot tolerate the noise and commotion of family gatherings.

Other students find social situations difficult because they lack the skills necessary for successful "typical" social interactions. For instance, individuals with autism may not be very good at reading subtle social signals. If a person yawns or begins putting on a jacket, most people would read this as a signal that the individual is getting ready to end the conversation and go home. For some individuals with autism, reading these subtle signs is a real challenge.

Students with autism may also struggle socially because those around them don't understand their attempts to be social or to interact. For example, one of my former students, Donna, often ripped paper from her notebook, crumpled it into a ball, and tossed it at her classmates. Students reprimanded Donna for this behavior and told her repeatedly, "Donna, don't throw garbage at your friends." When I told Donna's mother about the behavior, however, she gasped and then laughed. She then explained that Donna was imitating her brothers; when her older brothers wanted to play with her, they folded paper into little balls and pretended to shoot baskets through hoops they made with their outstretched arms. In Donna's house, play could be initiated by throwing paper in someone's direction; the appropriate response, of course was to arc your arms to make a "basket" for the shooter. From Donna's perspective, she was behaving perfectly appropriately; it was her classmates who lacked social awareness!

Lucy Blackman, a woman with autism, emphasized the importance of realizing the different ways students initiate social contact and interaction:

For me, successful "social" contact depended on someone else interpreting my own signals. Some of my attempts at communication were fairly conventional, as when I put my arms up towards a person with my hands stretched up because I desperately needed to be picked up or lifted over an obstacle. However Jay noted that if I turned my hands outward when I put my arms up to her, I was asking for a boost for a somersault, rather than some help in climbing up. If she interpreted wrongly, things could get very noisy. (2001, p. 11)

Learning Differences

Donna Williams, an author and woman with autism, related that she has many different types of processing difficulties. She refers to one category as "sorry, wrong address" or "misfires":

Messages can be sorted inefficiently so that they are related badly. This is like putting a call through to the wrong number or the next-door-neighbor's house instead of your house.

These are what I call "misfires." Some examples of these in my own life have been where I've come up with words or names that have a similar shape, pattern or rhythm to one I am trying to recall without being similar in meaning. I've had this trouble with names such as Margaret and Elizabeth because they seem to have the same feel and seem similar to me.

In the same way, I've said things like "I want my shoes" when I meant "I want my jacket" and been surprised to get things I apparently asked for. (1996, p. 89)

Sue Rubin, a woman with autism, reported that she has significant problems with memory:

I have a deficit in my thinking and I don't know if it is common in autism or is just unique to me. When I remember events, I can't tell if they really happened or I imagined them. I can actually picture events in my mind and I am sure they are real until someone points out that they couldn't have happened. Awash in embarrassment, I realize that I imagined the event. I even worry about imagined events that I think really happened. Waking nightmares may be a good description. Lasting problems can result from this. The problem with my memory does not affect my schoolwork. I learn what is in my books, what the professor says, and what everyone says in class. I admit I still have problems with assignments. I need someone to write them down for me because I cannot recall them. Assume my forgetting assignments is much worse than normal people's forgetting. (1998, p. 3)

Although many of the problems students have traditionally had are assumed to be problems with intellect, they are, in fact, remarkably similar to the types of struggles reported by individuals with learning disabilities (Gilroy & Miles, 1996; Mooney & Cole, 2000; Smith & Strick, 1997). In other words, teachers may assume that a student does not or cannot give a correct answer or respond to a direction correctly because he or she is incapable of understanding the task. In many instances, however, the student does not or cannot perform because of the way in which the information is presented, heard, or processed.

Interests or Fascinations

Many individuals with autism have a deep interest in one or a variety of topics. Some interests are commonly seen across individuals with autism (e.g., trains, horses, light switches); others seem more unique to an individual person. For instance, Sean Barron, a man with autism, once had a great interest in the number 24. At another point in his life, he became fascinated by dead-end streets (Barron & Barron, 1992).

Often, a student's educational team will focus on curbing a student's involvement with their interests or compulsions. Many a meeting has been planned and many a behavior program has been written to squelch a student's interest or engagement in something. As a person with many compulsions of my own—including the need to keep my book bag by my side at all times and to rub my hands on a soft texture like satin or taffeta when I am experiencing stress—I cannot imagine what it is like to have another person manage your "favorite things" for you.

Willey cautioned that it can be dangerous for people without autism to pass judgment about interests and obsessions. In fact, she noted, in many ways and in many circles, having intense interests is considered positive and even admirable.

At the base I have to wonder, are we so very different from marathon athletes, corporate presidents, bird watchers, or new parents counting every breath their newborn takes? It seems lots of people, NT [neurotypical] or otherwise, have an obsession of sorts. In my mind, that reality rests as a good one, for obsessions in and out of themselves are not bad habits. There is much good about them. Obsessions take focus and tenacious study. They are the stuff greatness needs. I have to believe the best of the remarkable—the artists, musicians, philosophers, scientists, writers, researchers and athletes—had to obsess on their chosen fields or they would never had become great. In some respects, then it must be said that obsessions do not have to be considered handicaps. (2001, p. 122)

Luke Jackson criticized that it seems okay for people without disability labels to have these interests in our society, but not those with labels:

I have a question for teenagers here.
   Q: When is an obsession not an obsession?
   A: When it is about football.
   How unfair is that? It seems that our society fully accepts the fact that a lot of men and boys "eat, sleep, and breathe football" seem to think that if someone doesn't, then they are not fully male. Stupid! (2002, p. 47)

Jackson noted the rigidity of society when it comes to issues of difference and normalcy.

I am sure if a parent went to a doctor and said that their teenage boy wouldn't shut up about football, they would laugh and tell them that it was perfectly normal. It seems as if we all have to be the same. Why can no one see that the world just isn't like that? I would like everyone to talk about computers all day actually, but I don't expect them to and people soon tell me to shut up. (2002, pp. 47–48)

In keeping with the suggestions from Willey and Jackson, teachers may want to allow the student with a specific fascination the time and space to pursue it if it is not disrupting the student's education or hurting them. Students often need these favorite materials, activities, behaviors, and interest areas to relax, focus, or to make connections with others. In addition, students will often find their own ways of regulating their compulsions when left to do so.

Of course, some students want and need help restricting behaviors or time spent with preferred materials or activities, especially if they are dangerous or extremely embarrassing (e.g., touching other people inappropriately). Some individuals with autism will have a desire to spend less time with or to get rid of these interests and in these instances the teachers should support the student in doing so. It is important to emphasize, however, that this process should be done in a respectful way and always in collaboration with the student.

Willey suggested talking to the student with autism about the "good and bad parts of obsessing." She shared a story of how she has helped her daughter, who has Asperger's syndrome, to learn how to live in concert with her interests.

Slowly, patiently, with tiny steps we are trying to help her find the good and the bad parts of obsessing. "It is good to play with your monkey collection when you feel badly about something that happened at school," we tell her. "Of course you can buy that book about monkeys because you worked hard to control your temper this whole week," we will say. "No, you cannot sort your monkeys right now, not until your homework is finished," we remind her. In time, she will do these things for herself. In time, she will know on her own how to share her life with her obsession. (2001, p. 125)

If the student is not interested in moving away from his or her interests, the teacher should proceed with caution. In many cases, some people in the student's life may want an interest to recede when the student does not. Eugene Marcus, a writer, teacher, and advocate with autism, has indicated that fascinations and interests often serve important purposes in the lives of individuals with autism. He has stressed that when possible, individuals with autism should be allowed to assess and control their own interests, compulsions, or fascinations:

Never mind that I am a slave to my compulsions. New people in my life always see me that way, and friends never worry about them, but never value them either. My own view is that my life is enriched and made livable by the habits that enslave me. My feeling is that my enslavement is a voluntary one in that nobody else forces me to be compulsive, or even gives me permission to be compulsive.

My wish is to one day be free of my compulsions, but not any day soon. By being an inconvenient and loud slave to compulsion, I have learned things I never would have through silent cooperation. I have tested the limits of my real and unreal friends (even those people who wanted to be my friends, but only when I was play-acting a role—not being myself). My compulsive behavior has allowed me to set my own agenda in situations where the most I could have hoped for was "eats and treats." My compulsive behavior is a long-playing defense against well meaning people who cannot guess what I really am thinking of or wishing for. How can I be a non-compulsive person but also not compulsively agreeable? Because I can see that in compulsive agreeing is a big risk of losing my path and my dreams. Being myself but also being my social self is a real complicated mess sometimes. (2002, p. 8)

THE SOCIAL CONSTRUCTION OF AUTISM

This chapter would not be complete without considering the role society plays in constructing disability. Many individuals with autism have experienced difficulties due to societal and cultural ideas of how people should look, communicate, interact, move, and behave. Although most people with autism will tell you that "it" is real, that they do experience things in different ways, that their bodies are uncooperative, or that they have sensory or communication problems, it might also be suggested that autism is in some ways exacerbated by an inflexible society. That is, autism is a social construction; it is a phenomenon that is created and recreated through culture, interaction, and social circumstances. For instance, people may feel more or less disabled on any given day based on whether appropriate supports are provided for them or whether they are expected to communicate in a conventional way. Jonathan McNabb, a man with autism, suggested that "neurotypical" individuals (people without autism) stop assuming that *difference* means *deviance* and start understanding the autistic experience from those who live with it:

Personally I find the basic stumbling block on which all the other issues stem is the assumption most Neurotypical people have that Neurotypical worldview is neutral and normative. The Neurotypical world is presented as a given. I would be very surprised if many would be aware of it being an issue. Autism is then seen in contrast to this given, natural, neutral, and normal society. The person with autism is then judged on his or her ability to conform to the values and standards of society.

The autistic person is then in the position of being in a society which does not understand autism and where the defining of autism [is] are controlled by those who have regularly not helped the position of autistic people and indeed much of the time have hindered them. The autistic person is then placed in position of how to cope within such a society. There are numerous solutions, some which are better for the person than others. Many are forced to take the pioneer role. (2001, p. 1)

People create or exacerbate disability when they have rigid values about the "right way" to do things, when they fail to provide the help that people may need, or when they expect all individuals to act in the same ways and need the same things.

When a person is unable to participate in our culture, it typically is because a context has not been created for that participation. For instance, a woman who is 80 years old may be frustrated when she can no longer walk to the corner and get her mail. Her frustration and "inability" is minimized or erased, however, if she can have a mailbox installed near her door, a neighbor starts picking up her mail for her, or she gets an electric wheelchair. For this woman, changing the context for her participation changes everything. Likewise, when a student with autism needs space to relax, extra time to make the transition between classes, or support from a peer, and these accommodations are provided, ability is emphasized and disability is diminished.

To illustrate the narrow ways in which individuals without identified disabilities often perceive ability, a Web site assembled by people with autism and Asperger's syndrome offers another way of seeing autism. The creators of this site have imagined a world where autism is the norm and being typical is a problem. This glimpse at how some people with autism see those without that label might help teachers, families, and all who support those with autism. Sit for a moment on the other side of the teacher's desk and consider this passage, written by the creators of this Web site:

Neurotypical syndrome is a neurobiological disorder characterized by preoccupation with social concerns, delusions of superiority, and obsession with conformity. Neurotypical individuals often assume that their experience of the world is either the only one, or the only correct one. NTs find it difficult to be alone. NTs are often intolerant of seemingly minor differences in others. When in groups NTs are socially and behaviorally rigid and frequently insist on the performance of dysfunctional, destructive, and even impossible rituals as a way of maintaining group identity. NTs find it difficult to communicate directly, and have a much higher incidence of lying as compared with persons on the autistic spectrum. NT is believed to be genetic in origin. Autopsies have shown the brain of the neurotypical is typically smaller than that of an autistic individual and may have overdeveloped areas related to social behavior. (Institute for the Study of the Neurologically Typical, 2002)

SUMMARY

Until the movie *Rain Man* (Johnson & Levinson, 1988) was released, few people knew what autism was and fewer still knew a person with that label. While the much-acclaimed motion picture gave the average person a glimpse into this little-understood disability, it also provided Americans with a range of stereotypes about autism and people labeled as having it. In the wake of the film, most viewers cam to believe that people with autism can read cards like a Las Vegas professional and count hundreds of toothpicks in an instant.

Today, more than a decade after the movie's debut, people's awareness of the autism spectrum has increased greatly. Because of widespread deinstitutionalization, the growth of community living for people with disabilities, and more accurate and varied accounts of people with autism in biographies, autobiographies, magazines, and television, most Americans understand more about what it means to have autism than they ever have before. And because of the inclusive schooling movement, an increased emphasis on learning about differences in the classroom, and more accurate and varied accounts of students with autism in pre-service textbooks and in teacher preparation classes, more classroom teachers (both special and general education) are learning about how to educate students with autism.

As I share in the introduction to this chapter, many educators are now learning about autism from their students. This chapter can serve as a primer on autism, but the best way to find success with a learner with autism is to get to know that individual and his or her family. If a student can talk or share ideas through speech or writing, this can be an avenue for meeting the student and learning something about autism. If the student cannot communicate reliably, the teacher will learn about the student by spending time, interacting, working, and teaching him or her. As Jasmine Lee O'Neill pointed out, getting to know students, appreciating them, honoring their individuality, and helping them to feel at home in the classroom is as important as anything else teachers may do:

Many autistic people affectionately, humorously refer to themselves as aliens. They feel displaced on a vast planet, which has a code of life, and understanding they can't even quite subscribe to. If they are welcomed, however, and cherished as the individuals they are, then there wouldn't be as much dissension on both sides. Aliens can become more comfortable and less paralyzed in fear, while still remaining who they are. Their essence stays the same. Then they don't have to despise their alien status, as if it were forced upon them. Instead, they can enjoy their uniqueness, just as others enjoy theirs. (1999, p. 125)

For More Answers and Ideas

Attwood, T. (1998). *Asperger's syndrome: A guide for parents and professionals.* London: Jessica Kingsley Publishers.

Donnellan, A., & Leary, M. (1995). *Movement differences and diversity in autism/mental retardation: Appreciating and accommodating people with communication and behavior challenges.* Madison, WI: DRI Press.

Gillingham, G. (2000). *Autism: A new understanding.* Edmonton, Alberta, Canada: Tacit Publishing Inc.

Waterhouse, S. (2000). *A positive approach to autism.* London: Jessica Kingsley Publishers.

Williams, D. (1996). *Autism: An inside-out approach.* London: Jessica Kingsley Publishers.

Undoubtedly, the best way to learn about autism is to learn from people with that label. Luckily, people with autism are sharing their experiences in increasing numbers. Teachers who want to prepare to have students with autism with disabilities in their classrooms or those who want to learn more about those already in their schools have a variety of texts from which to choose, including autobiographies of individuals with autism and Asperger's syndrome, "how-to" guides to teaching, and books written specifically for young people on the autistic spectrum. See also the Bibliography for a more complete list of books on autism by people with autism spectrum disorders.

CHAPTER 2

Understanding
Inclusive Schooling

All my life I was enrolled in classes for the
profoundly retarded. The pain of that isolation, I can't
describe. Some classes consisted of putting flashlights together
and then they would be taken apart for the next day's project. I never
spoke or made eye contact. I hummed and self-stim[ulat]ed. No wonder they
thought I was hopeless. I was always treated well but my intellectual needs were
never addressed because nobody knew I had any intellect at all. Sad to say, many
like me remain in that same hellish situation. (Treacy, 1996, p. 8)

Inclusive schooling stresses interdependence and independence, views all students as gifted, and values a sense of community (Falvey, Givner, & Kimm, 1995). According to Udvari-Solner, it also supports civil rights and equity in the classroom.

> [Inclusive schooling] propels a critique of contemporary school culture and thus, encourages practitioners to reinvent what can be and should be to realize more humane, just and democratic learning communities. Inequities in treatment and educational opportunity are brought to the forefront, thereby fostering attention to human rights, respect for difference and value of diversity. (1997, p. 142)

Like Udvari-Solner, I define inclusive education as something that supports and benefits all learners. I also see it as a social action and political movement. If "inequities in treatment and educational opportunity are brought to the forefront," for instance, teachers and community members might question practices such as tracking and standardized testing that segregate, stratify, and often harm students. If schools create "more humane, just, and democratic learning communities," then all students will be valued and seen as important members of the school including students from all racial and ethnic groups, students new to the school and community, students using English as a second language, students who identify themselves as gay and lesbian, and students marginalized for having different types of bodies (e.g., students deemed "too skinny," those with weight problems). Inclusion is *more* than a set of strategies

Table 2.1.   Important school practices, beliefs, and values for diverse, inclusive schools

Releasing intelligence rather than quantifying it

Nurturing effort rather than defining ability

Building strengths rather than sorting according to weakness

Developing dispositions and skills necessary for lifelong learning across all areas of knowledge rather than imparting particular information in a given subject area

Balancing concepts with meaningful content

Building on students' aspirations rather than circumscribing their dreams

Recognizing students as members of a learning community rather than as products of an assembly line

From Wheelock, A. (1992). *Crossing the tracks: How "untracking" can save America's schools.* New York: The New Press; reprinted by permission.

or practices, it is an educational orientation that embraces differences and values the uniqueness that each learner brings to the classroom.

CHARACTERISTICS OF INCLUSIVE SCHOOLS

Although every inclusive school will have a different look and feel, schools dedicated to serving all students will share some characteristics. Specifically, these schools will have committed leadership, democratic classrooms, reflective teachers, a supportive culture, engaging and relevant curriculum, and responsive instruction.

Committed Leadership

Administrators, school board members, and teachers in leadership positions (e.g., department chairs, teacher union representatives) play a critical role in inclusive schools (Keyes, 1996; Rossman, 1992; Villa & Thousand, 1990) by articulating a vision for inclusive schooling, building support for the vision, and working with the school community to implement strategies and principles that make the school successful. (See Table 2.1 for principles that support inclusive schooling.) In their study of teachers' impressions of inclusive education, Trump and Hange (1996) found that administrative leadership was considered to be the greatest support or the greatest obstacle to the success and development of inclusive schooling.

In a study conducted by Udvari-Solner and Keyes, administrators who were identified as leaders of inclusive education claimed that they needed to have courage to "relentlessly pose the difficult, the contrary, the controversial, and the seemingly unanswerable questions" (2000, p. 450). In addition, these principals and central office administrators stressed the importance of expressing their own personal values. Sue Abplanalp, an elementary school principal in the study, shared that she felt that being open and honest about her own beliefs was critical to the development of an inclusive community in her school:

> I guess the most important thing I can do is be an advocate by voicing my opinion, modeling and letting teachers know about best practices, and [by continuing to ask] myself the same question when I am not sure about what to do: is

this in the best interest of the child?...I have a desire to be an advocate for equality, regardless of age, disability, race, religion, sexual orientation, ability, gender, and anything else I forgot. It's part of my vision for justice. (p. 442)

Administrators and other leaders help students, staff, and the local community understand inclusion as a philosophy or ideology that will permeate the school; they help staff members when new ways of "doing business" are adopted; they provide encouragement and support as teachers take risks and try new approaches; they educate families and community members about the school's beliefs and their inclusive mission; and they help to celebrate day-to-day successes and problem-solve day-to-day struggles. (Van Dyke, Stallings, & Colley, 1995)

Democratic Classrooms

Cunat defined democratic education as "the vital and dynamic process of a learning community that recognizes and validates the individuality and responsibility of each participant." He argued that "the overall purpose of democratic education is to engage individuals in a process that will help them develop the skills and attitudes necessary to become people who can and will contribute to the making of a vital, equitable, and humane society" (1996, p. 130).

But how will this kind of democracy look in practice? Teachers interested in pursuing democracy in their schools can support students as they challenge institutional knowledge and create their own interpretations of classroom materials. Teachers can help students to see that knowledge is continually created and recreated through reflection and action. Both teachers and students in the democratic classroom see themselves as learners and educators and they understand education to be a cooperative task.

In a democratic classroom, students often "run the show." Consider a lesson in which the teacher works with small groups of students to present different aspects of content to the group. The teacher will work as a coach, mentor, or advisor to the groups as the students work to construct materials and design instruction that will inspire and educate peers. Students are active in constructing knowledge as they move from searching the web at the computer station, to interviewing local experts on the phone, to reading from encyclopedias, to developing a three-dimensional model that will eventually be used in a presentation their group makes to the class. Throughout these activities, the teacher may be consulting with groups and individual students, asking them how much time they should spend on the projects, engaging them in critical conversation about their work, and prompting them to evaluate the experience.

Students in democratic classrooms often share ideas, make rules, question classroom practices, help to create curriculum, and make decisions about their learning and their environment. In addition, they often direct their own learning experiences. In order to conduct these responsibilities, they must be able to talk, to move, and to share. Thus, a teacher interested in making his or her classroom more democratic might ask the following questions (Kluth, Diaz-Greenberg, Thousand, & Nevin, 2002):

- Where do students sit in relation to the teacher? That is, is the teacher always in the front of the classroom facing the students?

- Who is responsible for assessment? Does the teacher always grade and assess student work or do students have a voice in how/when they are assessed?
- Who determines classroom rules? How are rules set and enforced? Are rules constructed collaboratively by teacher and students?
- What does the classroom environment look like? When a stranger glances around the room, does the space appear to be a teacher's space (e.g., all of the writing on chalkboard is in the teacher's handwriting, work displayed is chosen by the teacher) or a space shared by the classroom community?
- Can students question decisions made by the teacher? Are students viewed as decision makers in the classroom?
- Who makes decisions regarding curriculum? Does the teacher make all of the decisions about topics covered, materials used, and ways in which instruction is delivered, or are students consulted on these decisions? Do students construct curriculum and design instruction?

In democratic classrooms, students and teachers can work as a team to educate one another and to co-create understanding of their shared world. Thus, a student with autism might educate her teachers about her own needs and strengths. She might write a letter to teachers sharing tips on "how to help me in the classroom," construct a portfolio complete with her favorite work samples and reflections on how her disability affects her education, or create her own adaptations for certain lessons.

Reflective Educators

When one enters an effective inclusive school, teachers can often be seen asking students critical questions, observing each other, critiquing lessons, and sharing stories of their practice. Inquiry, dialogue, and reflection are central to the work of the inclusive educator. Consider this definition of the reflective teacher:

> Reflective teachers willingly embrace their decision-making responsibilities, and they regularly reflect on problems they confront, and maybe they make mistakes, but they never stop trying. They are sincere and thoughtful professionals who constantly learn from their reflective experiences. They understand that receptiveness to further learning is the key to continued professional development and validity. (Henderson, 1992, p. 2)

While most teachers reflect on their work often—as they are driving to school, during lunch, or while they are working with a student—these incidents do not always result in learning or a deeper understanding of their work. Reflective teaching as it is being discussed here is not just the practice of remembering, rehashing, or musing. John Dewey (1910), for instance, suggested that those engaging in reflective action must bring to the act openmindedness, responsibility, thoughtfulness, and caution.

Nirua Regiane Henke (www.disal.com.br/nroutes/nr5/pgnr508.htm) suggested a sequence for reflection that can help teachers move beyond the logical and rational. She suggested beginning with an area of focus and selecting tools (e.g., journal, videotapes) to help with the study of the issue or event. Next, the teacher should describe the event or focus area in as much detail as possible. This processs is followed by asking "why" questions about the event, in order to understand the event or issue from different perspectives. Although some of this work can be done effectively by individuals, many teachers enjoy and prefer to engage in these exercises with colleagues. Some schools are now sponsoring discussion groups, professional reading circles, action research projects, peer teaching and mentoring, and other unique professional development activities that inspire contemplation.

Educators must be thoughtful workers, reflecting on their experiences and beliefs individually, but able to work effectively with others and approach teaching as a collaborative and dynamic learning experience. Reflective teachers seek opportunities to check their biases, challenge assumptions, question prejudices, and realize successes.

Supportive School Culture

Often, the culture of a school is apparent to visitors the moment they walk in the front door. School outsiders can learn a lot about a school by the ways the walls are covered, the types of teacher conversations overheard in the hallways, and the ways in which students are engaged. All of these elements are aspects of school culture.

Fullan and Hargreaves described school culture as the

> Guiding beliefs and expectations evident in the way a school operates, particularly in reference to how people relate (or fail to relate) to each other. In simple terms, culture is 'the way we do things' and relate to each other around here. (1996, p. 3)

Therefore, if the culture is open, accepting, and caring, inclusive schooling can thrive. If the school culture is competitive, individualistic, and authoritative, however, teachers will find it impossible to grow inclusive schooling. Cultivating a safe, positive, and robust school culture may be the most difficult piece of creating an inclusive school, but it is also, perhaps, the most critical piece. School leaders and educators concerned with creating an inclusive school culture might implement the following practices:

- Hold informal brown-bag lunches with small groups of teachers, staff members, students, and parents
- Invite parents and community members to visit classrooms, help with projects, and serve as resources
- Give students opportunities to teach and lead
- Use suggestion boxes and implement suggestions from all stakeholder groups in the school
- Give students and teachers opportunities to socialize
- Make time for school celebrations, both small and large

Peterson (2002) shared the story of how one principal was able to shape the culture of a new school. Shelby Cosner, the first principal of Wisconsin Hills

Middle School in Brookfield, Wisconsin, wanted to build a school culture that valued and sustained professional learning. Over time, the school staff developed a culture that nurtured and valued professional learning.

One strategy these educators used was to discuss and develop a set of core themes and values that guide learning. They scheduled regular "D" Days (staff development days) every other week. They always shared food during meetings, a symbol of collegiality and a bond for the group as it studied new approaches to differentiating instruction and integrating technology. Staff shared both personal and professional stories, sometimes about their students and other times about themselves. Eventually, teachers made storytelling into a contest, with the staff voting for the best funny classroom or school story. These stories were then shared in the school newsletter.

Engaging and Relevant Curricula

Teachers in inclusive classrooms must design curricula and instruction and engineer classroom activities that are personally and culturally appropriate, engage a range of learning styles, and are suitable for learners with various talents and interests. This is critical not only for students with autism and other unique learning or social needs but also for every learner in the classroom. Children grow and learn from the daily curricula and also from the ways in which schools respond to difference.

Teachers demonstrating good inclusion practices design curriculum and engage in pedagogy that reflects the diversity found in classrooms and communities. Units of study must be relevant and meaningful, themes of investigation must be interesting and motivating, and content must be appropriately challenging. Classroom materials should also be engaging to a wide variety of students. The classroom library must include books written by and about people with individual and group differences, for example. Furthermore, classroom lessons should include information about the diverse groups represented by the students. A teacher might achieve this by providing information about Thomas Edison's learning difficulties during a lesson on inventions or discussing the complexity and diversities of Chinese cultures when reading Amy Tan's novels.

Responsive Instruction

Teachers in inclusive classrooms are concerned about reaching and motivating all learners. In the best cases, they are versed in adapting materials, lesson formats, instructional arrangements, curricular goals, and teaching strategies (Udvari-Solner, 1996) and can meet both the academic and social needs of students. Therefore, a teacher in an inclusive classroom might give a struggling student some leadership opportunities in the school, engineer a cross-age mentoring relationship for a student who may need extra assistance, give personal checklists to those who need help with organization, structure cooperative learning lessons so active learners have time to move and share, or give a student with autism opportunities to pace in the back of the classroom during lectures and class discussions.

The idea that students learn in different ways or different styles is now widely accepted within the literature, if not uniformly implemented in practice

(Armstrong, 1997, 1994; Gardner, 1993; Ladson-Billings, 1994; Kliewer, 1998; Nieto, 2000; Paley, 1990; Smith & Strick, 1997; Taylor & Dorsey-Gaines, 1988; Udvari-Solner, 1996). The "myth of the average learner" has been shattered and teachers are recognizing the need to individualize and honor the unique profiles of all students. Inclusive schooling has been a catalyst for such a model and has prompted educators to differentiate instruction and attend to diverse learning styles as they plan and implement daily lessons.

INCLUSIVE SCHOOLING AS EDUCATION REFORM

Although many have understood inclusive schooling to be a reform implemented for the benefit of learners with disabilities, most of its proponents understand it as a movement that concerns all students (Kluth, Biklen, & Straut, in press). It is a way of thinking about and engaging in teaching and learning to benefit and support all students in public schools, and it is inspiring promising new practices, behaviors, supports, and ideals in American education. As Shapiro-Barnard illustrated, inclusion is a reform that can help all students feel a sense of belonging in schools:

> Inclusive education benefits school communities by bringing attention to the issue of belonging and by reminding us that the capacity of schools to host meaningful learning opportunities parallels our attention to this matter. Even if there were not students with disabilities, the culturing of inclusive schools would still be important because the entrance of students with disabilities into general education classes does not signify the presence of diversity in the school; it recognizes and affirms the diversity that has always existed. As a result, people are less bound by false ideals of normalcy, are less fearful of expressing their own uniqueness, and thus are more able to learn. (1998, p. 12)

The inclusive schooling movement is prompting teachers and administrators to attend to differences broadly and positively. The movement has much to share as we work to construct new models for education that challenge teachers to embrace, support, and understand *all* diverse groups. The philosophy of the movement helps teachers expand their thinking, expectations, and understanding of how students can learn and how teachers can teach.

Many students with significant disabilities have been successfully educated in general education classrooms. Students without reliable, functional, communication; those with significant behavior challenges; and even those who struggle to complete any classroom task or activity in a traditional way have received an education in inclusive classrooms.

Although students with more significant needs will require more creativity and invention on the part of classroom educators, this creativity often behooves and benefits all learners in the classroom. In many instances, teachers claim they become better at their craft after expanding curriculum and instruction to meet the needs of a wider range of students. Oftentimes when teachers create lessons to which all students can have access, they find that all students learn and achieve more.

I once worked with a high school team who supported Anne, a young woman with autism. Anne did not have a reliable communication system, and she often vocalized audibly during classes. Her American History teacher, a popular and animated instructor, was frustrated with her presence in the classroom; he had been using the same lessons for several years and was not prepared to make changes "just for one student."

Anne's teacher, a special educator, offered to work with the history teacher to create opportunities for Anne to participate in his lessons. At the time, the class was studying the Vietnam conflict. In order to teach this particular unit, the teacher was using a history textbook, a range of popular films about Vietnam such as *Apocalypse Now* (Coppola, 1979), *Platoon* (Stone, 1986), and *Hamburger Hill* (Irvin, 1987); newspaper clippings from the late 1960s and early 1970s; and a few fictitious accounts of the war. Although the materials were varied and interesting to most of the students, the teaching style was not. This dynamic instructor, although very funny and entertaining, delivered instruction through a lecture format every day. Although students did have opportunities to ask and answer questions during the lectures, they were not able to interact with each other, explore materials in-depth, solve problems independently, or create products. Some students were able to stay attentive during a lecture format; however, many others, including Anne, could not. By the end of the daily lecture, many students were falling asleep, writing notes to friends, or staring out the classroom's large wall of windows.

The special educator suggested that once a week, while the teacher was showing a movie, the students in the class would be offered an alternative activity. The teachers decided to collaborate on the activity. One teacher, they decided, would stay back in the classroom and supervise the movie viewing, while the other teacher would accompany a small group of students around the large high school, seeking faculty, staff members, and other adults in the school who would be willing to be interviewed about their memories of the Vietnam era. For the first few weeks, the special educator took the students on the school tour; five students including Anne marched through the halls, visited the teacher's lounge, and even canvassed the main office looking for family members who might be visiting the school. Because Anne could not speak, her job was to operate the tape recorder (a new skill she acquired at the onset of the project). She introduced the group to the person to be interviewed via a communication card reading "We are conducting a history project related to the Vietnam conflict. We are interested in interviewing people who remember the Vietnam era. Do you mind if we ask you a few questions?" Anne also participated in the interview process by handing question cards to the adults being questioned.

After 3 weeks, the history teacher decided he wanted to accompany students to the interviews and asked his special education partner to stay back in the classroom and supervise the film. The history teacher also decided that every student would need to participate in the interviews during the unit. The teachers designed a formal interviewing schedule for the class. Through the course of 6 weeks, the students interviewed seven parents, three custodians (one of whom did three tours of duty in the Vietnam War), all four school secretaries, the school nurse, both librarians, six cafeteria workers (one of whom lost a brother in the war), nearly every teacher in the building, the school social worker, and the police officer assigned to the high school.

The teachers and the students became so excited about the interviews that they spent 2 extra weeks on the unit, with the teacher adding questions to the interviews to spur new learning and to teach new content. Participants were excited, too; some teachers even signed up to be interviewed. As the students shared the results of their interviews, the class discussed, researched, and investigated topics ranging from women's roles in the 1960s to Watergate to the Black Panther Movement.

Both educators were pleased with the unit and the history teacher claimed that all of his students learned more, even those who could "handle" the lectures. He saw more complexity in all of his learners and felt that the interview activity allowed him to tackle more complicated topics and give students more opportunities to think critically. He did not have Anne in any of his classes the next semester, but he did continue to use the interviewing project as a central focus of the unit. In subsequent semesters, all students worked in groups to choose a specific focus for their interviews and to design questions. Furthermore, students were no longer asked to skip the film while conducting interviews; all learners went out into the school and neighboring community during the class period.

This unit was important for Anne. Anne was able to address all of her individual learning needs in a natural and authentic context. She needed more experience using her communication system, interacting with others, and making choices. She was able to practice all of these skills within the context of the history lessons. In addition, she acquired some new skills as a result of the unit. She learned how to operate a tape recorder and later used this skill to listen to music on the school bus and during study hall. Anne also learned about Vietnam, something she probably would not have learned had her teachers decided that the class was inappropriate for her.

Students with the most significant needs often foster teachers' creativity and stretch their ideas of what it means to reach all learners. Although a teacher can meet the needs of all students without ever having a student with disabilities in her classroom, these students are often a catalyst for change and creativity. Specifically, including students with autism may help teachers think more carefully about the choices offered to students; the design of the lesson; the ways in which students can participate in teaching and learning; and the comfort, engagement, and opportunities for all.

INCLUSIVE SCHOOLING AND THE LAW

Even though inclusive schooling has been part of American schooling for more than 2 decades, many students with autism are still separated from peers without disabilities. Perhaps these exclusions occur because teachers feel uncomfortable or unable to support students with communication or behavioral differences. Or maybe it is because traditionally, students with autism, especially those with significant disabilities, were educated in special programs and special schools. Despite relatively slow progress, students with autism are increasingly being educated in inclusive classrooms. Many of those same learners, however, are being excluded from rich and meaningful experiences in those classrooms, perhaps because teachers are unsure of how to include them, because they do not see all students as capable of benefiting from general education curriculum, or because they simply have not been introduced to ways in which instruction can be differentiated for diverse learners. Whatever the reason, some educators assume that segregated placements are more appropriate for learners with the label of autism.

What many teachers are beginning to see, however, is that students with autism and other disabilities are finding "unexpected" success when provided with opportunities to become members of the general education classroom (Kliewer, 1995; Kliewer & Biklen, 2001; Martin, 1994; Rubin, Biklen, et al., 2001). Certainly, accounts of such success alone should serve as motivators to invite students into general education experiences. If teachers need more inspiration, however, federal law can help.

The Individuals with Disabilities Education Act (IDEA)

In 1975, Congress passed the Education for All Handicapped Children Act (PL 94-142), guaranteeing for the first time that all students with disabilities would be provided with a public education. The Act promoted a free and appropriate public education (FAPE) for students with disabilities and mandated that the student must be placed in the least restrictive environment (LRE) to receive this education. This law has revolutionized American education policy. PL 94-142 was also developed to protect the rights (e.g., fairness, appropriateness, and due process in decision-making about providing education and related services) of students with disabilities and their families; to assess and ensure the effectiveness of special education at all levels of government; and to financially assist state and local governments in educating students with disabilities through the use of federal funds. Requirements of PL 94-142 included

- Procedures for referring children suspected of having a disability
- A team comprised of personnel from varied disciplines to determine eligibility
- Team development of an individualized education program (IEP)
- Specialized instruction and placement in an educational setting appropriate to the child's needs
- Procedures for parental notification and participation
- Time limits on how rapidly the eligibility/referral process happens
- Periodic reassessment of the student's eligibility
- Procedures for resolving disagreements and disputes (King-Sears, 1996, p. 89)

PL 94-142, later reauthorized as the Individuals with Disabilities Education Act of 1990 (PL 101-476), began a movement toward civil rights for students with disabilities and set the stage for inclusive schooling.

Free and Appropriate Public Education (FAPE)   The central focus of PL 94-142 and its subsequent revisions is the guarantee of a free appropriate public education (FAPE) for children and youth with disabilities; this means that every student with disabilities can receive educational supports and services at public expense. The passage of the law was a major victory for people with disabilities and their families. This provision was critical because, prior to 1975, many students were either not educated at all or were educated at the expense of their parents or guardians. In 1970, American schools educated only one in five students with disabilities, and more than 1 million students were excluded from public schools. Some states even had laws excluding certain students, including those who were blind, deaf, or labeled "emotionally disturbed" or "mentally retarded." (National Council on Disability; Back to School on Civil Rights, January 25, 2000; http://www.ncd.gov/newsroom/publications/backtoschool_1.html)

Individualized Education Program (IEP)   The IEP is another important tenet of IDEA. The IEP is the cornerstone of the law, providing a framework for the student's educational programming, curriculum, and instruction; it can be viewed as the educational road map for students with disabilities. The IEP document outlines the student's educational goals for the year and how the student will be supported to reach those goals.

An IEP includes the student's current level of functioning, a set of goals and objectives that will be addressed in the upcoming year, and a clear statement of all special services that the student will be receiving. The IEP team for each student with a disability must make an individualized determination regarding how the child will be involved and progress in the general curriculum and whether the child has any other educational needs resulting from his or her disability that also must be met.

Least Restrictive Environment (LRE)   Another important tenet of IDEA is the idea that students with disabilities must be educated in the least restrictive environment (LRE). The proper forum for making the decision regarding LRE is the IEP team. In making this decision, the team must consider the individual needs of the student and must take both academic and non-academic needs into consideration. Specifically, schools are supposed to ensure

> That to the maximum extent appropriate, children with disabilities, including children in public or private institutions and other care facilities, are educated with children who are not disabled, and special classes, separate schooling, or other removal of children with disabilities from the regular educational environment occurs only when the nature or severity of the disability of the child is such that education in regular classes with the use of supplementary aids and services cannot be achieved satisfactorily. (IDEA, 1990 PL 101-476, § 612[a][5])

These phrases from the law mean that *schools have a duty* to try to include students with disabilities in general education classes. The language of the law can be confusing, however, and is often criticized for being ambiguous. For this reason, it can be helpful when considering LRE to look to the courts for clues in understanding the intent of IDEA. In one of the best-known cases, Rachel Holland and her family spent years fighting in court for her right to be educated in a general education classroom (*Sacramento City School District v. Rachel H.*, 1994). The parents challenged the district's decision to place their daughter half-time in a special education classroom and half-time in a general education classroom, they instead wanted their daughter in the regular classroom full-time. The district court ordered an aide and special education consultant to work with Rachel's teacher and held that she should be placed in a general education classroom. The school district appealed this decision all the way to the Supreme Court; when they refused to hear it the lower court's decision was thus affirmed. The Holland family was engaged in pursuing an inclusive education for Rachel for more than 5 years (King-Sears, 1996; Villa & Thousand,

2000; Yell, 1995). According to Yell (1995), some important lessons can be learned from LRE-related litigation:

- LRE decisions are to be made by the IEP team and based on the individual needs of the student
- Children with disabilities have a presumptive right to be educated in integrated settings
- Schools will bear the burden of proof in defending LRE decisions.

Implementation of IDEA   Unfortunately, having a law and seeing it implemented are not one and the same, and many families in the United States are having to fight to get their child into a general education classroom and into inclusive experiences. Just as in *Brown v. Board of Education* (1959), the court decision that integrated schools in the 1950s, it took time—more than 25 years—for schools to catch up with the law. Although many schools and districts have successfully been educating students with disabilities in inclusive settings for years, nationwide implementation of disability law has been slow:

> In the period between 1977–1978 and 1989–1990, there was little or no change in placements of students with disabilities as a group at the national level. In 1977–1978, 68% of students with disabilities were in general education class and resource room environments compared with 69.2% in 1989–1990. Placement of students with disabilities in separate classes was 25.3% in 1977–1978 and 24.8% in 1989–1990. Separate public school facilities and other separate environments educated 6.7% of students with disabilities in 1977–1978 and 5.4% of students with disabilities in 1989–1990 (Karagiannis, Stainback, & Stainback, 1996, p. 23)

The National Council on Disability (NCD; 2000) released similar findings in their independent report, *Back to School on Civil Rights*. The Council found that every state was out of compliance with IDEA requirements and that U.S. officials are not forcing compliance. The investigators also found that children with disabilities are often taught in segregated classrooms and that, in many cases, schools are not following regulations meant to protect students from discrimination.

A student, Empris Carter, quoted in the NCD report, explained her frustration with the continued practice of educational segregation:

Early in the game I discovered that many of my teachers felt that I was a nice, respectful, and intelligent young girl. However, they had some doubts about my capabilities and immediately began to label and set limits on my future role in society. Instead of helping me to find ways to learn, they moved me to a special class where kids were not expected to learn. I would get angry about their doubts and my self-esteem was low. My mother would fight back with encouraging words and my self-esteem would rise again. After being encouraged by mother's words, I again realized that I am the key person in my future.

Learning comes easy for some and is more difficult for others. Education plays a major role in everyone's future. I, Empris Carter, have a place in the future. In order for me to function properly and be able to contribute something positive to our society, I, too, must have the opportunity to receive the best education possible (http://www.ncd.gov/newsroom/publications/backtoschool_1.html).

Even today, it is somewhat common for a student to be labeled as having a disability and placed immediately in a self-contained classroom. Likewise, young children with disabilities who enter kindergarten with a label regularly become members of self-contained classrooms without having an opportunity to experience general education. In other cases, students with disabilities may be moved out of general education environments and into segregated experiences when they move to a new school or district.

Is Anyone Paying Attention to the Law?

More than 25 years after the passage of PL 94-142, many educators and administrators remain unclear about how the law should be implemented and what responsibilities schools have to students with disabilities, their families, and school communities. In some cases, districts may be moving slowly toward inclusive education in order to make the transition smooth for families and students alike. Although this strategy can be an effective way to comfortably introduce teachers and students to change, "moving slowly" cannot be an excuse for stalling when a learner with a disability comes to school requiring an inclusive placement. Schools must move toward the adoption of inclusive practice when a student comes into the school needing such an educational experience. As Reed Martin (2001), a disability-rights attorney, stressed, students and their families have been patient. It is time for schools to learn the law and for government agencies to hold schools accountable:

> Our kids and their families are still having to fight to get simply what they are entitled to in public schools. They are not asking for charity, or asking for schools to feel sorry for them because they have a disability. The accommodations that we fight for are not "I can't be expected to do as much as typical kids do so you have to go easy on me." Our kids have a right to an end to the illegal and unconstitutional discrimination that every day bars students with disabilities from access to what typical students receive. (p. 1)

Common Questions and Answers Related to the Law

By answering the following questions, I will illustrate how the law affects schools, how the law has been interpreted, and how teachers can work toward offering an inclusive education for their students.

Question: Can Schools Choose to Offer Inclusion?

Answer: I often hear teachers and families talking about inclusion as if it is something schools can *choose* to adopt (or reject). For instance, I recently met a teacher who told me that her school "did inclusion but it didn't work" so they "put the kids back." Similarly, a parent sent me a letter explaining that she wanted her child to have an inclusive education, but her neighborhood school doesn't "have inclusion."

Since 1975, federal courts have clarified the intent of the LRE component of the law in favor of the inclusion of students with disabilities in general education. If a student with disabilities can be successfully educated in general education settings with peers without disabilities, then the student's school must provide that experience. Schools *cannot* claim that they do or do not "offer" or "do" inclusion.

From a legal perspective, a school is inclusive when a learner with autism (or any disability) who requires supports and services in his general education classroom begins attending that school. Special education is not a program or a place and inclusive schooling is not a way of doing business that schools can dismiss outright. As the law indicates, students with disabilities should only be removed from general education "when the nature or severity of the disability is such that education in regular classes with the use of supplementary aids and services cannot be achieved satisfactorily" (IDEA, PL 101-476, § 612[a][5]). Therefore, in cases where students can be educated in regular education "satisfactorily," the school must "offer inclusion."

Question: What if the School Isn't Prepared to Be an Inclusive School?

Answer: An important point is that schools cannot refuse to provide an inclusive education for learners because they "don't know how." As far as the federal law is concerned, not knowing is not an excuse for not doing.

Certainly, when PL 94-142 was passed in 1975, the professional literature was void of information or ideas related to inclusive education, differentiating instruction, curricular adaptations, collaboration between special and general educators, and positive behavior supports. Today, however, there are many resources to guide administrators and teachers as they build inclusive classrooms and schools including books, journals, web sites, conferences, and professional consultants.

Teachers and administrators may be occasionally stumped when supporting a student with autism or other unique learning characteristics—that is understandable. If teachers, therapists, or administrators do not have the skills and competencies necessary to educate a learner with disabilities, school leaders must provide these staff members with the training and resources necessary to be successful. Some teachers may work with families to learn about the student's disability. Others attend conferences and workshops. Still others may want to visit successful inclusive schools to observe useful practices.

In some schools, staff members learn inclusive strategies from each other. Speech therapists working in general education classrooms can show general education colleagues how to encourage student vocalizations. Special and general educators can observe each other working with individual students and provide feedback on these interactions. Often, however, the schools that have the most success are those that are prepared to work collaboratively and commit to an inclusive philosophy.

Question: Is Inclusion Right for Students with Significant Disabilities?

Answer: A special education teacher recently told me that she was really interested in inclusive schooling and that she decided to "try it" with one of her students. Patricia, a little girl with significant disabilities, began first grade that fall, but was moved back into a special education classroom by November. The teacher told me how difficult the decision had been and explained why educators had changed Patricia's placement: "The kids really liked her and she loved first grade…but she just wasn't catching on with the reading. She couldn't keep up with the other kids."

Some parents and teachers assume that some students with disabilities cannot be provided an inclusive education because their skills are not similar enough to those of students without disabilities. This is perhaps the most common misconception about the law that exists among families and teachers. Students with disabilities do not need to keep up with students without disabilities to be educated in inclusive classrooms; they do not need to engage in the curriculum in the same way as students without disabilities; and they do not need to practice the same skills as students without disabilities. In sum, no prerequisites are needed for a learner to be able to participate in inclusive education.

For instance, a middle-school social studies class is involved in a lesson on the Constitution. During the unit, the class writes its own Constitution and Bill of Rights and reenacts the Constitutional Convention. Malcolm, a student with significant disabilities, participates in all of these activities even though he cannot speak and is just beginning to read. During the lesson, Malcolm works with a peer and a speech-language therapist to contribute one line to the class Bill of Rights; the pair uses Malcom's augmentative and alternative communication (AAC) device to write the sentence. Malcolm also participates in the dramatic interpretation of the Constitutional Convention. At the Convention, students—acting as different participants of the Convention—drift around the classroom introducing themselves to others. Because he cannot speak, Malcolm (acting as George Mason) shares a little bit about himself by handing out his "business card" to other members of the delegation. Other students are expected to submit three-page reports at the end of the unit, but Malcolm will be assessed on a shorter report (a few sentences) that he will write on his communication device. He will also be assessed on his participation during the class activities, on the demonstration of new skills related to programming his communication device, and on how well he initiates social interactions with others during the Constitutional Convention exercise (Kluth, Villa, & Thousand, 2001).

The Constitutional Convention example illustrates how students with disabilities can participate in general education without engaging in the same ways and without having the same skills and abilities others in the class may have. In addition, this example highlights ways in which students with disabilities can work on individual skills and goals within the context of general education lessons. It is also important to note that the supports and adaptations provided for Malcolm were designed by his teachers and put in place to facilitate his success. Malcolm was not expected to have all of the skills and abilities possessed by other students in order to participate in the classroom. Instead, Malcolm's teachers created a context in which Malcolm could "show up" as competent.

In order for Malcolm to be successful in his classroom, his teachers need to provide him with a range of "supplemental aids and services." Aids and services might include curriculum that is differentiated to meet the needs of the learner, support from a paraprofessional, peer tutors, some type of assistive technology, use of an educational consultant, instruction from a therapist, different seating or environmental supports, modified tests and quizzes, adapted materials (e.g., talking books, visual organizers, computer touch-screen, pencil grips, personal schedule), or any number of other strategies, methods, and approaches. Although schools do not need to provide every support available, they do need to provide those needed by the student with disabilities.

The 1992–1993 case, *Oberti v. Clementon*, illustrated the responsibilities schools have to provide "supplemental aids and services." A U.S. Circuit Court ordered Raphael Oberti, a student with Down syndrome, to be educated in a general education classroom after the Court determined that Raphael's school had not supplied him with the supports and resources he needed to be successful in an inclusive classroom. The judge also ruled that appropriate training had not been provided for his educators and support staff. The school was, therefore, required to make greater efforts to educate Raphael in his classroom or explain why they could not. In upholding Raphael's right to receive his education in his neighborhood school with adequate and necessary supports, the court placed the burden of proof for compliance with IDEA's inclusion requirements squarely on the school district and the state (instead of on the family). That is, the school had to show why Raphael *could not* be educated in general education with aids and services; his family did not have to prove why he *could*. The federal judge who decided the case endorsed inclusive education by writing, "Inclusion is a right, not a special privilege for a select few."

Question: Don't Students with Autism Belong with Other Students with Autism?

Answer: A few years ago I went to my neighborhood school to vote. I was directed down a long hallway and into a classroom marked, "AUTISTIC CENTER." Although it was past 3:00 P.M., a teacher was still in the room working at a desk. I approached her and asked about the classroom. She told me that the room was used to educate all of the students with autism in the school district; this teacher was responsible for educating 11 students with autism.

Across the country, many school districts are still operating and in some cases developing new educational programs for discrete groups of students. Programs and separate classrooms exist for students with certain labels (e.g., emotional disabilities, physical disabilities) and for students with perceived levels of dis/ability. For instance, some districts have programs for students with "severe disabilities." In many cases, students are being placed in these segregated and self-contained environments without being provided with an opportunity to attend a general education classroom with "aids and services." Students are also often placed in such programs without regard for their needs and abilities—that is, students with autism are often educated together because they share a label, not necessarily because they have common needs.

In 1993, the *Roncker v. Walter* case challenged the assignment of students to disability-specific programs and schools. This case addressed the issue of "bringing educational services to the child" versus "bringing the child to the services." The case was resolved in favor of inclusive (versus segregated) placement and established a *principle of portability*. That is, "If a desirable service currently provided in a segregated setting can feasibly be delivered in an integrated setting, it would be inappropriate under PL 94-142 to provide the service in a segregated placement" (700 F.2d.at 1063). The judge in the case stated

> It is not enough for a district to simply claim that a segregated program is superior: In a case where the segregated facility is considered superior, the court should determine whether the services which make the placement superior could be feasibly provided in a non-segregated setting (i.e., regular class). If

they can, the placement in the segregated school would be inappropriate under the act (I.D.E.A.). (*Roncker v. Walter*, 700 F.2d at 1063)

The Roncker Court found that placement decisions must be individually made. School districts that automatically place children in a predetermined type of school solely on the basis of their disability or perceived "level of functioning," rather than on the basis of their educational needs, violate federal laws.

Question: What if the Family Does Not Want an Inclusive Education for Their Child?

Answer: The IDEA clearly states that whenever possible, a student with a disability should be educated in the school he or she would attend if not identified as having a disability. Furthermore, the law indicates that if a student can be successfully educated in general education environments with peers without disabilities, this experience should be provided. As the law states, students with disabilities should only be removed from the general educational environment "when the nature or severity of the disability is such that education in regular classes with the use of supplementary aids and services cannot be achieved satisfactorily."

Therefore, in cases where students can be educated in general education programs satisfactorily, the school districts have no legal responsibility to educate a student with a disability with other students with the same label or in a segregated or self-contained program, even if the parent is nervous about an inclusive situation or they don't feel the school is ready to provide an appropriate education for the child in an inclusive classroom. *This is not to say that the family has "no say" in their child's placement.* In fact, the family of a student with disabilities will have a voice in determining the question of whether an inclusive education experience can be "achieved satisfactorily" by their presence and participation on the IEP team. Therefore, if serious concerns exist, the discussion about placement should take place within this structure and between all team members.

Having answered the question about parent preference from a legal standpoint, I feel I should address this matter from a personal and professional vantage point, as well. It is quite understandable that families might not want their child to be the first or only child with a disability in a classroom or in the neighborhood school. Families may be nervous about having their child be the "test case" for inclusion in a particular school or district; this is a real and important fear. For these reasons, it is important that the law be implemented and that necessary supports are put in place to make the experience successful. It is the school's responsibility to prepare teachers effectively, put the necessary services and supports in place, and provide staff development opportunities for members of the school community.

Question: What if Teachers Do Not Feel Ready to Teach Students with Autism?

Answer: Although many general educators may feel unprepared when they begin educating students with disabilities in their classrooms, all teachers need to see themselves as "inclusion teachers." At any point, any general educator may be called on to serve as the classroom teacher for a student with a disability. Therefore, it is the responsibility of school districts and building administrators to prepare the staff to work with diverse learners and the job of teachers to acquire new skills and develop new competencies when necessary.

The 1997 amendments to IDEA call on general educators to participate more actively than ever before in the education of students with disabilities. For too long, general educators have been asked to participate in the education of students with disabilities but have not been given sufficient opportunity, in most cases, to engage in the planning for and evaluation of learners with disabilities. Finally, the law is respecting the work of general educators and including them as full participants in the education of students with disabilities.

The federal law demands that general educators participate directly in the development of the

> Statement of the special education and related services and supplementary aids and services to be provided to the child, or on behalf of the child, and a statement of the program modifications or supports for school personnel that will be provided for the child. (20 U.S.C. 1414[d][1][A][iii])

For students with more than one general educator (e.g., students in middle and high school), at least one teacher who has actually worked with the student and can therefore provide input regarding whether the educational team's assessment of the student's functioning is sufficient and whether the program being designed for that student seems to make sense. General educators are also vital members of students' educational teams because they are most knowledgeable about the curriculum and instruction in their own classrooms.

SUMMARY

In my own experiences as a teacher I have seen students with autism thrive when provided with opportunities to learn from classmates, participate in cooperative learning activities, engage in general education curriculum, and receive instruction from both general and special educators. Teachers in both elementary and secondary schools, in fact, are finding that students with autism, including those labeled as having "significant disabilities," are being successfully included in general education classrooms (Biklen, 1992; Downing, 1999; Farlow, 1996; Heeden, Ayres, Meyer, & Waite, 1996; Jorgensen, 1998; Kasa-Hendrickson, 2002; Kluth, 1998; Schmidt, 1998).

If success is possible for students with a wide range of needs, why is inclusive schooling not a reality for more students in the United States? I believe that one central reason for this discrepancy is the ways in which most teachers view inclusive schooling. Consider the possibilities that exist when educators view inclusive schooling as a verb—something we *do*, versus viewing it as a noun—something we *have*. Too often, inclusion is used as a noun, as in "We *have* inclusion here, but this child isn't successful in our inclusive classrooms."

An action-oriented understanding of inclusive education can push teachers to refine their practices continually and to become increasingly successful with their students. Seeing inclusion as an action may prompt educators to make inclusive schooling *happen* when they meet a student with challenging communication, behavior, and learning needs—a student who challenges their notion of who gets included in schools. Furthermore, teachers who see inclusion as a process might expect to have struggles as they implement inclusive practices; they expect progress for some students to be bumpy at times and appreciate the learning that may occur with such terrain.

Although understanding inclusive education, the laws related to it, and practical strategies are important, nothing is more helpful in learning about inclusive schooling than doing it. Teachers in today's schools must make a commitment to value the participation of all and to work toward good inclusive practices every day. It is my hope that readers will understand this chapter as a call to action, begin to see inclusive schooling as a verb, and help students with autism gain access to inclusive classrooms and educational experiences.

Perhaps the most important reason to pursue inclusive education, however, is to provide all students with an education that respects the diversities they bring to our schools. As one teacher commented, inclusive schooling is not for or about students with disabilities, it is for and about all learners: "I don't call it inclusive because of [my students with autism]. I call it inclusive because...I am a teacher for all kids. That's what it's all about anyway—teaching and valuing all kids" (Kasa-Hendrickson, 2002, p. 145).

For More Answers and Ideas

Anderson, W., Chitwood, S., & Hayden, D. (1997). *Negotiating the special education maze: A guide for parents and teachers.* Bethesda, MD: Woodbine House.

Capper, C., Frattura, E., & Keyes, M. (2000). *Meeting the needs of students of all abilities: How leaders go beyond inclusion.* Thousand Oaks, CA: Corwin Press.

Downing, J. (2002). *Including students with severe and multiple disabilities in typical classrooms.* Baltimore: Paul H. Brookes Publishing Co.

Fisher, D., Sax, C., & Pumpian, I. (1999). *Inclusive high schools: Learning from contemporary classrooms.* Baltimore: Paul H. Brookes Publishing Co.

Grenot-Scheyer, M., Fisher, M., & Staub, D., (Eds.). (1999). *At the end of the day: Lessons learned in inclusive education.* Baltimore: Paul H. Brookes Publishing Co.

Jorgensen, C. (1998). *Restructuring high schools for all students: Taking inclusion to the next level.* Baltimore: Paul H. Brookes Publishing Co.

Kliewer, C. (1998). *Schooling children with Down syndrome.* New York: Teachers College Press.

(continued)

(continued)

Kluth, P., Straut, D., & Biklen, D. (in press). *Access to academics: Critical approaches to inclusive curriculum, instruction, and policy.* Mahwah, NJ: Lawrence Erlbaum Associates.

Peterson, M., & Hittie, M. (2003). *Inclusive teaching: Creating effective schools for all learners.* Needham Heights, MA: Allyn & Bacon.

Sailor, W. (Ed.). (2002). *Whole-school success and inclusive education: Building partnerships for learning, achievement, and accountability.* New York: Teachers College Press.

Thousand, J.S., Villa, R.A., & Nevin, A.I. (2002). *Creativity and collaborative learning: The practical guide to empowering students, teachers, and families* (2nd ed.). Baltimore: Paul H. Brookes Publishing Co.

Villa, R., & Thousand, J. (Eds.). (1995). *Creating an inclusive school.* Alexandria, VA: Association for Supervision and Curriculum Development.

Villa, R., & Thousand, J. (Eds.). (2000). *Restructuring for caring and effective education: Piecing the puzzle together* (2nd ed.). Baltimore: Paul H. Brookes Publishing Co.

Wheelock, A. (1992). *Crossing the tracks: How untracking can save America's schools.* New York: The New Press.

CHAPTER 3

The Role of the Teacher

ATTITUDES, VALUES, AND ACTIONS THAT SUPPORT INCLUSIVE SCHOOLING

People are always looking for the single magic bullet that will totally change everything. There is no single magic bullet. I was very lucky to receive very good early intervention with very good teachers, starting at age 2½ years. I cannot emphasize enough the importance of a good teacher. A good teacher is worth his or her weight in gold. (Grandin, 1996b)

In every classic example of students finding "unexpected" success, we find a teacher who believes that all students can learn and who implements practices in order to make this expectation come true (Keller, 1954; Ladson-Billings, 1994; Matthews, 1988; Meier, 1995; Moses & Cobb, 2001). Clearly, teachers have incredible power to inspire learning and create important change in schools and in communities. Hiam Ginott summarized the amazing charge of teachers in this often-quoted philosophy:

> I have come to the conclusion that I am the decisive element in the classroom. It's my personal approach that creates the climate. It's my daily mood that makes the weather. As a teacher, I possess a tremendous power to make a child's life miserable or joyous. I can be a tool of torture or an instrument of inspiration. I can humiliate or humor, hurt or heal. In all situations, it is my response that decides whether a crisis will be escalated or de-escalated and a child humanized or de-humanized. (1972, p. 13)

NINE WAYS TO SUPPORT STUDENTS WITH AUTISM WHILE PROMOTING INCLUSIVE SCHOOLING

This chapter is dedicated to the role of the teacher as an educational leader and change agent and stresses how central are the attitudes, beliefs, and actions of teachers to the cultivation of inclusive education. I outline nine ways in which teachers can support students with autism while promoting inclusive schooling. These include the following:

1. Recognize differences.
2. Interrogate the use of labels.
3. Reconfigure expertise.
4. Preserve student dignity.
5. Look for complexity in learners.
6. Serve as an advocate and teach advocacy.
7. Act as teacher and learner.
8. Listen.
9. Practice subversive pedagogy, if necessary.

1. Recognize Differences

Sometimes seeing and understanding differences are complicated for a teacher; for example, teachers often say, "I don't see disabilities, all of my students are special" or, "If you walk into my classroom you can't tell which student has autism." Although these statements may be well intentioned, they are often misguided. It is, I believe, impossible to "not see" disability or ethnicity or race or the other differences that make up all of our lives; these elements are real and important; they are an integral part of who we are as individuals and as members of our communities. As Sapon-Shevin pointed out, accepting all learners is key, but ignoring differences may not be a desirable way to show such acceptance:

> If differences are minimized or covered up to meet a goal of making all students look the same, what messages are communicated to students about differences? Is it better to talk about Nadia's hearing aides and what kinds of help and support she needs, or should we discourage the other students from noticing that she wears them or that they sometimes squeak or that she has obviously missed a verbal cue? Is it best to accommodate Tim's diabetes and special dietary needs by inconspicuously giving him different treats at snack time so as to spare him the embarrassment of needing a special accommodation? (2001, p. 24)

"Not seeing" is not a positive response to difference. Recognizing, however, and doing our best to really understand how differences affect students' lives and educational experiences, helps us to better know and serve each individual student.

In inclusive schools, students are encouraged to express their individuality and to acknowledge "not only what is good and enjoyable in their lives but also what is painful and hard" (Sapon-Shevin, 1999, p. 35). As Sapon-Shevin stressed, teachers need to encourage students to feel comfortable with their differences, but to do so, they must first create a context for differences to be exposed and accepted:

> We want to create chances for students to share all aspects of themselves: the good, the laudable, the troublesome, and the confusing. Because community and cultural values and standards concerning what's appropriate to share are apt to vary considerably, it is important for teachers to be extremely sensitive in respecting children's differences. (1999, p. 36)

The inclusive schooling movement has inspired a paradigm shift in the field of education. This critical education reform has helped teachers conceptualize differences as essential and valued aspects of classrooms. Inclusive teachers *desire* differences in the classroom and view them as critical to student learning. In good inclusive schools, "the view that differences among individuals in education pose difficulties and need to be fixed, improved, or made ready to fit (i.e., homogenized) is replaced by the recognition that differences are valuable assets to capitalize on" (Stainback, 2000, p. 508).

2. Interrogate the Use of Labels

Teachers in diverse classrooms must recognize the benefits of celebrating student differences while working to know students as individual learners. During busy classroom days, teachers may rely on stereotypes, assumptions, and perceptions in their daily social interactions with students and in the planning of curriculum and instruction. Educators may also fall into the trap of using labels or simple descriptions of students (e.g., "the two autistics in my health class," "the slow kids in the ninth grade") in conversations with colleagues, in educational reports or other types of communication, and even in interactions with students themselves.

The labeling of differences presents a challenge. Although labeling and identity politics can certainly result in benefits such as self-affirmation, positive self-image, and connectivity with others, the limitations presented by labels are many. Labels can be constricting and limiting, and relying on them to describe students can lead teachers to see a student's autism before or instead of seeing the individual student. As Nancy Burns, a woman with a disability, pointed out, labeling often results in "othering":

As someone with a disability, I don't want to be thought of or treated like I'm special, stupid, a freak, different, the village idiot, an alien from outer space, a second class citizen or invisible. Treat me with the same amount of respect and consideration you would give to someone else—no matter what. Get to know the person on the inside and not just by the disability. I bet you'll find they are not that much different from you. (1998, p. 12)

In the staff lounge, at faculty meetings, and in educational reports, students are often described in one-dimensional and often unflattering ways. Consider the story of Xang, a first-grade student. One of his teachers gave me a report that made Xang sound very needy and incompetent: "Xang is very disruptive in class. He needs help to complete even the simplest of tasks. Academically, Xang is also experiencing problems. He is struggling in reading and writing in Hmong and in English." In this report and in conversations Xang was often seen as the slow English as a second language student instead of as the active, inquisitive, bilingual, and biliterate youngster that he was. Similarly, James, a student with autism in the same school, was often seen as anti-social, obsessed, and "in his own world" when he wrote and solved his own math equations. His mother and siblings, however, saw him as the brilliant academic learner he was.

Ayres (2001) called this labeling of students "a toxic habit." He illustrated the need to examine and carefully critique the ways in which students are described and ultimately perceived:

It's as if supervisors, coordinators, and administrators have nothing better to do than to mumble knowingly about "soft signs," "attention deficit disorder," or "low impulse control," and all the rest of us stand around smiling, pretending to know what they're talking about. The categories keep splintering and proliferating, getting nuttier as they go: L.D., B.D., E.H., T.A.G., E.M.H. It's almost impossible for teachers today not to see before them "gifted and talented" students, "learning disabled" youngsters, and children "at risk." (p. 29)

To combat labeling that is harmful, teachers must work to understand the uniqueness of each student. This might mean spending time with students one to one or asking them to share personal information during class. To see each student as an individual, the teacher should also consciously speak about the person with autism as an individual. Instead of comparing and contrasting descriptions of students with autism and talking about these learners as if they are one homogeneous group, teachers who resist the overuse of labels will share information about "Nathan's accomplishments," "Kevin's abilities," and "Anne's success."

3. Reconfigure Expertise

Too often, students with autism are told about their lives instead of having opportunities to craft their own stories. In order for inclusive education to thrive, teachers must be curious about and interested in the expertise and experiences of individuals with autism. Furthermore, teachers must act on the education they receive from students. Teachers should consider, also, the gifts and strengths that children with autism bring to the classrooms. True inclusive education looks at all students as individuals who can benefit from each other. It is not a specialized program meant to help only a few. The unique perspectives that children with autism can share with others can help their peers and teachers see the world in a new light.

In inclusive classrooms, the teacher looks to the students as the experts, asks them what they would like to learn, and invites them to teach and lead in the classroom. In doing so, the teacher examines his or her own expertise and power. Kliewer and Biklen called for a shifting in our understanding of expertise:

A part of the disability rights agenda has been to reconfigure the meaning of *expert* [italics added]. It demands that no research be conducted on, nor policy implemented for, people with disabilities without their participation. This is certainly a radical democratic stance, but one that comes on the heels of years of subjugation, objectification, and outright silencing at the hands of scientists and policymakers. In effect, people with disabilities are proclaiming to the scientific and policy communities, "Our rights are not yours to give away. The reach of professional prerogative stops at the tenets of democracy." (2000, p. 198)

Educators must shed their desire to be "in charge" and to make all decisions. This power shifting can cause discomfort, however. Danforth and Rhodes pointed out that "Seeking, hearing, and taking seriously the words and ideas of the persons served by special programs, although seemingly innocent enough, is often disruptive" (1997, p. 363).

Dan Reed (1996) relayed an example of such a disruption in his book, *Paid for the Privilege: Hearing the Voices of Autism.* He shared the story of Randy, a man who often hit others in his day treatment program. Reed explained that Randy was not a mean person; rather, he was easily startled and if someone surprised him, he might hit them. When the hitting began, the staff would immediately "get in Randy's space" to protect him and any others in the area. After learning to communicate through the use of facilitated communication, however, Randy was able to tell his team how to better handle the hitting outbursts: "Just give me room to breathe" Randy typed. The staff of the program decided to honor Randy's expertise and changed their intervention. Instead of moving toward Randy to intervene when the hitting started, the staff moved away and let him have room. Reed reported that "Almost without fail, he calms down in a few seconds—no interventions, no head-butts, no more loss of dignity" (p. 113).

Clearly, listening to students is not simply a matter of giving attention and providing opportunity; educators and others who support individuals with autism must respond to the voices of these individuals even when they present information or ideas that challenge authority or criticize institutional structures. Although Randy's request did, in a sense, challenge the way the staff had been responding to crisis in the program, staff members were able to hear that challenge and use it as a learning experience. And even though the suggested intervention was a significant departure from the typical interventions used in settings like schools, group homes, and day programs, this staff honored the suggestion and gave Randy the ability to design his own supports.

4. Preserve Student Dignity

Although every teacher, undoubtedly, wants to protect students and help them to build self-respect and self-esteem, these goals are sometimes inadvertently put on the educational "back burner" during busy classroom days. Ironically, when students are not achieving or participating, it is often because we have neglected our personal relationships with them. It is, indeed, in those moments when we pause to listen to our students and learn about who they are and what they need that we do the most to facilitate their learning.

Hutchinson suggested that "dignity requires that the creating of one's life be honored" and that "...marginalization is the antithesis of dignity" (1999, pp. 63–64). If we subscribe to Hutchinson's version of dignity, it stands to reason that it is the teacher's job to find space and time for students to shine and to reveal their complexities to others. It is also the teacher's job, then, to consider the ways in which students are marginalized and forgotten and to challenge the structures and practices that hurt students and prevent their full participation and membership in the school community.

Teachers who create comfortable and supportive classrooms in which students can be themselves allow for the preservation and sustenance of all students' dignity. In such classrooms, intimidation, taunting, and name-calling of students who look, communicate, or behave somewhat differently from the "norm" are questioned by teachers and students alike. As Nieto pointed out, behaviors that threaten student dignity can even be turned into a classroom lesson on social justice:

The name-calling that goes on in many schools provides a tremendous opportunity for teachers and students to engage in dialogue. Rather than addressing these as isolated incidents or as the work of a few troublemakers, as is too often done, making them an explicit part of the curriculum helps students understand these incidents as symptoms of systemic problems in society and schools. Making explicit the biases that are implicit in name-calling can become part of a "circle" or "sharing time," or can form the basis for lessons on racism, sexism, ableism [i.e., prejudice toward those with disabilities], or other biases. (2000, p. 356)

Even students in the most supportive classrooms, however, may need extra support. Some students with autism have experienced embarrassment, frustration, and even trauma in their educational history. Some, for instance, may have been physically punished by a teacher or excessively teased by peers. Students without identified disabilities may need support, as well. Shy students, students new to the classroom, or those who are experiencing difficulties of some kind may need more encouragement and attention than others. For these students, it may be especially important that teachers find ways to show compassion and caring.

Finally, dignity can be preserved when educators cultivate and maintain personal relationships with students. Students should feel comfortable showing their uniqueness in the classroom and bringing their personal life to the teacher and to classmates. As Cummins (1996) pointed out, the heart of effective teaching is knowing students: "Good teaching does not require us to internalize an endless list of instructional techniques. Much more fundamental is the recognition that human relationships are central to effective instruction" (p. 73). Likewise, Jasmine Lee O' Neill (1999), a woman with autism, believes that the best professionals are those who want to know students as individuals:

Good professionals in the field spend a lot of time getting to know each new autistic client or pupil. They respect that sensitive person's characteristic to live like a shy sea creature inside a vibrant, colourful, self-containing shell home. They are interested in each one as a human being. They delight in the surprises that unfold as they get to know the autistic individual. (p. 22)

5. Look for Complexity in Learners

Educators must constantly be scouting for student talents and seeking situations that highlight the abilities and support the needs of diverse learners. Teachers of students with autism must believe that students *are* competent and then they must "set the stage" for students to perform competently. For instance, I once worked with a high school teacher who taught Scott, a student with autism, in her computer class. This learner had limited speech and experienced significant struggles with movement; he often entered her classroom running and during lessons he typically paced up and down between the computer tables. This student was very skilled at certain computer games and could type some sentences on his own.

In order to highlight his complexities, the computer teacher set up her daily lesson to complement Scott's needs and abilities. All students spent the first 20 minutes of class listening to the teacher explain a new skill or concept. During the next 30 minutes, students worked individually or in teams to practice the skill. Scott was given a different schedule of activities to follow, however. Instead of working on the computer for the first 20 minutes, Scott listened to the teacher discuss the new concept as he paced in the back of the room. Then, when students began working on their own, Scott was allowed to pace between tables and stop at different stations to teach his classmates some of the computer games he had mastered. In exchange, students would review the daily work with Scott in a one-to-one format.

The arrangement seemed to benefit all students in the class. Scott's classmates appreciated learning something fun every week, and Scott had an opportunity to learn skills and concepts in a relaxed, small-group situation, which appeared to boost his understanding of the content. As important, Scott's classmates had opportunities to see their peer's talent for learning new software and mastering complicated computer games. Students who had never seen Scott excel at any activity were amazed at his quick reflexes and problem-solving abilities.

In another classroom, a teacher became curious about the behavior of Billy, one of his students who happened to have autism. Billy would come into Spanish class every day and stare at the map of Mexico. It took several reminders to get him to move away from the map and take his seat at the beginning of class. During the second month of school, Billy's behavior still had not changed. Instead of taking the map down as a colleague had suggested, Billy's teacher put a map of Spain next to the one of Mexico. Billy became equally interested in that map. A map of Puerto Rico followed until over a dozen maps filled the walls of the room. The teacher then gave Billy smaller versions of the maps to keep at his desk so he would be able to study the countries when he was listening to a lesson.

These examples illustrate how teachers build student learning and interest when they look for competence and see students as learners. The teachers built experiences from student strengths so that the learners with autism would succeed and so that all in the classroom community would be able to appreciate those strengths. Teachers can look for competence and complexity in learners in many ways—by helping an individual student shine during a lesson, studying a student's learning style and teaching to it, or exploring how a student expresses him- or herself and carving out a place in the classroom for that form of expression. Teachers looking for competence and complexity in learners should constantly consider the following questions (Ayers, 2001; Kluth, Biklen, & Straut, in press):

- Who is this student?
- Under what circumstances does this student thrive?
- What gifts/skills/abilities does this student have?
- What is this student's awareness of himself or herself as a learner?
- What effort or potential does this student bring?
- How can I help this student find success?
- What prevents me from/helps me to see this student's competence?
- How does this student learn?
- What does this student value?
- How and what can I learn from this student?

6. Serve as an Advocate and Teach Advocacy

One of the most important roles a teacher can adopt is to advocate for students. In many cases, teachers who have students with disabilities in their classrooms become responsible for teaching other educators about inclusive education or about specific disabilities. These teachers may also be responsible for answering the questions that families, the PTA, or the local community may pose about inclusive education. For these reasons, it is important that teachers remain aware of the laws as they relate to inclusive education and become familiar with some of the research related to inclusion and educating diverse learners. Teachers should also become familiar with advocacy groups such as The Association for Persons with Severe Handicaps (TASH) (www.tash.org) and Autism National Committee (Autcom) and the Autism Society of America (see the For More Answers and Ideas box at the end of the chapter).

Teachers need to study the greater school community; the curriculum; and the organization, politics, and culture of the school. Teacher advocates will also question their own education and look for opportunities to create change in their school communities through staff development, partnerships with the greater community, and political participation. For example, groups of teachers from Seattle to New York are resisting the standardized testing movement and advocating for the use of more authentic and meaningful assessments. Teachers involved in this anti-testing movement are particularly concerned with eliminating the racial, class, gender, and cultural barriers to equal opportunity posed by standardized tests, and preventing the damage caused by these liabilities to the quality of education. Many also feel that the tests are unfair to students with disabilities; these advocates feel that the tests assess the students' disabilities more than their academic abilities. Some teachers involved in this movement are refusing to administer the tests. Others are attending school board meetings to protest the assessments (Rethinking Schools, 2000).

In order to truly make a difference, teachers and students must be committed to inspiring change in a way that respects and values all participants equally. This means that in addition to serving as advocates, teachers must promote student self-advocacy. All students are capable of making contributions to their own education and most teachers do not know enough about experiencing disability to begin to answer to the multiplicity of issues that students face in their educational lives.

Self-advocacy involves students acting or speaking on their own behalf or on behalf of others with disabilities. To encourage self-advocacy, teachers might encourage students to run for student council, give them opportunities to present information about autism to teachers or to community members, help students find ways to contribute to their individualized education program (IEP) meetings and to other educational planning meetings, make sure students are given choices and consulted regarding the decisions related to their education (e.g., daily schedule, extracurricular activities), and provide them with opportunities to articulate their preferences and needs.

7. Act as Teacher and Learner

Schools need ways of bringing learners and teachers together and of becoming communities in which participants learn from each other. Teachers must have ways of renewing themselves, of being open to new ideas, and of trying out different strategies and approaches to learning. Some teachers may prefer to continue learning through professional development seminars or college or university courses. Others may seek opportunities in their own buildings. For example, one school I visited held "Share an Idea" workshops every month. Every staff person in the building was invited to present and to attend. A different teacher or team presented one idea during each session. Topics ranged from "Using Writing Workshops in the Inclusive Classroom" to "Co-Teaching with Your Speech Therapist" to "Stress Relief at 3:00 P.M." This gave teachers ways to grow as practitioners and helped the school to move forward with progressive practices.

Some schools have instituted book clubs for teachers and other staff members. In one of the schools in which I taught, the book club chose both professional selections (e.g., a book on cooperative learning) and personal favorites that were not directly related to schools and schooling. These experiences allowed teachers to keep current with professional reading and also provided opportunities to socialize and develop a community. In another school, I started a book club focused specifically on autism. This school had an unusually high number of students with autism and the teachers were constantly seeking opportunities to learn more and to exchange ideas on the topic. We initially focused on autobiographies of individuals with autism, and then teachers took turns suggesting other texts that would help them in their work.

For those teachers or educational teams who seem to lack common time to meet, web-based discussion boards might be used to share information. Discussion boards can be used to brainstorm lesson ideas, share positive behavior supports, or post teaching questions and success stories. During a school year when I worked on a grant project with a group of educators that spanned 12 different schools and 7 different districts, the administrators of the project set up an Internet discussion group to encourage conversation and idea sharing. Teachers shared a range of success stories ("Donald ate his lunch by himself today"), questions ("What ideas do folks have for helping a student who likes to fidget or doodle during classes? What kinds of toys or gadgets have others used?"), and thoughts ("I have started talking to students in a softer voice and they are responding. I am going to keep using this with Marie and Carol and will try it with Dottie today. I'll let everyone know how it works"). This structure not only gave our group a way to communicate ideas but it also served as a way to build a support system among educators who shared values and a common purpose but seldom had opportunities to meet face to face.

8. Listen

Teachers who are good listeners often find that students are able to provide them with an exceptional education about teaching, learning, and dozens of other topics. For example, consider this description of the perfect school written by Jamie Burke, a young teenager with autism, on his augmented communication device:

A school of good soft seats and desks that held wonderful books that told of love and kindness to each other. Kids would need to behave in a most kind manner and teasing would be a detention time. Everyone would be asked to join all clubs if desired and pleasing music would play everywhere. The teacher, good and many of them, would only be as we choose. Not assigned by computers. Courses chosen by love of subject and teachers must be excellent in that class. If homework was told to be done time more than one day is given. Lunch would be served in a room far from cooking so smells are not sickening. The lunch would be a time for peaceful eating and not loud talking and annoying bells and whistles which split my ears as a sword in use of killing monsters. All of the new kids would be treated to a monster movie. Dear parents are welcomed to meet really good all dear teachers to tell of kids powers. But my school is very good and people try both teaching and loving me and my autism. So I think I am fearing less now than younger times of my life and joy in life as a boy in a journey to a happy life is even a dream now seen. Respect comes with love and understanding each kid's abilities and the desire to teach so therefore teachers must have a desire to teach everyone. They must realize that their dreams are not ours ask us what we will need to be an independent person later in our life. Teach good skills in a respectful way. Conversations with me will tell you if I'm happy. (Burke, 1999, p. 4)

This passage is important for at least two reasons; first, it provides teachers with concrete ideas for supporting Jamie. An educator who is willing to learn from this student will carefully consider the seating used in his or her classroom or the types of materials available. Second, this description of school is incredibly poetic and introspective. A teacher who listens to Jamie's ideas is also learning about his great talent for writing and expression.

Teachers must also consider ways to listen to students with communication differences. Teachers and students in the inclusive classroom will need to consider how they might listen fully and generously to those who do not speak, those with limited English, those with different accents or linguistic styles, and those who struggle to be expressive in whole or small-group situations. Teachers might work with students to create listening adaptations in order to encourage the voices of all. For example, the classroom community might agree to make a very conscious effort to respond to the verbalizations and gestures of peers who do not speak. If a student with disabilities grunts, laughs, or yells out, peers might turn and say, "Patty, you sure seem to have a strong feeling about that. Can you tell us more using your communication device?" Adapting to all learners might also mean working as a group to learn more about the diverse communication styles and approaches in the classroom. The entire class might communicate for an afternoon using only written words, or learn storytelling gesticulations or sign language greetings and conversation starters.

Another way teachers listen is by tuning into students as they work and socialize. Teachers who participate in casual conversations at lunchtime or who "hang out" in hallways can learn about students in more holistic ways. What makes students excited? Worried? What are they knowledgeable about? Interested in? Afraid of?

Teachers may find keys to teaching and learning and discover ways to better support students by listening carefully and respectfully during informal but important moments.

My friend Eileen, a fifth-grade teacher, found ways to listen to her students by forming an "anyone-is-welcome" poetry club. She benefited as a teacher not only by participating in a social activity with students but also by eliciting their

voices through the poems they wrote. Other teachers listen to students by joining them for lunch, coaching a sport, chaperoning a dance, playing with them at
recess, or finding moments to connect with them individually in the classroom.

9. Practice Subversive Pedagogy, if Necessary

Janna, a teacher I know, was asked to set up a behavior management program
for one of her students with autism. Janna was told by a district behavior specialist to ignore this student if he bit his hands or screamed. If the young man
was able to refrain from biting his hands and screaming for more than 20 minutes, Janna was to reward him with a baseball card.

Janna refused to implement the program. She believed the student's hand
biting and screaming was happening because he was uncomfortable and scared
in his new school. Janna was very concerned about her student and was determined to learn what was causing the behaviors. Janna felt that ignoring the behaviors was cruel and she worried that this approach would negatively affect
her relationship with the young man.

In rejecting the specialist's program, Janna was practicing what some might
call *subversive pedagogy*. That is, Janna was rejecting common institutional practices in favor of those she saw as more humane and appropriate. Teachers who
practice subversive pedagogy "question the policies, procedures, and practices
of those who employ them and of these institutions that prevent individual opportunity and growth" (Lasley, Matczynski, & Rowley, 2002, p. 387).

Another example of subversive pedagogy comes from my own teaching
experience. During a short period of time when I was teaching in a district that
did not support inclusive education, I attended an uncomfortable meeting with
a family and an administrator. The mother and father wanted their son to be
educated in a general education fifth-grade classroom. The administrator told
the family that it would be too difficult to provide the child's education in such
an environment. She gave them several reasons but told them it was primarily
a staffing issue; she did not "have" a general education teacher knowledgeable
enough or even willing to support a student like their son. The family seemed
disappointed when they left the meeting but appeared to accept the administrator's answer. When I tried to talk to the administrator (my boss) about the
issue, she made it clear that the decision had been made. I left her office, went
back to my room, found a "Parents' Rights in Special Education" booklet in my
files, highlighted the sections of importance, and anonymously sent it to the
family in the mail. Days later, the parent advocate the family had hired called
the administrator to discuss inclusive schooling again.

Subversive pedagogy is not a new phenomenon; there is a long tradition
in education of teachers resisting practices and structures deemed oppressive
and/or harmful to students (Ashton-Warner, 1963; Ayers, 2001; Freire, 1970;
Holt, 1967; Kozol, 1967; Ladson-Billings, 1994; Paley, 1979). Ayers reported that
he once clipped the wires of the classroom intercom after a stream of senseless
announcements disrupted his teaching. Students were able to learn in peace
after this act of "creative insubordination" as the intercom was not repaired for
3 years (2001, p. 125).

Teachers in Ladson-Billings' study of successful teachers of African
American students also supported learners by resisting policies and structures

deemed oppressive. The researcher explained how the educators felt it was necessary to challenge structures with action:

> The teachers I studied work in opposition to the school system that employs them. They are critical of the way that the school system treats employees, students, parents, and activists in the community. However, they cannot let their critiques reside solely in words. They must turn into action by challenging the system. What they do is both their lives and livelihoods. In their classrooms, they practice a subversive pedagogy. (1994, p. 128)

These teachers in Ladson-Billing's study did everything from rejecting the classroom materials they were told to use (e.g., using trade books and literature instead of text books) to quietly sidestepping school policies they deemed inappropriate or damaging to their students. Ladson-Billings points out that even though it is sometimes difficult business to struggle against oppression, teachers must not "legitimate the inequity that exists in the nation's schools, but attempt to delegitimate it by placing it under scrutiny" (p. 130). She goes on to point out that sometimes "working in opposition to the system is the most likely road to success for students who have been discounted and disregarded by the system" (p. 130). When working with students with autism, then, subversive pedagogy may involve challenging IEPs or reports that contain insensitive or negative language; resisting behavior programs and plans that are undignified, hurtful, or fail to consider the student's individual needs and strengths; rejecting curriculum that does not engage or challenge the learner; or pursuing inclusive education when administrators discourage such actions.

SUMMARY

My sister once sent me a postcard that read, "No one forgets a good teacher." This simple phrase has been at the center of my work in teacher education ever since. When most of us think of our favorite teachers, we think about someone who knew us well, someone who took the time to learn from us, someone who liked us, and someone who thought that we were capable. Therefore, even though it is critical that our educators are knowledgeable and skilled, stories of favorite or most effective teachers are seldom about curriculum.

Although a good teacher certainly needs to know how to develop lesson plans and draw students into learning, the teacher's orientation toward the students is typically the most powerful predictor of success in the classroom. A teacher's beliefs matter. Her politics matter. Her language matters. Her relationships with students matter. Her values matter. In fact, these things matter in very real and very practical ways. Students surely know when and if the teacher believes they will learn and be successful. Consider the words of Stephen Shore, a man with Asperger's syndrome:

I was usually behind in math and reading by at least half a grade. The first-grade teacher said that I would never be able to do math. Nevertheless, somehow I learned and have even taught the subject at the college level. I believe this teacher would be shocked to learn that I went on to study calculus and statistics in college. (2001, p. 49)

Sadly, Shore achieved in mathematics *despite* instead of *in concert with* his teacher's expectation. There is no room for such pessimism in education. The teacher's belief in the learner is central to success in the classroom. The best lessons, curricular adaptations, and teaching strategies are useless if a teacher does not expect the learner to achieve, consistently question his or her own assumptions, and constantly reflect upon the attitudes, values, and actions he or she brings to the daily work of teaching and learning.

For More Answers and Ideas

Ashton-Warner, S. (1963). *Teacher.* New York: Simon & Schuster.

Ayers, W. (2001). *To teach.* New York: Teachers College Press.

Freedom Writers & Gruwell, E. (1999). *The freedom writers diary.* New York: Doubleday.

Ladson-Billings, G. (1994). *The dreamkeepers: Successful teachers of African-American children.* San Francisco: Jossey-Bass.

Michie, G. (1999). *Holler if you hear me.* New York: Teachers College Press.

Paley, V. (1990). *The boy who would be a helicopter.* Cambridge, MA: Harvard University Press.

Organizations

The Association for Persons with Severe Handicaps (TASH)
29 W. Susquehanna Avenue, Suite 210
Towson, MD 21204
(410) 828-8274
http://www.tash.org/

TASH's focus is on those people with disabilities who
- Are most at risk for being excluded from the mainstream of society
- Are perceived by traditional service systems as being most challenging
- Are most likely to have their rights abridged
- Are most likely to be at risk for living, working, playing, and/or learning in segregated environments
- Are least likely to have the tools and opportunities necessary to advocate on their own behalf
- Historically have been labeled as having severe disabilities
- Are most likely to need ongoing, individualized supports in order to participate in inclusive communities and enjoy a quality of life similar to that available to all citizens

(continued)

(continued)

Autism National Committee (Autcom)
Post Office Box 6175
North Plymouth, MA 02362-6175.
http://www.autcom.org/

An advocacy organization dedicated to "Social Justice for All Citizens with Autism" through a shared vision and a commitment to positive approaches. AUTCOM was founded in 1990 to protect and advance the human rights and civil rights of all persons with autism, pervasive developmental disorder, and related differences of communication and behavior.

Autism Society of America (ASA)
7910 Woodmont Avenue
Suite 300
Bethesda, MD 20814-3067

The ASA is dedicated to increasing public awareness of autism and the day-to-day issues of individuals with autism and others involved in their lives. The Society provides information, education, research, and advocacy.

CHAPTER 4

Connecting with Families

WITH EILEEN YOSHINA

"Mom," I said, "I'm autistic too, aren't I?"
"Yes," she said. We sat very still and looked at each
other for a long, long time. I had the strangest feeling, one that
was entirely new to me. All at once I knew that I could ask Mom anything,
say anything I wanted, and that it would be all right—
she would understand me. (Barron & Barron, 1992, p. 229)

As teachers, we should work closely with the families of students with disabilities, not necessarily because it is considered "best practice," or because families will often be the most willing and open collaborative partners to whom we can turn. These reasons are relevant, but the most important and compelling reason to build a strong home–school partnership is related to the intimate relationship that exists between children and their families; the parents of our students know them in ways teachers do not. Parents also *see* students in ways teachers do not. They can provide more rich and detailed information about a student than any professional we can ask or any report we can read.

Consider the story of Beth Kephart (1998), the mother of a school-age son with the label of pervasive developmental disorder (PDD). Beth tried to enroll her son in a preschool. When Jeremy showed up for a day-long visit to the school, the principal followed him around the school with a clipboard, making marks each time he struggled. Meanwhile, Kephart could only look on anxiously:

Jeremy tries—valiantly—to go along with the morning routine. Sits at the computer beside another boy, then attempts to take on the software himself. It's new to him. He fails, gets frustrated. The principal, watching from the corner of the room, strikes a check across her clipboard, and we're asked to move on and join the children in another room who are convening for a snack. There's only one slight problem with the principal's worthy plan—all but Jeremy have special, placarded chairs. When the principal asks Jeremy if he wants something to drink, he circles the room looking for space at the table, offers no answer, returns to me, hurt and teary-eyed. Another check, and we move on.

It's circle time. All the children from two to five gather in a darkened room to sing the songs they must sing every day. Adorable songs with charming hand motions and the inevitable *We all fall down.* The kids look so darling and chipper as they wag their yellow hair. They look so normal and zesty, kindled by the possibility of a glorious soloist spot. I know some of the songs, but I've never sung them to Jeremy and I don't believe they're staples at [his current school]. In the circles Jeremy sits and stares. He watches with magnificent patience and I am immensely proud, until the principal asks him if he wants to be the farmer in the dell, and pulls him to the center of the room. *What's a dell?* His eyes seem to be imploring, and what can he possibly do if he doesn't know the answer and the principal's not saying and the other children giggle until Jeremy finally sits down? Another mark on the despicable clipboard, and I throw a spear of hatred across the room.

Afterward it is time for recess, and Jeremy, genuinely relieved, gallops all around the yard, climbs the equipment with abandon, dances to his own dervish tune—demonstrating the grace and balance he's exhibited from his start. It doesn't matter. The performance falls on dead eyes. I am ready for the principal when she approaches with her news. "I've been thinking," she tells me, with a sugary, grandmotherly smile, "that we simply don't have room. The child with diabetes is taking all our extra time, and that means we could never do right by your son." (Kephart, 1998, pp. 164–165)

In this preschool scenario, it is clear how much the perspective of a parent matters. Without Kephart's interpretations, Jeremy's teachers may not know that using new software will be a challenge for Jeremy or that he *can* successfully participate in the school's snack time if given information about where to sit and how to engage in the routine or that he *does* know how to sing songs (just not those particular songs). Furthermore, it seems that only the parent sees Jeremy's "grace and balance" and knows how very hard he is working to be successful in the preschool activities.

Harry (1992) suggested that teachers must constantly ask the question "Do we assume that professional efforts constitute the only legitimate source of opinion, and that the role of parents is to give permission for professional activities and automatic approval for professional decisions?" If the answer to the question is "yes," then changes are essential as a true partnership with families cannot grow from such a belief system. If families are ignored, dismissed, or otherwise prevented from participating in the education of their child, the student's edu-

> Somehow, somewhere, an invisible barrier has been built between school and home. We all need to realize how much we both are an integral part of our children's education. What is done at home impacts what is done at school. What is done at school impacts what is done at home. Student progress would soar if we could all be on the "same page."
>
> As a parent, I feel that at times I've had to beg, borrow, and steal my way into the system. Unfortunately, the reality of "politics" is what I believe is the inhibiting factor to develop real partnerships. I do believe we are beginning to make progress in this area. Through numerous conversations and stating the importance of collaboration, we are beginning to work together, (staff/parent/student) on techniques and assignments. If I would ever be granted one wish to come true, it would be that a school/home partnership be identified and developed on the IEP prior to any goals/objectives.
>
> —Pat Wilson

All indented quotes are from parents of children with autism.

cation will suffer—skills and knowledge gained in the classroom may not be reinforced in the home; any competencies the child demonstrates in the home will not be practiced and, perhaps even seen, in the classroom; and new learning inspired by the synergy of a home–school partnership will never be realized.

This chapter is purposely near the beginning of this book; in placing it before the chapters on curriculum, instruction, communication, behavior, friendship, and other topics, we hope to communicate the idea that building partnerships with families is as or more important than anything else teachers can do in the classroom. The ideas outlined in this chapter are designed to push teams to work with families in new and creative ways and to move beyond collaboration that is passive or partial. We offer suggestions for learning about families and building school–home partnerships where power and responsibilities are shared and dialogue is encouraged.

LEARNING ABOUT FAMILIES

The first and most important step toward getting connected to students is learning about their families and the lives they share with those families outside school walls. Specifically, we recommend that teachers of students with autism make an effort to learn more about all of the individuals and groups that make up a family, recognize all of the diversities that families bring to the classroom, and rethink the idea of "difficult" families.

Think Beyond Mom and Dad

Some students are parented by a grandmother. Other students live with foster families. Still other students may come from homes with two mothers or two fathers. The nuclear family is no longer the norm in American life. Extended family members, family friends, or even organizations (e.g., group homes) may serve as guardians or primary caregivers for students in today's schools and should, therefore, be seen as part of the school community in the same way as would historically typical parents. If students with autism receive respite care or part-time foster care, the individuals providing this care should also be viewed as part of the home–school partnership. Community institutions may be part of the family structure in some cultural groups and neighborhoods; these relationships should be honored as well. A church may play a central role in the life of the family, for instance.

Our family is very close-knit; if our son is having a bad day, the whole family feels it. Early in our son's high school experience, our oldest daughter was also a student at the high school. She would often express concern when hearing her brother in the hallway during a meltdown. She would excuse herself from class to see what was wrong only to be sent back to class. We would hope that educators would see siblings as a resource. After all, the siblings might bring another outlook to the situation. Most of all, compassion is needed every day. By understanding that you can make a difference, you have the power through compassion to make every day a good day.
—Chris Van Boxtel

Finally, the role that siblings play in the life of a student with autism should be considered when working with families. Siblings might be asked to contribute thoughts or ideas to formal meetings or to give their parents suggestions to bring to discussions about their brother or sister. Often, siblings have knowledge about the student with autism that others do not. Siblings of individuals with autism may even have knowledge the parents do not have.

For example, one woman told me an amusing story about her son, Peter, and how his siblings support and understand him when his mother and father cannot. The family was having dinner when Peter, who has the label of PDD, yelled out "phooey" and spit a mouthful of chili all over the kitchen table. The woman and her husband were surprised and annoyed by this behavior and thought that Peter was trying to impress his brothers by misbehaving. Peter's brothers came to his rescue as they burst out laughing and told their parents that he was only imitating a Scooby Doo videotape he had watched that day. Peter frequently acted out scenes from his favorite cartoons and often appeared to use these scenes to communicate with others. The woman and her husband felt differently about Peter's spitting behavior when they got this piece of information from the boys and were able to talk to Peter about "how dogs eat hot chili differently than little boys do."

Recognize the Diversity of Families

In many schools in the United States, especially those in urban areas, the differences in culture, language, and life experience among students and teachers can be significant. In the early 1990s, the composition of the teaching force in the United States was approximately 87% Caucasian, 8% African American, and 3% Hispanic (National Education Association, 1992). Nearly 10 years later, teachers in America were still primarily English-speaking, middle-class, heterosexual, Caucasian women (Gomez, 1996; Knight, in press; Olmedo, 1997). At the same time, however, the United States and, therefore, the student population of this country, had become more racially and ethnically diverse (Delpit, 1995; Hernandez, 1989; Hodgkinson, 1985).

Social, racial, and cultural mismatches between teachers and students are problematic; every student in today's schools—including Caucasian students—would benefit from having more teachers of color. This is not to imply that Caucasian teachers cannot be effective teachers of students of color. Caucasian teachers can be effective with students of color, but only if they are committed to seeing and valuing the cultural, linguistic, and ethnic differences students and their families bring to the classroom (Knight, in press; Ladson-Billings, 1994).

My son's teacher is a very patient and sensitive person. She has called me numerous times at home, and I am pleased to say that the communication between school and home has been wonderful. I have been very impressed with how difficult situations have been handled at school. I am a teacher myself, and I understand how difficult it would be to have a student with challenging behaviors. Thanks to the kindness and patience of Yuuki's teacher, along with accommodations made by the administration, my son is able to succeed in school.

There have been occasions when Yuuki has hit, and at that time, he was suspended from school for three days. My son Yuuki loves school, and we've all come to the conclusion that when there is a break from school, he gets upset because he is such a creature of habit and he doesn't like having a break from school. If Yuuki is expelled, everyone has to go through the trauma of once again having to get used to the school routine when he gets back. I appreciate the school's efforts to work with me and my son.

—Midori Aoki

When teachers do not recognize and see family diversity, they are likely to jump to conclusions that are inaccurate and that threaten the home–school partnership. The dangers of rushing to judgment are highlighted in this reflection from a novice teacher:

It was a culture shock to teach at a school where students were black, white, Latino and Asian. Even though I felt like a competent teacher, I went through some changes because the children were different. Mai and Dou were both my students and one year apart in age. Mai would come to school tired, inadequately dressed, with dirty hair…while her brother was always rested, neat and clean. I knew about gender differences in Asian cultures but I was thinking, "When in Rome do as the Romans do." I lost it—got so angry—when she came to school on a snowy day with a T-shirt, shoes with holes in the bottom and without the coat I had gotten for her from a local charity. I asked where her coat was and she said that her mother had given it to her sister. I called and sent notes home but received no word back. I felt they were neglecting this child. Finally, the school social worker, a translator and I made a home visit. In the end, I was wrong…the mother was newly immigrated, did not speak English, was very concerned about both of her children, respected the expertise of teachers, and needed some help getting acclimated to a new world where her cultural practices were easily construed as abuse. (Knight, in press)

Delpit (1995) observed that the key to connecting with families is in attending to the ways in which they talk about and see themselves instead of trying to guess or, even worse, insisting that we know and understand who they are. Teachers must listen to families and work to understand their experiences, traditions, histories, rituals, and beliefs. Teachers will benefit from learning to understand how families view themselves, the students' school experiences, and the partnership between the school and the home.

Teachers should also explore how the family views the student's disability. In some cultures and, therefore in some families, disability may be seen as a natural human difference, whereas in other cultures, the same disability may be seen as a medical problem. Locust pointed out, for instance, that

Most traditional Indian languages do not have words for *mentally retarded* or *disabled* or *handicapped* and, rather than using such categories, may assign names of individuals that are descriptive of the disability, such as One-Arm, or One-Who-Walks-with-a-Limp. (as cited in Harry, 1995, p. 46)

Knowing how a student's family understands the disability and label can help the teacher make appropriate choices in designing supports, talking about the student and his disability, and making suggestions for supports and services outside of the classroom. Some families, for instance, feel more comfortable than others in talking about their child's differences as a disability. These preferences should, of course, be honored.

Rethink "Difficult" Families

Teachers sometimes muse about the "difficult" parents of students with disabilities. This label is often given to parents who call or visit often, ask a lot of questions, or those who often seem uncomfortable with or critical of the school, the teachers, or of their child's educational program. Although some of the clashes teachers have with families may be because of personality conflicts or differences of opinion, other struggles occur because teachers do not understand a family's history. Some students with autism and their families come to the classroom with a history of bad education-related experiences. Families may have felt unwanted in other schools, treated with indifference or contempt, or made to feel unimportant in some way. As one parent reports, "I was adversarial with Laura's educational system all the way through, but I had lots of questions that I couldn't get answers to" (Egel, 1989, p. 200). As Harry (1992) pointed out, many parents become "difficult" because their views are dismissed and their membership in the educational partnership is threatened. In these situations, parents feel that they have no way to express their views or to be heard except to be "difficult":

> Unless parent–professional interactions are based on dialogue, professionals may view themselves or the system as the source of truth—and they may cast parents' interaction within an adversarial framework. In this atmosphere, parents find that they must either passively cooperate or take a stance of confrontation. (p. 128)

The mother that calls twice a day to ask questions and criticize may be accustomed to years of feeling brushed aside. The father that starts a conversation with a threat of legal action may be living in fear of watching his child fall through the educational cracks. Teachers must keep in mind that many families come to the classroom having dealt with individuals and systems that have misunderstood or even rejected their child. It may take a lot of reassurance and effort to earn the trust of parents who have been insulted, ignored, or otherwise hurt.

One of the most powerful ways to support a wounded family is to listen to them and their stories. Asking the family to share such stories might help them to feel heard, but these accounts can also help a teacher understand the history that a student brings to the classroom. Biklen (1992) shared the story of a young man with disabilities who, every day at lunchtime, would scream and throw things. At first, the educational team and the young man's mother were stumped by this behavior. Eventually, however, the mother realized that her son was upset by the small cans of pudding distributed in the cafeteria. These cans of pudding, the mother realized, were the exact kind used to reinforce the young man's behavior when he lived in an institution months earlier. The cans triggered the young man's memory of the institution, a place he dearly feared. Without the input of the family and the knowledge of the student's difficult past, the teaching team would likely have never guessed that the lunch problem stemmed from the student's reaction to pudding cans and they would have very likely worked (unsuccessfully) on solving the problem for months.

Teachers and other educational team members should show the family of any student with a difficult educational history that they value the home–school relationship. Furthermore, the team should seek ways to demonstrate their commitment to the family through action, namely by working to create an effective partnership in the current school and situation.

ELEMENTS OF AN EFFECTIVE SCHOOL–FAMILY PARTNERSHIP

In order to design appropriate strategies and approaches, however, the elements of an effective home–school partnership must be developed. We suggest five basic elements that must be in place in order for educators and families to establish positive and productive relationships and collaboration structure:

- A welcoming school
- The belief that all students are important
- Communication that is open, constant, and productive
- A willingness and interest in learning from families
- Clear structures for information and knowledge sharing

A Welcoming School

Even if a teacher is warm and accepting, parents still may not feel at home in a school if the building and the staff are not welcoming to all families. Promoting an inclusive philosophy is an important part of this process of welcoming families. In many cases, families are still fighting to get their child an inclusive education. Although this phenomenon is less common today than it was 10 or 20 years ago, families across the United States are still struggling to find schools that will accept and understand their children with autism. Davern (1996) suggested that building relationships with families will involve long-term schoolwide plans to offer full membership to all students, not just offers to set up programs for students in response to the requests of individual parents.

Families should be made to feel that they are valued members of the school community; this is especially true in schools where inclusive schooling is a new phenomenon. In these schools, families may need extra support as many will be unaware of some of the norms and traditions of a "regular" school; they may be inexperienced in networking and meeting families of students without identified disabilities; and they may not be well connected to some of the typical child-centered community and neighborhood ac-

In the past few years I have been told that my son with autism "could be better served in a more specialized program, like a special school." I believe that it was this attitude that hindered his progress. Based on this past experience, we knew it was imperative to have the support of a regular education teacher with an open mind.

I used to believe that the most important component of a good, effective inclusion program was the special education teacher. Although I believe every member of an educational team is an important one, I now feel that the support of the regular education teacher is critical.

David's teacher this year has just that. His general education teacher has accepted him as a full participating member of her classroom community. She treats him like all of the other students, is able to be flexible and make accommodations if necessary. She accepts us, the parents, as equal members of the team and encourages our input. Most importantly she believes my son cannot only learn from his peers without disabilities but that he has a lot to offer them in return.

David is not only happier this year but progressing both academically and socially. We are extremely grateful for the support and acceptance of his classroom teacher, to which we attribute this success.

—*Jo Anne Califana*

tivities. If a family does not have other children without disabilities, they may need help "breaking into" the "soccer parent" circle or the car pool group.

For example, when a family one of us knew came to the school to enroll their young son (who happened to have autism), the principal of the school immediately suggested to the family that they join the PTA and reminded them to attend the open house, which was to occur on the following evening. When the family explained that their son was likely to "get very active" during the open house, the principal reassured them, "This is a school, not an art museum. We expect kids to be themselves here...and to act like kids. Please join us tomorrow night."

I believe that for inclusion to have a real chance to be successful, a working partnership must be established between educators and parents. If each is willing to admit that they don't have all the answers, then they should also be willing to admit that they can learn from each other.

Much like success in any interpersonal relationship, there needs to be a foundation established on mutual respect and trust. Parents should acknowledge the teacher's expertise, dedication and value. At the same time parents should be prepared to demonstrate what they know that teachers don't. As a parent I have an insight into my child's unique learning style and the characteristics of my child's underlying condition. I also know that my child can learn, can effectively relate with others, and can fit in...if supported and given the chance. I know this because I have already successfully included my child into my family and my community.

As a parent of a child who learns differently than his peers, what keeps me up at night are the unknowns in my child's future. As an adult, will my child fit in? Will he find a job? Will she marry and have kids of her own? Will he have friends? Will she become a productive and welcomed member of a community? The hope, and the dream, and the ideal, of true inclusion is that by making kids who are different real members of diverse school communities, when they reach adulthood each of these questions will be answered in the affirmative. To witness inclusion working, to see teachers, administrators, and fellow students enriched by and acknowledging the value in my child, is what lets me begin to really believe that there truly is a place for my child.

—Jeffery Cohen

The family must also feel that the student with autism is seen as a member of the school and classroom. The student should be invited to participate not only in the classroom but also in the life of the school, including extracurricular activities, evening events (e.g., dances, concerts, school carnival), and before- and after-school rituals and routines (e.g., hanging out in the hallway with friends, visiting the school store).

The Belief that All Students Are Important

Families should be able to expect that teachers will value their child and see him or her as an individual and as an important person. One of the most significant messages that can be communicated to a family is "We feel your child has something important to contribute to the life of the school." These types of messages are best communicated through actions. A mother we know, for example, was thrilled when the physical education teacher called the family to ask them if their son, Gordon, could join the after-school weight lifting team. As Gordon's mother shared, "It was the first time something really fantastic happened for Gordon that we didn't need to ask for."

Another way teachers can communicate their respect for a student is to think about the language they use in conversations, meetings, and written documents. If every meeting begins with a description of a student's struggles

As parents of a child with Asperger's syndrome, we realize the school staff needs our help and support to properly educate our child. Our experience with our son entering high school has been positive one. Because we got off to a slow start, there were days that we did not believe that we would make it to our son's senior year. But here we are with our son's high school graduation coming in May. Through trial and error our family, as well as the high school staff, have worked together to ensure a positive outcome. The doors of communication have always been open between our home and the school. It is always a joy for us to receive a phone call and or note saying things are going great at school. It is this positive feed back that can truly make our family's day or week. Positive reinforcement is not only great for the child but for the entire family as well.

—Chris Van Boxtel

and if every report written fails to include a student's strengths and gifts, it will be hard for a parent to believe that the teacher appreciates the student and sees him or her as a contributing member of the classroom. A parent of a fifth-grade student told us that she was in the education system for 6 years before any teacher said anything kind or positive about her daughter. When the teacher offhandedly shared that Rachel, her daughter, had "a beautiful smile and great energy" the mother burst into tears, startling the teacher. After learning of the reason for the mother's reaction, the teacher made it a point to keep sharing information about Rachel's abilities, gifts, skills, strengths, and accomplishments throughout the school year.

Consider the ways in which one mother describes the IEP meetings she endured that were deficit and program driven:

> The room would be filled with too many people, sometimes as many as 21, all eager to push for their own agendas. The meeting would begin with evaluations, present levels, and a list of things that Andrew could not do…Goals had been written by specialists who discussed how they were going to "fix" Andrew's problems, with the hopes of "getting him ready for a regular classroom" (7 out of 10 times, with 85% accuracy). (Dixon, as cited in Contract Consultants, Inc., 1997, p. 61)

Contrast that description with the meetings this same family attended after they moved their son into an inclusive educational setting and began working with professionals who believed meetings should be positive and focused on discussions of student strengths:

> We talk about a beautiful child and his gifts, the things he is learning and what other children are learning from him. When we set goals, no one cares that Andrew doesn't isolate his index finger on command 2 out of 3 times. We care that he is doing the same things as the rest of the class. We depend upon our dreams to set goals for Andrew that will help him succeed in society when his school days are over. (Dixon, as cited in Contract Consultants, Inc., 1997, p. 61)

As Biklen reported from his study of parents of students with disabilities, most families simply want people to care about and recognize the uniqueness of their children:

> The parent of a child with severe autism remembers her trepidation about sending him to a nursery school. Although her son is now nineteen, she still remembers vividly that she "didn't have to beg for entry; they wanted us." The director and the

teachers felt that Neil would be "good for the other children. They never made me feel I had to be grateful [to them] for taking him in." Furthermore, "they made it abundantly clear that they enjoyed and cared for Neil. I never had that 'if only I were the child's mother' feeling that one can get from professionals." (1992, p. 53)

Likewise, in a study by Davern (1996), parents reported that they valued the "ability of teachers to see different aspects of a child's personality aside from academic achievement." One parent in this study shared, "For teachers to say to me, 'I really like your kid,' or 'You know, he really has a great sense of humor'...lets me know that they really care about him as a person" (p. 61). Another parent shared that she was impressed with teachers who focused on the progress of individual students rather than comparing learners to each other: "So our child's not going to be the top of her class in gym. We understand that. Just take her for who she is. Find space for her" (p. 61).

As a parent with multiple children with many different learning abilities, I believe inclusive education shouldn't be thought of as just another thing a teacher has to try and do to accommodate a minority of students. Reaching all students with all kinds of abilities is the goal, and using curricular adaptations and a wide range of materials and strategies can help a teacher create the perfect classroom for all students. If a teacher used these creative ways to reach every student, my son could succeed along with every other child in his classroom. It is my hope that all of my son's teachers will teach in a multifaceted style, so that every student has a chance to learn in his or her most productive fashion.
—Lori Micheal

Communication Is Open, Constant, and Productive

Communicating with all families is an important centerpiece of education. When working with the families of students with autism and other disabilities, communication may be even more critical. Several reasons exist for this increased need for communication:

- Some students with autism cannot communicate reliably; therefore, all of the home–school communication must take place between the teachers and the family.
- Students may have special needs that require frequent exchange of information (e.g., sharing information about the impact of medications).
- When working with students with unique learning characteristics, families will often have valuable information about the learner and the disability that teachers cannot get from another source.

One of the most obvious ways to improve communication is to create opportunities and structures for sharing information and giving and getting support. In some partnerships, the stakeholders meet for coffee once per month; in other situations, the parties communicate back and forth with a weekly or daily notebook entry. Still other families and teachers may share information through e-mail, which is an ideal option for busy families and teachers. No matter how information is shared, the team should be sure to have an explicit conversation about the process. Some families cannot field telephone calls at work; others have many children and do not have much time to read and respond to daily notes. The communication systems put in place should meet the needs of all members of the partnership.

Other ways that communication can be enhanced are offered here.

Take the Time to Talk Most communication problems start with parents feeling out of the loop. A parent may feel especially dependent on the school for communication if a student does not have a reliable way to communicate or if he or she has speech or language difficulties. A mother of a kindergarten student was especially frustrated when her child's teacher called her at work to ask why her daughter, Lanie, who is nonverbal, did not have a lunch or permission slip for the day's field trip. The mother was frustrated because she had never been informed about the field trip. It is time-consuming to call parents on a regular basis, but it is worth the investment if the teaching team can avoid misunderstandings down the road. In the case of the mystery field trip, for example, consider that preparing the family for the field trip in advance would have taken approximately 10 minutes. Repairing the damage of a missed communication, however, took far longer and put a strain on the teacher–family relationship for weeks.

Setting aside 15–20 minutes each week or every other week to call parents for a friendly update can build bridges between school and home and provide an avenue for working through concerns or hatching future plans in small and manageable amounts of time. Teachers may call different parents every week, leaving messages for some and having a 5-minute exchange with others. A colleague of ours engages in this practice religiously and makes it a point to call the parents of every student in his classroom at least once during the year. For students with disabilities or other needs, the calls may be more frequent or supplemented with other communication systems or forms.

Involve Families in Solution Building When parents have a problem or concern, the teacher or a few members of the educational team should sit down and brainstorm a variety of possible solutions. When possible, educators should allow the family to make the final choice; the teacher or administrator might review all of the possibilities with the family and ask "Which of these options are you most comfortable with? Which seems most doable to you?" Whereas the family might have come in feeling powerless, they would now leaving with a myriad of solutions at their disposal, a clear plan of action, and the final decision over their child's education.

Sharing solution building also divides the responsibility for the situation between school and home. Often,

As a mother of a college-age child with Asperger's, all I can say is "we did it." When my son was 2 he scored a 72 on an IQ test, and we were told he was minimally retarded. His ability to count, add, and multiply at an incredibly early age were described as "splinter skills." We saw signs of intelligence and encouraged him to build on it. Math was always his strength. He scored an 800 on his Math SATs. Lots of therapy, lots of love, and a tremendous amount of social counseling have formed my son into the person he is. Some individuals with Asperger's tend to accumulate vast amounts of knowledge about topics that interest them. My son's focus is basketball. He has incorporated this interest into his education. At Seton Hall, he is majoring in sports management and is one of the student managers of their basketball team. He plans on taking his hobby and turning it into a profession.

My son's success did not just happen. We, meaning my husband and myself, his teachers, therapists, and so forth all built on the positives. Most of his teachers modified their social and behavioral expectations for my son well before differentiated learning and inclusion were even thought of as educational jargon. Our elementary school principal paved the way for him to take advanced math classes at our local middle and high school. It took teamwork in "our village" to make this work.

—Linda Malinsky

parents want to act but don't know how; this can lead to frustration and feelings of helplessness. If a parent helps to build solutions, the brainstorming
process is likely to be more rich and meaningful. When the family and the
school work as partners rather than as adversaries, it can make a significant difference in how the family feels and how a student is perceived. As one parent
shared:

Brainstorming together is an energizing process. It can make assessment and
planning look more like a celebration and less like a funeral. The focus of the discussion becomes giving families normal life opportunities rather than creating
'near normal' children. (Rocco, 1996, p. 57)

Accentuate the Positive   A mother we know claims that she tenses up at
work whenever her cellular telephone rings. Because her son's school is the
only party that has this telephone number, she knows that she will receive bad
news as soon as she answers the call. This pattern has become so regular and
predictable that this mother has grown to hate talking on the telephone at all
because she associates the ringing with frustration, anger, and pain.

Many problems are inherent in this woman's story. Certainly, the school
should reconsider the reactive nature of the relationship; a family–school partnership will surely fail if parents are only contacted to respond to negative situations. Furthermore, any telephone call made to a family member should be
done with care and compassion. If a student's behavior or health is in such a
state that a telephone call home is warranted, the parent will obviously be disappointed or even depressed to hear the news. The stress of such a situation
should always be considered; there is a huge difference between calling a parent to report, "You need to come over here. Tom is having a bad day again" and
calling a parent to say, "Do you have any time to help us? Tom is biting himself
and we can't seem to help him calm down. Do you have any ideas?"

Another way to build better relationships and avoid the fear-of-the-
telephone phenomenon is to avoid communicating ONLY in difficult moments.
Telephone calls, conferences, and notes home should be conduits for sharing all
types of news—good as well as difficult. Teachers and administrators should
write or call periodically to report success stories and share ideas that seem to
work. This practice is important and effective not only to build and sustain relationships but also to serve as a way to build better supports for the student
with autism.

A Willingness and Interest in Learning from Families

Teachers who do not connect with families and seek expertise or concrete
strategies from them may miss all of the rich opportunities for building on
skills that are already acquired and fail to capitalize on the important links that
can be developed among parents, communities, schools, and students (Taylor
& Dorsey-Gaines, 1988). Through families, teachers can learn about the materials that are familiar and valued, strategies that are effective, situations that
prompt learning, topics of conversation and discussion that spur discovery and
interest, and activities and issues that are relevant and have meaning in students' lives.

Students with autism are incredibly unique and their needs are unlike others with the same diagnosis/label. For this reason, teachers need to rely on experts who know the needs and abilities of the individual child they are expected to teach. Parents are virtually the only resource with this kind of expertise and knowledge, and educators must, therefore, use and learn from their ideas and suggestions.

One effective (and too-seldom used) way to learn from families is to get to know them outside of the classroom. Many teachers make it a practice to at least visit the communities and neighborhoods of all students in their classes—some teachers even try to visit the home of each learner in their classroom. This practice may be particularly necessary for students with disabilities.

When I was a new teacher, I visited the homes of all five of my students right before school started and then 1 week after school had been in session. These meetings were invaluable in getting to know families and in setting up partnerships with them. Furthermore, I was able to see students learning, playing, communicating, and socializing in a natural setting.

At the beginning of my career, I knew little about autism and my administrators and colleagues didn't seem to know much more, so I relied on these parents and siblings to teach me as quickly and as thoroughly as possible. One mother invited me to dinner and showed me how she was struggling to get her son to eat at the dinner table; I was instantly able to see what he could do (e.g., open his napkin, pour his milk) and what was hard for him (e.g., staying seated, cutting food). Another family allowed me to sit on the floor and play a favorite card game with their son; I immediately went out and bought this same game so this young man would have a familiar activity waiting for him in his new classroom.

As the year progressed and I got to know the families a bit better, I began conducting IEP pre-meetings in their homes. This gave me a chance to talk casually to the student and his or her family about ideas for a new IEP before all of us met with our full team and were faced with the formality of paperwork and protocols. These meetings seemed quite effective; parents started coming to IEP meetings as full participants, ready to share ideas, ask and answer questions, and give information to other team members.

Clear Structures for Information and Knowledge Sharing

Teachers use a variety of tools and strategies to reach, inform, and learn from families. Some send a classroom newsletter. Others host a series of open house class meetings. Still others may use telephone calls or e-mail to stay in touch. These structures can be incredibly effective in helping all parties stay aware of a student's needs and progress.

Teachers may find, however, that some students and the families of some students need more information or more frequent or personal interactions than typical classroom communication tools and strategies allow. Outlined here are three ideas for enhancing school–home communication and giving and getting critical information and knowledge.

Parent Reports   Harry (1992) suggested that parents be invited to participate in meetings in more meaningful and formal ways. One way to get information from parents and to let them know that their perspective matters is to ask them to present a report at the IEP or placement meeting:

> This report would constitute an official document, to be entered into the record and taken into account in decision making, along with the professional reports. This official parental role would not only increase the value that professionals place on parental input, but this role would signal to parents that their input is not only valued but needed. (pp. 128–129)

A parent report could be very formal or very informal. It might be 10 pages or a few paragraphs. Such a report might include information about the student's home life (e.g., new interests, changes in family routines), achievements he or she realized at home or in the community (e.g., has played her first video game with brothers, has been nominated to speak at church), skills taught in school that have been applied at home, and/or parent impressions of progress on IEP goals and objectives. Parents might also include any artifacts that would help the team better understand the learner (e.g., recent photographs, drawings, medical information).

Harry (1992) pointed out that in order for this suggestion to be effective, teachers and other educational team members will need to take seriously the charge of planning meetings that are family-friendly. This may mean that teams consider holding meetings outside of traditional school hours so that parent work schedules can be supported; finding places to meet where all stakeholders feel comfortable (e.g., school lounge, in the home of a family member), and making sure that all participants are encouraged to contribute ideas. One team ensured participation by all by setting a timer for 30 minutes and, when the bell rang, members took "inventory" of who had already spoken and who still needed to have "the floor."

Audiotape/Videotape Exchange   Some ideas are difficult to express and share through the written word; in these situations teachers and families may share videotapes or audiotapes. Audiotapes are especially helpful when the educational team and the family have a hard time connecting face to face or on the telephone. Audiotapes are best used in situations where a family member or educator needs to explain or ask something that is too complex or involved to write in a note. We know one family who communicated to their son's teacher through an audiotape every other week. The teacher listened to the tape as she drove home from work on Fridays and found that she got some of her best teaching ideas from this indirect exchange.

Videotape can be an incredibly powerful communication tool, as well. We have most often used videotape to record "trouble spots" in the day, by sending tapes home to families and asking if they had any ideas about the taped situation. For instance, a young woman, Shelley, was having a hard time in her high school physical education class. For 3 consecutive days the teacher videotaped the class and sent it home to her family. His father watched the tapes and gave this feedback:

- "She doesn't seem to understand the directions; maybe the teacher can write them down."
- "Kathy H. is in the class—maybe Shelley can be paired with her for some activities; she lives in our neighborhood and the two have known each other for years."

- "She got hurt playing volleyball in sixth grade so she might still be afraid of the game; she might need to take a more passive role during this unit."

All of Shelley's father's suggestions proved helpful; especially the information about volleyball being problematic. Sure enough, when the physical education teacher told Shelley she knew about the injury, she seemed to become more relaxed. The teacher stopped putting Shelley close to the net, and instead let her rotate through the back row for the rest of the unit. There was no way of knowing this critical bit of information without the input from Shelley's father.

Furthermore, Shelley's parents really appreciated seeing Shelley in the classroom without having to constantly visit the school. It gave them a chance to review the day with her and view her progress. The tapes also had an unexpected and positive impact on Shelley; she began to insist on watching the tapes frequently and seemed to grow calmer in the class as a result of visually rehearsing the classroom routines featured on the tape.

Student Learning Logs If the student can write or type, a daily learning log or reflection on the day's activities is both a valuable educational tool *and* a nice way for families to find out the answer to the question, "So, what did you do in school today?" If written communication is not possible for the student with autism (or any student) to undertake at the end of each day, a classmate can easily provide some support for this task.

When chapter author Eileen Yoshina taught fifth grade, all of the students were responsible for filling out a daily homework and reflection log before the final bell. Eileen and the students typically filled in the homework section together, and then discussed as a class some possible entries for the reflection portion of the sheet, which could include personal achievements, new skills practiced, or just anything interesting that happened during the day. Faith, a student with significant disabilities in the class, would dictate to her classmate, Trang, what she wanted to include on her reflection sheet. If the teacher mentioned any specific news or reminders for families (e.g., pack a lunch for the picnic tomorrow, remember to bring back library books), Trang would write that down too. Whenever possible, Faith would add a note of her own or embellish the day's entry with a drawing or with her choice of stickers.

When I consider how often I feel that people who describe my experience as the parent of a child with a significant disability "get it wrong," it humbles me. It helps me realize how imperfect are my poor attempts to understand my son's experience, or the experiences of families other than my own.

One thing they never told me is that there would be fun parts: that the child is a child, engaged in life, frequently charming. Autism for us is like family language—certain words, actions or juxtapositions take on inside meanings. Others wonder why we're laughing; but explaining a joke is hard, and often deflates the humor.

What saddens me most is how the rest of the world responds. It is so easy for any of us to ignore the things that really matter about someone if we are distracted by differences we think have to matter. We claim that a "need for sameness" is an autistic trait, but it is we who are unable to let go of difference, to become comfortable with others.

The real story about being anyone's parent is that children do not turn out to be who you expect them to be. This is as entirely true for my children without autism as for the guy with the label. Perhaps I was lucky enough to learn it sooner with the child who was "different." But things never turn out as anticipated: All of them outgrow us, disappoint us, surprise us, amaze us, and have the potential to delight us. And our children do all of this on their terms, not ours. If we're among the lucky ones, we might just learn to appreciate our offspring, and remain friends with them as they leave us behind.

—*David Smukler*

The learning log is a nice replacement for the communication notebook that is often passed from the teacher to the parent of the student with a disability because it gives the family an opportunity to receive classroom news as well as information about their child. Furthermore, it gives the student an opportunity to participate in the interactions between teacher and family while giving the learner an opportunity to practice both literacy and communication skills.

SUMMARY

It is exciting to contemplate the possibilities of forming strong and productive partnerships between schools and families. We may not yet realize all of the ways in which we can improve on curriculum, instruction, communication, social, and behavioral supports until we commit ourselves to working closely with families and to creating new models of working in concert with them. Ro and Jo Vargo, the parents of a woman with Rett syndrome, share the importance of such a commitment:

Our journey has taught us that we cannot work in isolation to accomplish Rosalind's inclusion. Rather, we must collaborate with others to make it work. It does not matter whether it is as simple as a discussion on the telephone about how to adapt arrangements for Rosalind to participate in a field trip (curriculum modifications) or convincing church officials to include her in a sacramental rite (intervention strategies) or as complex as advocating for more inclusive schools (e.g., collaboration, teamwork, normalizing environments). With little or no training, we still get the job done every day with the support of others. (2000, p. 243)

For More Answers and Ideas

Barron, J., & Barron, S. (1992). *There's a boy in here.* New York: Simon & Schuster.

Biklen, D. (1992). *Schooling without labels: Parents, educators, and inclusive education.* Philadelphia: Temple University Press.

Fling, E. (2000). *Eating an artichoke.* London: Jessica Kingsley Publishers.

Harry, B. (1992). *Cultural diversity, families, and the special education system.* New York: Teachers College Press.

Hart, C. (1989). *Without reason: A family copes with two generations of autism.* New York: Harper & Row.

Hart, C. (1993). *A parent's guide to autism: Answers to the most common questions.* New York: Pocket Books.

Kephart, B. (1998). *A slant of sun.* New York: Norton.

(continued)

(continued)

Mont, D. (2002). *A different kind of boy.* London: Jessica Kingsley Publishers.

Stehli, A. (1995). *Dancing in the rain: Stories of exceptional progress by parents of children with special needs.* Westport, CT: The Georgiana Organization, Inc.

Waites, J., & Swinbourne, H. (2002). *Smiling at shadows: A mother's journey raising an autistic child.* Berkely, CA: Ulysses.

Willey, L.H. (2001). *Asperger syndrome in the family: Redefining normal.* London: Jessica Kingsley Publishers.

CHAPTER 5

Creating a Comfortable Classroom

Why do you think I have so much trouble paying attention in the classroom?
I hear everything that goes on—every phone call that the principal makes in her
office; every single time an eighteen-wheeler truck gears down on the highway three
blocks away. I HEAR IT! I HEAR EVERYTHING!
(Bober, 1995, pp. 114–115)

When I sit down to write, it takes me about 20 minutes to prepare. I can write without the preparation, but my best work is done when I have created the optimal setting for myself. First, I make a pot of coffee or brew a cup of tea. Then I light great-smelling candles (blueberry is my favorite), turn on the television, and tune into something interesting that I do not need to watch. For instance, a football game will not work because I am too interested in the game and would need to follow all of the plays. Cable news usually works fine or even a somewhat engaging infomercial.

I can sit in either my office chair or on a couch (if I have my laptop computer). I take my shoes off (but keep my socks on) and sit on my feet or cross my legs so I am sitting with all body parts off the floor (no, I don't know why this is important to me).

Usually I work with all lights blaring; I turn even kitchen and bedroom lights on until the house looks like a runway or an interrogation room. Other times I turn off all of the lights and work only by the glow of the computer screen.

Every 20–30 minutes I stop working and do the following things: skip to Internet web sites, walk around my office, go into the kitchen to get a drink, or work on something else for a few moments. Every few pages I need to print what I am writing, see it on paper, and feel it in my hands.

Then I need to edit. Editing involves another set of rituals. In order to edit successfully, I need to leave the writing environment. If I am at work, I might go to a coffee shop or to the puffy armchair outside my office door. If I am at home, I will sit outside (depending on the weather) or simply switch rooms. Editing requires a big table or any size clipboard. I need to mark changes using a special pen—preferably a green felt-tip marker. After I have finished editing, I return to the computer to work.

I use this extended example to highlight the lengths to which many of us go in order to be as productive as possible in our work environments. Although some may feel my writing process is eclectic or strange, most readers will identify with some part of the process I described.

In order to be effective in my work, I need to make adjustments to my seating, the lighting, and sights and sounds in the room. I even need to create special smells in my environment. I am not alone. Many adults go to extremes to create an environment conducive to their work style, physical needs, and idiosyncracies; this is a critical point. We all make changes to our home and work environments to increase our productivity and comfort. It is helpful to remember all of these environmental favors we do for ourselves when we are planning for students in our classrooms.

Many times when I talk to my university students about creating adaptations or supports related to environment, someone will raise a hand and ask, "But is that the real world? If I let one student have water at her desk or give another student a special chair, isn't that special treatment? At some point this student has to learn that there is a real world out there and you don't get special treatment in the real world."

Hmmmmmmmmm.... What about the slinky on my sister's desk? Or the "Do Not Disturb" sign on my colleague's door? Or the coffee and bagels my colleagues bring to morning meetings? Or the desk lamp my friend uses instead of turning on her bold florescent room light? Or the rocking chair my boss keeps in her office?

Clearly, we do have choices and opportunities to get what we need "in the real world." Within most job environments, individuals have the power and freedom to make some adjustments to their work space, and although there are exceptions, most people have choices about the environments in which they work. In schools, however, students cannot choose the teachers, tasks, or classrooms that suit them best.

In most cases, for most people, school environments are more restrictive and less flexible than any other place in which they will function as adults. Consider all of the things individuals do to alter the work environment: drink a cup of coffee or have a snack at their desks, chew gum or eat candy, listen to music, place pictures of friends and loved ones on their desks, get up and use the bathroom at any time, or talk to others when they want to or need to. Although some jobs have more rigid restrictions than others and not every worker has a lot of freedom, adults still tend to have more control over their day and environment than do students.

In addition, it is important to remember that if a student has a serious environmental need that carries over into adulthood, he or she will need to choose a job that is conducive to that need. The individual will need to negotiate how to get the supports he or she needs at that time. Withholding support or adaptations during the school years will not make the student stronger or more capable; actually, providing effective, sensitive supports may give the student ideas that can be implemented throughout the school years and beyond. For instance, a colleague of mine noticed that Trent, a student with autism, had a hard time concentrating on school tasks on days when the Chicago Cubs played baseball. On these days, Trent spent the entire day asking, "When do the Cubs play? When do the Cubs play?" Although it was unclear whether he needed to know about the Cubs, he seemed to need to ask the question or at least he was unable to stop asking it. The teacher, curious to see if a certain strategy would help him, taped the Cubs' schedule to the chalkboard. From that point on, whenever Trent asked about the Cubs' schedule, his teacher or classmates pointed to the chalkboard. Eventually, he was able to check the schedule himself.

In subsequent years, Trent was able to use this adaptation in his classrooms. In middle school he did not need the Cubs information posted in his classrooms, he simply placed the schedule in the see-through cover of one of his binders and brought it to all of his classes.

CREATING A PLACE WHERE ALL STUDENTS CAN SUCCEED

Sometimes students are unsuccessful because they are uncomfortable or feel unsafe or even afraid in their educational environment. Providing an appropriate learning environment can be as central to a student's success as any teaching strategy or educational tool. Students with autism will be the most prepared to learn in places where they can relax and feel secure. In order to create environments that are most conducive to learning for students with autism and their peers without disabilities, teachers may need to examine ways in which classroom spaces are organized. Specifically, teachers should evaluate learning atmosphere, seating options, and the use of space.

Creating an Optimal Atmosphere

When you walk into my favorite up-scale restaurant, you can immediately smell fresh-baked bread. The lights are often dim and the music is soft and inviting. The waiting area is filled with huge comfortable couches, big glass bowls of fresh flowers and an enormous tropical fish tank. They have a huge, dimly lit dance floor and a wonderful five-piece jazz band that never seems to take a break. The food is excellent, and they never let you leave until you have seen (and sampled from) the beautiful dessert cart. Clearly, this establishment is working hard to create a certain atmosphere. They have created a space that inspires patrons to act in certain ways; they want customers to relax, dance, socialize, eat their food (and spend their money), and come back again—so they create an environment that motivates people to do those things.

Teachers also spend a lot of time cultivating a classroom atmosphere that inspires certain behaviors. Teachers want students to work hard, participate in activities, help each other, and pay attention to the lessons. In order to see these behaviors in all students, teachers may need to evaluate their classroom atmosphere and make adjustments to lighting, sounds, smells, or temperature.

Lighting Restaurateurs, photographers, casino managers, and directors of Broadway productions understand the impact of lighting on emotions and behaviors. Lighting can also have a powerful influence on learning. The right lighting can soothe, calm, energize, or inspire students. The wrong lighting can be annoying, distracting, and even painful for students with autism.

Some individuals with autism have incredible sensitivity to light (Attwood, 1998; Gillingham, 1995; Reed, 1996; Willey, 1999; Williams, 1996). Liane Holliday Willey, a woman with Asperger's syndrome, describes this sensitivity as "impossible to bear" at times:

Bright lights, mid-day sun, reflected lights, strobe lights, flickering lights, fluorescent lights; each seemed to sear my eyes…my head would feel tight, my stomach would churn, and my pulse would run my heart ragged until I found a safety zone. (1999, p. 26)

Children and adults with autism have reported problems with florescent lights in particular. Florescent lighting, the most common lighting used in classrooms, can affect learning, behavior, and the comfort level of students with autism. In order to determine whether florescent lights are problematic for a student with autism in your classroom, you may want to turn off the overhead lights for a few days to see if the change seems to benefit the student. If the fluorescent lighting does seem to be a concern for the student, you may need to experiment with different ways of using light:

- Try lower levels of light, if possible.
- Use upward-projecting rather than downward-projecting lighting (Williams, 1996).
- Experiment with different types of lighting. Turn on the front bank of lights but not the back, or turn on alternating banks of lights. In one classroom, teachers strung white holiday lights around their whiteboards and plugged night lights into different sockets around the room in order to give the classroom a more calm and peaceful feeling (Kinney & Fischer, 2001).
- Try different colors of light. Take one corner of the room and experiment with a pink or yellow lamp.
- Replace fluorescents with incandescent bulbs.

If the fluorescent lighting cannot be changed, try the following strategies:

- Some students find the use of sunglasses helpful. Glasses might be worn during recess or can even be tried indoors (especially near florescent lighting). Wearing a baseball cap can also help a student avoid direct exposure to light.
- Move the student's seat. Sometimes the problem is not the lights themselves, but the reflection of light on a wall or other surface.
- Florescent bulbs tend to flicker more as they age. If you must use florescent lights, use the newest bulbs possible.
- Some students find that it is particularly difficult to use white paper under florescent lights. Students may be bothered by the glare from the paper. Using colored overlays can minimize or eliminate the glare.
- Some students are more distracted by the sound than the sight of florescent lighting. In these cases, the student may want to use earplugs while studying. In some instances, simply moving the student farther away from the noise may help.

Teachers might also experiment with the use of natural light in the classroom, especially in those classrooms with several windows. Natural light is not only a cost-saving measure but also research has suggested that students—not just those with disabilities—may perform better in classrooms with natural light (Kennedy, 2002).

Sounds   You know that horrible nails-on-a-chalkboard sound? Even thinking about such an unpleasant noise makes some people wince. For some individuals with autism, nails-on-a-chalkboard discomfort happens every day with even the most common of sounds (Grandin, 1995; Jackson, 2002; O'Neill, 1999; Robinson, 1999; Shore, 2001; Stehli, 1991; Waites & Swinbourne, 2001).

Students with autism might be troubled by the sound an air conditioner makes, the shuffling of feet as another class passes by in the hallway, or the soft scratching of pencils moving across papers.

Some students with autism will not only struggle with sounds most of us view as annoying (e.g., car alarms, sandpaper on wood), but may also react negatively to sounds most of us would filter out or even find pleasing. Some may also fail to react at all to the banging of a door or the scream of a siren. Wendy Robinson, the mother of a young man with autism, remembers how stunned she was at her son's uneven reactions to sounds:

One evening he was seated on my lap on the hall floor while [his brother] bounced and punched a very large balloon around him. Suddenly the balloon burst by Grant's side, which sent my heart into a flutter. However, Grant did not flinch or even turn his head to the noise. Later, when I had my electric whisk in operation, he ran screaming from the kitchen and I had to stop what I was doing to find and console him. He had the same reaction to the Hoover and other loud electrical equipment. (1999, p. 43)

Consider the following ways in which some individuals with autism and Asperger's syndrome have described their sensitivities to sound:

The following are just some of the noises that still upset me enough to cover up my ears to avoid them: shouting; noisy, crowded places; polystyrene being touched; balloons and aeroplanes; noisy vehicles on building sites; hammering and banging; electric tools being used; the sound of the sea; the sound of felt-tip or marker pens being used to colour in and fireworks. (Jolliffe et al., cited in Attwood, 1998, p. 15)

It happens to me that I am very sensitive to voices. (Mukhopadhyay, 2000, p. 72)

I can detect all sounds that the neurotypical person can hear, including very low and very high-pitched sounds. I have always had a strong aversion to loud music or high volume on the TV set. As a result of this, I often find it awkward to ride with those who crave loud music in their cars, particularly heavy metal or rap. I have always loathed crunching and chewing sounds while other people are eating. Our family has meals in the family room with trays rather than the conventional dinner table gathering. I can tolerate restaurants and cafeterias because the background noise suppresses these bothersome sounds. (Hamrick, 2001)

When I was little loud noises [were] a problem, often feeling like a dentist's drill hitting a nerve. They actually caused pain. I was scared to death of balloons popping, because the sound was like an explosion in my ear. Minor noises that most people can tune out drove me to distraction. When I was in college, my roommate's hair dryer sounded like a jet plane taking off. (Grandin, 1995, p. 67)

I have strong sensitivities to sounds. When I was in grade school, my classmates used to call my name as softly as they could to see if I could still hear them—I could hear them from across the room and often even into an adjacent classroom. One time a teacher did something similar. He stood behind me and barely whispered my name. I still sensed his presence and looked around. The whole class, teacher included, had a good laugh. (Shore, 2001, p. 1)

One of the ways teachers can help students cope with sounds is to simply ask families about which sounds are hardest for the learner. If Grant Robinson's teachers knew about his fear of sounds related to vacuum cleaners and electrical equipment, for example, they would think twice before signing him up for a woodworking course and could keep him away from things such as the electric pencil sharpener and stapler.

Consider these additional ideas for helping students deal with sounds:

- Once a disturbing sound has been discovered, helping the student can be as simple as moving him or her as far away as possible from the sound source.
- Use a soft voice when possible. Instead of shouting to get a student's attention, try whispering.
- Try earplugs or headphones for some activities or for use in some parts of the school building (e.g., gymnasium).
- Reduce classroom noise. Echoes and noise can be reduced by installing carpeting. Carpet remnants can sometimes be obtained from a carpet store at a low cost. Some teachers cut tennis balls open and place them on the bottoms of the chair or desk legs; this adaptation muffles the scraping sounds created when furniture is shuffled around (Grandin, 1998).
- Change the sound, if possible. For instance, if a student cringes when he hears clapping, students could develop another system of appreciation for student presentations, birthday celebrations, and assemblies.
- Prepare the student for the sound. If you know the school bell is about to ring, cue the student to plug his or her ears or simply tell the student to get ready.
- In noisy or chaotic environments, allow students to listen to soft music using headsets or play soft music (e.g., classical, environmental) for all students.

Many students have effective ways of coping with problematic sounds. Some learners will concentrate on an object or scribble on paper when they are bothered by sounds, for example. Pay attention to these strategies and avoid interfering with them, if possible. Although a student's coping mechanisms may not be apparent to all, teachers should be open to the possibility that behaviors such as hand flapping and finger flicking may be helpful to the learner and that preventing the student from engaging in these behaviors may cause him or her more strife.

It is important to remember that students with autism may find some sounds very helpful or pleasant and may in fact need or want to hear certain sounds in order to cope or relax. Wendy Lawson, a woman with autism, reports her relationship to sounds in this way:

Tunes and music or a gentle low-pitched voice can temporarily relieve moments of fear and anxiety. You'll still catch me humming, singing, whistling, and even talking out loud in an attempt to dispel confusion or unease due to change. The strategy enables me to think and calm down. (1998, p. 4)

Many students with autism report finding solace and joy in music. Music can be used as both a teaching tool and as a curricular adaptation to support the learning of students with autism. Music plays a central role in many pre-school, elementary, and secondary classrooms. Some teachers use music as part of the curriculum. For instance, a high school teacher might play "When Johnny Comes Marching Home" or "John Brown's Body" when the class studies the Civil War. A third-grade educator teaching a unit on oceans might play students the complex and beautiful song of the humpback whales. Some teachers play music in their classrooms as students study quietly or work on projects. Teachers may play music to help students relax. For example, a teacher might play Mozart while students paint or draw at the end of a busy day. Teachers also use music to energize students. Rock-and-roll or hip hop music might be played as students exercise in physical education class or build sets for a school production.

Teachers might experiment with different types of music (e.g., instrumental, chanting, rap, classical, popular) to see how students respond. Tonal qualities in songs or instruments may upset students with autism more easily than they do other students or adults. If the student with autism responds negatively to some of the music selections, the teacher may need to find other types of music. Playing different types of music can give the teacher an opportunity to expand the experiences of learners, to change the energy of the classroom, and to inspire and interest students. For instance, in one classroom, Sally, a student with autism, was constantly singing the song, "The Yellow Rose of Texas." Eventually the teacher and all the students learned that Sally's grandmother was from Texas and that the song was a family favorite. Sally seemed thrilled when all of the students in the class learned to sing "her" song. The teacher then asked all learners to bring in a song that meant something to each of their families.

Smells   Whereas some (all of us?) might associate a few smells—chalk dust, peanut butter, new crayon—with schools, some individuals with autism associate dozens or hundreds of smell with schools. A student with a heightened sensory system may take in dozens of smells in just a few moments—the wet shoes of a classmate, the icing on a friend's cupcake, the stale odor of a musty locker, the dirty shavings in the hamster cage, the teacher's hair gel, and the rubber cement being opened across the classroom.

Echo Fling (2000), the mother of Jimmy, a young man with autism, reported that her son's sense of smell was so acute that he was able to use it as a tool for identifying his possessions! She recalled an incident that occurred when Jimmy was just 7 years old. Jimmy was playing with his Star Wars action figures with neighborhood boys who had their own collection of the same toys. When the boys were done playing, they realized that their two Luke Skywalker figures had gotten mixed up during the game. As Fling related,

The boys paused, not knowing which Luke belonged to whom. To solve this dilemma.... Jimmy held each one up to his nose, took a quick sniff, and immediately told the other boy, "this one is yours." (p. 146)

Although this illustrates potential benefits of a heightened sense of smell, this sensitivity can also be a struggle. As one individual with autism describes, smells can often be overwhelming and cause extreme discomfort:

I still have trouble with [animals] ... Dogs and cats and smells like deodorant and after-shave lotion, they smell so strong to me I can't stand it, and perfume drives me nuts. I can't understand why people wear perfume, and I can smell hand lotion from the next room. (Stehli, 1991, pp. 197–198)

Other school smells that may bother students include paint and other art products, school supplies (e.g., "smelly" stickers, markers), chalk, cleaning agents, class pets, and plants or flowers.

What can teachers do about smells, though? Teachers may not even be able to detect the smells that might cause a student anxiety and discomfort. Teachers can take a few precautions, however, and minimize some of smells that are often problematic for learners with autism:

- Many individuals with autism report that perfume and other personal products cause problems. If a student seems to avoid a particular person or if she will only interact with that person occasionally, consider that the student may be reacting to that person's perfume, lotion, hair gel, aftershave, cologne, or shampoo. If a student is very sensitive to these types of smells, teachers and other professionals working in the classroom should avoid—as much as possible—the use of products with heavy smells.
- Food smells are incredibly distracting for some students with autism. One of my former students could smell a sweet treat two classrooms down from ours. Although he loved the smell of chocolate and baked goods, once he smelled them he could not focus on his work. In order to support him, all teachers in our hallway agreed to serve birthday treats at the very end of the school day. Parents agreed to bring all treats to the office and the school secretary offered to hold our brownies, cookies, and cakes until 2:45 in the afternoon.
- In rooms that have strong smells (e.g., art room, cafeteria, science lab), students might be seated near the door or an open window. Or a student might be able to use a small personal fan to minimize the impact of the smell.
- If students seem to rely on their sense of smell to learn or to explore the environment, allow them to do so when it is possible and when the behavior does not hurt or disturb others. When Echo Fling's (2000) son, Jimmy, was smelling her hair one day, she asked him, "What are you doing?" He replied, "I'm remembering you." Realizing her son's need to smell, she did not forbid or discourage this interesting behavior. She simply instituted a social rule for Jimmy at school: Don't sniff people without their permission (p. 147).
- Ask custodians and administrators to order and use unscented cleaning materials and products when possible.

Just because a smell is strong does not mean that a student with autism will react to it, however. In fact, many school smells may be pleasing and even comforting to students. If these pleasant and helpful smells can be identified, they might even be used to support the learner with autism. For instance, I knew a young man with autism who could be calmed by the smell of mint. His teacher kept mint gum and candies in her desk in case he needed a treat to relax.

Liane Holliday Willey (1999) brings her own "smell adaptation" with her wherever she goes. She has suggested putting a bit of a favorite smell (if such a thing can be found in a liquid or paste) on the end of a cotton ball or on the inside of the arm. This way, when the person with autism gets overwhelmed by certain smells they can minimize the impact by sniffing the cotton or their arm and inhaling something pleasant.

Temperature Some students struggle to concentrate or relax in rooms that feel too warm or too cold to them. Consider the words of Dave Hamrick (2001), a man with autism:

I often get uncomfortable when I go to other houses or businesses in the summer months where the temperature is above 75 degrees. Many people set their thermostats between 75 and 80 degrees during the summer and I'm comfortable in a 70-degree environment. As you might expect, I get really excited when the temperatures start falling in autumn. Blasts from an air conditioner or heater can feel painful to some and soothing to others.

Classroom temperature is difficult to adjust to individual student needs, so teachers will need to give each student ideas for keeping him- or herself comfortable. If the student is often cold, he or she might be asked to keep a sweater or sweatshirt in the classroom. If the student is often warm, he or she might be given opportunities to sit in a cooler part of the room (near a door or window) or to keep a bottle of cold water at his or her desk.

Providing Appropriate Seating

Providing appropriate seating in the classroom and around the school is another important part of classroom organization. Consider your own seating needs as you plan for the learners in your classroom. Think how it feels to sit on a high stool when your feet don't touch the metal or wooden supports, or when you try to fit into a movie theater seat that is too small, or when you fold yourself into an airplane seat that doesn't have sufficient leg room. You may physically squirm around and reposition your body. You may even be unable to keep track of a conversation as you focus on your discomfort.

Appropriate seating may not be a teacher's first consideration when planning for a student with autism, but for some students, comfortable classroom furniture is pivotal to their success. One of my former students couldn't sit in a desk for more than a few minutes but he could sit in a beanbag chair for 40 minutes at a time. We soon purchased several beanbag chairs for the school (a few for the library, two for the music room, a handful for hallways, and one for the office) so that this student could be at ease throughout the school and so that all students could enjoy a change in seating now and then. Not every student with autism will need or like the feeling of a beanbag chair, however. In most cases, finding appropriate seating is a matter of trial and error. Another one of my former students, Kelly, seemed unable to settle into his metal desk, but he also did not respond to our beanbag chairs or to the rocking chair we kept in the back of the room or to the pillow pile we kept in the "living room" area of the classroom. After experimenting with many different chairs, materials, and strategies, we finally found that Kelly could sit for over an hour at a time if we tied a cushion of woven wooden beads (the type you often see in taxicabs) to the back of his chair.

Having a few different seating options in the classroom can potentially improve the educational experiences of all learners. Seating that may appeal to learners with and without autism include

- Rocking chairs
- Seat cushions (the type that can be tied on to the rungs of the chair can be purchased for a few dollars at discount stores)

- Reading pillow (large cushion with arms that props the user upright)
- Floor/exercise mats (individual mats can be made cheaply by sewing a stack of newspapers in between two large sheets of vinyl) or large floor pillows (also easy to make with stuffing from a fabric store and a few yards of material)
- Lawn chairs
- Old car seats
- Couches, loveseats, armchairs, or large footstools
- Body or exercise ball

Some teachers like to adapt the environment by installing a carpet sample into one area of the classroom or by putting a few armchairs in a special part of the room. I taught with a kindergarten teacher who brought an old-fashioned, claw-foot bathtub into her classroom and filled it with small colorful pillows. A high school teacher with a very small classroom clustered the desks together in groups of four and cleared nearly half of the classroom for a community area. This section of the room contained an old coffee table; two loveseats; an old turntable and stacks of folk records; and a huge, upholstered footstool. Teachers of young students might provide space in a classroom with pillows, carpet squares, and stuffed toys. Other items that might be placed in this area include a fish tank, music magazines, an audiotape or compact disc player, photograph albums, and small games (e.g., Jenga, Etch-a-Sketch, Tic/Tac/Toe).

Some students (with and without autism) may prefer to sit on the floor for some part of the day. To assess student response to this arrangement, teachers can design instruction that calls for students to sit on the floor. Even in my college classes, I occasionally use this arrangement. We might sit in a circle for a discussion or spread out and work on projects. Some lessons are very well suited to this type of arrangement. Students might sit on the floor when working in small groups or when they need to spread out to manage materials.

In some cases, students might be given the option to sit on the floor or at their desks. Students who prefer to sit on the floor or in a chair without a desk can work on clipboards or use lap desks. Beanbag lap desks can be purchased for a few dollars. I often cut them open, drain the soft beanbag material out, and replace it with sand or another similar substance. Many students appreciate the weightier material and some find that it helps to keep them centered and to be more aware of their bodies in space.

Other students may prefer to stand instead of sit for some part of the day. This is an adaptation I have made for students with autism in elementary and secondary classrooms and more recently in my college classroom for students who are pregnant or those with back problems or arthritis. Students can be provided with a lectern and a desk at the back of the classroom and they can alternate between the two as needed.

Teachers may also want to consider how the placement of a student's desk or seat in the classroom can affect learning and behavior. One teaching team found that Becky, a student with autism in their classroom, had difficulty sitting at her desk until they let her sit in a different area of the room. Previously, Becky had sat in the back of the classroom next to a large heat register. In this arrangement, Becky had few chances to interact with peers because she was positioned behind most of them. In order to get Becky more interested and involved in the classroom, the teacher changed all of the desks, moving the students so that there were two rows on the right side of the classroom and two rows on the left side. She then turned the rows so they would all be facing the center of the room; students on the left were now facing the students on the right and vice versa. This arrangement worked exceptionally well for Becky because she could easily see other students at work and learn from their actions and habits (Heeden, Ayres, Meyer, & Waite, 1996).

You may also encounter students who are distracted by the sight of others. A seating adaptation can help this type of student, as well. For those who get too distracted by the sights around them, teachers can construct study carrels from cardboard. A large piece of cardboard (about $1\frac{1}{2}$ feet tall) folded into thirds can be placed on the student's desk to shield him or her from other students, from classroom materials, and from visual information around the room. Because these carrels are easy and inexpensive to construct, a teacher could make them available for any student in the classroom. Another option is to bring one or two study carrels (the type often found in college libraries) into the classroom and let any student work in the sheltered space when privacy or some focused study is needed.

Organizing Learning Space

Although the classrooms of the past were characterized by students acting as passive learners in rows and columns facing the teacher at the front of the room, in classrooms today students are often more active and more likely to be involved in collaborative work. Sometimes, when a teacher changes the ways in which spaces are used, student learning is enhanced and the use of more intrusive adaptations are minimized.

Classrooms that best suit students with diverse learning needs have flexible learning spaces. Teachers may need to think "out of the box" to invent new possibilities for learning environments. For instance, teachers in two neighboring classrooms could co-teach for all or part of the day and use both rooms to teach all students. This would allow the team to allocate one room for quiet study and one room for active projects. Special and general educators can also work together to reallocate space. Old resource rooms can be changed into quiet study rooms, available to any student at any point in the day. When I was teaching second grade as a special educator, my colleagues and I revamped the resource room by giving it a new name (The Learning Lab) and a new identity. Any student needing a place to study or do independent work could use the room and when we were co-teaching, we used the room to engage in project-based instruction. Try these additional tips for making the most of the learning spaces in your classroom:

Make Quiet Study Areas Available for Any Student   Students with autism often need time away from the noise and chaos of the classroom to meet their needs. Most teachers do not have as much space as they need or want. Overcrowding, especially in urban areas, is common. In most schools, spare classrooms do not exist, but when they are available, an administrator might be willing to convert some space into a full-day quiet study area to which any student can have access. In crowded schools, teachers might work with the school librarian to create a space just for studying or projects, or spaces in the hallway might be used for quiet study. A few chairs and even a small table might be set up in the hallway (depending on fire codes of the school) for any student who needs a break from the chaos of the classroom.

Keep Some Students Moving   Although many students have the need for quiet, others need movement, activity, and interaction. A student who cannot sit in a desk or keep a low voice in a classroom can still participate by working on course material in a different part of the room, in a different environment with a few classmates or on a related lesson in a community environment with a small group. One student in a high school English classroom was unable to sit through long lectures and readings of *Romeo and Juliet*. Instead of making the young man fidget through the hour, the teacher asked him to make costumes for a class production of the play. Two students at a time (including the student with autism) were then allowed to work quietly in the back of the classroom while the rest of the class rehearsed the lines of the play and discussed the story.

A paraprofessional told me about a student with autism who could not sit in his desk during his science class. Although the student wanted to listen to the teacher's lessons, he could not remain in a chair for more than a few minutes. The teacher agreed to let the student pace during the lessons. Eventually, however, the pacing became distracting for some of the students because the young man was often crossing back and forth in front of the teacher and the chalkboard. The teacher's solution was to turn the back of the room into the pacing and thinking area. She taped off two areas with masking tape; one was named "sit and learn" and one was named "move and learn." The student was told he could pace anywhere labeled "move and learn." He was instantly able to follow the simple rule; in fact, it was so successful that the student asked for designated "move and learn" spaces in other classrooms.

Create Different Areas for Different Activities   Many students with autism learn best in spaces that are highly organized. One way to make the classroom extremely easy to navigate is to set up different areas for different activities. For instance, a high school teacher might have an area just for storage and teacher materials, a small library area, and an activity table. An elementary school teacher could have a puppet show theater/drama center, a reading corner, and a whole-class gathering place. When possible, areas can be sectioned off (by using furniture or masking tape, or by painting the floor different colors) or labeled clearly to help all students understand how spaces are to be used.

Keep Learning Spaces Free of Congestion   A student with autism may become frustrated if students are constantly walking past his desk or crossing in front of a chalkboard he or she is trying to read. Whenever possible, the pencil sharpener, classroom library, and supply cabinet should be kept in separate areas and in places least likely to interfere with class functioning and activity or at least away from the students who are the most easily distracted.

Manage Materials   Look around a typical classroom and you may find 20–35 desks (with sweatshirts or backpacks hanging off the backs of a few chairs), a few globes and a pull-down map, crates full of student portfolios, a few computers, dozens or hundreds of books, two bulletin boards filled with student work, a handful of tape recorders, a television and a videocassette recorder, and maybe a few plants or a hamster in a habitat. Although all of these materials are central to teaching and learning, it is important that they are well organized, easily accessible, and visually manageable.

Kindergarten teachers often have "a place for everything and everything in its place" so that students can easily find materials and learn how to participate easily in managing the classroom. Teachers in upper grades often abandon this type of organization, however, assuming that learners no longer need this kind of predictability. Most students profit from being educated in an organized environment and from knowing how and where to get educational materials.

One way to support learners with autism is to avoid visual clutter. Ask students to be especially conscientious about keeping the classroom neat and about storing their materials in their desks and lockers. Younger students might need a desk map to find and replace items independently (Goodman, 1995). The teacher or the student can draw a map of all items in the desk on a small index card or a sheet of paper. The map can then be taped to the top of the student's desk or attached to the inside "ceiling" of the desktop. A similar type of map can be created for the classroom, in general, or for a student's locker.

Because many struggle to organize materials, you might provide all students explicit suggestions for keeping things orderly. For instance, instead of asking all students to clear their desks for a test, ask them to put their notebooks in their backpacks or to put their markers in their supply box. These types of direct and specific statements remind students that their supplies have a "home" and may help them learn organization skills over time. You might give some ideas on how to organize desk tops, lockers, cubby holes, or backpacks (e.g., "Keep your protractor in your pencil bag and only in your pencil bag, then you will always know where to look"). I know of one teacher who taught a student with Asperger's syndrome to color code his materials when he was in seventh grade (e.g., math papers in red folder, writing assignments in yellow folder). The student is now in community college and is still successful using this organizational system.

In order to make the maintenance of the classroom as easy as possible, you can give all students classroom jobs. For instance, a few students can be responsible for keeping bookcases orderly. Such an activity can even be parlayed into an academic learning experience. Younger students can practice alphabetizing and older students can learn the Dewey Decimal System or create their own categorical system. Students can also be responsible for caring for plants, keeping the pencil jar stocked, cleaning chalkboards, organizing bulletin boards, and keeping desks orderly and floors neat.

Finally, to keep the classroom working efficiently, keep important information posted clearly. You might keep a calendar, a clock, and a daily schedule in one area of the classroom (especially important for students with autism who seem to need this information readily available). Students of any age can be held responsible for writing the date daily, changing the calendar when needed, and even writing out the schedule and other information (e.g., stock quotes, weather) each morning.

SUMMARY

I open this chapter by detailing some of my own needs related to work environment. Although I can now see how central these supports are to my productivity, I fought implementing many of them for years. When I was in graduate school and learning how to write, I felt that serious academics would write at a desk in an office-like environment. I knew that the library was considered an appropriate environment for studying and writing, so I tried in vain to work in silence at a long wooden table. When I got my first university job, however, I began to see the diverse ways in which my colleagues tackled their work. Some only wrote at home while others had to be in their offices with the door open and National Public Radio programs buzzing in the background. Only then did I give myself permission to craft my own work environment; as a result I soon became more relaxed and capable as a writer.

Teachers may also find that adapting the learning environment gives them opportunities to be with students in new, different, and important ways. In my college classrooms, for example, I find that I understand students in a more personal way when we are all seated in a circle on the floor. Likewise, a teacher may act in ways that are more informal and relaxed when he or she provides instruction while seated on a couch.

Clearly, making adaptations to the learning environment can help all of us feel more at ease and work more effectively. These adaptations can also be educational. It behooves individuals to learn about themselves and their learning needs from even the earliest years of school. Students who are given choices about their learning environment and are asked to express their preferences regarding factors such as lighting, sound and noise, organization of materials, and furniture arrangement will come to better know themselves as learners. They are also likely to be more prepared to get the environmental supports they need at school and, perhaps will be more capable of setting up an appropriate study area in their homes.

Although teachers may not be able to please every student every day, those who experiment with various aspects of classroom atmosphere and organization can create a learning place that meets as many individual needs as possible. The teacher cannot engage in this work alone, however. All of the students need to work together and communicate to make the classroom conducive for learning. Whatever supports are deemed necessary should not be provided "in secret." In fact, students often make realizations about their own learning style and needs when they learn about the style and needs of others. After learning about his fifth-grade classmate's need to wear headphones to tune out noise, one young man (without an identified disability) claimed that he thought he needed the same adaptation. When provided with the headphones, he did indeed seem to work for longer periods of time and become less distracted.

Some environmental supports involved compromise and conversation with all learners. For instance, the teacher may need to poll students to find out if all students can tolerate music during independent work time or if they like windows open or closed on warm days. Other supports are specific to one student and can be easily implemented without interfering with the learning experiences of other students. If a student is uncomfortable sitting in his or her desk all day, he or she can alternate between sitting at a classroom table and working on the carpeted floor.

In other instances, the student with autism will need the help of his or her classmates to be successful in the environment. For example, George, a student with Asperger's syndrome, was struggling to sit through classes because of the strong perfume his classmates wore. He was especially disturbed by the scent of patchouli, which seemed to be a popular scent for girls in his high school. In one of his classes alone, four girls wore the fragrance regularly. When the teacher and the young man brought this problem to the class, the girls agreed to avoid wearing a lot of perfume or to sit far across the room from the student when they did. The teacher agreed to use a flexible seating chart so the girls could switch seats when necessary. Interestingly, the young man reported that the girls stopped wearing perfume for the entire semester even though he had not asked them to do so in the class meeting.

Alice, a first grader with the label of pervasive developmental disorder, was having problems participating in physical education class because she could not tolerate the teacher's whistle. To solve the problem, students were asked to think of different ways the teacher could get their attention. Students suggested that the teacher could wave her hands, sing a song, ring a bell, play a trumpet, act like a monkey, wave a yellow flag, or squeeze a rubber squawking chicken toy. The teacher, in response, tried each one and gave students the option of picking the ones that worked best (the chicken, of course, came out on top). Everyone in the classroom benefited from the creative brainstorming process and from the act of building a community that was comfortable for all classroom members.

Certainly, it takes time and thought to engineer many of these adaptations, but teachers often find that creating a good learning environment minimizes that need to provide other, more-restrictive supports. For instance, if the illumination of the classroom feels painful to a student and no adaptations are made related to the lights, the student may leave the classroom for long stretches of time and thus lose valuable learning time.

Perhaps most important, educators may also learn about students when they offer different types of supports related to learning environment. By assessing and, when necessary, changing the atmosphere and the learning spaces throughout the school to better meet student needs, teachers can learn about the motivation and learning styles of learners and give students more opportunities to be successful. It is not unusual to hear about a student whose disability appears more or less severe or a student who seems more or less gifted when he or goes from one teacher's classroom to the next. In education, context matters, and teachers who attend to environment may be surprised to see that student profiles change and learners shine in new ways as the classroom environment begins to work for them as learners.

For More Answers and Ideas

Feldman, J.R. (1997). *Wonderful rooms where children can bloom.* Peterborough, NH: Crystal Springs Books.

Gillingham, G. (1995). *Autism: Handle with care.* Edmonton, Alberta, Canada: Tacit Publishing.

Kaufeldt, M. (1999). *Begin with the brain: Orchestrating the learner-centered classroom.* Tucson, AZ: Zephyr Press.

Williams, D. (1998). *Autism and sensing: The unlost instinct.* London: Jessica Kingsley Publishers.

CHAPTER 6

Friendships, Social Relationships, and Belonging

How peaceful it is to withdraw from the complicated world of human relationships! I do however enjoy the presence of a friend and feel so content in the company of one who is willing to take me as I am. My friends have been willing to see me this way and I am so grateful to have been given the opportunities to discover life in the real world. (Lawson, 1998 p. 100)

For most students, the best part about coming to school is seeing and spending time with friends. For students who struggle to make social connections, however, going to school can be a lonely and frustrating experience. Many students with autism who are being educated alongside their peers without identified disabilities are indicating that they need more than an inclusive classroom to feel successful; students with autism are increasingly asking teachers to facilitate the development of friendships and provide them with access to social opportunities (Burke, 2002; Kluth, 1998). In this chapter, I outline ways in which teachers can build classroom communities that encourage relationships and connection. I also provide suggestions for facilitating social interaction in the diverse classroom. Finally, I provide ideas for supporting the social lives of individual students with autism.

BUILDING COMMUNITY IN THE CLASSROOM

Although no teacher can *create* friendships among students, every educator can create conditions in the classroom that will give students opportunities to strengthen social relationships, learn about and from each other, and get and give support. The hope is, of course, that these opportunities will eventually lead to the development of friendships.

Developing and sustaining a school community requires that educators use strategies and practices that purposefully encourage and teach sharing, learning, interdependence, and respect. For example, teachers might encourage community through cooperative learning experiences, conflict resolution opportunities, games, class meetings, service learning, social-justice education, cross-age and same-age tutoring and mentoring, and school and classroom celebrations (Sapon-Shevin, 1999). Teachers can also cultivate community by working for whole-school change. By lobbying for smaller classes, challenging competitive school structures (e.g., homecoming court, spelling bees, sports teams that cut or exclude students), and developing ways to connect students across classrooms and grade levels (e.g., in-school e-mail pals), for example, teachers can not only strengthen the classroom community but also help the school as a whole become more responsive to a wider range of learners. A sense of community can also be developed and sustained through curriculum.

Build Community Through Curriculum

One of the most effective ways to create a classroom community is to offer curriculum and instruction that is responsive and respectful. Many teachers have effectively built community by framing lessons around issues of democracy and social justice. For example, when Erin Gruwell, a high school English teacher in a struggling urban community, confiscated a racist drawing from one of her students, she decided to reshape her curriculum to respond to the incident:

> When I got ahold of the picture, I went ballistic. "This is the type of propaganda that the Nazis used during the Holocaust," I yelled. When a student timidly asked me, "What's the Holocaust?" I was shocked.
>
> I asked, "How many of you have heard of the Holocaust?" Not a single person raised his hand. Then I asked, "How many of you have been shot at?" Nearly every hand went up.
>
> I immediately decided to throw out my meticulously planned lessons and make tolerance the core of my curriculum. (Freedom Writers & Gruwell, 1999, pp. 2–3)

Gruwell built her entire curriculum around students, their experiences, their concerns, and their ideas. She supported their interrogation and critique of institutions and authorities in their communities. Gruwell's students thrived on the discourse of social justice that she cultivated in her classroom. Students in her classroom became involved in community service and political action as Gruwell helped them connect their own experiences to history. They raised money to bring Miep Gies, a friend of Anne Frank's, to visit their school; they held a peace demonstration; they co-taught a college class on diversity; they visited the Holocaust Museum in Washington D.C.; they conducted a candlelight vigil honoring friends and family lost to violence; they mentored local elementary students; and they collectively wrote a book about their experiences.

In another classroom, Yolanda, a student with autism, was frightened of a mural hanging in the school's gymnasium. The mural—a picture of children walking in the woods that included the image of a snake coiled on the ground—scared Yolanda because she was afraid of reptiles. The mural had been painted years ago and the principal had often thought of replacing it because other students had expressed a fear of it in years past. Futhermore, the principal and teachers had, at different times, expressed irritation because all of the children depicted in the mural were Caucasian. They did not feel it repre-sented the student body, which was comprised of many different racial and eth-nic groups.

When Yolanda came into the school, the principal volunteered to paint over the mural to soothe her intense fear. Yolanda's teacher had a better idea, however; students in the class were charged with designing and creating a new mural that would be both appealing to the students and representative of the multicultural population of the school. Students worked with an art teacher to learn about mural painting. They studied colors, designs, and styles of murals. Yolanda was on the committee to choose a new design, and although she could not speak, her peers paged through books with her to find images that inter-ested her. Over a 6-week period the students painted a beach scene with images of children from racially and ethnically diverse groups. The mural also in-cluded a picture of a mermaid, because The Little Mermaid was Yolanda's fa-vorite character from a book.

Painting the gymnasium certainly inspired further study of murals—the students explored content ranging from the murals painted during President Roosevelt's New Deal to the connections between mural painting and social revolution in Mexico—but the painting also brought students together as a community. The art gave students a voice and a forum for expressing them-selves. Everyone participated and everyone's ideas were incorporated into the final project. The art teacher found that painting the mural not only helped stu-dents to learn more about Yolanda but also it brought the whole class together as a group. One student, Armando, who was often teased for being "nerdy," became a leader for the class for the first time as soon as his classmates saw his artistic talents. Throughout the project, students approached him for new techniques.

Community-Building Activities

Students of all ages will profit from experiences that give them opportunities to connect with other students and learn about the class as a group. It is fairly easy to incorporate community-building and team-building exercises throughout the day and year. Not only will students with autism need such opportunities to improve social skills and learn in non-threatening ways but also teachers will always have new students in the class who want the chance to get to know classmates. Students who already know each other will benefit from the op-portunity to connect with classmates in more meaningful ways.

A variety of community-building exercises such as those listed here can be implemented to enhance relationships in the classroom, encourage friendships, and foster student-to-student learning opportunities. Although all of these ac-tivities can be used at the beginning of the year to help students become famil-iar with one another, they should not be abandoned thereafter. Community building and team building are not achieved by having students engage in a few games or icebreakers. True team building takes time and involves mean-ingful and continuous interaction over the course of the school year (and, it is hoped, over the course of the school career).

Group Résumé A résumé describes an individual's accomplishments, whereas a group résumé, or collective profile, highlights the accomplishments of a team (Silberman, 1996). A group-résumé writing exercise involves a teacher explaining to students that the classroom includes students with talents, experiences, gifts, and interests. The class is then divided into small groups, and every team is given chart paper or newsprint and colored markers. In these groups, the students are asked to create a group résumé such as the one illustrated in Figure 6.1 to advertise their accomplishments. The teacher then invites the groups to present their collective résumés to the class. The teacher can end the exercise by hanging the résumés on the wall. This display can serve as a visual reminder of the collective gifts of the class.

Asking students to create a collective profile is an entertaining and effective way to promote reflection and self-assessment. The group résumé is also a quick and easy team-building strategy; students not only find out about each other but also about themselves. It is important for even the youngest students to evaluate and realize their abilities. The résumé helps students form skills of self-promotion and evaluation. It also guides them to focus on the classroom as a teaching and learning community and helps all learners understand the resources they have in their classmates. The résumés can be general or tailored to content (e.g., Creative Computer Consultants, The Four Readers & Writers) and can be used to start the year or to summarize learning at the end of a unit.

Women Who Leave an "Impression"

Krisi, Nancy, Jen, Kana, Kim, and Katia

Qualifications

- Familiar with Impressionism
- Can compare the styles of Impressionist painters (especially Renoir, Monet, Manet, and Degas)
- Have read autobiographies of Mary Cassatt and Cezanne
- Have successfully completed six high school art classes
- Have knowledge of
  - Watercolor painting
  - Sculpture (wood and clay)
  - Furniture painting
  - Collage
  - Oragami
  - Print making

Other skills

- Sign language
- Word processing
- Can sing every song from *My Fair Lady*

Hobbies and interests

Reading, watching old movies, listening to music (especially movie soundtracks), and karate

---

Figure 6.1.   An example of a group résumé, which builds friendships and social contacts by highlighting the accomplishments of a team.

In order to be sure that all students participate, the teacher should give students ideas on how to elicit information from peers. Students could be shown how to informally interview one another and how to ask questions that will allow all students to contribute something. For example, if a student does not have reliable expressive communication or claims he or she cannot think of anything to add, the other team members might share their contributions first, give the student time to circulate the room and get ideas from other teams, or draw or sketch ideas instead of naming them.

Other versions of this community builder include the following:

- Revise and update the résumés throughout the year
- Complete a video or audio résumé
- Generate a list of questions and conduct a round-robin interview of each other before assembling the résumé

Pass the Compliment   Even after being out of high school for 10, 20, or even 50 years, most adults remember being teased, ridiculed, or insulted when they were children or teenagers. For many, name calling is part of what it means to be a kid. Students with autism may be at an increased risk for this type of verbal bullying because of their social, communication, and behavior differences. Teachers, however, have the power to change that culture and inspire a different kind of "name calling" in classrooms.

"Pass the Compliment" is like the old telephone game many have played at childhood sleepover parties (Loomans & Kohlberg, 1993). Students are asked to think of a compliment they would like to pay to the person sitting directly in back of them (or next to them, or in front of them). The first person in the row begins the game by turning around and whispering a compliment to the second person in line ("I think you are creative"). The second person in line then turns to the third person in line and repeats the first compliment and gives a new one ("I think you are creative and funny"). The third person in line turns to the fourth person in line and shares three compliments, and so forth. When the compliments get to the end of the line, the teacher calls on those in the back row to relay all of the compliments from the entire row ("I think you are creative, funny, independent, a good cartoonist, and gutsy"). Row members then let everyone know if the message got through or if some of it got lost in the process.

Other versions of this community builder include the following:

- Set up a compliment box in the classroom and pick some to read aloud every week.
- Pick one or two students at the end or beginning of the day or week and have five classmates give those individuals compliments. Compliments can be general or specific. For instance, a middle school teacher might read a student's story and ask her classmates to provide five compliments related to the story (e.g., "Student gave the story a creative title," "The ending was a surprise," "The part on the staircase was really suspenseful").
- Begin or end the day or the class period by asking students to give themselves a group compliment ("We created amazing poetry this week").

A Truth or a Lie   A Truth or a Lie is fun and energizing and can be integrated into the classroom as a "get to know you" exercise, a weekly exercise in creativity and collaboration, a curriculum preview or review, or a way to immerse students in content (Bennett, Rolheiser, & Stevahn, 1991). This may be an especially useful activity for some students with autism who need practice in understanding abstract concepts. For younger students, use of this activity will help them differentiate between the ideas of "truths" and "lies" and give them opportunities to engage in storytelling and verbal expression.

Students simply write three statements on a slip of paper. Two of them are truths and one of them is a lie. Students then get into pairs or into small groups, read the statements aloud, and ask their classmates to guess which statements are lies and which are truths. Time is often provided for students to share short stories related to their truths and lies. Other versions of this community builder include the following:

- Ask students to focus on specific topics for the exercise. For instance, students can be asked to share two truths and a lie related to the Middle East, sharks, woodwind instruments, or triangles.
- Ask students to share one truth, one lie, and one wish.
- Instead of writing two truths and a lie, have students pantomime three ideas.

Paper Bag Interviews   Paper bag interviews are a great way to facilitate interactions between students and to provide them with opportunities to ask and answer questions. It is also a fun way to engage all students. Instead of one or two students having a chance to speak during a lesson, paper bag interviews give all students time to share. This activity can be used to teach younger students turn-taking or reading simple sentences. Older students can learn actual listening skills or ways to ask clarifying or follow-up questions.

To engineer paper bag interviews (Gibbs, 1995), the teacher writes a series of questions related to classroom topics and places them in small lunch bags or cardboard boxes. The teacher then puts students into small groups of three to five students and hands each group one bag or box. Students then take turns drawing questions from the container and answering them. At any point, a student may decide to pass on a question and draw a new one.

Paper bag interviews can be used regularly throughout the year. Teachers can either use this activity to give students opportunities to learn about one another or to comment on different topics of study in the classroom, or questions can give students a chance to do both. For example, the question, "How are you most like Crazy Horse?" prompts students to disclose something about themselves while they consider information they have about this historical figure.

Other versions of this community builder include the following:

- Have students generate the questions.
- Ask students to take turns answering questions using different types of expression, including sign language and gestures, original drawings and illustrations, and facial expressions.
- Put questions in the bags that relate to student interests. If a student in the group has just become an uncle, include a question about this big event. If a student is really interested in the Beatles, include a question about 1960s rock and roll.

- If students in the classroom receive support from a speech-language teacher, this might be the perfect time for that professional to work in the classroom and help all students improve skills related to turn-taking and asking and answering questions.

FACILITATING SOCIAL INTERACTIONS AND RELATIONSHIPS IN THE DIVERSE CLASSROOM

Once teachers establish a classroom community, they can focus on developing and using specific strategies that will encourage social interaction and relationship building. Specifically, educators should create spaces for sharing, respect different ways of socializing, rely on students to support each other, support relationships through activities, and provide opportunities for social connection beyond the classroom.

Create Spaces for Sharing

Teachers who seek information about students' experiences, dreams, interests, and needs can use it to better educate their students and to facilitate relationships between them. Too often (especially in secondary schools), students are educated in the same classrooms day after day without developing personal relationships. When I was observing one middle school classroom, I asked a young man to tell me the name of one of his classmates. "I don't know his name" the student replied. "I've never talked to him." I later found out that these two students had been in the same classroom for 2 months and had never had a conversation.

Students' voices must be central to classroom work and time must be carved out for communication and idea sharing. Teachers interested in incorporating students' voices might begin by increasing forums for student participation and leadership. For instance, students might be asked to lead weekly class meetings.

In Kim Rombach's first-grade classroom, students have ample time and space for sharing; they are even in charge of managing conflicts. Rombach facilitates this process by providing two "talking chairs" that are available to any two students who engaged in a disagreement. Students in this classroom don't go to the teacher to have their recess scuffle assessed; instead, they secure permission from the teacher to use the talking chairs. In the chairs they discuss their issues and try to find a solution or explain their feelings. One boy explained the purpose of the chairs this way: "Sometimes it takes us a long time, but we try to get to be friends again" (Sapon-Shevin, 1999, p. 139).

Another specific strategy that can be used to encourage sharing is dialogue teaching. Dialogue teaching involves educators and students engaged in a discussion focused on critical problem solving. Student ideas are the center of the dialogue, with the instructor acting as an active listener and facilitator. Teachers using dialogue teaching will prompt students to think critically and listen openly. For many teachers, dialogue teaching is tricky because it looks and feels so different from traditional classroom discussion: "...the dialogue cannot be reduced to the act of one person's 'depositing' ideas in another nor can it become a simple exchange of ideas to be 'consumed' by the discussants" (Freire, 1970, p. 77).

Part of the challenge of being a skilled dialogue teacher is investigating the verbal style and linguistic habits of the students. This may be particularly important for the teacher in the inclusive classroom, in which some students may have minimal speech and in which a variety of students communicate in different ways. In addition, students in diverse, inclusive classrooms will most likely have many different practices. For example, some students will be speaking native English, while others are learning English as a second or third language. A teacher interested in dialogue teaching will attend to these differences in order to inspire the richest and deepest conversations possible. Specifically, teachers will want to

- Consider pace of the dialogue: Are all students having opportunities to join the conversation? Do some learners seem to need more time to think before providing responses? Does the group need to build in "think time" or strategic pauses for some students?
- Consider how students are contributing: Are some students dominating the conversation? Is the group monitoring how time is used? Is the group providing opportunities for all to participate? Is the group valuing different types of contributions—including laughter, gestures, typed words on a communication board, verbalizations, and so forth?
- Consider topics of conversation: Do all students feel comfortable chiming in? Are topics relevant and important to the group?
- Consider who is contributing: What does the dialogue dynamic look and sound like? How are issues of race, gender, ability, and class affecting who is speaking or given space to speak?

Whether students are working to solve a classroom social problem or a more academic task, teachers using dialogue teaching must be careful not to overshadow their students by directing them or by using language all learners cannot understand. The students, meanwhile, must be attentive to the needs of every participant—watching carefully for communication initiation and allowing for the full and uninterrupted expression of each speaker. Students might need some instruction in active and compassionate listening. In order to prepare students for dialogue teaching, teachers might provide opportunities to practice active listening, engage in community-building exercises, and debrief issues related to team building and cooperation. Teachers and students might role play examples of good listening or thoughtful feedback.

Dialoguing may be the perfect activity for students who have been the object of study—students with disabilities, students of color, those labeled "at-risk"—or who have been rewarded for compliance and silence for much of their lives. The student will enter a new and unfamiliar role in dialogue teaching. He or she will no longer have an authority to follow, nor will he or she need to attend to commands. Dialogue teaching is an especially important strategy to use with heterogeneous groups of students who can benefit from diverse perspectives.

Respect Different Ways of Socializing

Some individuals with autism struggle to make friends and socialize in ways that are conventional and familiar to others. For example, some students with autism may be uncomfortable with touch and, therefore, unable to shake hands with others. Teachers must cultivate a classroom environment that encourages different types of social participation. As Wendy Lawson, a woman with autism, illustrates, asking a person with autism to socialize and behave like "everyone else" can be painstaking and frustrating:

Over the years, I tried to contain my excitement and joy over life's happenings and watched to see what makes other people happy or sad. If they laughed or were unmoved, then this was my signal that it was alright for me to do likewise. This process was hard work and although it helped me to be more observant of others, it robbed me of spontaneity and enjoyment of the richness of my own experience. (1998, p. 116)

Teachers of students with autism will want to clearly communicate to students that there are many ways to engage in conversations, play and socialize, and participate in class. In a second-grade classroom, Cindy, a student with autism, liked to watch some games and play activities before or instead of joining in; students in the classroom grew accustomed to Cindy's participation and on occasion, Greg, another student without an identified disability, joined her in quietly watching the classroom commotion.

Dan, a student with the label of autism who was nonverbal, often introduced himself to others using a photo album he had created. Whereas other students started their days by chatting in the cafeteria as they waited for the first bell to ring, Dan began his day by circulating around the cafeteria tables showing students the newest pictures in his album. Because Dan and his mother changed the pictures every Sunday, he had new "stories" to share every week. In Dan's school, students became so interested in this mode of socializing that they began bringing pocket-size photo albums to share with Dan and with each other.

Rely on Peers to Teach and Support

I worked with one young man by the name of Jason. For 2 years, his family and teachers hoped that he would learn to greet his peers in the morning with a wave or a handshake or by communicating "hello" in some way. This goal was listed on his IEP and addressed by his educational team each day for months. Then Jason began attending second-grade with his peers. Instead of going into his general education classroom for only a few hours each day, he became part of his classroom by spending all day with peers in the second grade! Peers began clustering around Jason each morning, slapping him on the back and wishing him a "good morning." In only a few weeks, Jason was looking up at his friends, initiating handshakes.

Peer support is an essential part of inclusive schooling. In some cases, students succeed in supporting other students or helping them achieve when teachers cannot. Often, peers will learn quite naturally how to support a friend with autism. They will know how to calm, teach, and encourage a classmate without any direction or interference from adults. In addition, peers are valuable resources because they tend to understand each other in ways authority figures or adults do not. Even the best teachers lack the same degree of intimacy with students that students share with each other. Students know each other's secrets and fears. They often recognize each other's needs and gifts in ways not seen by teachers. This type of help and mutual support is also great preparation for adult life for both or all participants.

In the popular and important book, *The Dreamkeepers* (1994), Ladson-Billings writes about a teacher, Pauline Dupree, who keeps community issues at the center of her classroom practice. Dupree fosters unity in her classroom and reports that she expects her classroom to be both a center of serious learning and a place of comfort and cooperation. Dupree teaches teamwork in her classroom and asks students to serve as resources for one another:

From the day that they walk into my room they know they have to select a buddy. This is their learning partner for the year. A lot of times when a student is having a hard time I'll call the buddy to my desk and really give him or her an earful. "Why are you letting your buddy struggle like this? What kind of partner are you? You're supposed to be the helper." Within a couple of months I begin to see them looking out for one another. One student will hesitate before he turns in his paper and will go check to make sure the buddy is doing okay. Eventually, they begin to check very carefully and they may discover some errors that they themselves have made. (p. 72)

The beauty of this example provided is that the students are engaged in a reciprocal partnership instead of in a helper–helpee relationship (Bishop, Jubala, Stainback, & Stainback, 1996; Strully & Strully, 1989; Van der Klift & Kunc, 1994). It is critical that teachers seek such opportunities to give all students the chance to both give and receive help and support. As Bishop and colleagues pointed out, students with and without identified needs profit from reciprocal relationships:

In contemporary society, a healthy, well-rounded individual may be considered to be someone who is able to both give and receive help as necessary for continued growth and self-esteem. The ability to perceive oneself as both the helper and helpee in any friendship is valuable to the maintenance and growth of that relationship. Too often, people with disabilities are presumed to be able to participate in relationships only as the helpee, which is detrimental to the depth and longevity of the relationship. (pp. 163–164)

Students with autism must, then, be given opportunities to offer support to classmates. Relationships in which some individuals are always helped while others are always helping are neither natural nor particularly helpful in building a classroom community. It is a teacher's job, therefore, to cultivate a classroom culture that allows all students to give and get support. As Eugene Marcus (2002), a man with autism, pointed out, the best relationships can only emerge when peers serve as supporters of each other, not as "bosses or role models":

Peers are people who are in the same boat as we are, and who are our equals. That means people who must follow the same foul rules as we do. And who have ways of coping that we need to know about. Role models are expected to be perfect, but peers can fumble and make mistakes just like we do. Peers are fully human, and that welcomes us to be our fully human selves. Do not think you confuse us by telling us about your mistakes and failures. Those things are what make us feel close to you.

Good peer support is always from people who are eager to learn and that means people who don't mind being wrong a lot of the time. (p. 1)

Classroom activities can be structured in several ways to encourage reciprocity. For example, in one seventh-grade classroom, the teacher asked each student without an identified disability to serve as a "peer buddy" for Julie Ann, a young woman with Asperger's syndrome. Within weeks of implementing the program, however, Julie Ann, who was an expert map drawer and geography buff, was helping all of the students in the classroom with their social studies homework. When the students began asking to have Julie Ann serve as *their* "peer buddy," the teacher knew it was time to change the system. Instead of having class members sign up to be a helper for Julie Ann, *every* student had to develop an advertisement and a help-wanted poster to hang on a classroom bulletin board. On the advertisement, students had to list all of their strengths and specifically highlight the things they would be willing to teach others. On the "help wanted" poster, students had to list the things they needed or wanted to learn or things they needed help doing. With the new system in place, all students were able to see the gifts and abilities and the needs and struggles that *all* students brought to the classroom.

Support Relationships Through Activities

Some students who find conversation and "typical" ways of socializing a challenge are amazingly adept at socializing when the interaction occurs in relation to an activity or favorite interest. Dane Waites, a man with autism, had few same-age friends until he took up weight lifting. After finding both athletic and social success in that sport, he began cycling and running for pleasure and again found he was able to develop relationships through these activities (Waites & Swinbourne, 2001). Jasmine Lee O'Neill, a woman with autism, suggested using common interests to facilitate relationships:

Anything can be used as a stepping stone for forming a relationship. Art and music are superb for that. Use things the autistic individual enjoys to spark her interest. If she likes music and hums to herself, use music as an introduction to relating to other people. It is a falsehood that autistics do not relate. Rather, they relate in their own ways. (1999, p. 83)

One of my former students, Patrick, had few friendships and seldom spoke to other students until one day a new student came into the classroom wearing a *Star Wars* T-shirt. Patrick's face lit up on seeing the shirt and he began bombarding the newcomer with questions and trivia about his favorite film. The new student, eager to make a friend, began bringing pieces of his science fiction memorabilia to class. Eventually, the two students struck up a friendship related to their common interest and even formed a lunch club where students gathered to play trivia board games related to science fiction films.

Stephen Shore, a man with Asperger's syndrome, pointed out that building relationships based on interests or activities can reduce the stress sometimes associated with getting to know others:

Building a relationship with a person via an activity as the catalyst proved help-ful. While this may hold true for most people, it is especially so for those on the autistic spectrum. Having an activity as the focus of the interaction reduces the reliance on being able to detect, accurately encode, and respond appropriately to nonverbal social cues. (2001, p. 74)

Provide Opportunities for Social Connection Beyond the Classroom

In order to support the development of relationships in the classroom, teach-ers may need to help students find social opportunities outside of the class-room. Although most schools offer activities to meet the needs of all students, other schools need to develop a wider array of activities so that every student can find an extracurricular activity in which they feel at home. Some schools, for instance, have moved beyond the traditional sports-based and arts-based extracurricular options to offer clubs and activities related to academic content (e.g., book club, chess club), political issues (e.g., conservation groups, Students Against Drunk Driving [SADD]), and social support (e.g., anti-drug groups).

All schools must be conscientious about offering options that will interest, engage, and be available to a range of students in the school. This means ex-amining whether all students can afford certain clubs or activities, whether meeting times are convenient for students who may have after-school respon-sibilities, and whether students can get the appropriate supports they need to participate in after-school activities. In a middle school, a student with autism wanted to join the track team but needed to have some individualized support to be able to attend practices and games. As the student's educational team was trying to develop a solution to the problem, two high school stu-dents volunteered to serve as junior coaches and give extra support to all of the students. This type of creativity is key.

In elementary schools in which typically there are few school-sponsored extracurricular activities offered, teachers and school administrators might work with families and community members to offer a few clubs or activities open to any student. Or schools might investigate after-school options available in the surrounding area and help families connect to these activities. For in-stance, if the local recreation center offers after-school arts classes, the school might offer to do some staff training for the facility around issues of support-ing diverse learners.

SPECIFIC STRATEGIES THAT HELP STUDENTS WITH AUTISM

Students in the most welcoming, social, comfortable, and accepting classrooms may still need extra support and guidance when navigating social relation-ships. Having a strong classroom community and using a range of approaches to facilitate relationships are always prerequisites for building and sustaining relationships and supporting students' social worlds, but students with autism spectrum disorders will very often need or want help understanding and ne-gotiating social situations. Specifically, students with autism may need ideas for approaching and interacting with peers and understanding social cues.

Social Stories

Many teachers, families, and students with autism have found social stories (Gray, 1994, 2000) to be useful tools in learning about relationships and personal interactions, coping with difficult situations (e.g., hearing loud noises), and getting information about novel situations (e.g., visiting a museum for the first time). Social stories give the student information about a situation and provide ideas or guidance on what to expect or how to respond to that situation. Many individuals with autism report that the social stories method or related types of written preparation help them to learn, understand, and cope with puzzling, new, or complex situations. For instance, if a teacher was writing a story about going to the school play, he or she would want to include information about intermission and the clapping that is sure to occur at that time. The story would most likely also include information cueing the student to join in with the clapping when he or she hears it or—in the case of a student who is sensitive to loud noises—to plug and protect his or her ears as soon as the curtain goes down.

A social story can be "written" in a number of ways; students can be asked to formally co-construct the stories with the teacher or the teacher can ask the student to lead the activity by sharing—in any way possible—information he or she may have about a given situation. For instance, if a student needs to write a social story about going to a pep rally, the student may be asked to draw or act out anything they already know or think they know about school assemblies or athletic events. Social stories can be "written" with photographs, drawings, magazine clippings, or words alone. Stories can also be put on audiotapes or even on videotapes, with the student's teacher or the student him- or herself reading the story.

Social stories can be implemented in a number of ways. Teachers might read the stories to or with students. The stories might be sent home to be reviewed with the family. The stories might be kept in a desk, locker, or personal notebook so the student can read the stories often and keep them handy for quick review. In some instances, the student may only need to review the story once or twice to feel calm and comfortable with a situation. In other cases, the story may need to be read and reviewed daily for weeks at a time. Once the student successfully enacts the skills or appropriately responds in the social situation depicted, use of the story can be phased out.

Many individuals with autism report that the social stories method or related types of written preparation help them to learn, understand, and cope with puzzling, new, or complex situations. Dane Waites (2001), a man with autism, uses the stories not only to learn about unfamiliar situations but also as a way to reduce stress or anxiety. Dane's mother explains the process he uses to construct and use his stories:

Before I discovered the Social Story technique, I used newspaper clippings, magazine cuttings and photographs to try to explain issues to Dane. Social Stories, however, can be devised to suit Dane's specific needs. If necessary, they can be illustrated with computer-generated photographic images of real people.

Dane now has a folder of prepared social stories covering various contingencies. The following extract is from a story that helps Dane overcome his difficulty in changing from weekend activities to work on Monday mornings, and it also helps him to follow his list. He has named it "A Time for Work and A Time for Interests'":

Not everybody has an interesting life. I have an interesting life. Many people don't have a job. They don't get paid my wage each week. I don't get bored. I am paid to do all the work on my list. I am paid to finish my list and do a good job. When I finish work for the day I can do other things, like sport. Mum has to follow her list. If Mum did not follow her list, who would cook the meals, do the washing and keep the house nice for her family? When Mum finishes her list she can do other things, like reading. (Waites & Swinbourne, 2001, p. 196–197)

For Dane, social stories convert his own words into reality. He creates and takes ownership of a social story, and when he reads it again it gives him a mechanism to work with. For months, Dane studied 'A Time for Work and A Time for Interests' every Monday morning to remind him why he wanted to work and why he must follow his list. This story also reminds him that after work he can go the gym, or for a run or ride his bike.

Role Play

Role play is another strategy that many students find helpful when learning to socialize. Students may need only a quick verbal role play to get through a situation (e.g., rehearse the steps involved in ordering lunch from the cafeteria) or a full dramatic role play can be used in which the teacher or other students take on different parts.

In a high school business class, the students engaged in role play to practice skills related to job interviews. William, a young man with Asperger's syndrome, was taken with the exercise and asked his father to practice the role play with him several times at home. William's father even videotaped the role play so his son could watch it whenever he needed to be reminded of the language and behaviors associated with interviews. When William eventually landed a job interview (with the help of his teacher), he navigated the process with ease and was offered a position as a retail clerk at a music store.

William found the role play so helpful and was so successful with it that his family and teachers began using it across environments and contexts. The business teacher, in the meantime, was so impressed with the effectiveness of the strategy for all students that he began using role play in other areas of his curriculum. Students in the business class engaged in role play to learn strategies for dealing with irate customers, for learning ways to share ideas in a business meeting, and for making small talk with new business contacts.

Role plays can be used to practice a specific situation (e.g., singing in a concert, going to the first day of middle school) or to improve certain skills (e.g., greeting people). One of my former students often asked his brother to role play "teenager conversations" with him. The student's brother would bring up a topic, and the young man with Asperger's syndrome would practice entering and staying in the conversation.

Let Students "In" on Social Secrets

For many learners with autism, participating in a social interaction is like playing a game without knowing the rules or the objectives. Some individuals with autism report that the social demands of making small talk or walking into a party can create stress, anxiety, and panic. Students report that they often feel as if everyone else knows the social secrets necessary for success and they do not. For these reasons, it can be very helpful to explicitly teach students about social situations. Liane Holliday Willey (1999), a woman with Asperger's syndrome who also happens to have a daughter with Asperger's syndrome, explained the significant stress she experienced when trying to figure out the social requirements of planning a party for her daughter:

The most simple-sounding duties blew me away. For example, what exactly did it mean to plan a child's class party? With no precise guidelines or definition of terms in tow, I had no answer but plenty of questions. Was any kind of entertainment acceptable or did I need to hire a dog and pony act? Could I provide any sort of snack or was I expected to bring in fully nutritious main course meals? Was I supposed to poll the parents and ask them for their thoughts? Was I supposed to invite them to attend? If I planned a craft, were there rules about which materials the kids could use? I did not know where to begin or worse, how to end. The experience was terrifying to me. (p. 101)

Likewise, Wendy Lawson, a woman with autism spectrum disorder, shared how confusing social rules and norms can be. She illustrated how the requirements of even the most basic and common of social situations can be puzzling:

"Can I buy dessert now?" I asked. We were at McDonald's, my favorite eating place, and my main meal was over.
"Wendy, you don't have to ask my permission to buy dessert," my friend said. "You are an adult, you can do what you want."
But that is how it is. Due to being constantly unsure of required behavior, I always ask my friends what needs to happen next. Some actions are routine and I understand what is required, but others are always changing. (1998, p. 100)

Sharing secrets may involve giving students information as situations arise. For instance, if a student is at a school dance and seems confused about what those at the dance expect of her, the teacher might approach her and suggest that she get a snack, approach some friends to talk, or join other students on the dance floor. Some students may even want these options in writing.

Another way to share secrets is to routinely give students information about a variety of social situations. For instance, students may want to receive instruction on aspects of making small talk (e.g., how to enter a conversation). Liane Holliday Willey has constructed a set of rules to help her child learn about communication and socialization:

- When in doubt, think it but don't say it.
- If you don't have anything nice to say to someone, do not say anything at all.
- Write in your journal when something really bothers you, rather than exclaiming it to the world. Then bring your journal home and let Mom and Dad help you figure out what to do with the thought. (2001, p. 41)

Similarly, Stephen Shore finds that emotionally charged situations, in particular, are more negotiable if people are sensitive but direct enough to give him the information he needs:

When dealing with emotionally charged situations with other people, I find it helpful if others can say exactly what they mean along with creating a feeling of safety and trust. If this happens, I feel freed from the concern of having to create an appropriate response. Some phrases that I keep in my response repertoire for these situations include "What can I do to make you feel better about this?" or "Look, I sense that you have some strong feelings about _____. Can we talk about it?" While having an algorithm or method for handling these types of situations helps, it does not approach the facility others off the autism spectrum seem to have for these emotionally charged situations. (2001, p. 110)

It is important to remember that sharing social secrets is important even for students who do not speak or have reliable communication. Just because a student cannot express confusion related to social situations does not mean he or she will not be puzzled about them. To err on the side of caution, teachers should provide information about social situations to every student.

Promote Acceptance and Belonging

Too often, individuals with autism are asked to make accommodations, to use "typical behavior," and to learn "appropriate social skills." Instead of asking students with autism to make all of the adjustments, teachers and students without identified disabilities can rethink their ideas about concepts such as "typical" and "appropriate" and question whether conforming is *always* the best way to support students with autism. For instance, instead of asking the student with autism to study all of the social norms of attending a basketball game (e.g., sitting on the bleachers, cheering when the home team scores), all students and teachers in the school might expand their notions of what appropriate participation looks like. This exact question arose when one of my former students, Tawanna, attended her first varsity game. Even though the teachers had talked to her about appropriate social behavior for the game, Tawanna appeared unable or unwilling to follow the social rules that had been outlined for her. Instead, she paced rapidly up and down the court during the game (perhaps in imitation of the schools' coach) and waved a colorful flyswatter (a favorite possession) when the home team had the ball. When the special education teacher tried to stop Tawanna from pacing, students stopped the teacher and pointed out how other students were stomping on the bleachers, waving pompoms, and shouting at the players. A few students were even dressed as hornets (the school mascot), making the flyswatter a natural part of the scene! The teachers in Tawanna's school began to think more critically about what types of social supports they provided for her. Although Tawanna still wanted information about social situations and often did want to "fit in" to the life of the school, there were moments when she was relieved to be accepted with all of her differences and uniqueness.

Likewise, Jim Sinclair reported that part of forming true friendship is finding individuals who believe that relationships require "adaptation" and understanding on the part of both individuals:

I had a friend—not a parent driven by love and obligation to want to reach me, not a professional who made a career of studying my condition, but just someone who thought I was interesting enough to want to get to know better—a friend who, with no formal background in psychology or special education, figured out for herself some guidelines for relating to me. She told me what they were: never to assume without asking that I thought, felt, or understood anything merely because she would have such thoughts, feelings, or understanding in connection with my circumstances or behavior; and never to assume without asking that I didn't think, feel, or understand anything merely because I was not acting the way [one] would act in connection with such thoughts, feelings, or understanding. In other words, she learned to ask instead of trying to guess. (1992, p. 296)

SUMMARY

On my first day of teaching, one of my students with autism spent 6 hours running around the classroom. Every 30 minutes or so, he would get tired and collapse in my lap for a short 10-second rest. One of the paraprofessionals in the school walked in on this scene and remarked, "He can't be autistic. Kids with autism don't like to be near people." The paraprofessional was, of course, sharing one of the many myths related to the social lives of individuals with autism.

Certainly it is true that some people with autism need more time alone than others. Some even note that they are more comfortable alone or with animals than they are with people. Other individuals with autism crave social interaction and social situations, however. Of course this range of preferences parallels those of people without identified disabilities, so caution must be exercised when talking about a social preference or need as "autistic-like."

What does seem true about learners with autism and socializing is that their needs and preferences are as varied and individual as the students themselves. For this reason, teachers will do well to support the student with autism and all other students by creating a classroom community and cultivating opportunities for connection and interaction within that classroom. Within this context, then, individual supports and adaptations can be made to meet the needs of the individual student.

It was within the social context of such an inclusive classroom that a young first-grade student, Ian Drummond, was inspired to write the first story of his life, through typed communication. His words should help teachers consider the ways in which inclusion and social interaction are enmeshed and how student stories and voices must drive the work we do and the ideas we have about autism:

THERE WAS A SBOYH WHO HAD AUTISM. HE HADF A HAFTD TIME DOING THINGS THAT OTHER KIDS DID BUT JHE HAD F5RIENDS. HE LIKED EDDIE AN TRISTAN AND ALL THE MKIDS. THEY WERDE HAPPY TOGETHERY. (Martin, 1994, p. 241)

For More Answers and Ideas

Developmental Studies Center. (1997). *Blueprints for a collaborative classroom.* Oakland, CA: Developmental Studies Center.

Gibbs, J. (1995). *Tribes: A new way of learning and being together.* Sausalito, CA: Center Source Systems, LLC.

Gray, C. (1994). *Comic strip conversations.* Arlington, TX: Future Horizons Inc.

Gray, C. (2000). *The new social story book: Illustrated edition.* Arlington, TX: Future Horizons Inc.

Kagan, L., Kagan, M., & Kagan, S. (1997). *Cooperative learning structures for teambuilding.* San Clemente, CA: Kagan Cooperative Learning.

Lewis, B. (1998). *What do you stand for?: A kid's guide to building character.* Minneapolis, MN: Free Spirit.

Loomans, D., & Kolberg, K. (1993). *The laughing classroom: Everyone's guide to teaching with humor and play.* Tiburon, CA: H J Kramer.

Sapon-Shevin, M. (1999). *Because we can change the world: A practical guide to building cooperative, inclusive classroom communities.* Needham Heights, MA: Allyn & Bacon.

Schniedewind, N., & Davidson, E. (1998). *Open minds to equality.* Needham Heights, MA: Allyn & Bacon.

Snell, M., & Janney, R. (2000). *Teacher's guides to inclusion: Social relationships and peer support.* Baltimore: Paul H. Brookes Publishing Co.

CHAPTER 7

Building Communication Skills, Competencies, and Relationships

i love language more than anything
it links people
a language gives us dignity and individuality
i am not without language
(Sellin, 1995, p. 154; written using facilitated communication)

Educators who are preparing to teach a student with autism for the first time often ask, "Where do I start?" I always suggest beginning with communication. If the student does not have a reliable way to communicate, the educational team will need to experiment with strategies, systems, materials, or devices that might be effective. If the student does have reliable ways to communicate, the team should focus on building the student's communication skills and competencies and giving him or her opportunities to participate in class, engage in curriculum, and socialize using those skills and competencies. Supporting a student's communication is critical; if a teacher in an inclusive classroom wants to develop better curriculum and instruction for a student, find more effective and sensitive ways to support his or her behavior, or learn more about his or her social needs, that teacher needs to be able to gain access to that student's voice.

METHODS OF COMMUNICATION

Students with autism communicate in a variety of ways. Teachers are charged with learning about these communication efforts so that they can respond to them. As Gail Gillingham (2000), an educator and autism advocate, shared, the role of the teacher is not to teach communication but to find it, listen to it, and build sharing and understanding between the person with autism and others:

In all of the time I have spent with autistic people, I have not made any effort to "teach" autistic children and adults how to communicate. This does not mean that I do not communicate with them. We communicate all the time. I do not take any credit from "teaching" them how to communicate. I believe that their desire and willingness to communicate with others is the same as that of any other person in the world. They reach out to us in so many different ways, clearly communicating with those in their presence at all times. They may not be using words. Their gestures many not exactly match ours. Their behavior may appear "inappropriate." All of this is communication. If and when we take the time and make the effort to observe and to listen, we can and will understand. (p. 111)

Educators can support students by seeking to understand all of the ways in which students communicate and helping them to build on and enhance the strategies and approaches they already employ successfully. Two ways in which students with autism often communicate are explored here: 1) speech and 2) augmentative and alternative communication (AAC).

Speech

Some students with autism can use speech reliably. Others, however, use speech in ways that seem idiosyncratic and unreliable. For instance, some students can recite all of the words from a song or videotape but cannot ask for a drink of water when they need one. Another problem experienced by some individuals is that they can use a few words functionally (e.g., "Hello," "My name is Larry") but have difficulties using speech for conversation.

Uses and Purposes of Echolalia Some students repeat phrases or expressions over and over again. They may repeat words, phrases, or expressions immediately after hearing them. For example, if the teacher says "Good morning, students," the student may also say "Good morning, students." This phenomenon is called *echolalia*. If the student uses the words or phrase immediately after hearing it, the behavior is considered *instant* or *immediate echolalia* and if the student repeats something said minutes, days, or even weeks after something is said it is called *delayed echolalia*. When a student repeats a phrase from a movie, a line from a song, or a teacher's utterance ("We don't behave like that in the eighth grade!") repeatedly, that is considered delayed echolalia.

Different people seem to experience echolalia in different ways at different times. This means that for some people with autism, the purpose of echolalia—when there is one—changes across the day and across contexts. Some people report, however, that their echolalia often serves no purpose; it "just happens." That is, they sometimes say things they don't want to say or speak when they do not mean to do so (Burke, 2002; Donnellan & Leary, 1995; Kluth, 1998).

In some instances and for some individuals, echolalia is helpful. Some individuals with autism use echolalia because it can be pleasing or relaxing (Gillingham, 2000; Grandin, 1995; Webb, 1995). Jasmine Lee O'Neill, a woman with autism, reported that some of these sounds bring "a peaceful inner feeling":

In those who speak, they will often talk to themselves, chatting away about almost anything, and echoing tunes, phrases, or words that sound pleasing to them. The sounds of certain words can roll about deliciously and provide auditory stimulation. Even in completely non-verbal autistics there is a rare child who makes no sound at all. Each child picks and utters key noises to himself. (1999, p. 25)

Students often use echolalia in very functional ways. That is, students who cannot control or access all of the speech they need for a given situation seem to "borrow" words or phrases that they can gain access to and control. Grandin (1995) explained that some individuals with autism often echo words or phrases that are associated with the words they do want. To illustrate this point, Grandin used the example of Jessy, a woman with autism who always uses the words "partly heard song" when she means "I don't know." Grandin hypothesized that at some point in Jessy's life a partly heard song was associated with not knowing.

Individuals with autism may use echolalia to take a turn in a conversation, answer a question, or process information (Prizant & Duchan, 1981). Susan Stokes, a consultant who works with people with autism, shared an example of how one young man used echolalia to converse with his teachers:

A student with autism became upset with his teacher over completing a task. He then verbalized loudly, "Go to hell lieutenant!" His parents reported that he had been watching the movie "A Few Good Men" quite frequently. This movie contains this exact same utterance in the emotional context of anger. This child with autism was unable to spontaneously generate language to communicate, "I'm upset and I don't want to complete this assignment," but could pull forth an echolalic utterance which he had processed in the context of the emotional state of anger. (Stokes, www.cesa7.k12.wi.us/sped/autism/verbal/verbal11.html)

Students may also use echolalia to make requests. A mother I know told me that her son often puts records on the living room stereo and subsequently will turn to anyone else in the room and ask, "Do you want me to leave you alone?" (something he often hears from his family members) which the family has grown to understand means "Leave me alone, please."

Finally, the student with autism may use often-heard phrases to initiate conversations. Eric, a young man with autism I know (who is Caucasian) shared a locker space with two popular young men in the school (who are Latino). Every day when Eric came to the locker space, his two classmates would greet him by saying, "Qué pasa, man." Over time, Eric began to greet his family, classmates, teachers, and even his mailman with these same words.

Perceptions of Echolalia   Echolalic behaviors are sometimes seen as intentional or even as "interfering" or "challenging." Students who struggle with speech are sometimes blamed for saying inappropriate things or for not trying hard enough to "speak the right way." People with autism often report that they have little or no control over their speech, however. Even those who sometimes use echolalia in functional ways may be unable to control how and when they use it.

Sue Rubin, a woman with autism who uses both speech and facilitated communication to communicate, shares that her speech is unpredictable:

When I use speech alone I sometimes mean what I say and other times I don't. My awful echolalia is…an example of movement of thought (problems). I say a word or sound and am unable to switch it off or change to a different sound. (Rubin et. al., 2001, p. 421)

She also notes that her echolalia "disappears somewhat" when she is cognitively engaged.

Therese Joliffe, a woman with autism, also claims that she cannot use words reliably or easily:

Speaking for me is still often difficult and occasionally impossible, although this has become easier over the years. I sometimes know in my head what the words are but they do not always come out. Sometimes when they do come out they are incorrect, a fact that I am only sometimes aware of and often pointed out by other people. (Joliffe, Lansdown, & Robinson, as cited in Donnellan & Leary, 1995, p. 52)

I have observed this phenomenon in my own experience; many individuals with autism have told me that speech is difficult to control and, therefore, interactions are challenging. I know a young man, Cedrick, who continually asks people, "What are you doing tonight?" In many instances, Cedrick uses this phrase when he means to say something else. Because the question is a reasonable and socially appropriate one, however, his conversation partners often answer the question repeatedly. One day while I was walking around a conference with Cedrick, he typed on his communication board, "Tell them not to answer me" after he had asked his question dozens of times throughout the morning. As we walked around the conference together, I informed everyone we met that they didn't need to answer his question, but people seemed uncomfortable with this unusual suggestion. Therefore, Cedrick spent most of the day asking his question and getting more and more "stuck" as people answered the question and asked him the same. (See Table 7.1 for suggestions on supporting people with echolalia.)

It is not uncommon for people who speak unusually to be presumed to be incompetent and even intellectually impaired. For instance, a teacher who hears a student repeat "The sky is falling, the sky is falling" for weeks after the class reads the story of Chicken Little might assume that the student is not smart enough to know that his speech is "inappropriate" or that it sounds silly. In our society, people often assume that a lack of speech or verbal communication translates to ignorance or stupidity (Crossley, 1997; Donnellan & Leary, 1995; Rubin et al., 2001).

In fact, the widely used *Diagnostic and Statistical Manual of Mental Disorders–Text Revision* (DSM-IV-TR) stated that, "During the early childhood years [children with severe mental retardation] … acquire little or no communicative speech…" and that, "During the school-age period, they may learn to talk" (American Psychiatric Association, 2000, p. 43). Likewise, Winner (1996) cited exceptional oral language as one of five early indicators of the "Globally Gifted High-IQ Child." She indicated specifically that, "These children speak early, often progressing directly from one-word utterances to complex sentences. They have a large vocabulary and a large store of verbal knowledge" (p. 27). In other words, the story that guides professionals in fields from medicine to teaching is this: The more you talk, the smarter you are. Despite evidence to

Table 7.1. Supporting students with echolalia

Reassure the speaker	Sometimes just assuring people that you hear them and want to understand them can be a comfort. When I work with a person who uses a lot of echoed speech, I might tell him or her any one of the following things:
	"I can see that you are trying hard to tell me something; let me see if I can figure it out."
	"I think you are trying to tell me _____, and I apologize if I'm getting it wrong."
	"I hope you will be patient with me as I try to figure out what you want."
	"I know you sometimes say _____ when you (feel/want/need) _____; is that what you (feel/want/need)?"
	"I can see that you want to tell me or ask me something. Let's see if we can figure out together what it is."
Go to the movies	If a student often uses phrases from a favorite movie or cartoon, familiarize everyone on the staff with it. This is especially helpful if the student uses the phrases in functional ways. For instance, a student who watches *The Wizard of Oz* frequently might say "Lions and tigers and bears" when he is frightened because the characters chant this phrase during a scary scene. A teacher would need to know the film to guess that the child might be afraid of something.
Make a "key"	Create a "key" to help others decipher a student's speech. Make a list of all of the phrases and words the student commonly uses. Then, work with the student's family to "translate" them. For example, a student I know often says, "the King of Rock and Roll"; this often means that he wants to listen to music. All of his teachers have been informed of this translation.
	The key should contain all possible meanings of given words and phrases as educators and families will often be guessing at the meaning of the utterances. If a word or phrase is sometimes used in different ways across different situations, that information should be included as well.
Switch to writing	Sometimes when I am working with a person who is using a lot of echoed speech, I stop talking to them and begin writing to them using a computer or paper and pen. If a person is using echoed speech because they are confused or cannot understand his or her partner's speech, this strategy may be very helpful.
	Another way to use the written word is to ask the person with autism to communicate using typing, writing, or pointing. If the person is using echoed speech because he or she cannot get the right words out, this strategy can be helpful. One young woman I know communicates most effectively when the teaching staff writes questions to her and gives her opportunities to circle an answer (from a choice of three or four options).
Whisper	Gail Gillingham (2000) has noticed that some of her friends and colleagues with autism use echoed speech when they don't understand what she is saying to them. She has found that repeating her words verbally in a whisper is sometimes helpful.

the contrary (Bauby, 1997; Crossley, 1997; Robillard, 1997; Rubin et al., 2001; Tavalario, 1997), this myth persists.

Augmentative and Alternative Communication

Of course, some students with autism do not use speech at all. Chammi Rajapatirana, a man with autism who uses typed communication, shared his frustration with not being able to speak and the pain that comes from being treated differently because of it:

Being mute is like having your brain gouged out. Autism/apraxia took away my voice, and a world that equates muteness with stupidity took everything else. Yes it really is as if my brain were gouged out. It hurts so much I want to scream. Pouring all my pain into my voice I want to scream till that searing sound fills my body, my soul and my world shattering us all into a million fiery shrieking pieces.

As an experiment, just try keeping your mouth shut for a day. Just try keeping your mouth shut while they talk about you, telling your mother to put you away in an institution. You want to scream "no no no" but you are mute. (1998, p. 2)

Individuals like Rajapatirana must be supported through the use of AAC communication supports and strategies. AAC refers to communication that enhances, augments, or supplements speech and covers a broad range of methods and strategies, from sophisticated, computer-based systems with synthetic voices to teacher-created letter boards. Other examples of AAC include writing, drawing, gesturing, body movements, eye-gaze/pointing, facial expressions, and sign language.

All of us use various forms of AAC in our daily lives. We may, for instance, raise a hand to be recognized in a classroom or scribble a note to a friend during a quiet church service. For a person with unique communication needs, however, AAC is more than a convenience. For those with disabilities or communication differences, AAC systems, devices, and techniques typically mean increased access to voice, control, freedom, and power. For some, in fact, AAC strategies and techniques are the only way to tell a joke, order a cheeseburger, sing to a child, or write to a love letter. Sharisa Kochmeister, a woman who uses AAC to communicate and to pursue her work as an author, poet, and activist, claimed that AAC has liberated her, given her opportunities for expression, and "shattered walls" in her life:

Almost as much as my various "disorders" disable me, typing enables me. It allows me to communicate with and exist within a world where I was and would otherwise still be a total stranger. It lets me show other people that I (and therefore, possibly other "non-verbals") am alive and smart, understand, think, feel, hope, plan, and dream just like verbal people. (1997, p. 1)

Even those who can use speech may prefer to use AAC to supplement it. This preference or need should be honored. Individuals with autism may need a variety of ways to express themselves, and those without disabilities should be cautious about making judgments about the value of one over the other.

Some communication differences have little to do with anxiety. The real anxiety comes from working with so-called experts who make assumptions about communication.

Sign Language and Gestural Systems

Some students have found communication success by using some type of sign language. The most common system is probably American Sign Language (ASL), which is the language system used by those who are deaf or hard of hearing. Students might also use Signed English or Signed Exact English. Still others may use "home" signs, which are gestures and signs created and used by an individual. For instance, I knew one student who could not go anywhere without his watch. When he couldn't find it, he signed for it by squeezing his right wrist.

Although some students with autism may use ASL because they are deaf or hard of hearing, most use sign language because they cannot speak. The advantage, of course, to using sign language is that the user does not need an aid or piece of equipment. The main drawback to using any sign system, however, is that many communication partners do not know sign language, especially if the student uses some signs or gestures that are unique to his or her communication.

A manual sign system for some individuals with autism may also be tricky because of problems some students experience with movement. Some students may simply be unable to use signs accurately or predictably because of problems with initiation, volition, or modulation of movement. Some students, for instance, use ASL but move very quickly or use only approximations of the signs. These students can be quite successful with sign and gesture systems if those around them understand their movements as communicative acts and work to understand the individual's unique system.

Of course, none of these cautions should prevent a teacher from using signs or gesture systems in the classroom; if a student seems able to imitate signs and learn new language this way, it should definitely be pursued. Consider the case of my friend, Rick, a single father, and his son, Wyatt. For several months Rick asked Wyatt's teachers to introduce sign language to his son; Rick had seen evidence at home that Wyatt could learn and functionally use different gestures and thought it was worth pursuing. School staff resisted the suggestion and cited the student's motor control problems and "low IQ" as reasons he wouldn't be able to learn a complicated symbol system. Rick stopped pestering the school until the day Wyatt got a new babysitter. The young woman wanted to know why Wyatt couldn't talk. When Rick explained, she asked why he could not use sign language. Then Rick explained why Wyatt did not use sign language. The sitter who was not a teacher or even an adult then asked, "Well, do you mind if I try?" Rick encouraged her to try and using only a workbook she bought at the bookstore, the young woman soon had Wyatt communicating using more than 30 words. The last time I spoke with Rick, Wyatt was using hundreds of words—not only to make requests or label items but also to hold conversations with his father and others in his life.

For students who do not use conventional signs and even for students like Wyatt who use "real" signs that others may not know, teachers may want to assemble a gesture dictionary for use by all of the classroom staff and for students, as well (see Table 7.2). A gesture dictionary acts as a "translation guide by describing a student's gestures along with [his or her] meanings and suggestions for appropriate responses" (Mirenda, 1999, p. 120). If the dictionary is used consistently, the individual with autism may be less frustrated and more comfortable initiating communication with teachers and peers. In addition, educators may see a more complex profile of the student emerge as they begin to accumulate evidence of the various ways the learner gets his or her needs met and communicates information.

Objects and Pictures

Some students communicate by using objects. A student may bring his teacher the chalk if he wants her to write on the chalkboard. Or he may bring her his

Table 7.2.   Sample gesture dictionary for Marv, a student with autism

What Marv does	What it seems to mean	How to respond
Makes an "uh-uh" sound	"I need some help."	Show him the manual sign for help and then provide help.
Grabs another student's hand or arm	"I like you."	Explain the meaning to the student's friend and help them work together, if possible.
Bangs or taps his desk	"I'm bored; I don't understand what's going on."	Quietly explain to him what is happening, using simple language and graphics if needed.

From Downing, J. (1999). *Teaching communication skills to students with severe disabilities.* Baltimore: Paul H. Brookes Publishing Co., p. 121; reprinted by permission.

boots if he is ready to go outside. Although this type of communication is not sufficient in that it does not allow the learner to express complex thoughts and ideas, it should not be overlooked as an important supplement to other types of communication. In some situations, communicating through objects is enough. If a student can bring her teacher a cup to indicate that she wants water, she may be confused if the teacher asks her to show the same thing on her communication board in order to get a drink.

Students may also communicate by interacting with pictures, either by handing pictures to a communication partner or by pointing to pictures. Students may use different types of pictures to communicate, ranging from simple line drawings to complex and detailed photographs. Students may use pictures and photographs for a range of purposes including communicating quick requests, making choices, or starting conversations. A student may, for instance, point to items on a communication board to choose a snack.

Objects and pictures are commonly used to create communication boards that students can use to make choices or express ideas. Teachers might also use the pictures from these boards to create daily schedules or stories for the student, thus giving him or her opportunities to better learn the pictures by using them across situations and environments.

One formal system of picture communication is the Picture Exchange Communication System (PECS) (Bondy & Frost, 2002). In this method, students present pictures to another person or form picture sentences on a board as a means of communication. Students typically keep pictures in a portable notebook so they can bring their "voice" with them in different situations (i.e., across environments).

The six phases of teaching PECS are as follows: In phase one, students are taught to initiate communication. The second phase expands the use of pictures. In the third phase, students make specific choices between available pictures. During the fourth phase, the student learns to build simple sentences. The fifth phase involves helping the student answer the question, "What do you want?" and in the sixth phase, students learn to comment about items and activities.

Although many students have found success in learning the PECS approach, this method, like all others, should be part of a total communication system. The biggest drawback to using a system like PECS is that students are limited by the pictures available to them. Therefore, this method may need to be supplemented with other strategies.

Communication Devices

Students with autism may come into the classroom with a variety of devices that can be used for everyday conversations and to engage in classroom lessons. Many students enjoy using communication devices (versus pictures or gestures) because many of these devices "talk." For students who do not speak, the device can serve as their voice. Some devices are very simple and carry only one or a handful of messages, whereas other devices have many "levels" and can carry thousands of phrases. Some devices are designed only to carry and deliver a message, whereas others feature a variety of functions and features including calculators, printers, and memory capacity for storing large amounts of text.

Although there are many drawbacks to using such devices to communicate (e.g., they can be cumbersome, they can break down), if a student is successful in using a particular device, the benefits outweigh the drawbacks. Students using devices may not only gain access to a voice but also some may hone additional academic skills and competencies as they become proficient with their particular device. One of my former students had the use of speech but could only express simple needs and wants. When he began supplementing his speech by using a communication device, he was able to compose more complex and detailed thoughts. In addition, he became incredibly adept at programming the device and was able to get extra credit from his computer teacher for learning that skill.

Some students are even making gains in literacy, in part, through the use of communication devices. Jamie Burke, a student with autism, learned to talk by reading the visual display on his communication device:

[Jamie's device] can be programmed to say each letter aloud as it is typed, read each word aloud when the space bar is pressed, and read whole sentences or paragraphs aloud when the speak bar is pressed. When the speak bar is pressed, the sentence scrolls by on the bright green visual display as the device reads it aloud. Jamie initially began incorporating speech that seemed related to his typing by intermittently repeating aloud individual words after the [device]. Shortly thereafter, he began repeating aloud phrases and eventually whole sentences as they scrolled by, without the added support of repeating after the [device's] voice output. [Jamie's mother] describes Jamie's reading aloud as beginning"once he got the [device] and the use of the computer....and all of a sudden [he] started reading back, and repeating after the machine had said it, that just opened the floodgates." (Broderick & Kasa-Hendrickson, 2001, p. 17)

Writing

Beginning in the 1960s, a woman named Rosalind Oppenheim (as cited in Crossley, 1997) taught a group of nonverbal students with autism to communicate through writing. The students, previously assumed to have mental retardation, were soon able to "talk" on paper. Oppenheim noted that putting pressure on the student's hand seemed to be the key to writing success for those in her group:

We believe that the autistic child's difficulties stem from a definite apraxia… There seems to be a basic deficiency in certain areas of his motor expressive behaviour. So, in teaching writing, we find that it is unusually necessary to continue to guide the child's hand for a considerable period of time. Gradually, however, we are able to fade this to a mere touch of a finger on the child's writing hand. We're uncertain about precisely what purpose this finger-touching serves. What we do know is that the quality of the writing deteriorates appreciably without it, despite the fact that the finger is in no way guiding the child's writing hand. "I can't remember how to write the letters with out your finger touching my skin" one nonverbal child responded. (p. 40)

Although writing is not a common augmentative communication strategy used by those with autism, Oppenheim is not the only person to discover success with it. In Douglas Biklen's (1993) important book, *Communication Unbound*, he reported on the work of Mary Bacon, a special education teacher in Tucson, Arizona. Bacon described how she began using handwriting with her students:

I got a little perturbed with him when he wouldn't point to the ABC's for me. I slapped my hand on my side and said, "Garrett, you know the ABC's as well as I do. Now point to the W." That he did. He pointed to each one of them. I turned the page over and I said, "now, we're going to write the ABCs and I'll help you." All I did, I put my hand on his and my god, he wrote them all. (p. 96)

Tito Rajarshi Mukhopadhyay (2000), a young man with autism who also uses writing as AAC, has been writing independently since age 6. His story is interesting because Tito does not have verbal communication that is well understood by others: "I can speak although many people cannot follow because it is not clear. Sometimes I need facilitation to begin my speech like opening a speech door in my throat. To facilitate me mother has to wave her hands" (p. 76).

In the foreword of Tito's book, *Beyond the Silence*, Lorna Wing, a notable psychiatrist, describes her first impression of this young man:

> [When he arrived] Tito's observable behaviour [sic] was exactly like that of a mute child with classic autism, ignoring people but exploring the objects that took his attention. [His mother] settled him down and wrote the alphabet on a piece of paper. We asked questions and Tito pointed to the letters to spell his replies. He did this independently, without any physical guidance from his mother. He replied to questions in full sentences, including long words used appropriately. He also spontaneously told us, in handwriting, that he wanted the book he had written to be published and demanded a promise that this would happen. (2000, p. 2)

Tito's story is also interesting because he shares thoughts and ideas that would be considered sophisticated for a person twice his age; he is a gifted and talented poet and writer. He describes his autism in many of his writings:

Men and women are puzzled by everything I do
   Doctors use different terminologies to describe me
   I just wonder
   The thoughts are bigger than I can express
   Every move that I make shows how trapped I feel

Under the continuous flow of happenings
The effect of a cause becomes the cause of another effect
And I wonder
I think about the times when I change the environment around me
With the help of my imagination
I can go places that do not exist
And they are like beautiful dreams
But it is a world full of improbabilities
Racing towards uncertainty (Mukhopadhyay, 2000, p. 99)

Facilitated Communication

Facilitated communication, commonly referred to as FC, is a communication strategy being used by people with verbalization and motor skill difficulties. Specifically, FC is "...an alternative to speech that involves a communication partner who provides physical and emotional support to a person with a severe communication impairment as he or she types on a keyboard or points" (Biklen, 1990, p. 293). Facilitated communication is provided in several ways. It may entail a facilitator providing pressure to the speaker's shoulder or arm to support someone as they type or point to a communication device, board, cards, or objects. It can also involve a facilitator providing physical counter pressure to the speaker's wrist, hand, or elbow; or it may take the form of the facilitator being physically present, observing the speaker's communication, or simply sitting next to him or her.

Through the use of this facilitated communication, many students with autism and other disabilities who have limited use of words or who have never previously communicated with words were able to express their first thoughts, ideas, desires, needs, and feelings to family members, care providers, therapists and educators (Biklen, 1990; Crossley, 1997; Martin, 1994). FC is complex and involves more than physical contact. It requires emotional support and creative problem solving, as well. Many practical considerations are related to the implementation of FC. Facilitators are responsible for ensuring that the client is comfortable, watching the FC user and communication board/device and giving feedback about the typing process (e.g., reading off individual letters as they are typed, reminding the individual to look at the target, making suggestions about the individual's posture), and providing prompts and cues that will help the FC user communicate his or her message (e.g., asking clarifying questions such as "I don't understand what you typed there. Can you try it again?") (Biklen, 1990; Shevin & Chadwick, 2000).

Questions About Facilitated Communication

Although people with movement differences and other disabilities have long communicated with a variety of physical supports, the dawn of facilitated communication drew unprecedented attention. The unique nature of the method—having to support someone as they communicate through a device, board, cards, or objects that may entail physically supporting a person's body—instantly raised questions and concerns throughout the special education and disability rights communities. Also, some question the validity of the communication. Because of these concerns, many of the published studies about FC from the last decade have focused on the validation of the strategy and authorship of written communications (Biklen & Schubert, 1991; Calculator & Singer, 1992; Cardinal, Hanson, & Wakeham, 1996; Simon, Toll, & Whitehair, 1994; Szempruch & Jacobson, 1993; Weiss, Wagner, & Bauman, 1996).

In authorship studies, many researchers have found that facilitated communication is a valid strategy and that individuals with disabilities produce original communications (Biklen, Saha, & Kliewer, 1995; Cardinal et al., 1996; Janzen-Wilde, Duchan, & Higginbotham, 1995; Simon et al., 1994; Vasquez, 1994; Weiss, Wagner, & Bauman, 1996). Other researchers have reported that students could not produce original communication through FC (Calculator & Singer, 1992; Green & Shane, 1994; Hirshorn & James, 1995; Jacobson, Mulick, & Schwartz, 1995; Myles & Simpson, 1994; Regal, Rooney, & Wandas, 1994). Since these papers have been published, researchers, educators, and individuals with autism have studied the various reasons why individuals with autism might have "failed" the validity tests and have provided suggestions for studying the phenomenon more sensitively and effectively (see Biklen & Cardinal, 1997).

Some struggled with authorship/validity tasks and tests because the assessment conditions were uncomfortable or even threatening. For instance, some individuals with autism feared they would lose access to their communication if they did not perform as expected. As noted earlier, FC requires emotional support such as treating the FC user with respect and reassuring the individual as her or she types. Biklen described why this type of support is so important:

> Not surprisingly, people who have had a history of difficulty with motor planning will lack confidence in their ability to carry out new tasks. Imagine what it must be like to have significant problems with motor planning and indeed any kind of voluntary action and to have this problem from a very early age. In effect, you will have never enjoyed success in getting your body to do what you want it to do when you want it and often have your body respond in ways that make you feel embarrassed! And imagine what it would be like to be evaluated on the basis of your nonresponsiveness or your impulsiveness. Hence the importance of being supportive to help the person develop confidence that he or she can develop the ability to be successful in communicating through typing. (1993, p. 11)

Sue Rubin, an FC user who can type independently, has noted how the facilitator's encouragement and expressions of confidence have not only helped her to type but to become independent in that typing:

Confidence makes independence happen. I can now type independently with people I have just met because I am confident I can do it and they are confident it can happen because they see me typing independently with others. I gained confidence over time by being successful with each level of fading; however, independence still eluded me for the first five years of typing. (1999, p. 5–6)

Authorship

An issue that was overlooked by some during discussions of validity was the fact that many students had validated their communication naturally through daily communication (Biklen, Saha, & Kliewer, 1995; Kluth, 1998; Martin, 1994; Olney,

1997; Sellin, 1995; Weiss & Wagner, 1996). One study conducted in 1996 focused on how teachers confirmed the authorship of their students' typing (Biklen et al., 1995). The teachers identified several different types of evidence they had informally collected on each student. This information was gathered beginning with each student's first FC experiences. The authors call this type of validation a portfolio approach because different types of evidence are collected over time instead of "testing" students on only one occasion or pressuring them to perform during unnatural, scheduled sessions. (See Table 7.3)

In addition, some FC users have silenced naysayers' doubts by learning to type independently. That is, many FC speakers who started "speaking" by being physically supported at the hand or wrist are now typing without any physical support (Burke, 2002; Crossley, 1997; Gambel 2002; Kochmeister, 1997; Rubin et al., 2001). Rosemary Crossley (1997), who runs a communication clinic in Australia, reported that within several years of introducing FC to several individuals with disabilities, 30 typed independently, although some of them re-

Table 7.3. Validating facilitated communication using the portfolio approach

Attention to typing	One way students demonstrated communicative competence was through their attention to typing. Students who previously could not sit for more than a few seconds were able to remain sitting and visually attend to a computer, keyboard, or other communication device. Due to the previous behavior of these students, this sign of attention and ability to control some movement was enough evidence to convince some individuals in speakers' lives that the communications produced were valid (Biklen, Saha, & Kliewer 1995).
Relationship between typing and speaking	Another way communication was validated by the teachers in the study was through observing the relationship of student's speaking to their typing. Some students typed words and letters that match their verbalizations. Other times, students typed words or phrases related to their verbal communications. One student typed out "CAN I GO" and verbally said, "castle room" at the same time, indicating the place he wished to go (Biklen, Saha, & Kliewer 1995, p. 63).
Form, content, and style of communication	Attending to the communication form, content, and style of students' communications was another way evidence of authorship was gathered. Some students used unique, idiosyncratic, or unusual phrases or spellings of words. One student in the study frequently substituted the letter "y" for the letter "i" in a variety of different words. She used these same types of spellings across facilitators and across communicative contexts. Students also typed about the same topics or themes over time and across facilitators (Biklen, Saha, & Kliewer, 1995).
Message passing	Message passing, or the conveying of accurate information previously unknown to a facilitator was also used by the teachers in the study and has also been, perhaps, the most discussed and cited form of natural validation in other studies and narrative personal accounts (Biklen, Saha, & Kliewer, 1996; Biklen, Winston Morton, Gold, Berrigan, & Swaminathan, 1992; Crossley & McDonald, 1980; Weiss & Wagner, 1997). Students may pass information from home to school or vice versa. Information can also be passed across teachers, other students, or other educational staff. For instance, a student told his teacher that he had gotten a new bowling ball. On another occasion, he typed that his father was getting married on a certain date. The student's mother confirmed that the boy did indeed have a new bowling ball and that his father did marry on the date specified by the boy (Biklen, Saha, & Kliewer, 1996).

From Biklen, D., Saha, S., & Kliewer, C. (1995). How teachers confirm the authorship of facilitated communication: A portfolio approach. *Journal of The Association for Persons with Severe Handicaps, 20*, 45–56; reprinted by permission.

quired a light touch on the head or back. Some of those typing independently are even attending 4-year colleges, speaking at national conferences, and engaging in research on their own typing (Broderick & Kasa-Hendrickson, 2002; Burke, 2002; Harrison, 2000; Kochmeister, 1997; Rubin et al., 2001). As Hitzing indicated, arguments over the *validity* of FC should be moot:

> Imagine, if you can, the following situation. You and I are arguing about whether people with autism can fly. I say that they can, at least some of them... you argue strongly that they can't. Suddenly, in the middle of our debate a person with autism flies through the open window. The argument, as currently constructed, is over. Now, you could quite reasonably change the terms of the argument. You could, for example, argue that the person who just flew in the window is the only person in the world with autism who can fly. We could also argue about what it takes to teach a person with autism to fly, etc. But, unless you want to postulate that the person who flew through the window was misdiagnosed, or that the appearance of flying was the result of some sort of special effect, some slick illusion, you have to stop denying the validity of the "autistic" flying phenomenon. . . .Some of these folks are "flying!" It is indisputable that some studies have validated the communication abilities of people who are being physically assisted to communicate, whereas other people have progressed from physical dependence to independent communication. (1994, pp. 2–3)

CREATING A CONTEXT FOR COMMUNICATION

Whether a student talks nonstop or does not use spoken words at all, teachers can structure the classroom and engineer lessons to both recognize and inspire different types of communication. Teachers can be supportive through their own actions and by creating an environment that encourages diversity of expression and interaction.

Communicate with Students and Expect Them to Communicate with You

When teachers are working with students who do not have a reliable communication system, they sometimes ask me, "How can you tell how much she understands?" The truth is, teachers may not know how much a learner understands if he or she does not have a way to communicate understanding. The rule should always be, when in doubt, assume that students can learn and want to communicate. We have no other choice.

Historically in the United States, "experts" have been tragically wrong about the learning potential and intellectual abilities of many different groups of people, including women, poor people, those from different racial and ethnic groups, people with physical disabilities, those with mental illness, those who are deaf and hard of hearing, and many others (Gould, 1981; Sacks, 1973; & Selden, 1999). This history is important as we will undoubtedly repeat our mistakes if we do not assume our students are capable, can communicate, and want to connect with us.

Some teachers may feel uncomfortable or unsure of how to interact with a student who does not speak or one who communicates in a way unfamiliar to him or her. This is understandable, but feeling uncomfortable is not an excuse for not learning new ways of interacting and communicating. One of the most important ways to make a student feel included in the classroom is simply to communicate with him or her and expect the student to communicate with you. Gillingham has stressed the importance of holding these values:

> Whenever I am with an autistic person, I communicate with them and I fully expect them to communicate with me. The fact that they do not respond in the exact way that I approach them, does not mean that I cannot understand them. When I go into a home and say "hello" to an autistic person, they do not have to reply "hello" for me to feel that they are responding. Whether they approach me or withdraw to another room tells me something. I read an increase in repetitive behavior as an indication that they are excited to see me, and I verbally tell them that it feels good to see their excitement. I follow their lead if they take my hand to show me something. If they speak with garbled sounds, I acknowledge their efforts and openly admit that I don't quite understand what they are trying to say. As I spend time with them, I am continuously aware of what they are doing and how they are responding to me. It doesn't really matter to me, exactly how they are communicating. My focus is how I can respond to their message respectfully, not on what is wrong with them or how to fix them. (2000, pp. 111–112)

These beliefs and behaviors inspire trust in relationships and allow teachers and students to get to know each other and build communication opportunities and skills. As Gillingham went on to share, "Concentration on acceptance of what is, instead of trying to fix what appears wrong, leads to improved communication" (2000, p. 112).

In communicating with students and expecting communication, it can be helpful to reflect on what assumptions a teacher might have about his or her student. Shevin (1999) noted that in his role as a communication ally, he always begins with "default values" on which he acts until receiving specific information to the contrary. His own assumptions about individuals with communication differences are that they

- Are highly intelligent
- Have a deep interest in fostering relations with others
- Have stories they would like to tell, if the circumstances are right
- Have positive images of themselves that they wish to present as part of their communication
- Are paying attention to when others interact with them

Although every teacher will want to establish his or her own values and assumptions, those offered by Shevin (1999) should be carefully considered as this particular way of thinking of people can inspire positive actions. For instance, a teacher who believes his or her student is intelligent will creatively include that student in lessons and respond to that learner in moments when the student seems particularly interested in a topic or idea.

Pay Attention to the Communication Skills Students *Do* Have

Too often, professionals focus on what students cannot do instead of what they can do. All students with autism have some ways of communicating even if they do not use spoken words. Does the student point to objects she wants? Does she use facial expressions to indicate distress, pain, or happiness? Can she use an object or a picture to make a request (e.g., grab her lunchbox when she is ready for lunch)? Can she accurately use a gesture to communicate a need, a want, or a feeling (e.g., clapping hands when she wants to hear music)?

Although teachers, therapists, and others who work with a student will certainly want to help any student build on and enhance his or her communication strategies, support should begin by exploring and honoring the skills and abilities students already have. Teachers may not be able to accurately identify ways in which learners are communicating after knowing them only a few days or weeks, therefore, families must be interviewed and consulted about their child's communication strategies. If the teachers and other team members are unable to generate a lot of useful information by simply meeting with the family, the group might sit together and view a few videotapes of the student (at home and at school). The purpose of such a viewing is to allow various members of the group to ask questions and share answers about how the student communicates across various activities. For instance, as the team watches a tape of the student getting ready for school, the student's mother might point out how he taps his head to ask for his hat or how he vocalizes "buh" to ask for his favorite book.

Teach All Students to Use Augmentative and Alternative Communication

If a learner with autism uses a picture board to indicate choices, the teacher might ask all students to use a picture board for choices at some point in the day, thereby teaching another method of expression and communication to all. Likewise, students in the inclusive classroom might learn to use sign language or a laptop computer if these are communication systems used by the student with autism. A teacher might consider giving all students a spelling test using the sign language alphabet, for instance. And instead of having students shout out answers, they can be asked to write answers on paper or to indicate a sign for yes and no answers.

In teaching all students to use alternative modes of communication, teachers encourage expression and introduce learners to a wider range of choices they can make when communicating, creating, composing, and expressing. I worked with one young man without a disability who came alive as a poet when he started using another student's "talking board"—an augmentative communication device with a voice synthesizer. Another learner wrote and performed a one-person play using only dance, role-play, and gestures to communicate.

Create Communication Opportunities

Students with and without disabilities should have time to interact, share, and communicate with the teacher and peers throughout the day. In some classrooms, a handful of students dominate small-group conversations and whole-class discussions. Although it is important for these verbal and outgoing students to have a voice in the classroom, it is equally important for other students—including shy and quiet students, students using English as a second language, and students with disabilities—to have opportunities to share and challenge ideas, ask and answer questions, and exchange thoughts. To ensure that all students have opportunities to communicate, teachers need to put structures and activities in place that allow for interaction.

In one classroom, the teacher started every morning with a "whip" (Silberman, 1996). She pointed to each student in the class and asked him or her to give a three- to five-word phrase related to her prompt of the day. One morning, for instance, she asked students to report on something they learned on the previous day's fieldtrip to an art museum. Responses ranged from "Picasso was a sculptor" to "Dancing is art" to "Kids can be artists."

Another way to inspire communication is to ask students to "turn and talk" to each other at various points in the day. A high school history teacher used this strategy throughout the year to break up his lectures and to give students time to teach the material to each other. After giving mini-lectures of 15–20 minutes, he asked students to turn to a partner and answer a specific question or re-explain a concept he had taught. For instance, after giving a short lecture on the presidency, he asked students to discuss, "What qualities do Americans seem to want in a president?" and "How has this list of desired qualities changed over time?"

Teachers can also provide opportunities for communication by giving all students "airtime" during whole-class discussion. One way to do this is to ask for whole-class responses to certain prompts. For instance, instead of asking, "Who can tell me what H_2O is?," the teacher might say, "Stand up if you think you know the common name for H_2O." This strategy not only gives all learners a chance to give an answer, but it allows for some teacher-sanctioned movement, something often welcomed by students with autism.

Another way to engage all students in whole class work is to prepare the student with autism for his or her participation. The teacher might give the student a question or prompt before the class starts so that he or she can formulate a cogent response and respond with confidence. Although preparing the student in this way is often helpful for any student with autism, it can be especially useful for individuals who use AAC. The extra time gives the student more opportunity to formulate an answer and to prepare it by writing or typing it out.

ON BEING A SUPPORTIVE COMMUNICATION PARTNER

Open any textbook on autism or disability and you will find several pages and perhaps several chapters dedicated to improving the communication skills or capacities of students with autism. Less common, however, are pages and chapters dedicated to the necessary skills, attitudes, beliefs, and abilities of the communication partner. This paradigm or view of seeing "communication improvement" as a task for only one person in the communicative act is puzzling because communication is undoubtedly a social act. Therefore, supporting a student's communication will involve more than engaging in an assessment or encouraging his or her participation in a small group discussion. Supporting communication also involves reflection, self-examination, and collaboration with each individual student.

Do Not Insist on Eye Contact

When teachers want a learner's attention, many expect eye contact. Many who have taught students with autism, however, understand that eye contact can be irritating or even painful for these students. Wendy Lawson (1998), who has Asperger's syndrome, has claimed that for her, making eye contact with a speaker can result in a breakdown in communication:

How much easier it is to hear someone if you can't see his or her face. Then words are pure and not distorted by grimaces and gestures. I can listen better to the tone of someone's voice when I am not confused by the unwritten words of their facial expressions. (p. 97)

Jasmine Lee O'Neill (1999) and Luke Jackson (2002) offered similar advice and insight about the use of eye contact:

Autistics often avoid eye contact, so don't assume you're being ignored or treated rudely if you're not looked at directly.

Autistic people often glance out the sides of their eyes at objects or at other people. They have very acute peripheral vision and a memory for details that others miss. Gazing directly at people or animals is many times too over-whelming for the autistic one. Eyes are very intense and show emotions. It can feel creepy to be searched with the eyes. Some autistic people don't even look at the eyes of actors or news reporters on television. Eye contact must never be forced! (p. 26)

When I look someone straight in the eye, particularly someone I am not famil-iar with, the feeling is so uncomfortable that I cannot really describe it. First of all I feel as if their eyes are burning me and I really feel as if I am looking into the face of an alien. I know this sounds rude but I am telling it how it is. If I get past that stage and don't look away, when whilst someone is talking I find myself staring really hard and looking at their features and completely forgetting to lis-ten to what they are saying. (Jackson, 2000, p. 71)

Some students purposely avoid eve contact as a strategy for *enhancing* communication. As one man told me, "I can only participate in conversation if I'm looking at nothing." Stephen Shore explained how avoiding eye contact can help communication for some individuals:

With most people, the nonverbal communication supplements or enhances the verbal communication. The two channels are processed together to give a deeper meaning to the communication. With people having autism and Asperger syn-drome, however, the nonverbal component can be so difficult to decode that it interferes with getting meaning from the verbal channel. As a result, very little, if any communication occurs. This may be one reason why many people on the autism spectrum avoid eye contact when maintaining a conversation. The energy involved in reading the nonverbal data may interfere with getting the meaning from the verbal data. (2001, p. 130)

Consider Voice Volume and Tone

Any teacher can attest to the powers of the voice. When I taught high school students, I often found that the best way to get the attention of a noisy room of teenagers was to whisper. Surprising them with this tone of voice seemed to unarm them. When I taught kindergarten, I often gave directions in a sing-song voice. This, too, caught students off guard and appeared to capture their interest.

Playing with voice volume, quality, and tone can be a tool in connecting with any student, including those with autism. Gunilla Gerland, a woman with autism, indicates that whispers are extremely helpful as a communication tool:

But whispers came rushing at me from a long way off, always straight into my head, easily passing through all the passages in my ears, sliding directly up into my mind and rousing it. I didn't have to be on guard for whispers. I didn't have to wait to let them in. Whispers had their own key. So if people whispered when I was cutting out my little bits of paper, I looked up. Then I heard them. (1996, pp. 31–32)

Gail Gillingham, who shares the "whispering strategy" with people in her international workshops on autism, has received reports of success from her workshop attendees:

A father tells his son "it's time to put on his pajamas" in a soft voice and the son turns off the television and heads to his room. A mother tells her child that he has to stay close beside her, as the store is so busy today, and the child sticks by her side. A mother tells her child that "the bus is coming" and he turns off his video game, puts it away and goes to find his backpack, things she did for him in the past. (2000, p. 118)

"Listen" to Augmentative and Alternative Communication System Users

The communication act is incredibly dynamic when an AAC system is being used, therefore, the AAC user may have a difficult time interrupting, interjecting, or even initiating a conversation if the communication partner is not sensitive to communicative behaviors beyond speech. For example, an AAC user may begin a conversation by pointing to a word on a board. Such an initiation will be missed if the communication partner does not attend visually to the AAC user and look for signs (e.g., placing a hand on a communication board, shifting the body) that he or she wants to join the conversation.

A communication partner should also be aware of and open to changes in the pace of conversation. Many times, a communication partner will cut the AAC user off in mid-sentence because she thinks she knows what is going to be typed, indicated, or signed next or she may grow impatient with the AAC users' attempts to communicate and prematurely end a conversation. These types of communication clashes are often reported by people using AAC (Bauby, 1997; Brown, 1954; Crossley, 1997; Robillard, 1997; Tavalaro & Tayson, 1997). Mayer Shevin, an activist and researcher in disability studies and special education, encountered such a clash first-hand when he was hospitalized for a surgery related to his oral cancer:

For a week after the surgery, I breathed through a tracheotomy, was unable to speak, and communicated by slowly and shakily writing notes on a stenographer's pad. My mouth and throat were filled with a seeming ocean of mucus following the surgery; I relied for my survival on the wall-mounted suction machine, with its long hose and hard plastic mouthpiece. The hose and mouthpiece often clogged; I would clear them by dipping the mouthpiece in a glass of water. When that didn't work, and the hose or mouthpiece needed to be replaced, I had only a few minutes "breathing space" before I would begin choking.

One afternoon, the hose and mouthpiece both clogged, and I waited an endless-seeming 15 minutes until the nurse responded to my buzzer. When she asked me why I had buzzed, I started to write, "My suction is clogged—the tube and mouthpiece need to be replaced." I wrote MY SUCTION IS... and the nurse started out the door, saying, "Oh, I see—you need a new mouthpiece—I'll get it for you." I knew that merely replacing the mouthpiece wouldn't work, and I was already gasping for air. I flung my notebook at her, and hit her in the back of the head. Startled and angry, she came back to yell at me; I kept pounding my pencil on the tabletop and gestured, until grudgingly she returned my notebook to me. I scrawled my panic-stricken message in its entirety, making sure she did not leave until I was done. "Oh," she snorted, and with ill-grace returned a few minutes later with my precious suction hose. I'm sure she went home that night to tell someone about the rude patient who had attacked her. (1999, p. 1)

Although Shevin's story holds lessons about the need to humanize the medical profession, it is also a powerful story about communication. When Shevin's nurse turned away from him, she did more than engage in poor nursing practices; she took his power and his voice. Shevin illustrated the need for our society to become informed about individual differences and to examine the ideas that people have and prejudices they hold about diverse forms of communication.

Consider some of the problems of typed communication, for instance. Typed words do not always reflect tone, inflection, and emotion. It can be difficult to detect sarcasm, irony, anger, joy, or surprise in the written word. Furthermore, facial expressions and body language may be of little help in interpreting messages when the physical movements of the participants are unpredictable or unintentional—as they often are in the case of individuals with autism. A careful communication partner is observant—watching closely for the initiation of communication and allowing for the full and undisturbed expression of the AAC user. The purpose of these precautions is to minimize the dominance of the communication partner and maximize the involvement of the AAC user. Whereas some AAC users have sophisticated equipment with voice output, an ability to store messages, and a digital screen with a spell-check function, others work from simpler systems like paper communication boards or phrase cards. For this reason, some AAC users—especially those with simple systems—will need some feedback from their communication partner. For instance, a student using typed communication may need a communication partner to ask clarifying questions if he or she has a lot of misspellings or types only in sentence fragments. One of my former students, Michael, would often type one or two sentences at a time and then stop to see if I understood his meaning.

The results of the time-consuming and complex work involved in preserving the integrity of typed messages was illustrated by Jean-Dominique Bauby (1997) in his book, *The Diving Bell and the Butterfly*. Bauby, the French editor of the fashion magazine, *Elle*, experienced a massive stroke and had to invent an AAC system to use for casual conversations, formal writing, and other tasks. In his book he shared a comical side of the struggle to communicate intact messages:

It is a simple enough system. You read off the alphabet...until, with a blink of my eye, I stop you at the letter to be noted. The maneuver is repeated for the letters that follow, so that fairly soon you have a whole word, and then fragments of more or less intelligible sentences. That, at least, is the theory. In all reality, all does not go well for some visitors. Because of nervousness, impatience, or obtuseness, performances vary in the handling of the code (which is what we call this method of transcribing my thoughts). Crossword fans and Scrabble players have a head start. Girls manage better than boys. By dint of practice, some of them know the code by heart and no longer even turn to our special notebook—the one containing the order of the letters and which all my words are set down like the Delphic oracle's.

Indeed, I wonder what conclusions anthropologists of the year 3000 will reach if they ever chance to leaf through these notebooks, where haphazardly scribbled remarks like "The physical therapist is pregnant," "Mainly on the legs," "Arthur Rimbaud," and "The French team played like pigs" are interspersed with unintelligible gibberish, misspelled words, lost letters, omitted syllables. (p. 21)

To minimize "gibberish, misspelled words, lost letters, omitted syllables" and the potential for miscommunication, the teacher may need to work closely with the AAC user to decipher and confirm their communications. A teacher might read or listen to the AAC user's communication and ask questions related to the tone of the message (e.g., "Are you joking here or is this a serious point?") or the meaning of the text (e.g., "Is this the abbreviation for football?" "You asked for the scissors but you have them. Is there something else you wanted?"). This type of technical work is an important piece of listening to AAC.

Experiment with Indirect Communication

One night as Echo Fling was tucking her son, Jimmy, in bed, she picked up a puppet and used it to ask the little boy a question. Jimmy, who was not typically talkative, proceeded to participate in a long conversation with his mother about a range of topics. Fling described the experience as "shocking":

What's your name?' I asked in a squeaky cartoon-type voice, and got the expected response. Jimmy had just recently requested that everyone call him 'Jim,' instead of Jimmy and began to lecture the puppet on his newfound preference. I asked the usual static questions about his family, and what he liked to do. Jimmy and I had a nice back-and-forth discussion about all the characters in the Ghostbusters movie. I was pleased with how well he was maintaining the conversation. I decided to push further to see what more I could learn.

"Who are some of the kids in your class?" To my amazement, Jimmy began to rattle off some of the boy's names. Why would he be able to talk to the puppet and not me? (2000, p. 89)

Fling went on to share that the talks continued for several weeks. The two conversed about everything from Jimmy's fears to school issues and eventually, Jimmy was able to have these conversations without the aid of the puppet.

Many individuals with autism feel uncomfortable having direct conversations or engaging in direct interactions. Donna Williams, a woman with autism, shared that she prefers to interact and socialize in ways that are more indirect or detached:

The best way I could have been given things would have been for them to be placed near me with no expectation of thanks and no waiting for a response. To expect a thank-you or a response was to alienate me from the item that prompted the response.

The best way for me to have been able to listen to someone was for them to speak to themselves about me out loud or about someone like me, which would have inspired me to show I could relate to what was being said. In doing so, indirect contact, such as looking out of a window while talking, would have been best. (1992, p. 216)

In the wonderful and readable book, *The Boy Who Would Be a Helicopter*, Vivian Paley (1990) witnessed the power of using indirect communication with one of her students. Jason, a child enamored with helicopters, helicopter houses, and helicopter blades, seldom talks to peers, appears to ignore typical types of play, and repeats the same stories over and over again. Though he clearly has a unique approach to learning, Paley never described Jason as a youngster with a disability. Despite the way Paley did or did not characterize Jason, however, we can learn a lot about negotiating communication with students from this teacher's interactions with this student.

At one point in Paley's account, Jason was disrupting other children and the classroom community by continually running on to the stage that students use to perform plays. At first, Paley sat back, interested in why Jason seemed to need to "crash" the stage so often. After he repeated this behavior several times, Paley decided to problem-solve the situation with a few students, including Jason:

"Jason, sometimes you still run into the stage even if it's not your turn."
    "My blades are spinning."
    "But it seems as if your blades spin more in the story room than in the blocks."
    "Because he makes a airport there to land," Samantha [another student] points out.
    "Could that be the reason?" I wonder.
    "Yeah, it really is the reason," Joseph states with assurance.
    "Aren't you sad because you don't have a airport in here to land? To stay landed?"
    Jason is surprised by the question, but Joseph interprets his silence as agreement. "See, I told you. He's sad because there's no airport. His helicopter needs one." (Paley, 1990, pp. 57–58)

The students went on to decide that Jason should build a small heliport near the stage so he could have a place to park that wouldn't be the middle of the stage. The whole group managed to find a solution to a tricky problem without blaming or isolating anyone and, as important, they were able to communicate about something serious without involving Jason in a direct and potentially stressful interaction. That is, the students avoided scolding or warning their classmate. The entire conversation that takes place is about finding a space for a helicopter, not about the behavior of a boy named Jason.

Teachers can learn a lot from Paley and her students. Donna Williams (1998) suggested that teachers use costumes, foreign accents, conversation-songs, rhymes, and puppets to cultivate interactions that "encourage expression in a way that allows some degree of personal distance." Williams suggested that these props and activities help students "develop self-awareness in a self-controlled and self-regulated way" (p. 306). Indeed, Junee Waites, a mother of a man with autism, shared in her book *Smiling at Shadows*, that she couldn't get her son to engage in household routines until she sang to him:

I sang "We're sweeping the floor, sweeping the floor! We're making the bed, making the bed! Would you like…dah de dah…a drink of milk…la la la…?"

[The] scheme worked. I sang merrily and Dane began to point to what he wanted—and he would look to me. (Waites & Swinbourne, 2002, p. 41)

If a student seems unable to answer direct questions, the teacher might sing the question or say it in a rhythmic way. Stephen Shore, a music teacher with Asperger's syndrome, uses singing to connect with his students: "All of my communications with one particular child with Asperger's are sung. If I mistakenly lapse into a typical conversational tone, he loses focus, engages in self-stimulatory activities, and drifts away" (2001, p. 65).

A variety of other ways to make communication less direct can be employed. If a student does not want to read in front of the group, perhaps giving her a toy microphone or a special hat will give her the confidence and inspiration to do so. If a student does not like to answer peers who wish him a good morning, the entire class might say hello through handshakes, high-fives, or by learning greetings in other languages.

Help Students Understand and Decipher Language

Some people have trouble understanding certain aspects of speech. A student may not respond to his or her own name or may produce a fork when he was asked to get a spoon. In most cases, students who behave in these ways are not experiencing hearing problems. Rather, they are struggling with processing difficulties. That is, they have a hard time making sense of certain sounds, words, or sentences they hear. Because of these problems, the learner may seem inattentive or stubborn at times.

Students with autism also have difficulty understanding some types of language. For instance, some students interpret language quite literally. I learned just how literal some students are when I took one of my students swimming. As Tom entered the pool area, he began walking straight for the deep end. I shouted at him to turn around as he got to the edge of the pool, thinking that he would know to turn his back to the water in order to climb down the metal ladder leading into the deep end. I was puzzled, but quickly understood when Tom began twirling in circles. He was "turning around" as I had asked. Gunilla Gerland, a woman with autism, related that she often gives literal answers to questions, confusing her communication partners:

My attitude to questions was quite concrete. "Can you...?" I answered with a "Yes" which meant, "Yes, I can..." But that it should also mean "I will" or "I shall..." was a totally alien concept to me. If I said "I can," then I meant just that and nothing else. So the effect of my "Yes" to the question "Can you tidy your room?" was not the required one. I didn't at all understand why they were so cross at me. (1996, p. 85)

Stephen Shore reported that slang can also be confusing:

During the third grade I remember a classmate telling me that he felt like a pizza. I couldn't figure out what made him feel that way. Besides he certainly didn't look like a pizza. Eventually I realized he meant that he felt like eating a pizza. (2001, p. 53)

Students with autism may need help interpreting figurative language like idioms (e.g., "sitting on the fence," "hold your horses"), jokes or riddles, metaphors (e.g., "he was on fire"), phrases or slang expressions with double meaning, and sarcasm (e.g., saying, "good work" to someone who has just spilled a glass of milk). Teachers might offer support in the following ways:

- Double-check with all students to make sure directions or questions are understood.
- Provide opportunities for students to learn about language (e.g., present a "metaphor of the week").
- Use visuals to help students remember the meanings of figurative language (e.g., draw a picture of an angry person literally "flying off" of a handle).
- Encourage the student to keep a personal dictionary or encyclopedia of "puzzling language," every time the individual is confused by a word or the use of a phrase, explain it and have them add it to their dictionary.

SUMMARY

Although students with autism will have communication differences, students experience these differences in a variety of ways. Some students see their communication differences as problematic, whereas others feel their ways of communicating make them unique and interesting. Jasmine O'Neill cautioned that those without autism should not judge different communication to be deviant communication:

Many people consider there to be an "abnormality" in autistic communication. Call it whatever you will. I am against using the words "abnormal" and "normal."

Abnormal is derogatory. I feel the same about using the term, "a failure." Autism doesn't imply failure. (1999, p. 47)

Being unable to communicate in conventional ways may be frustrating for students with autism, but the attitudes and beliefs of those without autism may be even more frustrating than the inability to communicate reliably. Many assumptions are made about people who do not have reliable communication. For instance, if a student cannot speak, he may be seen as unable to think or understand the communication of others. For some, getting "outsiders" to understand these differences can be as challenging as the differences themselves.

Perhaps the most important message of this chapter is that teachers must respect the communication diversities that students bring to the classroom in order to help those learners acquire new skills. Educators much constantly seek ways to connect and communicate with their students. This includes watching and listening for communication from the student and providing students with opportunities to listen to the stories, ideas, thoughts, and experiences of the teacher.

Communication impacts everything else. Therefore, helping a student with communication can also serve to make other aspects of schooling easier. For instance, the more complex a student's communication becomes, the more meaningful the curricular adaptations will be and the less likely the student will be to share needs and wants through challenging behavior. Perhaps the most important reason for supporting a student's communication, however, is to help him or her direct his or her own schooling and life. I close by sharing the words of Richard Attfield, a man with autism and AAC user, who stressed in this letter to a colleague, just how important this kind of liberation is:

Four months roughly now. I am now finally able to communicate and express my opinion. Recognize for myself communication with other people will also allow me to control my life. Decide for myself what the future will be. Give me a right to be heard. Long have I waited for personal freedom. (1993, p. 11)

For More Answers and Ideas

Beukelman, D.R., & Mirenda, P. (1998). *Augmentative and alternative communication: Management of severe communication disorders in children and adults.* (2nd ed.). Baltimore: Paul H. Brookes Publishing Co.

Biklen, D. (1993). *Communication unbound: How facilitated communication is challenging traditional views of autism and dis/ability.* New York: Teachers College Press.

Biklen, D., & Cardinal, D. (1997). *Contested words, contested science.* New York: Teachers College Press.

Bondy, A., & Frost, L. (2002). *A picture's worth: PECS and other visual communication strategies in autism.* Bethesda, MD: Woodbine House.

(continued)

(continued)

Crossley, R. (1997). *Speechless: Facilitating communication for individuals without voices.* New York: Dutton.

Downing, J. (1999). *Teaching communication skills to students with severe disabilities.* Baltimore: Paul H. Brookes Publishing Co.

Flodin, M. (1991). *Signing for kids.* New York: Perigee.

CHAPTER 8

Seeing Students with Autism as Literate

BEYOND SIGHT WORDS

The boy was so interested that he was ready to learn more.
He was ready for the New World that was in front of him. But the
boy waited for the numbers to be taught again. Mother wanted to try out the
alphabets in the same way. They were learnt fast as usual. The boy knew by the end of the
day that he had a wonderful memory—something to be proud of. (Mukhopadhyay, 2000, p. 68)

In a 1998 study, I asked three high school students with autism and "autistic-like characteristics" to evaluate the curriculum and instruction they had received throughout their educational careers. All three students reported emphatically that they wanted and needed more literacy experiences. The students, in fact, appeared desperate for more access to books and reading opportunities, more dialogue and interaction, and more writing and composition experiences. One student in the study, Michael, expressed interest in pursuing a career as an author. Despite his constant pleas for a more academic and challenging curriculum, however, he was unable to successfully convince his teachers to respect his intellect and to help him improve his writing skills (Kluth, 1998).

Michael's story is not unusual. Historically, many individuals with disabilities—particularly those with significant disabilities—have been left out of literacy instruction. When instruction was provided for these learners, it was often focused on the acquisition of single words (Ault, Gast, & Wolery, 1988; Browder, Hines, McCarthy, & Fees, 1984; Lalli & Browder, 1993). Recently, however, there has been more attention paid to offering students with a range of dis/abilities access to phonics and whole language instruction and to a wider range of literacy activities, strategies, and materials (Colasent & Griffith, 1998; Erickson, Koppenhaver, & Yoder, 1994; Kliewer, 1998; McMaster, Fuchs, & Fuchs, 2002).

INVITATIONS TO LITERACY:
OPPORTUNITIES FOR STUDENTS WITH AUTISM

Colasent and Griffith reported in their study of three students that "children with autism can respond to stories in a very positive way that enhances their literacy skills" (1998, p. 416). A teacher in that study read three stories around a rabbits theme to the students and gave them opportunities to engage in a range of literacy activities related to the theme (e.g., drawing pictures related to the story). Each one of the three stories was presented over a 3-day period.

The students who had previously been exposed only to a curriculum of functional life and community skills bloomed when given the opportunity to listen to and discuss the thematic stories. Data from the study suggested that the students were able to attend to the stories and offer relevant comments during discussions. The researchers also reported that the students were able to "state a title, state their favorite character, and describe their personal feelings" after all three stories (p. 416). Furthermore, all three students wrote longer passages and longer sentences and used more sophisticated vocabulary after listening to, writing about, drawing, and discussing the three stories.

This study is provocative for several reasons. First, it is clear from the study procedures that all of the students had many skills and abilities related to literacy and that they were able to increase their skills as a result of the study activities. Second, these students were able to make strides in literacy without "special" interventions or strategies; students were simply given opportunities to engage in common classroom literacy activities. The third and perhaps most interesting finding of this research, however, is that teachers realized quick success with students who, before the study, "had received no reading instruction; their IEPs (individual education programs) included no reading goals and, in fact, stated that they were 'essentially nonreaders'" (p. 415).

This important study begs these questions: How had the students' abilities and skills been overlooked prior to the study, and how did these clearly capable learners come to be seen as nonreaders unable to benefit from literacy instruction? In my experiences in classrooms, I have observed that students are too often dismissed from the literate community (Kliewer, 1998). Although students with autism are increasingly being educated in general education classrooms, they are often excluded from rich and meaningful literacy experiences such as reading and writing stories, joining book clubs, acting and performing, journaling, and participating in whole-class and small-group discussions. It is not unusual for students with autism in these classrooms to follow a different language arts curriculum than the one offered to their classmates. Students with autism might, for instance, be asked to practice memorizing "sight words" while classmates are writing poetry or reading popular fiction.

Students may fail to receive literacy instruction because teachers are unsure of how to support and include them. Some teachers do not view all students as capable of literacy learning (Koppenhaver, Evans, & Yoder, 1991), or they simply have not been introduced to ways in which they might differentiate or adapt instruction for diverse learners. As Chandler-Olcott (in press) illustrated in her account of teaching two students with disabilities in her secondary English classroom, teachers may also exclude students from literacy experiences because of social constructs of disability. That is, many teachers limit expectations for students with disabilities because they understand disability as a fixed reality instead of as a construct that is constantly negotiated and socially and culturally generated:

> My shortcomings were partially attributable to a lack of knowledge and experience. Having had only one course in writing instruction and none in reading, I was ill equipped to identify students' literacy strengths or to provide the kinds of teaching that would have moved them forward. I knew a lot more about literacy devices and genre than I did about developmental literacy and diagnosis. I'm convinced, however, that at the time, I lacked something even more important: an explicit appreciation of the kinds of literacy growth all learners might achieve in my care. My perceptions of student's disabilities limited my ability to see their potential literacy development. (Chandler-Olcott, in press).

Extending an Invitation to All Students: Valuing and Building on Multiple Literacies

Kliewer (1998) suggested that in order to provide literacy opportunities for all students, teachers may need to "reconceptualize the literate community"; they may need to reject assumptions about disability and adopt an orientation of viewing all students as learners. In classrooms in which all students are accepted in the literate community, "all children are considered active participants in the construction of literate meanings within specific contexts. This assumption of literate value then serves as the core from which literate capacities are realized" (Kliewer, 1998, p. 100). In such classrooms, teachers challenge and question school practices that marginalize learners (e.g., exclusion, tracking) and create communities that encourage all students to teach each other; showcase talents; take risks; create; collaborate; and see themselves as readers, writers, and thinkers.

Furthermore, in order to best support students with a wide range of needs and abilities, teachers must understand reading and literacy as a broad and complex set of behaviors. Consider this definition from Edwards, Heron, and Francis:

> An ideological model of literacy expands the definition of literacy from the ability to read and write to the practice of construing meaning using all available signs within a culture, including visual, auditory, and sensory signs (Eisner, 1991; Gee, 1996; Neilson, 1998). To become literate, then, students must develop a critical awareness of multiple texts and contexts (Gee, 1996; Neilson, 1998). This involves an ability to understand how social and cultural ways of being and understanding affect how meaning is construed and conveyed (Brown, 1991; Gee, 1996; Eisner, 1991). (2000, p. 1)

According to these authors, students demonstrate literacy when they act out a scene from a favorite movie, page through a book, have a conversation, listen to the teacher read a poem, illustrate an idea, tell a joke, or learn to use a communication board or sign language system. Recognizing such abilities, skills, and behaviors as literacies is especially critical when teaching students who struggle with traditional reading and writing activities (e.g., writing sentences, turning the pages of a book).

Too often, students who do not follow a typical developmental sequence of literacy are considered unable to profit from academic instruction related to reading, writing, speaking, and listening. When teachers expand their understanding of literacy, however, they can facilitate the development of a range of abilities, build on the skills that students *do* have, and craft learning experiences that meet students' unique needs and capitalize on their strengths. I taught a second-grade student who was fascinated with Eric Carle's (1969) popular picture book, *The Very Hungry Caterpillar*. Every day, Jason—who did not speak—came into his classroom, grabbed the book from the classroom library, threw it on the floor, rotated it 360°, flipped through the pages (often when the book was turned upside down), licked or pressed his cheek to the cover, and stared silently at each illustration. Although some of Jason's teachers found these behaviors bizarre and problematic, Jason's general education classroom teacher, Ms. Knight, saw Jason's actions as purposeful, complex, and literacy-related. She, therefore, made efforts to enhance his skills and knowledge through this activity. She asked the school librarian to bring other books by Eric Carle into the classroom and slowly introduced Jason to new pictures, vocabulary, story settings and plots, and characters. She then asked Jason's mother to identify literacy-related behaviors that she saw at home. Jason's mother told Ms. Knight that her son often sat in his red beanbag chair when he wanted a story. Ms. Knight, therefore, bought a red beanbag chair for the classroom and shared this "story signal" with other teachers and students so they could respond when Jason wanted to read. Ms. Knight also introduced Jason to the felt board and told him the caterpillar story using this tool. Because Jason was such a kinesthetic and tactile leaner he was instantly drawn to the board and began creating his own stories with the felt objects and characters.

Clearly, embracing multiple literacies means that teachers must abandon the metaphor of the literacy ladder. That is, teachers must dismiss the idea that students develop in the same ways and reject the notion that literacy skills develop in a linear fashion. Luke Jackson, a young man with Asperger's syndrome, illustrated just how inadequate is the literacy ladder model when he shared the story of how he learned to read:

Reading was not something that I did at an early age but I did have some problems with reading when I was younger. The school gave me all sorts of extra help with reading and I couldn't even remember one letter from the other. However much anyone taught me, it just would not sink in. I had an assessment by an educational psychologist when I was seven years and eight months old and my reading age was not assessable because I just couldn't read anything. The next day Mum got a phone call from the school asking her to come in and see them.

She told me that she was very worried as that usually meant that I was having a massive tantrum, but when she got there the teacher had something that they just couldn't wait to tell. I had picked up a copy of *A Midsummer Night's Dream*, which the teacher was using to show how plays are written. It seems that I opened the book and began to read it fluently. How weird is that? (2002, p. 117)

Jackson isn't quite sure how he learned to read; he told his mother and the school that one day someone had "switched a light on" in his head. His advice for those working with students with autism is to "never give up on a child who seems unable to learn to read" (p. 117).

Although certainly amusing, Luke Jackson's story is not particularly unusual. Kliewer and Biklen (2001) have observed many students who seem to follow unique and highly individual literacy paths. Due to these variances, these researchers suggest that educators "reconstitute the ladder to literacy" and that instead of focusing on a sequential model of development, they consider a new metaphor:

> We suggest a new imagery for conceptualizing the social generation of an individual's symbolic presence, that of a web of relationships that forms a community. Written language and other symbolic tools constitute fibers in the strands that make up the web. (p. 11)

If teachers dismiss the literacy ladder and adopt the "web model," students won't need to acquire a certain skill set before being invited to participate in the curriculum and instruction in general education classrooms; learners won't be expected to develop, behave, and learn in the same ways; and individual differences in learning will be supported and appreciated. Adopting the web metaphor also means that teachers will come to know their students as complex thinkers and capable learners. They will look for gifts in every student and become talent scouts in their own classrooms; value diverse ways of interacting with materials, expressing knowledge, and communicating; and embrace the uniqueness of their students and of the skills those students bring to the classroom.

Expanding the Invitation to Include All Learners: Ideas for Inclusive Classrooms

I have found success using the following strategies with *some* students with the label of autism and feel that these ideas may be a take-off point for designing lessons that are appropriate, appealing, and challenging for every learner in the inclusive classroom.

Incorporate Interests When I worked with Trey, a student with a love of horses, I had a difficult time getting him interested in typical classroom materials. He seemed disinterested in storybooks, textbooks, workbooks, worksheets, games, computers, and art supplies. I thought I would coax Trey into classroom activities by buying him some horse magazines. I hoped that he might be able to look at the magazines during breaks or after he finished classwork. When I got the magazines and showed them to Trey, however, the plan crumbled. Not only did this strategy fail to engage my young student, it made the situation worse. Although we were thrilled to see Trey so excited about his new "schoolbooks," he seemed unable to concentrate on classwork when the horse magazines were in the room. He would rummage through his desk to find them the moment he came into the classroom and would pour through them during daily lessons.

Trey's second-grade classroom teacher and I solved the problem by creating classroom books using the magazine pictures. We made a social studies book from horse pictures (the topic was transportation, so we cut out pictures of horses pulling carts and people riding on horses). The math book contained addition and subtraction problems related to horses (2 ponies + 3 ponies = 5 ponies). For the reading book, we took vocabulary from class lessons and created a short story about horses. The adapted materials were a hit; Trey was able to stay with the class during lessons and could flip through his books if he needed to fidget. He was also able to learn new vocabulary and concepts by reading and rereading the horse books with teachers and classmates.

Students with autism often have interests that occupy their attention for long periods of time. Some enjoy trains, others love to study maps, and still others may be fascinated with light switches. Stephan Shore (2001), a man with autism, shared that, at some point in his life, he has had the following special interests: airplanes, medicine, electronics, psychology, geography, watches, astronomy, chemistry, computers, music, locks, shiatsu, bicycles, mechanics, hardware, rocks, cats, yoga, earthquakes, electricity, tools, geology, dinosaurs, and autism.

Such interests can easily be folded into the curriculum of an inclusive classroom. A student fascinated with airplanes might be asked to write a story about transportation, research the history of aviation, or do an independent research project on pilots Bessie Coleman or Charles Lindbergh. Teachers might then use these interests to introduce students to new topics and interests. For instance, I know a student who loves talking about the weather. His English teacher turned this interest into a literacy activity by showing the young man where he could find the daily weather in the newspaper each morning. She then introduced the student to other sections of the newspaper. Over time, he became interested in the sports section and began to look forward to checking information about and scores of local sports teams. Eventually, the teacher was even able to interest this learner in sports biographies.

Tapping into interests can help teachers to better connect with students and design curriculum and instruction that has meaning for them. It can also help teachers appreciate and make sense of the work students produce. As Stephen Shore explained, understanding interests can also give educators ideas for providing more appropriate and effective supports:

In second grade, for a class assignment, I wrote a story about some kittens that alternated between existing as little cats and puppies. In fact they were so much in demand that they fetched $47,000 each; or the price of a house at the time. The ideas for this story were spun out of my current life events. Cats were a special interest at that time. One of my family's many cats had recently given birth to five kittens, we had acquired a puppy, and our house was on the market for the same price as these mythical felines sold for.

My teacher discounted the assignment as being babyish. However, if she had asked me where my ideas for the paper had come from, perhaps she would have been more understanding and helpful in getting me through the writing assignment. (2001, pp. 74–75)

Use Visuals Although students with autism may benefit from verbal instruction, some also require an additional avenue of input as they learn. Teachers can provide this input by using a range of visuals as they lecture, conduct discussions, and explain daily lessons. As Donna Williams, a woman with autism, related, "I could read a story without difficulty, it was always the pictures from which I understood the content" (1992, p. 25). Williams also shares that she "took to" the study of psychology in part because it interested her and was connected to personal experiences (she had been evaluated by many psychologists and psychiatrists), but also because her course materials were filled with visuals:

A lot of psychology had to do with finding out how things worked. The subject of the mind was, for me, like the study of an object that worked according to a system. Systems were relatively predictable, the sort of things that came with guarantees. I could respect this sort of knowledge. The textbook had a lot of pictures and diagrams, which made the rest of the text easy to follow. (p. 119)

　　Table 8.1 provides a list of visuals that support student learning. For example, when students are studying a novel, the teacher might provide the student who has autism (and perhaps the entire class) with a pictorial timeline of the events in the story. A Venn diagram might be used to show learners how to compare and contrast two time periods in history. Photographs or drawings might be used to illustrate the meaning of new vocabulary words (e.g., show a picture of an angry, red-faced person when introducing the word *indignant*). Students might participate in creating these illustrations in order to boost understanding for everyone in the class and to give artistic and visual learners an opportunity to shine.
　　Temple Grandin, a woman with autism, noted that those with autism may struggle to learn things that cannot be thought about in pictures:

The easiest words for an autistic child to learn are nouns, because they directly relate to pictures.
　Spatial words such as "over" and "under" had no meaning for me until I had a visual image to fix them in my memory. Even now, when I hear the word "under" by itself, I automatically picture myself getting under the cafeteria tables at school during an air-raid drill, a common occurrence on the East Coast during the early fifties. (1995, p. 2)

　　Abstract concepts and language are challenging for many students with autism. Teachers may want to use visuals to teach any lesson, but especially when introducing abstract concepts and ideas (e.g., *beauty, communism*), figura-

Table 8.1. Visuals that support student learning

Physical objects (e.g., globe, puppet, three-dimensional model)

Charts

Graphs

Diagrams

Photographs or drawings

Teacher- or student-created pictures on chalkboard

Graphic organizers (e.g., story maps)

Slides or overhead transparencies of lecture

Gestures (e.g., holding up three fingers while instructing students to take a three-minute break)

tive language (e.g., "a gem of a person," "raining cats and dogs," "hopping mad"), slang (e.g., "what's up?", "get out of here") or words with multiple meanings (e.g., *watch, park*). Many students with autism also need help interpreting jokes and other types of humor (e.g., knock-knock jokes, plays on words, sarcasm).

Write It Down   Graphics are not the only way to clarify speech and communicate more effectively with students with autism; the written word can also be used as a visual support. If a teacher is giving verbal directions, she might also provide the same directions on the chalkboard. Students might take turns writing assignments on a classroom homework chart. A daily schedule might be posted and maintained by teachers and students together (with icons representing activities, if possible).

Many students with autism, in fact, seem to comprehend written text better than they do speech. Wendy Lawson, a woman with autism, provided insight on why one is easier than the other:

I find the written word much easier to comprehend than the spoken word. It takes me a lot longer to process conversation and work out the meaning behind the words than it does to scan the words on a written page. I think this is because I must also read the expressions on a person's face and study their body language. (1998, pp. 9–10)

One student I know found the written word so important to his success that he asked me to converse with him on paper whenever possible. During even the shortest exchanges, he preferred to talk on paper. He would type short answers, and I would write to him in longhand. Although we could not engage in conversations in this way every time he requested it, I tried to dialogue this way with him when time allowed. He found these exchanges on paper to be more calming, comforting, and easier to comprehend than those in which he participated verbally.

The student's middle school teachers also found that the written conversations were perfect opportunities to contact him with lessons related to literacy. For instance, we would add new vocabulary to our written messages every week. We would also take advantage of these natural opportunities to teach him about written expression. Because typed and written words do not always reflect tone, inflection, and emotion and because cracking, raised, or booming voices are not available in these texts, we needed to teach this young man about how to send those messages to his communication partners. We were able to use this absence of verbal communication to teach the student the use of ending and quotation marks and the importance of descriptive language. This student was then able to teach his classmates about communicating clearly using written language, which helped all students improve the e-mail messages they sent weekly to their cyber pen-pals. Keefe (1996) suggested that these "written conversations" be used to help all students develop individual strategies for comprehending, organizing, and storing information. She recommended that students engage in conversation together with their completed scripts.

Read Aloud   Almost every teacher, elementary or secondary, shares a book or some passage from a text with students during the school week. Including students with autism in this simple activity is one of the easiest ways to promote language learning. The development of literacy skills in individuals with disabilities is enhanced when they are exposed to individuals using printed materials (Koppenhaver, Coleman, Kalman, & Yoder, 1991) and when they have opportunities to interact with others around written materials (Koppenhaver, Evans, & Yoder, 1991). Reading to students can improve their fluency (Blau, 2001), help them gain access to content (Blackman, 1999; Mukhopadhyay, 2001), and expose them to a range of genres, especially those they would not choose on their own.

In addition to enhancing literacy development, reading aloud can also help students with autism learn more about language and human interaction. Because many learners with autism struggle to read bodies and emotions (Blackman, 1999; Lawson, 1998; Shore, 2001), listening to the teacher read with expression may help students better understand postures; facial expressions; and uses of volume, tone, and inflections in speech as well as the text being shared. When the teacher reads about a child fighting with his brother, the student has an opportunity to review the language that is associated with anger and, if the teacher reads with feeling, the facial expressions and body language that an angry person might use.

Reading to students can also help them better understand print and learn to read on their own. Tito Rajarshi Mukhopadhyay, a young man with autism, illustrates how his mother's habit of reading to him helped him not only to get information but also to read independently:

Mother's voice was the main source of learning. Mother had to read out everything from text books to story books because I could not keep my eyes on any page for a long time. However we need to improve our performances and cannot stay where we are. [A teacher] helped me to learn how to read…When she read, I had to naturally follow the words in order to keep pace with her speed. Slowly my concentration improved and I could keep my eyes fixed on a page without getting distracted. Mother practiced it at home and within a month I read a two hundred page book, reading about seven pages a day, reading in chorus with my mother. (2000, p. 75)

As Mukhopadhyay suggested, reading *with* students can also be a useful teaching tool. Students can be asked to engage in either "echo reading," in which the teacher reads a line and students repeat the line, or "choral reading," in which the teacher and all students read the text in unison. These strategies not only promote reading fluency (Blau, 2001) but also encourage participation of all because some students may feel less self-conscious about their reading performance when acting as a group. Although echo reading and choral reading may be more common in the elementary classroom (e.g., chanting rhymes), creative secondary teachers can also find ways to bring these practices into the classroom. A math teacher I know asked his students to do a "call and response" exercise with a chant called "Talking About Angles":

Teacher and Students:	Talking About Angles!
Teacher:	Angles
Students:	Angles
Teacher and students:	Please define

Teacher:	An angle is formed
Students:	An angle is formed
Teacher:	When two rays have the same endpoint
Students:	When two rays have the same endpoint
Teacher:	How many rays?
Students:	Two rays
Teacher:	What is the endpoint called, I ask?
Students:	Vertex
Teacher and Students:	The common endpoint is the vertex.
Teacher:	Vertex?
Students:	Vertex!
Teacher:	One ray forms the initial side.
Students:	The initial side
Teacher:	One ray is the terminal side
Students:	The terminal side
Teacher and Students:	Talking about angles!

Students were invited to stand and move around and even to "rap" during the exercise. Eventually, learners were asked to write their own verses, chants, or raps related to math content.

Seek Natural Opportunities for Instruction   When Bob came to school on the first day of September, his classroom teacher, Ms. Shey, was stunned to learn that her 12-year-old student could not read or write more than a few words. Bob had never received formal reading instruction and, according to his mother, had been educated in a classroom for 5 years that had only 12 books! Ms. Shey immediately began designing curriculum and instruction that would help Bob gain literacy skills across environments and academic subjects. She also began seeking natural opportunities to boost her student's literacy abilities throughout the day. For instance, Ms. Shey began asking Bob to find a joke or poem of the day from a book in the classroom library and write it on the chalkboard each morning. Bob came into the classroom a few minutes early each day to perform this task, giving his teacher a few extra moments to give a 5-minute mini-lesson on topics ranging from punctuation to pronunciation to use of literary devices (see Table 8.2).

Another colleague, a biology teacher, supported the literacy development of her student, Shu-li, by asking the young woman to announce the "vocabulary word of the day" to all students in the class. While Shu-li read the word and definition, different students took turns trying to illustrate the word on chart paper. This artistic and collaborative exercise often drew laughter from the class as students attempted to draw terms such as *photosynthesis* and *meiosis*. This exercise, although designed primarily to support Shu-li, enhanced the vocabulary of all learners and eventually proved useful in all of the teacher's science classes.

Class routines and jobs can also serve as opportunities to practice literacy skills. In one elementary classroom, Maria, a student with autism, was sometimes given the classroom chore of completing the lunch count. Counting the raised hands and having to record the right numbers in the right spaces helped to build both Maria's literacy *and* numeracy skills. To help Maria engage in this highly valued classroom job, teachers highlighted important parts of the lunch

Table 8.2. Natural opportunities to promote literacy development

Allow time for telling jokes and sharing short personal stories.

Institute a class newsletter, a traditional print version or electronically on the web.

Ask students to write information on the chalkboard (e.g., date, weather information, riddles, fact of-the-day, trivia question of-the-day).

Give students time to write or type personal notes to each other.

Ask students to draw or graphically map a class lecture or whole-group discussion (on board or at their desks).

Have students hand in two- or three-word notes describing their impressions of the day's lesson.

Ask different students to come to the front of the room to introduce guest speakers or classroom visitors.

Read directions on tests and worksheets aloud for those who need the support.

Ask students to perform literacy-related classroom jobs such as lunch count, calendar, taking attendance, checking feeding schedule for class pet.

Install a class suggestion box and rotate responsibilities for reading comments.

form and gave her an opportunity to take a "practice run" at reading the menu before conducting the count in front of her classmates (Kinney & Fischer, 2001).

Another natural way to weave literacy learning into the school day is to review a daily schedule with students (see Figure 8.1). Using a daily schedule or time map provides a routine that includes and informs students while providing them with opportunities to communicate, listen, share, and read. Furthermore, many students with autism (and many students without identified disabilities) feel comforted when they are given a schedule for the day and when they know what to expect. As Wendy Lawson, a woman with autism, related, having information and using routines is an important coping and organizing strategy: "I have been told, 'what you don't know won't hurt you,' but boundaries, rules, regulations and concrete structure provide understanding, and therefore enable an appropriate response" (1998, p. 110).

Reading and reviewing a daily schedule can give everyone in the class an organizational "heads up" while serving as a literacy exercise for those who need extra support. Some students may even want to copy the schedule into a notebook so they can review it throughout the day and be reminded of the day's events. If a student cannot write reliably, he or she might be provided with a written copy of the message.

Offer Multiple Texts A common myth about people with autism is that they have no imagination and lack the ability to think creatively (Kanner, 1943). For this reason, some teachers may believe that students with autism or Asperger's syndrome will be uninterested in listening to or reading fiction. Kenneth Hall, a young man with Asperger's syndrome, who is a huge Harry Potter fan, reported that he and many others with Asperger's enjoy works of fiction:

I spend a lot of time reading because it is one of my favourite [sic] things to do. I've read hundreds of books in my life and if books were food I would be very fat. I wasn't ever taught how to read. I just discovered how when I was very young and I have enjoyed it ever since. I have over four hundred books which I keep in alphabetical order by author.

Figure 8.1.   An example of a daily schedule that can serve as an important support for students with autism.

Some people say AS [Asperger's syndrome] kids prefer to read factual books. This is definitely untrue. I would reckon about 97 per cent prefer fiction. I like adventure stories best. I would love to be a character out of an adventure in one of my books. Sometimes I like to read the same book over and over many times. I have read some of my favourite books approximately 50-55 times. (2001, pp. 35-36)

Others with autism and Asperger's syndrome, however, do report that nonfiction reading materials are somehow more comforting and easier to negotiate than stories or other works of fiction. Consider the words of Liane Holliday Willey, a woman with Asperger's syndrome:

By around eight years old, I had become a very proficient comprehender as well as word caller. So long as the material was of a factual nature. Fiction was more difficult for me for it forced my thoughts to go beyond the literal. I preferred biographies and eventually made my way through every biography we had in our library, despite the librarian's repeated request that I check out something new and different. I like reading about real live people and their real life experiences. It didn't matter if it was a story about Babe Ruth or Harry Truman or Harriet Tubman. I wasn't attracted to baseball or government or social issues so much as I was attached to the reality of the words I was reading. Even today, as I find those same biographies on the shelves of libraries, I return to that old comfortable place in my mind where those words meant so much to me. (1999, p. 24)

Having a range of texts available and investigating what types of materials students prefer increases the likelihood that every student will connect with text during the school day. Texts of different genres, reading levels, and even formats (e.g., newspapers, pamphlets) should be made available at all times. Although this recommendation may seem common sense to some, one of my former colleagues did not appreciate how vast a range of materials she would need to make available until she encountered a student who loved to read cereal boxes more than any other "text" she offered him during the year. In order to meet his needs, she collected dozens of boxes and designed learning experiences around them. Eventually she coaxed the student into designing his own cereal boxes based on classroom literature. His products included "Sounder's

Sugar Pops," "Charlie and the Chocolate Factory Crisps," and "CoCo Puffins." Similarly, Kim Peek, the man with autism who inspired the film *Rain Man*, enjoys reading fiction and nonfiction books, record jackets, CD labels, information on cassette tape boxes, catalogs on both classical and contemporary music, almanacs, telephone books, and encyclopedias (Peek, 1996).

Give Students Comprehension Support   Many teachers tell me that their students with autism can read but don't understand anything. Responding to such statements is tricky because many students with autism *do* understand what they read but cannot effectively express what they know. That is, some students with autism only *appear* incapable of comprehending text. Because students with autism have movement and communication differences, they may struggle to answer questions and express ideas in traditional ways. Some students might be unable to "find" the words needed to answer comprehension questions (or any question for that matter). Others may know the words but be unable to answer questions when directly asked to do so. It may be hard for some teachers to understand that a student could fluently read a text, know exactly what it means, and be unable to communicate that information. And those who do understand these gaps may be hard pressed to engineer other ways to help the student show what she knows.

If a teacher is confused about a student's ability to comprehend, he or she should give the students many ways to demonstrate understanding. When asking comprehension questions, teachers may want to try the following strategies: Give students plenty of time to answer (even a minute or more); say the questions and present them in written form; let students write their answers or circle them rather than saying them; and sing the questions or ask them using a funny voice or foreign accent (Williams, 1996).

When students seem completely unable to answer comprehension questions, teachers might offer other ways to show understanding. They might ask students to draw or point to pictures (which may also be challenging for students with autism), use signs, gestures, or pantomime to "illustrate" a scene from a book, make a diorama of a key scene, or create a collage or painting related to the text.

If a teacher uses all of these strategies and still cannot assess a student's comprehension, the student should not lose access to books, reading, and opportunities to learn academic content. Students with autism often demonstrate understanding in their own way. For instance, a high school teacher who works with a young man with significant disabilities began reading *Thinking in Pictures* (Grandin, 1995), the autobiography of a woman with autism, to him. Before he was introduced to the book, the student was able to remain seated for no more than 15 minutes at a time (for reading purposes or for *any* activity). When the teacher read him a book on autism, however, the student sat rapt for more than 50 minutes. The teacher reported that she had never seen him sit so still or so quietly. The teacher interpreted this behavior to mean that he was interested in and able to understand the text. She then chose other books to read to the young man and found that the student had a similar positive reaction to other texts she chose—especially those related to autism and disability studies. While she continuously worked to assess his comprehension of the text, the student did not lose access to books during her search for new ways to learn about what he understood.

But what about those students who do need comprehension support? Having shared some information about students who know more than they can demonstrate, it must be acknowledged that many students with autism (and those without) need help comprehending text (Rosinski, 2002). Students with autism may have problems making predictions; visualizing the events of a text; and identifying a purpose for reading, for instance. As one mother learned, some students with autism also have a hard time separating main ideas from details:

In fifth grade my son was assigned to write a paper on Benedict Arnold.
I looked at his rough draft, I noticed that he had included all of the important
facts about Arnold's life except for one—the fact that he had betrayed the
Revolutionary Army to the British for 10,000 pounds and a commission in the
Royal Navy! I asked him whether he hadn't left out something important, to
which he replied, "But all of it is important!" (Rosinski, 2002)

To boost comprehension, teachers can help students monitor their own understanding as they read. One common strategy teachers often use in a whole-class format is the think-aloud (Harvey & Goudvis, 2000; Wilhelm, 2001). A think-aloud involves the teacher reading a text to the class and modeling his or her own comprehension strategies such as asking questions, making inferences, determining importance, and making connections to personal background knowledge. The text or selected passage should contain information, concepts, and words that students may find difficult. The students should be encouraged to read the passage silently as the teacher is reading aloud.

A teacher might start reading a book by saying, "The title of the book is *Tales of a Fourth Grade Nothing* so I think it will be about a kid in the fourth grade. When I look at the picture on the cover, I think maybe the main characters will be a boy and a girl. The cover has a picture of a classroom, so I think a lot of this book will take place in a school." Some teachers even write their thoughts on chart paper so students can see *and* hear the process.

Teachers may follow up by practicing the think-aloud strategy with their students. Small groups of students can read a text together, discuss their thinking with each other, and offer their own strategies as they read (see For More Answers and Ideas for additional information on the think-aloud strategy).

Comprehension can also be bolstered when teachers teach a story or a piece of text using drama. A teacher might have students act out parts of a text as it is being read, for instance. Younger students can perform scenes from a storybook while older students might be encouraged to act out a scene from history as the class reads in the social studies textbook.

Students can also be asked to help each other understand text. Some teachers ask learners to engage in "reciprocal teaching" (Palinscar & Brown, 1984). Reciprocal teaching is essentially a dialogue that takes place between teachers and students. The dialogue is structured by the use of four strategies: summarizing, question generating, clarifying, and predicting. The teacher and students take turns assuming the role of teacher in leading this dialogue.

Once students are comfortable with the strategies, they are invited to become "the teacher" and conduct reciprocal teaching dialogues with new material. At this point the teacher's role shifts from providing direct instruction to facilitating student interaction, monitoring progress, and providing feedback. As students become more skilled with the strategy, they can work in pairs or small groups to coach one another, ask questions, summarize, predict, clarify, and think aloud about what they are reading.

A WORD ABOUT LITERACY AND STUDENTS WITHOUT RELIABLE COMMUNICATION

In his landmark book, *Schooling Without Labels,* Biklen (1992) described a boy, Melvin, who lived in an institution during some of his childhood years. Melvin, who did not have reliable speech, was seen by many at the institution as a "hellion" and as "having severe mental retardation." When he was adopted at age 8, however, his new mother saw a different person than the one described in his records. According to his mother, he emerged as a "bright little kid" (p. 24) after gaining membership in a home, school, and community. One of the most striking aspects of Melvin's story is how he was viewed as incapable of learning although he demonstrated complex literate behaviors from an early age. For instance, while he was still living in the institution, Melvin (who at the time knew only five sign language words) managed to escape from his ward and order lunch from a neighborhood restaurant:

> When he was still only 5 years old, he left his unit at the institution, went down to the ground level on the elevator, got past the receptionist at the admin desk and out the door. An hour later the receptionist took a call from the local McDonald's, two blocks away but across two busy streets. "There is a little boy here demanding a hamburger and I think he is one of the kids that has come down here with your folks," the caller announced. When the institution staff went to retrieve him, they found him making the sign for "eat." Obviously he knew where he was going. He knew what he wanted. (1992, p. 21)

After Melvin was adopted and moved from the institution to his family's home, his literacy development continued. His mother marveled at his skills and abilities:

> [His mother] had taken him to church with her. The service was signed, so Melvin was paying attention: within three months of his moving in with her, he had learned two hundred signs; he had begun with only five. (1992, p. 22)

In another instance, Melvin's mother observed her son examining a book and stared at him, stunned at his engagement in the process. Once again, he was demonstrating literate behavior, and more importantly, confirming his mother's suspicions that he was a complicated, aware, and intelligent person:

> He was sitting on the couch quietly with a book open, just crying. I couldn't imagine what was happening. He had never had quiet moments like that at that point or at least very rarely. I just looked and didn't say anything. He was looking at Burt Blatt's book, *Christmas in Purgatory* [1966, an exposé of abuse in mental retardation institutions]. He looked up and said "big house." It was like

he recognized that this was about where he had been. I sat down and we went through the book together. He just cried. At this point he had very little language. It was just amazing to me....He has shown me time and time again, "Don't underestimate me and don't judge me by your outside perceptions." (1992, p. 28)

Melvin's story is noteworthy for so many reasons. As Biklen pointed out, it is an important story about having an inclusive philosophy; it is also a story of seeing student strengths, questioning what we *think* we know about learners, and following the lead of a student who has limited ways to show us what he knows (Kliewer & Biklen, 2001). This story illustrates how vital it is to support the literacy development of students without reliable communication no matter how slow, challenging, or tentative the process may be.

One way to support learners without reliable communication is to presume competence (Biklen, 1990) and provide literacy instruction even in those instances in which the student cannot demonstrate what she or he knows. Curriculum for students with disabilities should be based on the "least dangerous assumption" (Donnellan, 1984). That is, experiences should be designed with the belief that the "individual with a disability is a 'person first,' deserving the same considerations and concern as would be given a person without a disability" (p. 98). A teacher considering the least dangerous assumption should always be considering, "What would an education for this student look like if I viewed him as a literacy learner?" and "What does it mean to give this student the benefit of the doubt educationally?" All students, regardless of label, must be provided with literacy experiences. This education should include opportunities to communicate through drama, art, and movement; to explore a range of augmentative communication strategies and techniques; to socially interact with peers; to listen to lectures and discussions; and to see, hear, and examine a range of books and other materials.

Perhaps the most critical piece of supporting the literacy development of learners without reliable communication is inclusion in the classroom community. Consider the example of Rebecca, a "primarily nonspeaking" fifth-grade student with autism considered "preliterate" by professionals who had evaluated her (Kliewer & Biklen, 2001). The classroom teachers, determined to include their new student in classroom life, asked students to brainstorm ways to include Rebecca throughout the day. Some of the girls in the class thought of notes (the type that students typically pass to each other during class to socialize). The teacher recalls that students started passing notes to Rebecca, unfolding them for her, and then reading them to her. Over time, the teachers noted how interested Rebecca became when notes were read to her. Sometimes the notes would include questions such as "Do you like James? Yes? No?" and the students would ask Rebecca to answer. After Rebecca started nodding her head at some of the questions, the teaching team constructed a yes/no board and built a range of literacy experiences around the note-passing experiences.

Within the course of a single school year, Rebecca had gone from being perceived as nonsymbolic to constructing symbolic interactions with her classroom friends. Rather than requiring proof of symbolic competence prior to the development of relationships, Foster [the teacher] had turned the traditional equation on its head. Entrance into interaction constituted the terrain on which

Table 8.3. Supporting the literacy development of students without reliable communication

Include words/labels on picture schedules and communication systems.

Use close-captioning function when showing students videos or educational television shows.

Read to students and have students (e.g., classmates, cross-age tutors) read to each other.

Encourage students to support each other, talk to each other, share ideas with each other.

Keep the student involved in *all* aspects of classroom life (e.g., sharing secrets, telling jokes).

> symbol literacy was recognized. In this sense, social engagement in specific, lo-
> calized situations preceded demonstrations of intellectual competence and a
> more abstract definition of Rebecca as a thoughtful, engaged, and engaging
> human being. (2001, p. 6)

Strategies for supporting the literacy development of students without reliable communication are listed in Table 8.3.

SUMMARY

Jamie Burke, a teenager with autism, claims that resource-rich, inclusive environments allowed him access to an academic education and literacy learning.
He also credits these experiences with fostering his ability to communicate
using a device and with helping him learn to speak: "EXPOSURE TO THE
PRINTED WORD IS LIKE WATER TO THE DESERT. ONLY BOOKS COULD
LEAD THE WAY TO GAIN UNDERSTANDING HOW TO SAY SOUNDS"
[sic]. (Broderick & Kasa-Hendrickson, 2001, p. 22). Jamie's mother also feels
that inclusive schooling was a crucial part of her son's academic success and his
speech breakthrough:

> I think that being in a classroom where everybody is reading, speaking, and I
> think the use of overheads, seeing print and not have everything read to the
> class, but a big visual display… I'm thinking too, probably his drive to be like the
> other students, that's such a huge motivator for him. (p. 22)

Providing students with an inclusive education is a critical part of linking
students to literacy opportunities. Inclusive classrooms offer activities that inspire academic learning and an environment rich in print and filled with books
and other resources. In addition, students in these classrooms serve as natural
supports; they serve as models for speaking, listening, reading, and writing;
and teach new skills to each other as they play, socialize, and work together.

Teacher attitude and expectation is another factor that is closely tied to
helping learners with autism become literate. In many biographies and autobiographies, individuals with autism demonstrate "unexpected" skills and competencies when they are given an opportunity to participate in literacy experiences. When introduced to augmentative communication, a German teenager
became a published poet (Sellin, 1995). Temple Grandin (1995), a successful
professor and talented animal scientist, learned to read because her mother believed in her ability and spent hours teaching her through the use of concrete

objects and plastic letters. Paul Robinson helped his son to tolerate and eventually appreciate different types of literature by reading to him using different funny accents (Robinson, 1999).

Clearly, it is time to *expect* such success and competence from learners with autism. High teacher expectation has long been recognized as critical to student achievement (Brophy & Evertson, 1981). When teachers tell students that they will succeed and then create a context to help them do so, students so often become successful.

Inclusive education and high expectations—both of these conditions must be met before any of the strategies and activities suggested in this chapter can be effective. Inclusion and high expectations are not enough, however. The final ingredient necessary for giving students with autism literacy opportunities is action. This may mean bringing students into inclusive classrooms who are currently not being offered such an experience; changing curriculum and instruction to meet the needs of a wider range of students; or questioning the beliefs and values that permeate schools. If we are committed to inclusive schooling, we will consider how to provide all students with opportunities to gain access to reading, writing, listening, and speaking activities and experiences. One of my former students, a young man with autism, expressed it best when he wrote, "The deserving people with disabilities have to be treated the same as everyone else and have the same ways of learning with books and teachers and students" (Kluth, 1999, p. 7).

For More Answers and Ideas

Harvey, S., & Goudvis, A. (2000). *Strategies that work: Teaching comprehension to enhance understanding.* York, ME: Stenhouse.

Keefe, C.H. (1996). *Label-free learning: Supporting learners with disabilities.* York, Maine: Stenhouse.

Kliewer, C. (1998). *Schooling children with Down syndrome.* New York: Teachers College Press.

Moline, S. (1995). *I see what you mean: Children at work with visual information.* York, Maine: Stenhouse.

Oelwein, P.L. (1995). *Teaching reading to children with down syndrome: A guide for parents and teachers.* Bethesda, MD: Woodbine House.

Parker, K. (1997). *Jamie: A literacy story.* York, ME: Stenhouse.

Taylor, D. (1991). *Learning denied.* Portsmouth, NH: Heinemann.

CHAPTER 9

Rethinking Behavior

Positive Ways
to Teach and Support

Until you stop trying to make us normal and work on acceptance and understanding about us individually, your attempts will be impossible. (Cutler, 1998)

Because the concept of "supporting behaviors" is so tricky, conceptualizing this chapter was difficult. In the special education literature, in teacher preparation courses, and in daily language, educators often use words and phrases that seem to suggest that behaviors such as screaming, hand-flapping, and head-banging occur in a vacuum or worse—that they are located inside students. In reality, behavior cannot be set apart from curriculum, instruction, teaching and learning, relationships, school culture, classroom community, and hundreds of other factors and issues. Because behavior is so complex, I attempt to discuss it as a phenomenon that is interpreted; all behavior is perceived differently by different individuals—including the person who is experiencing it. I also treat behavior as contextual in this chapter; all behavior occurs under circumstances, in settings, and with people.

An example that may help to illustrate the importance of understanding behavior as both interpreted and contextual comes from the autobiography of Lucy Blackman (2001), titled *Lucy's Story*. Blackman, a woman with autism, describes how her behaviors can be confusing and even frightening to others if they are framed without an understanding of her life, her explanation, and information about the given situation. In this passage, she described how she would behave "as a small child" if someone tried to treat her as a friend:

Angrily I would play on the situation, or become even less socially competent. The strange thing was that I could see the ridiculous and comic scenario in my mind's eye, but I could not alter the behavior. As the other person got more and more embarrassed, I became more and more "autistic." Once when I was 18 I was walking home from school. An elderly lady stood next to me at the pedestrian crossing. I assume she was concerned at my odd movements. She asked me if I were all right. Confused by the fact that she expected me to respond, I started running in a little circle.

153

My would-be benefactor was standing aghast, with the attitude of an affable bird mesmerized by a newly hatched snake.

So my weird social overtures (for that is what that behavior was) created inappropriate responses in others. This made it even more difficult for me to respond appropriately in return. I still do not turn and speak or sign when someone speaks to me.

I know that I should say, "Goodbye!" to the speaker after these one-sided conversations, but cannot spontaneously look at someone and speak. Instead I glance sideways and walk off, or wait for someone else to tell me that this is the moment to say farewell.

Occasionally when I am very relaxed and pleased to see someone in a place where I am comfortable, a wonderful flash of enchantment takes over. (pp. 41–42)

Behavior as Interpreted Phenomenon

As Blackman rightly pointed out, her own perspective is critical if outsiders are to understand her behaviors in social situations. Without her interpretation of the bus stop incident, for instance, we might assume Blackman is not interested in other people or that she is incapable of understanding how to socialize with new people. Observers might even conclude that she is dangerous or violent.

Blackman's interpretations are key; she helps us understand more about her body, her behavior, and her individual needs. Blackman also gives us an increased understanding of how some people experience autism. It is important to remember, however, that her behaviors and the interpretations of those behaviors may be different from how other students experience the same exact behaviors. For instance, one student may run out of the classroom every day to escape the sound of the pencil sharpener, whereas another learner may run because of an intense need to move and be active. For these reasons, teachers must always be acutely aware of behavior as an interpreted phenomenon. Often, teachers misinterpret behaviors when students do not or cannot interpret their own actions or when teachers do not seek such interpretation and instead make assumptions. For instance, a teacher might think a student who fails to follow verbal directions (e.g., "Please line up at the door") is noncompliant, stubborn, or difficult. Another teacher may see the behavior and believe that the learner doesn't understand the directions. A parent may come into the classroom, observe the same behavior, and attribute the lack of response to his or her child's fear of transitions. Unless the learner can communicate reliably and interpret his or her own behavior, teachers who are observing, discussing, and attempting to support behaviors will only be hypothesizing about the nature of that behavior.

Behavior as Contextual

As Blackman stated, sometimes when she is very relaxed and pleased to see someone in a place where she is comfortable, a sort of magical feeling occurs. With this statement, she illustrated how much context matters; her behavior improves when the setting feels right. Of course, all of us experience fairly significant differences in behavior across environments. Our behaviors may also be influenced by the presence or absence of certain individuals, the time of day, the ways in which others are reacting to and interacting with us, and hundreds of other factors.

Considering context is critical; when a student is held responsible for "exhibiting a behavior," he may actually be communicating in the only way he can, responding to pain, asserting himself, escaping from an unpleasant or intolerable situation, or resisting the way he is being treated. A student may also be tired, frustrated, embarrassed, hungry, hurt, angry, cold, excited, or sad. Clearly, any and all of these are possibilities and should be considered when framing behavior.

GETTING STARTED: IS THERE A PROBLEM HERE?

When a student with autism behaves in a way that is unusual or unexpected, or that presents a challenge to the student or those around him, at least two important questions must be answered before appropriate supports can be provided: 1) Is the behavior a problem; and 2) If a problem exists, where is it? Each question is examined next.

Is the Behavior a Problem?

A longstanding tradition exists in special education of eliminating or changing behaviors deemed challenging by professionals. Many people with autism are contesting this behaviorist paradigm and suggesting new ways of coping with behaviors and bodies that work in atypical ways.

Often, when a student exhibits an unusual behavior (e.g., hand flapping, singing loudly, rocking), professionals move toward extinguishing it. Although it might be appropriate to help the student minimize some behaviors (especially those that may hurt the student with autism or other students), perhaps it is more appropriate to accept the behavior or to work to understand it better.

A high school student, Marcus, played drums in the school band. He could not read music but could learn the songs after hearing them played a few times by other drummers. He was a skilled drummer and could easily follow along as the teacher conducted the band, but he often repeated the conductor's commands loudly. The teacher might say, "Okay, get your instruments ready," and Marcus would say the same in a voice loud enough for all band members to hear. The repetitive speech didn't appear to bother the band members, but it upset the teacher a great deal and Marcus was asked to leave the band.

Who has a problem in this scenario? Although Marcus was somewhat ashamed of his outbursts, he found that he had little control over them. The other students did not seem bothered by the extra directions, but the director could not tolerate Marcus and his differences. What other solutions might have been generated in order to support Marcus in the band?

- The band teacher might have ignored the utterances.
- The band teacher might have asked Marcus to introduce some of the songs.
- The band teacher might have asked all students to shout out the names of the songs.

- The band teacher might have asked Marcus and his family about the utterances.
- Students might have tried giving Marcus different cues to speak more softly (e.g., touching him on the shoulder).

Dozens of other possible solutions to these types of perceived problems are possible if stakeholders are creative and open-minded.

The following questions should always be considered: Is this behavior really a problem? What makes us believe it is a problem? Is it a problem for everyone involved? If educators fail to study behaviors in this way, they will offer "support" that is not supportive. Furthermore, they may attempt to change some behaviors that are problematic for teachers, but important or helpful to the student with autism. For instance, a student who flicks his fingers may be using this behavior to tune out outside noise. A student who continuously spins or drops his pencil may be using the activity to relax or calm down after a difficult moment. A student who "refuses" to look at the teacher may be doing so in order to *listen* to their *words* more carefully (Jackson, 2002). A student who rocks back and forth when asked to sit for long periods of time might find this behavior comforting. A student who mumbles to him- or herself throughout the day might be doing so to process new information.

Furthermore, teachers should consider that they may be focusing on the behaviors of students with disabilities more so than those of other students. Reid and Maag (1998) found that, in some cases, teachers expected students with disabilities to behave *better* than students who were not labeled or seen or as having behavior challenges. For example teachers expected students with attention-deficit/hyperactivity disorder (ADHD) to sit quietly and pay attention longer than students without this label.

One of my former students, Amir, experienced such discrimination when a few educators asked that he not ride the school bus with other students. These well-meaning teachers felt that Amir needed more supervision than the driver could provide. Most of us who knew Amir well felt that because he always seemed to relax when riding in vehicles he would be very successful on the bus and quite able to handle noise and chaos. We felt that he might need some additional supervision and had considered assigning a paraprofessional to the bus, but given this extra support, Amir's family and his classroom teacher felt he should ride the regular school bus. To calm the nerves of all involved, a district administrator offered to ride the bus and observe Amir in order to put both the teachers and the family at ease. The results were quite interesting; the administrator reported that the bus ride was indeed chaotic, but that Amir was one of the only students sitting quietly and following the driver's directions!

By sharing this story, I do not mean to imply that Amir did not perhaps need more supervision than the bus driver could provide or that he did not sometimes exhibit behaviors that posed a challenge to him and to others. I do mean to point out, however, that our ideas about problem behavior are often influenced by our students' labels and reputations.

If a Problem Exists, Where Is It?

I was asked to consult with a school district about Phinney, a young man with autism. I went to visit the young man in his high school. He was being supported by two paraprofessionals for most of his school day because of his "severe behavior problems."

After observing the young man for a few hours, it became clear that he did, indeed, struggle throughout the day. He sometimes hit staff members; he often slapped and bit himself; and on more than one occasion during the month he had thrown another student into a locker. This young man struggled as much with his schooling as he did with his body, however. He did not see his educational supports as helpful and he found his environment and daily routine challenging. For example, Phinney thrived when he was allowed to interact with other students, but he spent most of his day separated from his peers. Whereas many teachers and administrators saw Phinney as a student with challenging behaviors, other teachers saw him as a struggling student who was working hard to cope under difficult circumstances.

When I told the building principal of my concerns about Phinney's education, he answered, "I brought you here to give us support and to deal with the problem. First you need to tell us what to do about Phinney, then we can take the time to look at his program." I didn't know how to respond—Phinney was seen as the sole issue or problem, so the approach to the problem had to be some type of response *to* him or treatment *of* him.

I was stunned and felt I could offer little to this team in the way of support or suggestions. It was, in my opinion, impossible to do anything to Phinney that Phinney or his team would find useful. Clearly, many aspects of the situation would need to be examined. The problem was not in Phinney and did not belong to him.

Phinney's behaviors, in my opinion, would not be reduced by creating a behavior plan for him. In this situation, changes in environment, curriculum, and educational program were clearly necessary. The team may have started brainstorming solutions to their struggles by locating the problem. Was the staff frustrated? Did they feel safe and prepared? Were they trained and knowledgeable? Was the school ready for inclusive education? Were team members working collaboratively and effectively? Were some of Phinney's needs going unmet? As long as this educational team viewed Phinney as owning the problem, they were blocked from making changes that would help him and make their work with him more productive, successful, and enjoyable.

TEN POSITIVE WAYS TO SUPPORT STUDENTS AND BEHAVIORS

If a student with autism and his or her team decide that a particular behavior is problematic, there are several different ways to support the student and help the team. I offer ten ways to understand, cope with, and learn about student behaviors. By considering some of these suggestions, a teacher may be able to appreciate a student's behavior in a new way or help him or her to make changes to it. These ideas are not offered as a recipe or as part of a linear problem-solving model. Rather, they are presented as a set of reminders or considerations that individual teachers or educational teams may want to review before a behavior plan is constructed or individualized education program (IEP) goals related to behavior are drafted. These ideas may help teams as they reconsider their own attitudes and values related to behavior and help the student with autism become more successful and comfortable in their classrooms and schools.

1. If Possible, Ask the Student About the Behavior

Ryan was a high school student who loved to swim and work out at the YMCA. Although he seemed to love swimming and using the gym equipment, his teachers could not get him to use the showers in the locker room. As Mr. Steib, his teacher, explained, swimming became a struggle for both Ryan and his teachers:

We had tried to get him into the large pool at the YMCA, and he just hates it; I never really understood why, and I talked to his former teacher and a lot of his former teachers and they had the same struggle. He never really seemed to get into swimming, or if he would, then he would just kind of stand there, but he loved the hot tub. That was like this huge thing to him—pie in the sky—sitting in the hot tub, but in order to get into the hot tub or pool you have to shower first. It's a Y rule, and it had been brought to our attention that Ryan needed to also follow those rules. So how were we going to get through the whole shower thing, because he fought the shower? I had turned it on to what I thought was an appropriate, comfortable temperature or whatever and he wouldn't even get in there. It was a struggle the first couple times. (Kluth, 1998, p. 108)

When Ryan gained access to reliable communication through the use of facilitated communication, he was able to give his teachers an explanation for his resistance to the shower. Ryan's "tips" not only solved the immediate problem but also gave Mr. Steib and Ryan's other teachers enough information to prevent difficulties in the future. Mr. Steib explained:

One of the days when Ryan was really "on" and able to communicate, I was able to ask him about why he didn't like to shower. Then he typed that it was too cold, that the shower was too cold and he said that he likes it extremely hot, so it's almost, not scalding, but extremely hot and now I don't even have an issue of going in the shower... because we turned that shower to hot. Now he goes in and he just grins ear to ear when he's in there. (Kluth, 1998, p. 108)

In this instance, Ryan was using behavior to communicate his discomfort in the best way he could. Ryan's story is an important reminder to examine every behavior from the perspective of the student, if possible. How does the student interpret the behavior? Is it hard or easy to control? Is it purposeful? Is it painful? Is it useful? Does the individual need it or want it in his or her life? Does the student want to stop engaging in the behavior? Does he or she view it as problematic? Is it something he uses to cope? Is it something he needs to stay calm? Often, individuals with autism engage in behaviors that look strange to others but serve an important purpose. Consider some of the ways in which people with autism interpret their behaviors:

Sometimes I had to knock my head or slap it to feel it. (Mukhopadhyay, 2000, p. 73)

My failure to modulate or express emotions appropriately also makes me appear retarded. When someone comes to see me and I am happy, I sometimes run through the house or else I go to my room. I am happy, but the emotions overwhelm me.

Appearances also contribute to the assumption of retardation. Many people with autism look quite normal, but some of us look goofy. We are also not well coordinated so we move inelegantly. We are trying to get our bodies where we want them to go, but our bodies have minds of their own. (Rubin, 1998)

Sean Barron, a man with autism, couldn't resist the urge to ask everyone around him if they had "been to" different U.S. states. Sean would ask houseguests, "Have you been to Arizona? To Oregon? To Utah?" His mother explained that when Sean started asking these questions "no other conversation was possible." Sean explained:

These questions were also a form of escape for me. When I asked about Montana, for example, I would picture myself there instead of where I really was. I may not have had a very accurate picture of Montana in my mind, but I did know that it was far away from Ohio, and consequently, from me. So, in a way I was at least temporarily removing myself from the pain of my present situation. (Barron & Barron, 1992, p. 106)

Here is how some other people with autism described their behavioral experiences:

I would move my hands a few inches from my eyes for hours on end, and feel at one with the leaves fluttering against the white pergola. In time the movement became a form of self-expression, so that even as an adult woman, when I feel very content, my fingers twitch in a formalisation of that movement. However, originally the finger movement gave me a means of analysing near and far, and could lend coherence to light and shade, much as a spinning peep-show did in a nineteenth-century fair booth. (Blackman, 2001, p. 11)

[Rocking, hand-shaking, and chin-tapping] provide security and release, and thereby decrease, built-up inner anxiety and tension, thereby decreasing fear. (Williams, 1992, p. 213)

Screaming was my only way of telling Mother that I didn't want to wear the hat. It hurt. It smothered my hair. I hated it. (Grandin, 1996, p. 17)

Ronny, who would raise women's skirts over their heads, said he did so to keep people from getting too close to him. Close touching, he claimed, made him feel as if he were being smothered. He knew if he took the offensive, people would avoid him. His actions helped by keeping them away, but he also hurt because he was alone. (Reed, 1996, p. 94)

These descriptions are insightful and, in some ways, surprising. An outsider, for instance, might not assume that by lifting a skirt a person may be communicating a need to be left alone or that rocking and hand-shaking can provide security. These accounts from individuals with autism have helped us to learn more about the dis/ability itself, uncover myths and misconceptions about why individuals do what they do, and help craft supports that individuals will truly view as supportive.

2. Talk to the Student's Family

I am always amazed at how family resources are underused. Parents offer free expert advice, and teachers must take advantage of it. When I taught kindergarten I became really stuck on how to support a little boy who did have speech but wouldn't or couldn't talk at school. He also seemed confused when we gave him directions or asked him questions. I called his mother and asked, "Could you come and work with me for a day or an afternoon or an hour?" She agreed and this collaboration led to powerful problem solving. She initially seemed reluctant to provide suggestions, but after I asked her to watch me and take notes, she came up with several ideas that I was able to draw on throughout the year. Among other things, this parent told me to use a louder voice with the student. She told me, "I don't whisper or use such a low voice, so I think he expects a little more volume when he is being asked to do something." She also suggested that if I wanted him to talk more, I should, "ask him about his dog— he loves his dog." This feedback was incredibly helpful—like a key opening a lock. Although this parent's suggestions may not seem especially earth-shattering, the information was exactly the type of feedback I was seeking and the advice turned out to be more helpful than anything I could have learned from a professional.

In another instance, I called on a parent to help me with a student's spitting behavior. Every day during lunch, Mike, one of my students, would take a big gulp of his milk and then spit it out, sometimes on the table and other times on his classmates. I was confused; the parent survey I collected at the beginning of the school year reported that Mike often drank milk and that he wasn't allergic to it.

At first, his classmates were understanding and tried talking to him about the incidents. Over time, however, students began to avoid sitting near him. Because Mike was new to the school, I was desperate to find a solution quickly; I felt that every day I failed to help this student, I was jeopardizing his chances for social success. Mike did not have much reliable speech, so it was difficult to get information from him about the spitting. Because I had only been teaching a year, I was reluctant to ask his family for help. I feared that they would see me as incompetent.

I tried talking to Mike; maybe if I could explain how he was upsetting other students, he would stop spitting. That didn't seem to work. Then I hypothesized that the cafeteria was too loud for him. I removed him from the lunchroom and instead, invited a few students to join him for lunch in the classroom each day. Mike didn't seem to mind eating in the classroom; however, the spitting continued. Finally, I placed a bucket next to Mike during lunchtime to see if, perhaps, the behavior had become part of a routine he couldn't stop; I didn't think the bucket would stop his behavior, but I thought I might learn more about what was happening with the spitting episodes.

When none of these supports seemed effective, I relented and called Mike's mother. I invited her to school to talk and review Mike's program, in general. Mike's mother agreed to visit the school, but I was still too insecure to ask for her advice directly. Instead, I asked her to sit in on some of Mike's classes and give me general feedback. Mike had never been educated in an inclusive setting before, so I felt she would appreciate an opportunity to review his day and activities. (I also hoped she would be able to help me without having to admit my ignorance.) Mike's mother was pleased with the morning and agreed to follow me to the lunchroom. We arrived in the lunchroom as Mike was about to open his milk. At this point, I mentioned the spitting to his mom in a nonchalant manner: "Oh—I almost forgot—does Mike ever spit out his milk at home, because he has done that once or twice here." As I spoke, we both turned to Mike at the moment he spit a mouthful of chocolate milk all over the young woman sitting next to him. His mother turned to me and said, "Oh that's easy. He hates chocolate milk."

I love this story because there are so many lessons in it. This is a story about learning to be an effective teacher and approaching problems from different angles. It is also a story about locating the problem; we may assume that a student has a problem when in reality, it is the situation that is problematic. Finally and most important, it is a story about listening to families. Families possess what Kliewer and Landis (1999) have called local understanding, which Kliewer and Biklen described as "a radically deep, intimate knowledge of another human being" (2001, p. 4). Families can often tell us a great deal about autism, but more important, they can tell us about *their child*. In the case of the chocolate milk described above, Mike's mother knew that her son automatically drank liquids when they were put in front of him, even if he didn't like the taste of them. She also knew that he spit when he tasted chocolate and that he typically felt embarrassed and upset after spitting in public. Only this mother could help our staff understand Mike's behavior and help us to see the struggle and frustration he must have been enduring throughout the chocolate milk ordeal.

3. Make the Most of the School Community

I once worked with a first-grade student who was tormented by the sound of crying. If a parent brought a crying baby into the school or if a peer started whimpering or shouting, Gino came unglued. He would wail and scream and drop to the floor in agony. Although these episodes decreased gradually, they were difficult for Gino and heartbreaking for his teachers. During the episodes themselves, nothing seemed to calm Gino—even his parents were at a loss for solutions.

In one instance, Gino was walking down the hallway with his classmates when a child from the preschool class came running in from the playground with a bloody lip. The child was sobbing, and soon Gino was too. Two teachers rushed to calm Gino, but nothing seemed to relax him. At that moment, Jerry, the school custodian, was walking by and stopped to help. We told him Gino would be fine and encouraged him to continue with his work. Jerry made no move to leave and we became flustered by his attempts to help. Three of us were now surrounding a tiny 6-year-old boy and, gauging from Gino's reaction, none of us were offering any comfort. Suddenly, Jerry began singing to Gino in Italian. Before we had time to tell Jerry that singing wouldn't work, Gino had stopped screaming and was staring at Jerry with his huge brown eyes. Jerry finished one song and sang another while helping Gino to his feet and walking him back to his classroom. My colleague and I looked at each other with amazement.

If Jerry taught me anything, it was that students with autism can and should be supported by all members of the school community. It certainly takes a village to educate students with autism (and those without), and every member of the school community should be considered a potential collaborative partner. Support for learners with autism might come from a school secretary, a lunch or recess monitor, the school librarian, a volunteer, a PTA member, a social worker, the school nurse, or a campus security officer.

Students can also be great supports for each other. Many, many insightful teachers I know use peers as resources and help all students understand that they have a responsibility to one another. Although students are not often viewed as collaborative partners, they often thrive in this role. Sometimes students see and understand things that adults don't.

I worked with a little girl named Yee who loved to go to physical education class, but hated to leave. When it was time for students to line up at the door, Yee would wail and run into the supply closet. She told us that she "loved the gym" and wanted to stay all day. In order to make Yee more comfortable, we had the physical education teacher visit her kindergarten classroom to give suggestions about how we might give Yee more opportunities for movement during daily lessons. The physical education teacher also let Yee lead some of the clean-up activities so she would have a concrete way of transitioning from one classroom to the next. Both of these supports seemed effective, but the most powerful support came from a little girl named Jillian. Jillian noticed that Yee was getting distressed after physical education class and offered to buddy up with her during that transition time. Without being asked, Jillian started approaching Yee after class and whispering in her ear, "Okay, Yee...we need to leave pretty soon. Okay Yee? Okay?" We wouldn't have predicted that this foreshadowing would work; yet these simple interactions worked wonders for Yee. The girls began pairing up for clean-up activities and then leading students out of the gymnasium as a team.

How did a child provide something an adult could not? Maybe Yee was comforted by those specific calming words or by Jillian's small, caring voice. Maybe Yee was confused about the routine and Jillian helped—in just the right way—to ease her through the sequence of events leading up to leaving the room. Maybe Jillian provided understanding or compassion in a way others could not or did not. Maybe Jillian disliked leaving the gymnasium too, and Yee was calmed by the act of providing a type of support to her friend.

Pinpointing why this peer support works so well is certainly difficult, but any teacher who has worked in an inclusive classroom has seen it and some have been a little stunned by it. Students often offer words, actions, behaviors, and gestures to one another that teachers and other adults cannot. Sometimes students are able to humor or help one another because they share experiences and "speak the same language." Although many teachers work hard to keep up with clothing styles, lingo, music, and other aspects of student culture, it is difficult for even the most observant professional or interested outsider to be as tuned into this culture as are the student "insiders." Educators, even the most well-meaning and attentive, remain anthropologists of—not participants in—student life.

4. Focus on Connection and Relationships

Perhaps the best way to better understand behaviors is to seek ways to connect with students and work hard at building relationships with them. This is especially important when students do not have a reliable way to communicate; these students cannot easily express thoughts and feelings, so teachers must form relationships with them and their families in order to support them in meaningful ways.

Lovett (1996) pointed out how making connections with those whom teachers are hired to support is central to any other work they might do related to behavior support. He highlighted the importance of educators showing their feelings and their very humanity to those they support:

> A positive approach [to behavior issues] invites people to enter into the same sort of relationship that most of us have and treasure: ongoing, with mutual affection and regard. In such relationships, we all make mistakes, are all in some ways inadequate, and yet it is not the level of success that makes the relationship so satisfying to the people involved; it is the ongoing commitment. In the context of relationships, the success and failure of our work becomes harder to assess because the key element no longer involves simply quantity but the more complex issues of quality. We professionals have routinely overlooked the significance of relationships. (p. 137)

Connecting with students can be accomplished in a number of ways. Some teachers make it a habit to explicitly convey caring. Expressing care can be especially important for those students who are struggling academically or socially or for those being ridiculed or teased because they are "different." Gallagher (1997) wrote of one teacher who took the charge of showing concern so seriously that she initiated a systematic program of expressing caring in her classroom. This teacher became conscientious about greeting students as they entered the classroom. She also made a list of words and phrases to describe students, of which she found the following to affect the students the most in term of conveying caring: "responsible, worthy, valuable, brave, courageous, treat, special, thoughtful, and on the edge of greatness" (p. 7).

Listening is another important part of relationship building. For students who can speak, listening will involve giving students time to share of themselves; eliciting stories from them; encouraging them to express themselves through drama, art, or writing; and getting to know them across contexts (e.g., in school, at home). For students who do not communicate reliably, listening may involve some of these same practices, but teachers will also need to pay special attention to a student's body language and behaviors. For example, if a student cries or screams, the teacher might listen by giving the student some attention and showing concern, trying to interpret her distress, or simply letting her know she is being heard.

5. Be Gentle in a Crisis

Recently I was visiting a friend at the preschool where she teaches. As I walked in the front door, I immediately heard the piercing cry of a young child. I couldn't yet see the child, but any teacher or parent hearing this wailing would recognize it as "the real thing." In other words, these screams did not belong to a child who was merely tired or cranky. These screams belonged to a distressed, frightened, angry, or otherwise wounded child. I listened for the teacher's voice. Was the child being punished? Was someone scolding him? Was he even with a teacher? I began to walk faster.

As I rounded the corner, I relaxed as I saw the child sitting on the floor in the arms of a teacher. I immediately understood why I didn't hear her voice amidst the screams; she was talking to him but she was whispering. I stood watching them from a distance, touched by this gifted teacher's poise and grace. The boy's sobs subsided as she stroked his back and continued whispering to him. She had a compassionate look on her face and her body communicated acceptance.

After 3 or 4 minutes, the child was calm and the two stood and walked back into a classroom. For the rest of the day I thought about how gently she had treated his crisis.

To be gentle in crisis, a teacher need not hug or hold a student, although this is sometimes quite appropriate. A teacher might also touch the student's hand, arm, or back in a reassuring way; ask the student how he or she wants to be helped; sing a favorite song or repeat a calming phrase; or simply keep his or her own body relaxed.

Consider the last time you lost your temper. Did you yell? Scream? Did you cry? Did you say things you would later regret? How did you feel when you were engaged in these behaviors? Embarrassed? Furious? Lonely? When most people are in this type of crisis, they need gentle support to calm down. They may need to take a short walk, curl up with a favorite book, find a place to be alone, or call someone who will listen to their problems. An individual experiencing stress will most likely not be helped by

- Loud voices
- Punitive statements (e.g., "You had your chance," "You made your choice, now you need to leave class")
- Confiscation of preferred or comforting materials or activities
- Physical redirection
- Angry tone or body language

Although a student experiencing challenging behaviors might need to know how the behavior is being interpreted or might benefit from information or teaching related to the behavior, it is seldom, if ever, appropriate or useful to intervene in these ways while the behavior is taking place. One of the most critical skills a teacher can have is the ability to be calm and comforting in a crisis situation. When a student is kicking, biting, banging her head, or screaming, she is most likely miserable and scared. The most effective and human response at this point is to offer support, act in a comforting manner, and help the person relax and feel safe.

6. Consider Perception and Language

When I was teaching elementary school, all of the educators in the building were asked to take turns supervising students from 3 o'clock until the buses arrived, a task that lasted about 15 minutes. Teachers often griped about this responsibility because students could get pretty loud and active as they unwound at the end of the school day. In order to make the task of watching 90 students manageable, some teachers engaged students in a quiet game. Others asked them to sit and read silently. I sometimes used the time in these ways, although I was just as likely to let students socialize during those few minutes. One day when I was in charge of pre-bus duty, students asked if they could "just talk" and I agreed. A few moments later, a veteran teacher walked by and, hearing loud voices (some were very loud) and laughter, took it upon herself to help me out. "Ladies and gentlemen, you WILL behave for Ms. Kluth," the teacher said. The students became instantly silent and attentive. My colleague whispered, "Don't be afraid to put your foot down," and walked away.

I was surprised and a little embarrassed. I did not understand the students' behavior as disrespectful or negative in any way. I was, in fact, learning a lot from their conversations and enjoying talking individually to some of the students that I didn't often see during the day. My colleague, who had less information about the context and my intentions, saw chaos and assumed that students were misbehaving. Her assumptions were based on the ways in which she had conducted and experienced bus duty and perhaps by the way she felt the supervision should be handled.

I use this story to highlight how behaviors can be created through values, biases, and perceptions; through the ways in which individuals interpret situations and read student actions, choices, and movements; and through the ways people name and talk about situations. When my colleague came into the bus area and saw students being loud and active, she saw bad behavior. When she addressed the students and gave me advice, she named the behavior and helped it become a reality. It became real to me in that my first reaction was shame. I felt for a moment that I had been doing something wrong myself. I suddenly felt incompetent as a teacher. It became real to the students in that they instantly became quiet and responded to her command. No student questioned her interpretation of the situation. At least for a few moments, undesirable behavior was invented by nothing more than perception and language.

My example of bus duty may seem, in some ways, to be simplistic. I certainly do not mean to imply that teachers are never really faced with challenging situations. I do want to suggest, however, that all behavior is seen and interpreted differently by different people. Recognizing the power of perception and language may not solve a difficult problem for a team, but it may help educators and students better understand situations they are facing and, in some cases, come up with more effective solutions when problems do arise. For example, I once met with a team of middle school teachers who worked with a student named Jim. Although Jim did not have an identified disability, it was clear from conversations among his teachers that some of them struggled with teaching him. Two of his classroom teachers complained about Jim's constant activity. One sighed, "He never sits down; he is a jackhammer—he bounces around constantly." Another remarked, "He gets up in the middle of my lessons to sharpen his pencils and he twists around in his seat so much that it distracts the other students." Most of the teachers nodded in agreement with these assessments; however, two of the educators at the table seemed confused by this information. The physical education teacher claimed that she didn't have "any problems" with Jim and that, in fact, he was one of her strongest students. She saw him as an active and athletic student, a leader, and as an asset to her class. He participated fully in all activities and seemed to try hard to acquire new skills. The science teacher also described Jim as an active learner and called him "cooperative and inquisitive." In short, some saw Jim's energy and activity as an asset whereas others saw it as a problem.

One way to support Jim would be to have members of the team help all of his teachers see and inspire his strengths. Teachers who had success with Jim might be able to share useful strategies with those who were struggling. The physical education teacher, for instance, might share her ideas on how Jim learns best. The science teacher might tell or show others about some of Jim's best assignments or class contributions. Teachers might even agree to co-teach a few lessons together or observe each other's classes.

Jim's story illustrates how the ways in which students are perceived affect teachers' practices and attitudes. In this case, Jim's teachers could have re-framed and solved their problem simply by sharing their perceptions of him and listening to and learning from the ways in which other colleagues had labeled and understood him. Jim's teachers might also have learned a lot about their biases by examining how their perceptions influenced their language and how their language may have affected their practices.

Language is a powerful tool that can help or harm a student. In his powerful and important poem, "The Language of Us and Them," Mayer Shevin, a disability rights activist, highlighted the ways in which language has been used to stigmatize, ostracize, and—in some cases—dehumanize individuals with disabilities:

The Language of Us and Them

We like things.
They fixate on objects.
We try to make friends.
They display attention-seeking behavior.
We take breaks
They display off task behavior
We stand up for ourselves
They are non-compliant
We have hobbies
They self-stim
We choose our friends wisely
They display poor peer socialization
We persevere
They perseverate
We like people
They have dependencies on people
We go for a walk
They run away
We insist
They tantrum
We change our minds
They are disoriented and have short attention spans

We have talents
They have splinter skills
We are human
They are ???
(Personal communication, March 20, 2002)

Why do we use language in these ways that privilege some and label or hurt others? Why is it that students with autism who have extraordinary talent are called "savants" whereas students without identified disabilities are called "gifted," "talented," or "geniuses"? Why is the label *at-risk* used primarily for poor students (usually poor students of color), whereas wealthier students who struggle are thought to have learning disabilities or academic needs (Coles, 1987; Sleeter, 1986)? Perhaps it is the same reason we call young, socially disadvantaged women, "unwed mothers," but would never use this term to describe the single Hollywood star who gives birth or who decides to adopt.

The importance of examining these labels is realizing that language does matter. It has an impact on the way we see a student and it can facilitate or prevent us from offering meaningful support to learners. One way to think about perception is to use the Lead to Gold framework developed by Armstrong (1987), which encourages individuals to consider the negative language used to describe a particular learner and think about how the language, and therefore, the perception of the learner might be changed. For instance, a student who is described as "lazy" might also be seen as "relaxed." A student who vocalizes when she is afraid might be described as "a screamer" or someone who "sometimes communicates through screaming when she is scared." This questioning of the discourse of schools (Ayers, 2001; Henderson, 1992; Udvari-Solner, 1995) is critical to the work of a caring educator. As Henderson noted,

> Language is a product of our culture. Because we live in a society fraught with overt and subtle social, economic, and political inequities, our language reflects those inequities. It becomes tainted by them. Suppose, for example, you are a male middle school math teacher, and you have been raised to think of women as "too emotional" for the exacting logic of mathematics. If you have female students in your class, how could this sexist language possibly help you confirm their best selves? If you take this language seriously, haven't you already decided that, as a math teacher, you can only confirm boys and not girls? If you don't question this language, aren't you likely to be a sexist math teacher selectively caring for your students? (p. 37)

The point of questioning discourse is not to hide important information but to closely examine the perceptions that educators bring to teaching. Other examples include the following:

- A student described as "hyper" might also be seen as active and engaged
- A student described as having obsessions might also be seen as having interests
- A student described as being self-involved might also be seen as intrapersonal or introspective or pensive
- A student described as stubborn might also be seen as independent and steadfast

- A student described as unable to stay on task for 10 minutes might also be seen as a child able to remain engaged for 7–8 consecutive minutes

When I ask my undergraduate students to use this framework with a student they know, they often suggest that I am asking them to "sugarcoat" the description of the student or that I am ignoring "real problems." I explain to them that I don't mean to suggest that difficulties they encounter in the classroom are not real or that teaching is easy if you just have the right frame of mind. I do think this framework is helpful, however, because behaviors or characteristics of learners can often be perceived in many different ways, and, in many cases, the revised label is more useful. I often ask students to compare their initial and revised descriptions of learners and then I ask them, "Is the revised version as true or perhaps closer to some truth than the initial version?" Consider how one college student used the Lead to Gold framework to shift her perceptions of a learner. When asked to describe a student who challenges her, a student wrote this profile of Ron, a middle school student with the label of Asperger's syndrome:

- Unmotivated by academic work, hates math
- Bothers other students, disturbs others constantly by asking questions
- Obsessed with Michael Jordan
- Resists transitions, won't leave class when the bell rings

When I asked this student to assess the language she used in her profile, she realized that she used a lot of negative descriptions. We also discussed her feelings about Ron. She was feeling frustrated by not knowing how to help him and this feeling of inadequacy was seeping into her perception of him.

When she rewrote her description of Ron, I asked her to think about other ways Ron might be described. I asked her to concentrate specifically on things Ron could do and on his strengths, but not to hide his struggles or needs. This is the revised profile she wrote:

- Very motivated by working with peers; learning about basketball and car racing; and reading books about magic, wizards and warlocks, and time travel
- Very social; enjoys working with others; thrives in group situations
- May need help to focus when working independently
- Inquisitive; will initiate conversations
- Is an expert on basketball—especially knowledgeable about Michael Jordan. He is very interested in lessons related to sports (e.g., calculating shooting percentages in math) and is willing to teach others about sports.
- Needs support when moving from one activity to the next. Five minutes before class ends, a peer should remind him that it is almost time to go. This seems to make transitions less stressful

In both of these descriptions of Ron, the same individual and the same characteristics are presented. In the revised description, however, Ron's gifts and abilities are highlighted. As important, his needs are accurately described but not characterized in a negative way. From a practical perspective, the revised profile is also more useful. A teacher reading the first profile will not only feel immediately discouraged about teaching such a student with so many problems but also will have absolutely no ideas about how to teach the student. A teacher reading the second profile, however, will most likely feel excited about teaching such an interesting person and will have a variety of ideas for engaging, supporting, helping, and educating Ron.

Attending to issues of perception and language are central to providing effective supports for learners with disabilities because our beliefs about students affect the way we teach. Brophy and Evertson (1987) found, not surprisingly, that teacher expectations were tied closely to student achievement. Specifically, they learned that teachers' expectations that students will learn curriculum are positively related to student achievement. Therefore, educators must engage in constant reflection and interrogation of these ideas so that they may see a more complete and complex picture of their students.

7. Teach New Skills

One of my students, Jeff, always struggled during recess. He loved the slide and, given the opportunity, would play on it after lunch every day for the entire 30-minute play break. Seeing Jeff feeling so content during recess was wonderful; however, I was concerned that he never tried any other games or activities. Jeff's classmates were also frustrated. Because our playground only had one slide, Jeff was often accused of "hogging" one of the most prized pieces of playground equipment. When classmates attempted to take a turn on the slide, Jeff shrieked uncontrollably. He often collapsed to the ground, throwing himself face first into the piles of wood chips at the base of the jungle gym.

Initially, I tried to work with other students to give Jeff as much time on the slide as he needed. For several months we avoided Jeff's screaming by letting him use the slide for as much time as he wanted; usually this meant that all of the other students had to go without using this piece of equipment. Although the students were understanding and patient, I wasn't sure this arrangement was the best way to support Jeff. I did, after all, want him to learn a bit about turn taking and perhaps teach him some strategies he could employ while waiting.

The next thing we tried was letting Jeff use the slide for 10 minutes, asking him to take a break for 5 minutes, and letting him use the slide again for another 10 minutes. During the wait time, I showed him how to follow the minutes on a digital watch and encouraged him to walk around the playground until his turn came around again. This strategy was somewhat successful, but Jeff still appeared upset and preoccupied with the slide. Although I wanted Jeff to learn to take turns with the slide, I didn't want the lesson to cause him undue stress.

The situation came to a crescendo when we had a big overnight storm and the slide and entire jungle gym area was flooded. The custodians put barriers around the area and for the next four days, students were barred from using the equipment. When Jeff came outside and saw the barriers, he was inconsolable. I tried to comfort him, then tried to walk with him and engage him in conversation.

Finally, the students solved the problem. Kristi, a shy girl who sat next to Jeff in the classroom, approached him while he walked around the playground and invited him to play four-square. Jeff resisted at first, but after two days of Kristi's encouragement he joined her on the black top. She taught him how to play the game and when she discovered he was struggling with the rules, Kristi and her friends changed them slightly to accommodate Jeff. The second graders also taught Jeff to turn a jump rope and play a game of tag they called "King on the Grass." Jeff still pined for the slide and began using it again when the water disappeared, but he had learned many other skills and began to enjoy a wider range of activities during recess thanks to Kristi and other students in the class.

I learned a lot from Jeff and his classmates on the playground. While I was being reactive and trying to prevent Jeff from "having a behavior" (thinking of how to decrease time on the slide), his classmates were being proactive and focusing on expanding his experiences and building his skills. The lesson Jeff and his friends teach is an important one. Sometimes teachers focus on addressing a behavior when it would be more useful to focus on addressing the individual's needs and on building the student's competencies. Students may need to learn a new skill or to obtain information about something in order to feel more competent and comfortable. Table 9.1 includes some ideas of positive ways to meet students' diverse needs.

8. Be Willing to Adapt

I was asked to visit a middle school and observe a student named Micky. The school principal told me that Micky was disturbing other students because he often chewed on his notebooks; he, in fact, ate them little by little. I asked if the staff had tried asking Mickey about the "problem." The principal told me that they had asked Mickey and he said he needed gum or candy to chew when he felt the need to move his jaw. This sounded reasonable to me and I told the principal as much. She told me that while it did seem to be an appropriate response to the chewing, it could not be implemented because the school did not allow students to have candy.

Consider also the story of Guy, a young man who was very capable academically but needed some simple adaptations to make it through the school

Table 9.1.   Ideas for supporting behavior by teaching new skills

Student need/concern	Skill that might be taught
Student is afraid of stairs or escalators.	Teach student to use a quick relaxation strategy before taking the first step.
Student is frustrated when asked to do written work.	Teach student to type on a computer or typewriter.
Student cries when he or she is not understood.	Taught to use sign language or facilitated communication.
Student gets flustered in a noisy environment.	Student is taught to use headphones and operate a CD player.
Student feels uncomfortable and anxious in new social situations.	Teach student a few conversation starters and give information about the expectations in different environments (e.g., "Parties are a good place to tell jokes or share funny stories").

day. Guy constantly disrupted lessons because he arrived late to his classes, struggled to find a place to sit, and often did not have the necessary course materials. Although some of his team members suggested a few simple adaptations, seeing them implemented would not be so simple:

> After discussions between his mother and the Head of Special Needs it was suggested that he should be allowed to have a fixed desk at which to sit in every lesson—preferably at the back of the class where he would be less of a distraction to other pupils. In each classroom the desk would also contain the minimum equipment necessary for him to cope with the lesson (paper, pens, ruler, etc.). Some teachers were happy to implement these suggestions and in their classes Guy's behavior improved rapidly. Others refused to change long-established teaching practices and in these classes his behavior remained highly disruptive and erratic. (Howlin, 1998, p. 244)

Both of these stories illuminate how behaviors are facilitated or even created when students are not allowed access to adaptations and supports that they need. In the beginning of this chapter, I noted the importance of seeing behavior as interpreted and contextual. Guy's situation is a perfect illustration of how behaviors are *not* fixed realities; when teachers work to understand students and their needs, undesirable behaviors can be minimized or eliminated. Guy's "behaviors" disappeared or were facilitated by each teacher's willingness to provide him with the seating he needed.

A meeting I had with a student's family and my building administrator helped me to understand the potential power of creating adaptations and working toward solutions instead of focusing on problems. The team was concerned about Matt, a young man who would frequently run out of his classroom and into the schoolyard. Once there, he would jump on the swing, at which point he would burst into tears if his pursuer refused to push him on the swing. Matt repeated this behavior approximately five times each day. When we tried to lock the doors near his classroom (terrified he would run into the street at some point), he would make a break for the library and jump on the hammock hanging in the corner.

Everyone felt that Matt must need the input the swing could provide, but none of us wanted him to continually miss out on the activities, interactions, and opportunities provided in his general education classroom. My boss, a district administrator, piped up during the meeting, "Matt shouldn't have to go to the swing, the swing should go to Matt," and proceeded to draw out plans for installing a hanging basket swing in the back of the first-grade classroom. All of us—the first-grade teacher, Matt's mother, my boss, the school principal—got excited about the idea and began planning ways in which we would naturally integrate this piece of equipment into the classroom. We decided that the swing would become part of a reading corner and that all children would have opportunities to use it when Matt was taking a break from it.

I left that meeting upbeat and with a new understanding of how teachers could think about adaptation and inclusive education. It was the first time I had seen a team of professionals treat "inclusive schooling" as an action (versus as a phenomenon that was or wasn't appropriate for a given student). That is, the stakeholders in Matt's education—especially the administrators—challenged themselves to make inclusion happen for him; they worked toward including him until it happened instead of declaring that inclusive schooling wasn't *for* Matt because he needed too many adaptations.

9. Do Something Else

Supporting behaviors is often trying work. I have driven home from work in tears on more than one occasion, frustrated by behaviors I didn't understand, terrified that I was hurting a student by not being able to respond to his or her needs appropriately, and frightened that those around me would see that I didn't know what I was doing after all. During one of these low periods in my teaching career, a friend read me an attitude-altering story:

I'm listening to the desperate sounds of a life-or-death struggle going on a few feet away. There's a small fly burning out the last of its short life's energies in a futile attempt to fly through the glass of the windowpane. The whining wings tell the poignant strategy: Try harder.

But it's not working.

The frenzied effort offers no hope for survival. Ironically, the struggle is part of the trap. It is impossible for the fly to try hard enough to succeed at breaking through the glass. Nevertheless, this little insect has staked its life on reaching its goal through raw effort and determination.

This fly is doomed. It will die there on the windowsill.

Across the room, ten steps away, the door is open. Ten seconds of flying time and this small creature could reach the outside world it seeks. With only a fraction of the effort now being wasted, it could be free of this self-imposed trap. The breakthrough possibility is there. It would be so easy. (Pritchett, 1993, p. 222)

This simple anecdote helped me to understand the need to continuously approach problems from different angles, to step back and view the difficulty in another way, and to occasionally resist the urge to "do something" when a struggle arises. Sometimes thinking outside of the box can help individuals and teams find solutions that they could not uncover by doing more or working harder. Doing something else might involve

- Doing nothing. Think: Is action required? Is it okay *not* to act?
- Consulting with someone new (e.g., the student's grandmother, an adult with autism, the crossing guard, the student's best friend)
- Using humor
- Trying to understand the behavior another way, from a completely different perspective (e.g, how would an artist, an athlete, a priest, a CEO see this behavior?)
- Quietly observing the situation for a few days instead of intervening
- Confiding in the student, telling him or how you are feeling about the situation
- Journaling or writing about the concern to see if an answer emerges, or have the student journal or write about the concern
- Scheduling a series of lunch meetings or soda breaks with the student or with a student and a friend so you can all get to know each other better

10. Take Care of Yourself

When I was student teaching, I formed a close relationship with a high school student in my class. Patrick was a dynamic and engaging young man. Typically he was full of energy and quite personable. One day, however, he had a falling out with friends and came into the classroom grunting and frowning. After explaining to him that he would need to calm down, he picked up a chair and threw it in my direction. Although the chair missed me by more than a foot, the incident was upsetting and frightening and I went home shaken and frustrated.

When I got home, my host teacher called to check up on me. We talked for an hour; she shared some of her worst teaching moments and told me funny stories about her own student-teaching experience. This talk turned into a regular Thursday afternoon social engagement. We sometimes went to dinner or had coffee at a local bookstore. Other teachers and paraprofessionals in the department sometimes joined us. While we typically talked about our lives outside of the classroom, these outings were also used as a time to process events from the work week.

These Thursday get-togethers became a way for me to get teaching ideas from my more seasoned colleagues, but they also served as a model for how to cope with stress and stay fresh and focused as a teacher. Teaching can be a very exciting but very exhausting job. When the educational team is coping with a behavior problem, the work can be even more tiring and frustrating.

Noddings wrote, "An ethic of caring is a tough ethic. It does not separate self and other in caring....If caring is to be maintained, clearly, the one-caring must be maintained" (1984, pp. 99–100). Those who are engaged in a profession as intimate and dynamic as teaching need to pay attention to their personal needs and hone their coping skills. Some relieve stress by confiding in trusted colleagues. Others might listen to calming music or exercise. At times, educators may also want to practice quieting their minds. With so much going on during the typical school day, it can sometimes be helpful to tune out inner distractions completely and try to be mentally still for a few moments.

Teachers engaged in self-care also pay attention to inner dialogue. Educators should ask themselves, What kinds of messages am I sending myself? Do I focus only on what is going wrong or can I see progress and what is going right, too? Do I plan concrete ways in which I can improve things in the future? Richard Carlson (1998), the author of *The Don't Sweat the Small Stuff Workbook*, suggested that a productive way to reflect is to think of problems as potential teachers. He suggested that "when we accept our problems as an inevitable part of life, when we look at them as potential teachers, it's as if a weight has been lifted off our shoulders" (p. 160). For example, a parent may call and express dissatisfaction with the way her child's behavior issues have been handled. The teacher can get angry or defensive or she can reflect on the parent's concerns and see if there is another way to interpret the remarks: Is the parent scared for her child? Has the school staff explained their viewpoint on the situation to the mother? The teacher might also consider whether she has approached the situation in the best way. Perhaps a principal or counselor should be involved? The teacher might learn a lesson about communication, listening, family needs, or teacher responsibilities.

CAUTIONS IN SUPPORTING BEHAVIOR

While it is typically most useful to consider practices that may be helpful versus those that are potentially problematic, a few cautions must be issued in order to adequately address the topic of supporting behavior. In my work as a teacher educator and as a consultant to schools, I typically try to help teachers form solutions to behavior based on the ten ideas outlined throughout this chapter, but I typically begin problem-solving sessions by outlining three cautions: realize the limitations of behaviorism, avoid removing students from the classroom, and do not focus on compliance as a goal. Although I could share a range of other cautions in addition to these, I choose to share these three consistently because these approaches are so common across schools and across the United States; and when teachers do not heed these three cautions, it becomes difficult to create behavior supports that are positive, student-centered, and as humane as possible.

Realize the Limitations of Behaviorism

Behaviorism is the philosophical position that says that psychology, to be a science, must focus its attention on what is observable; it is a theory of learning that focuses on objectively observable behaviors (Skinner, 1976). Many educators have challenged the usefulness of behaviorist technologies, but Herb Lovett suggested that it is the application of behaviorism that is often found reprehensible and *not* behaviorism itself:

> There is no reason we cannot pay attention both to research and to social realities. In working with persons labeled retarded, for example, we can use task analysis to make what is complex simpler. But my experience is that many persons using behavioral interventions reduce complex social situations too simply. (1985, p. 64)

Certainly, sensitive practitioners have used elements of behavioral technology to support behaviors and to help students enhance quality of life (Donnellan & Leary, 1995; Lovett, 1985). In these cases, supports are designed in consultation with the person experiencing difficulty, are gentle and natural, and are grounded in positive relationships.

One reason to be cautious in the use of behaviorist technology is related to human nature. Behavior is complex and behavioral approaches must account for this. Even when the person designs his or her own behavior plan, the technology may backfire. Sue Rubin, a woman with autism, explained why behaviorism does not always work for her:

Often [aggression and self-abusive behavior] are triggered by specific events, but sometimes they just happen. Maybe it is some kind of chemical imbalance. So if you are looking for an antecedent and plan on giving a consequence, that might be unfair. A negative consequence will change the behavior, but it will just be replaced by a different awful behavior. I actually asked for lost privileges to help control my behavior, but always understood that they were only bandaids and would be good for a short time. (Rubin, 1998)

Another reason to look beyond behaviorism is related to its history and misuse. Behaviorist technology is too often used to hurt, humiliate, or manipulate learners. For example, those who misuse behaviorist methods might ask students to perform skills that make them feel physically uncomfortable (e.g., "Keep your hands at your sides," "Make eye contact") or try to change behavior by taking away materials or activities that the student needs in order to feel calm (e.g., making a student earn time on the computer). Furthermore, behaviorist technology is often interpreted and implemented in ways that clash with students' cultures. McIntyre (2002) pointed out, for instance, that many cultures including some American Indians and Hispanics value self-determination over compliance and conformity. He claimed that some in these groups reject the "power-oriented and controlling conceptualization upon which behaviorist practices are based." These groups are more likely to advocate for "acceptance of non-standard behavior with little in the way of interference or attempts to control it." In some of these cultures, in fact, variations in behavior (if non-violent) are respected and self-determination is valued (Brendtro & Brokenleg, 1993; Good Tracks, 1973; Kallam, Hoernicke, & Coser, 1994; McIntyre, 2002; Slaughter, 1976). Two approaches that are often used in behaviorist programs are rewards and reinforcement and punishment. I will examine both of these techniques and outline ways in which each can be misused.

Using Rewards and Reinforcement   Many of us use rewards and reinforcements in our own lives to alter our behaviors. We may buy tickets to a sporting event if we manage to stay within our budget for 2 months in a row or treat ourselves to a rich dessert on Saturday night if we eat healthy food during the week. These types of rewards can be very effective because we design them. Furthermore, we are in control of monitoring our own progress and deciding on when and how we should follow through on the rewards.

When an outsider is involved in reinforcing and rewarding us, we may be less motivated and, therefore, less effective in meeting our goals. If my sister decided how much healthy food I needed to eat in order to get my dessert or if my mother determined how strict I had to be with my budget or how much I could spend on the sports tickets, I might well lose my urge to "behave." As Herb Lovett explained, we need to pay attention to our own behaviors and our own lives when supporting people with disabilities:

> Think of some chore around your house that you do not much like. Suppose you can cope with house chores except for making the bed, doing the laundry, or shopping for groceries—something basically trivial but eventually unavoidable. Do you think you would do it more often if others around you automatically said, "Good bed making Karen!" (1985, p. 65)

In general, using rewards and reinforcement to change a student's behavior results in frustrated teachers, "unsuccessful" students, and a lot of lost time and energy. And when students *are* successful, the problem may not be solved. A student who is rewarded when he doesn't pinch for 10 minutes might learn to quit pinching but begin kicking or hitting if the purpose of his pinching behavior was to initiate a conversation with others.

Human behavior is more complex than most rewards and reinforcement plans would have us believe. Consider the case of Joan:

> Joan loved music. Each day when she returned home from school she would sit quietly for awhile listening to her favorite tapes. Her parents met with a psychologist to design a behavior program for Joan's behavior of destroying property. He started by asking her parents to list those things Joan found reinforcing. Music was at the top of the list. It was decided that her parents would hold Joan's cassettes. When Joan did not destroy anything all day she would be offered her choice of a cassette to listen to for a half-hour before bed. Joan's psychologist was shocked when the program was criticized—"but it's all based on positive reinforcement!" he insisted. (Weiss, 1999, p. 22)

In Joan's case, the program was anything but reinforcing and positive. The ways in which the psychologist used behaviorism failed to help Joan and her family understand her tendency to destroy things; it certainly did not provide Joan with any new skills or strategies; and it served to potentially eliminate one part of her day that already was calm, quiet, and relaxing. Instead of being helpful, this plan was disrespectful and counterproductive.

Dan Reed (1996) also shared a story about the way reinforcements can be construed as punishments:

> At Ted's annual meeting, the staff of the group home where he lived was talking about the previous year and making plans for the following one. The discussion was about weekend activities, what to continue and what to change. Ted had been getting pizza every Friday night. The staff thought that since he seemed indifferent to the pizza, perhaps another Friday night activity was indicated.
>
> Ted reached for his letterboard and demanded to be heard. DON'T TAKE MY PIZZA AWAY, I LOVE PIZZA.
>
> The surprised staff responded, "Since you never seemed to enjoy it, we thought you didn't care for pizza."
>
> IF YOU KNEW I LOVED IT, YOU WOULD HAVE MADE ME EARN IT. (Reed, 1996, p. 96)

Ted's critique of the program illustrates how different the vantage points of professionals and individuals with disabilities can be. In this story, the behavior program was so useless that the individual who should have been benefiting from it had to design a behaviorist strategy of his own to cope with it!

Using Punishment   Punishment, in behavioral terms, is defined as the application of an unpleasant or aversive consequence immediately following an undesirable behavior. Common punishments include making students stay after school or assigning them extra work. Punishment follows a behavior and is intended to decrease the likelihood that the behaviors will occur again. Therefore, if a student who is sent to the principal's office for talking during a lesson continues both the talking behavior and the visits to the principal's office, the consequence is not serving as a punishment.

Many common criticisms are given regarding using punishment in classrooms. One of the main objections to punishment is that it doesn't teach students what to do; it only teaches them what *not* to do. Spanking a child, for example, can be very effective in stopping a toddler from fighting with his sister, but it will not teach him anything about sharing toys or using words to communicate. In addition, the spanking may result in the child fearing the parent and, ironically, learning that it is sometimes okay to hit other people to solve a problem. Likewise, a student who is punished for getting out of his seat repeatedly may be able to stay in his chair after a punishment, but if he was getting out of his chair because he craved movement, he may feel anxious, restless, and unable to concentrate on the rest of the day's lessons.

Punishment is also criticized because it can cause students to distrust or fear adults. It may cause students to feel disconnected from the teacher and hurt the teacher–student relationship. This may be especially true for students with autism who have experienced physical punishment in the past.

Despite criticisms of punishment, teachers often use it because it is familiar. Sometimes behavior plans are developed because of the belief that students "have to learn" to behave. One of my former students often kicked and bit staff members and as the days passed without much change in these behaviors, so did the frustration and anger of the teachers and paraprofessionals supporting him. Even teachers who did not support him directly felt angry and approached me to suggest proper ways to discipline him. One teacher told me that I shouldn't let him "get away" with the behavior.

It became apparent after some time that the school community wanted this student to be punished—not necessarily for his benefit—but perhaps to "do something." Perhaps they wanted a punishment in order to cope with their own stress. Because staff members were being hit and kicked, they may have— consciously or unconsciously—wanted this student to be punished so that they could respond in some way to being hurt. Although it *is* certainly frustrating and upsetting to be injured, punishing students typically does not make teachers feel better in the long run and it does little to inspire new learning and build classrooms in which all students can feel safe and comfortable.

Avoid Removing Students from the Classroom

I was visiting an elementary school when I passed a little boy sitting on the floor in the hallway crying and sucking on his wrist. When I asked another teacher about the child she told me, "Oh that's Peter. He's out there more than he's in the classroom. He can't handle it."

I fear there are a lot of Peters out there waiting for opportunities to re-enter the inclusive classroom. Many students who are included in general education environments are only allowed in for a portion of the school day. Others are allowed in on a contingency plan; they can stay as long as they can behave.

During my first week of teaching, I was in a fifth-grade classroom co-teaching with a veteran teacher. Although she had never been a teacher in an "inclusive" classroom before, Ms. Goldman had been teaching for more than 25 years and had experience with students with a wide range of abilities, needs, skills, and gifts. During the first 10 minutes of the day, George, a student with autism, began to show signs of anxiety; he threw his notebook on the floor and then stood up and spilled the wastebasket. I was so anxious for Ms. Goldman and others to see how well inclusive schooling could work and was mortified by the situation. I walked over to George and began to guide him out of the classroom for a "break." At this point Ms. Goldman began chattering away, "Okay, well things get spilled in the classroom. George, can you sit down again please and we will get started." She got the students started on an activity and then walked over to him and helped him put the garbage back into the basket.

While they worked she gave him a little information about activities the students would be engaged in that morning. Without hesitation, he helped her to clean the mess and took his seat.

I was surprised by George's reaction, but Ms. Goldman, the more experienced teacher, was not. She had been teaching long enough to understand that students are often scared during the first week of school. Furthermore, by handling the situation in the classroom, she showed George that she valued him and wanted him to be a part of the community. She also helped him to become more comfortable in his new environment by encouraging him to join the group. Over time, Ms. Goldman was able to teach George ways to calm himself in stressful situations; she looked for signals that he was becoming agitated or overwhelmed by noise or activity and helped him to self-manage by taking deep breaths or by pacing in the back of the room.

Any student may need to leave the classroom for a variety of reasons throughout the day, and it is important for students to have this option when they feel upset, sick, or angry. Furthermore, students may need to leave the classroom at times so that their dignity may be preserved and protected; if a student needs privacy or wants a break, it should be provided. There is absolutely nothing wrong with having a place of harbor where any student can go to relax, calm down, or have a few minutes alone. In fact, all students should be given this option, and when a situation escalates, a student can be calmly reminded that he or she can use this space.

Students should not, however, be escorted out of the classroom every time they struggle or every time a teacher struggles *with* them. Too often, students with autism are asked to leave the classroom or are escorted out of educational environments without their permission. Faber and Mazlish (1995) asked people to put themselves in the place of a student who is isolated. "As an adult you can imagine how resentful and humiliated you would feel if someone forced you into isolation for something you said or did" (p. 115). For a young person, however, this type of rejection can be even more serious because she may come to believe "that there is something so wrong with her that she has to be removed from society" (pp. 115–116). Vivian Paley (1992) reminded us that teachers send powerful messages of exclusion and rejection when they isolate learners. These messages, in turn, affect students and the classroom:

Thinking about unkindness always reminds me of the time-out chair. It made children sad and lonely to be removed from the group, which in turn made me feel inadequate and mean and—I became convinced—made everyone feel tentative and unsafe. These emotions show up in a variety of unwholesome ways depending on whether one is a teacher or child. (p. 95)

This tendency to send the student away from the group is incredibly problematic. When at all possible, it is best to support and address challenging situations in the environments in which they occur. Removing students from places where they should feel that they belong is detrimental to the building of community and, often, to the processes of teaching and learning.

One of the primary reasons students should not be removed is related to the definition of inclusion; students should feel without question that they are members of their classroom community and they should not have this membership constantly threatened. Asking or forcing students to leave an educational environment may even cause new problems—both for them and for teachers; students removed from the classroom may feel rejected, hurt, or confused and, in response, may struggle academically, socially, or emotionally. Students who are removed from the classroom also lose valuable content when they are away. Students miss instruction, lose work time, and have fewer opportunities to interact and learn from peers.

Furthermore, students need to learn to negotiate behaviors in the most natural ways possible. Students cannot learn social skills without opportunities to make friends. They cannot learn communication skills without interacting and working with classmates, and they cannot learn competencies related to behavior if they are not allowed to solve problems and work through difficulties with others in natural and authentic environments.

Finally, removing students from the inclusive classroom frames the behavior as the student's problem and prevents students and teachers from understanding behaviors as complex and socially situated. If a student is removed from the classroom, the teachers and the students are unable to see how the classroom community, the environment, the behaviors of others, and the curriculum and instruction might be affecting a student's actions, feelings, movements, and moods.

Do Not Focus on Compliance as a Goal

The word *compliance* is often found in the school records of a student with disabilities. It is not as common in the records or reports of students *without* disabilities, however. Although general educators might assess the engagement, citizenship, or listening skills of a learner without disabilities, they typically do not talk about or report on how compliant students are. At some point, this term and concept became part of the discourse and values system of human services and special education and over the years has driven many a behavior plan and educational program. Weiss (1999) addressed problems with compliance by detailing the story of a young student named Laura:

> Laura was in a regular fourth grade classroom but, because of her disabilities, her teacher didn't include her in many of the learning activities in which the other children participated. The teacher had selected a few activities for Laura that she felt were better suited to Laura's abilities. These included sorting pegs by color, putting together a puzzle, and matching objects to pictures on a grid. Laura showed curiosity about the activities of other children. Their activities were generally of a more active and participatory nature. Laura would often wander around the classroom disrupting the work of the other students. When she was redirected back to her seat and her activities, Laura would often become upset, throwing her materials on the floor and occasionally even pushing and hitting the teacher.
>
> Laura's teacher enlisted the help of the school's behavior specialist to develop a program to encourage Laura to stay in her seat, attend to her work, and to reduce Laura's aggressive behavior. She told the behavior specialist that Laura was noncompliant. The behavior specialist was happy to begin designing a careful system of reinforcement to assist Laura to achieve these behavioral goals. The ethical questions are clear. Simply because the technology exists to

train Laura to be compliant in an inappropriate environment doesn't make it eth-
ically acceptable. An astute teacher or behavior specialist would recognize
Laura's behavior as one of the most objective critiques of service quality that
they are ever likely to receive. (Weiss, 1999, p. 27)

The story of Laura shows how a focus on compliance can shift attention away from what really matters and prevent teachers from forming solutions that are creative, meaningful, and related to enhanced teaching and learning.

Another problem with compliance is that it teaches students the wrong things. Compliance can teach students to obey without question and to listen to adults at all costs. Students who learn to be compliant not only may be confused about why they are to do what they are asked to do—but some students may also learn to comply with requests that are inappropriate or even dangerous. For instance, a student who is taught to be compliant might fail to question a fellow student who tells him to pull the fire alarm or worse, a student who is taught to blindly follow any adult's direction might follow a stranger's directions as willingly as those of a teacher.

Instead of compliance, students should be taught a curriculum of self-determination. Students who are taught self-determination will be able to protect and advocate for themselves. Furthermore, students who learn choice-making, decision-making, problem-solving, and goal-setting skills will be better able to help themselves around issues of behavior and may be able to help others offer the most appropriate supports.

SUMMARY

On his first day of third grade, one of my former students, Todd, ran through the building, crawled under tables, banged his head against the cement floor of the locker room, and screamed every time he heard the fire alarm. Teachers in the building were apprehensive. Todd, who had been educated in segregated, special education schools for several years, seemed scared and confused in his new inclusive school. During this time at least two colleagues approached me to ask if I thought our school was the right place for Todd.

I was certainly nervous about working with Todd; I desperately wanted him to be successful and was unsure of where to begin in supporting him but I was certain that our school was the best community for him. When my colleagues challenged Todd's placement, suggesting that he needed a more restrictive environment, I pointed out that it was most likely the more restrictive environments that had facilitated the development of so many of Todd's behaviors. What he needed, I insisted, was a chance to be a member of a school community.

Indeed, Todd had been educated with several nonverbal students for years and was, therefore, unaccustomed to typical classroom behaviors. He was educated with two students who banged their heads and he, therefore, adopted head-banging behavior. He was never given instructional materials to handle on his own, so he was unaware of his new teacher's expectations. He had been educated all day in one room, so changing environments during the day and "traveling" through such a big school was quite confusing at first.

Changes came slowly but consistently for Todd. Teachers, however, were cautiously optimistic, hopeful, and open-minded. They watched and waited for success and it came.

After spending a lot of time observing other students and engaging in typical school routines, Todd was able to use some speech and sign language to request a drink of water or a trip to the bathroom. Students learned his communication system and began socializing with him. Very slowly, his head-banging went away.

Todd also learned where to put his belongings and materials in the classroom and began using a picture schedule to learn about daily activities. After a few weeks, he learned where he was supposed to be at different points in the day and stopped running around the building. His teacher then acquired a few small rocking chairs and some floor pillows and Todd stopped crawling under desks, opting instead to sit in his desk, on the chairs, or propped up against the pillows.

Teachers and students helped Todd to prepare for the annoying fire drill sounds. Two students flanked Todd the moment the alarm sounded and they modeled how he could put his hands on his ears as he walked out of the building. Although he never grew accustomed to the noise, Todd's screaming ceased and he was able to tolerate the sporadic drills.

It took several months for Todd to acclimate, but after only a few weeks the staff marveled at how different this young man looked and acted. He continued to make impressive gains and by his fifth-grade year, Todd was participating in all aspects of classroom life, participating in the general education curriculum, and working collaboratively with peers. He became a member of the track team and sang in a school musical. Although he once had a paraprofessional sitting next to him at all times, Todd could now work in his classroom with only occasional "spot-checks" by a paraprofessional or special education teacher.

It wasn't until the school hosted a team of visitors from another district that the teachers understood how important their commitment to inclusion had been. The visitors, who were hoping to learn more about inclusive schooling, peered into Todd's classroom and watched him working for the better part of a morning. But as the group conferenced in the principal's office later that day, they lamented that "our model" of inclusion simply "would not work" for their teachers and their school. When our principal pushed them to elaborate, they explained, "Well, you are doing a great job here but you have to admit that is easy to include kids like Todd." Curious, the principal pressed on, "Kids like Todd?" One of their group clarified, "You know, kids that are so capable... so easy."

Behavior is often cited as a reason why students with autism *cannot* be included in general education classrooms. Todd's experiences in an inclusive school, however, should cause teachers to question this rationale. If Todd had been seen as "the problem" then teachers would not have created adaptations for him; they would not have given him time to learn about his surroundings; and they would not have adjusted their own expectations or practices. Todd's teachers did not see him as "the problem," though. Instead, they viewed *the situation* as challenging and collaborated with Todd to make the school a familiar and welcoming place to learn.

As I have attempted to convey in this chapter, we will not be able to support students effectively until we begin to treat behavior as something that is interpreted and contextual. Too many students are excluded because they are thought to "own" their behaviors and because these behaviors are assumed to be problematic and unchangeable. Teachers need to question these beliefs and this tradition of exclusion seriously. Although behavior can certainly pose a challenge to individuals with autism, their peers, and their educators, it should not serve as a barrier to inclusive schooling. In fact, inclusive schooling may be exactly what students like Todd need most. The story of Todd teaches us that ultimately, we need to face challenges with ideology and develop ways of supporting students that resonate with the beliefs and values we want to promote in our inclusive classrooms and schools.

For More Answers and Ideas

Johnson, L. (1999). *Two parts textbook, one part love.* New York: Hyperion.

Kohn, A. (1996). *Beyond discipline: From compliance to community.* Alexandria, VA: Association for Supervision and Curriculum Development.

Lehr, D., & Brown, F. (1996). *People with disabilities who challenge the system.* Baltimore: Paul H. Brookes Publishing Co.

Lovett, H. (1985). *Cognitive counseling and persons with special needs.* Westport, CN: Praeger.

Lovett, H. (1995). *Learning to listen: Positive approaches and people with difficult behavior.* Baltimore: Paul H. Brookes Publishing Co.

McGee, J. *Feeling at home is where the heart must be: Home making for children and adults with broken hearts.* (Retrieved 11/17/02 from (http://www.gentleteaching.com/sitenew _book/default.asp).

Nelson, J., Lott, L., & Glenn, H.S. (1993). *Positive discipline in the classroom.* Rocklin, CA: Prima.

Smith Myles, B., & Southwick, J. (1999). *Asperger syndrome and difficult moments.* Shawnee Mission, KS: Autism Asperger Publishing Co.

CHAPTER 10

Inclusive Pedagogy

PLANNING LESSONS
IN THE DIVERSE CLASSROOM

*Before I came to an inclusive school, I never got a chance
to learn in a classroom that taught academics but I was all ready to learn. It
made me feel so sad and angry. (F. Wilson, personal communication, May 2, 2000)*

A colleague of mine, a second-grade teacher, once asked me to observe her class-room. A student with autism, Jalen, had just joined her class and my colleague was concerned about providing an appropriate education for him. I observed her 50-minute lesson on prisms and light. She began the lesson by outlining in-structions for an activity; the students were going to spend the afternoon creat-ing kaleidoscopes and making observations about light and color. The lesson was clearly explained before students were asked to begin their work. She cir-culated around the room as she gave the directions. The teacher provided both verbal and written directions (complete with a few simple diagrams). She set paper, markers, and other supplies out on a table and sent the students up in pairs to retrieve materials. Jalen and his partner, Ty, were sent to the table first. During the activity, the teacher rotated from student to student, answering ques-tions and giving assistance when necessary. Jalen and two other students in the classroom seemed to need a lot of help assembling the small parts of the kalei-doscope so the teacher asked all of the students to work on the assignment with their partners. Each pair had to answer questions about the activity and fill in a worksheet. Because Jalen had a difficult time filling in the worksheet that ac-companied the activity, Ty filled in the answers while Jalen (along with the teacher) asked questions verbally in several different ways to give him an op-portunity to show his understanding of the material.

After the lesson, the teacher asked me what I thought. She was sure that I would be able to tell her some way to enhance her lesson and she was equally sure she had done *something* wrong. With this particular lesson and this partic-ular student, however, I could not think of any way to improve this educator's lesson. Although any teacher can find some way to improve any lesson, I found the kaleidoscope activity to be extremely appropriate and engaging for Jalen,

Ty, and all of the other students in the classroom. The teacher created an active and interesting lesson that incorporated the needs of all students and provided some individualization for Jalen when he needed it. The teacher was using what I am calling *inclusive pedagogy*.

INCLUSIVE PEDAGOGY

Since the inception of inclusive schooling, scholars and practitioners have used many different terms to describe curriculum, instruction, and assessment that meets the needs of diverse learners. Udvari-Solner (1996) proposed a reflective decision-making model for creating curricular adaptations and responding to all students. Tomlinson developed a model of "differentiating instruction" to illustrate ways in which teachers can "shake up" what goes on in the classroom and give students "options for taking in information, making sense of ideas, and expressing what they learn" (1995, p. 3). Oyler (2001) has used the term, "accessible instruction" to describe the use of democratic practices and the development of learning experiences that challenge and support all students. In this book, I use the term *inclusive pedagogy*, which incorporates tenets drawn from all of these models to describe a process of meeting the needs of all learners in diverse classroom.

The first time a general education teacher finds a student with an identified disability on his class list, he or she may feel unprepared to support a learner with such a label. I have often heard teachers say that they are "not trained in special education" and, therefore, cannot be effective with students with disabilities. Although it can be beneficial to know about autism before teaching students with that label, often teachers are effective when they show acceptance, look for strengths in learners, provide personal attention when necessary, and allow for differences in the ways students approach tasks and complete classroom work. That is, teachers are often practicing inclusive pedagogy when they are simply engaged in good teaching.

- When a teacher allows students different ways to express their understanding of a novel (e.g., taking a written test, designing a piece of art related to the book, giving a speech about comparing the novel to other works), she is using inclusive pedagogy.
- When a teacher uses cooperative learning approaches and assigns students' roles that will challenge them as individuals, he is using inclusive pedagogy.
- When a teacher provides students with a range of materials to teach photosynthesis (real plants, plastic models of plants, encyclopedias, interactive software), she is using inclusive pedagogy.
- When a teacher makes informed decisions when grouping students for instruction, he is using inclusive pedagogy.
- When a teacher allows some students to stand or sit on the floor during whole-group instruction, she is using inclusive pedagogy.
- When a teacher gives students opportunities to support and teach each other he is using inclusive pedagogy
- When a teacher shows students how to complete an assignment by demonstrating it and by providing the directions in writing, she is using inclusive pedagogy he is using inclusive pedagogy

- When a teacher designs lessons around the interests and experiences of students he is using inclusive pedagogy

Table 10.1 provides a list of statements applicable and not applicable to inclusive pedagogy.

USING INCLUSIVE PEDAGOGY TO PLAN LESSONS

A step-by-step guide to lesson planning for inclusive classrooms is outlined in this section. Lessons planned using this framework will support the needs of students with and without autism and other disabilities; students with a range of gifts, talents, and interests; and students who are ethnically, linguistically, and culturally diverse.

STEP 1: CHOOSE CONTENT THAT MATTERS

A teacher writes the question "Were the ancient Egyptians black?" on the chalkboard. Students begin a discussion about the question. They wrestle with the relevance of the question and talk about how race is treated, hidden, or highlighted in history. The teacher breaks the students into groups to begin a

Table 10.1.   Defining inclusive pedagogy by what it is and is not

What inclusive pedagogy is	What inclusive pedagogy is not
An approach that benefits all learners including those who are racially, culturally, and linguistically diverse, and those with a range of skills, gifts, strengths, needs, abilities, and disabilities	An approach designed primarily to meet the needs of students with disabilities
Curriculum, instruction, and assessment that is carefully designed to incorporate the needs of all learners *up-front*	Adaptations that are "tacked on" to pre-developed lessons
A reform that intersects with and ideologically fits with dozens of other current reforms and approaches including cooperative learning, authentic assessment, co-teaching, constructivist teaching, project-based instruction, active learning, culturally relevant teaching, community-based instruction, and multicultural education	Another disconnected model/approach for teachers to implement and fit into the school day
Creating diversity in instruction and continuously changing and creating lesson formats, materials, groupings, teaching strategies, and personal support for all learners	Changing pieces of the lesson for one or two students
Something that most teachers are doing already, perhaps without realizing it. Teachers who offer a range of assessment choices, assign diverse roles to students in cooperative groups, or offer enhancement to learners who need extra challenge are using differentiated instruction. For most teachers, using an inclusive pedagogy will simply involve expanding strategies and approaches already used in the classroom	A new and unfamiliar approach to teaching and learning

month-long investigation of the question with different teams taking on different pieces of the research. The students raise questions about Egypt and learn why it was regarded as a great civilization. In doing so, they explore contradictory information and learn that even the experts disagree sometimes in matters of science and history (Ladson-Billings, 1994).

Students in Boston take a ride on the subway (the "T"), construct models and draw pictures of the trip, and discuss and write about the experience (this part of the lesson includes personal stories). Teachers then teach mathematics during the trip by asking students about directionality and distance (e.g., In what direction and how many stops is Park Street Station from Central Square?) (Moses & Cobb, 2001).

When two students find a field contaminated with "ooze" near their school, it leads to an intensive investigation of the health hazards found in their own backyard. Students videotape toxic sites, collect soil samples, and engage in discussions with the Moore Oil Company (the group responsible for the pollution). Eventually, students inspire the company to clean up the mess (Miller & Opland-Dobs, 2001).

What do all of these lessons have in common?

- They engage students in real-world problem solving or connect them to authentic work.
- They ask students to participate actively in their own education.
- They allow students to arrive at answers, gain understanding, and participate in many different ways.
- They are challenging, interesting, meaningful, and relevant to students' lives.
- They are multidimensional.
- They offer opportunities for students to address individual goals.

When planning a lesson or unit for a diverse, inclusive classroom, the first and perhaps the most important aspect is choosing content that is motivating and available to all. Great content is the best tool for keeping students engaged and involved; planning lessons that matter to students often minimizes or eliminates the need for other types of adaptations or special supports.

When I was a student teacher, I supported students in a general education "remedial" math class. When I walked into the classroom, almost every student was slumped in his or her chair; one was sleeping, two students were not working at all, and two others were being "shushed." The teacher sat at her desk and encouraged students to approach her if they had a problem. Although the teacher seemed very caring and seemed to have high expectations for the students, the classroom content did nothing to communicate her belief that they were capable and skilled. Students were completing worksheets related to money skills. High school students were solving problems such as "If you buy a baseball hat and a pair of cowboy boots, how much will you need to spend? How much could you save by buying tennis shoes instead of cowboy boots?"

I couldn't help thinking how differently students might have responded to the same types of math problems had they been in charge of purchasing for the school store or investigating the wages local businesses pay to sub-groups of teenagers (e.g., comparing by gender, race, or ethnicity) or helping a local nonprofit organization analyze the types of donations they received in the past year. This type of content communicates respect for learners. It demonstrates caring through challenge and shows students that teachers expect and trust them to work hard and demonstrate capability. It also shows them that teachers want to learn from them and know their ideas.

Consider Authenticity

Learning about the three branches of government can put some learners to sleep, but learning it as you petition for a new state law can grab the attention of even the most reluctant student. Measuring lines and assessing area can be dull, but measuring materials and assembling tires, boards, and metal bars to create a new playground is very exciting. Likewise, writing an essay per week for the teacher can seem less than inspiring at times, but creating a screenplay for a movie the class will film can be quite interesting.

Students understand from an early age the difference between real work and those tasks that are manufactured. Authentic work is more engaging, interesting, and worthwhile because students who work for a real audience can also get real-world feedback. For instance, a teacher needing some books on tape for his middle school classroom asked a handful of girls to give a dramatic reading of Sandra Cisneros's 1991 novel, *The House on Mango Street*, the story of a young Mexican-American girl growing up in Chicago, into a tape recorder. The students became completely spellbound by the project and learned about issues of culture and identity through their storytelling experiences. Their inventive teacher was so impressed with their reading that he took them to a professional sound studio to record the final version of the audiotapes. The girls were so enthusiastic about their work that they wrote to Cisneros to invite her to the school. The students were both surprised and delighted when Cisneros came to give a special lecture at their school (Michie, 1999).

Certainly there are enough real issues to explore, problems to solve, and tasks to complete to keep all students busy throughout their school careers; teachers need not invent work. Consider the story of Hunter Scott and how his attention to an existing problem stirred the awareness of thousands and brought peace to dozens of brave World War II veterans. In 1996, Scott watched the movie *Jaws* and heard one of the characters talk about how he had survived the sinking of the *USS Indianapolis*. The *Indianapolis* was torpedoed in the South Pacific in 1945, shortly after delivering part of the atomic bomb that would be dropped on Hiroshima.

Scott became curious about the event, and the 11-year-old soon found himself interviewing nearly 150 survivors of the *Indianapolis* and reviewing hundreds of documents related to the incident. As part of his research, Scott surveyed all of the survivors about the court-martial of the captain of the ship. He quickly learned that the survivors did not feel that their captain, Charles B. McVay, should have been court-martialed. After conducting his initial research, Hunter dedicated himself to clearing McVay's name.

What began as Hunter Scott's history project has turned into a national crusade. Since Hunter Scott began his research, he has attended the survivors' reunions in Indianapolis; joined a group of survivors in Hawaii for a short trip on the nuclear submarine the *USS Indianapolis*; traveled—more than once—to

Washington to meet with politicians; and testified in a Senate hearing. As an indirect or direct result of Hunter Scott's work, Congress eventually decided that Captain McVay's record should reflect that he was exonerated for the loss of the *Indianapolis*, representing acknowledgment at last by the federal government that he was not guilty for the tragedy that led to his conviction.

Although most teachers will not be able to facilitate a project as grand as Hunter Scott's, this young man's adventure might inspire teachers to connect learners with problems that matter and people who need them. Authentic problems often inspire students in ways typical class work does not. Even the most "unmotivated" learners often "show up" as competent and complex when teachers invite them to address real issues, contemplate and solve real problems, create real products, or educate a real audience.

Plan with Students

To ensure that curriculum resonates with students, include them formally or informally in the planning process. Even students in preschool and kindergarten can participate in curriculum design by making choices about what they want to learn and bringing questions into the classroom. They may want to further develop their gifts and strengths (e.g., fishing, making tamales, scrapbooking, dancing, writing poetry, drumming). They may want to tackle curriculum that gives them answers or makes them feel useful (e.g., researching neighborhood homeless problems, nutritional value of school lunch, quality child care in the city).

They may want to pursue topics that they view as central to their lives. Students in rural areas might want to investigate new farming technologies; a Native American student may want to study the storytelling traditions of a local tribe; a group of girls in the class may want to examine how gender affects their own educational experiences; and students with autism may want to learn more about their own disability or study human and civil rights issues related to disability.

Many individuals with autism suggest using personal interests or hobbies as a teaching tool (Grandin, 1996; O' Neill, 1999; Shore, 2001). Students with autism may be fascinated by anything from the 50 states (Barron & Barron, 1992) to double garage doors (Hundley, 1971) to music boxes (Robinson, 1999). A student who knows a lot about using tools may insist that some lessons focus on building or creating things. A student who is interested in a certain movie may ask that a lesson be built around the film.

I once worked with a young man who struggled constantly in his English class until his teacher encouraged him to use the class to pursue one of his primary interests: Asperger's syndrome. Inspired, the young man constructed his own web site on his label and diagnosis. He wrote a few essays for his site, and when the class began the poetry unit, he wrote a sonnet about his experiences as a person with Asperger's syndrome.

Teachers of both elementary and high school can plan with students in informal ways by incorporating their interests and concerns into curriculum and instruction. Teachers can also plan with students in more formal ways by working with them to explicitly design units of study. Teachers might share planning by asking students to generate content ideas or to choose ways in which the class will approach topics of study.

Develop a Central Question or Problem

Perhaps the easiest way to differentiate for all learners is to frame lessons and units as questions, issues, or problems (Bigelow, 1994; Onosko & Jorgensen, 1998; Simon, 2002). Lessons posed as problems can accommodate the needs and skills of many learners, and they tend to be more challenging and interesting than those that are structured as topics. Think of the typical fifth-grade unit of study. In one classroom, the teacher introduces the topic of "poetry." In another classroom, the teacher tells students they will be thinking about ways in which poetry has influenced American politics. Which group will be more motivated and, perhaps, more likely to engage in higher order thinking? Onosko and Jorgensen pointed out that using problems, questions, or critical issues as the base of a lesson or unit helps the teacher to narrow the topic and reduce the likelihood of "fragmented and superficial treatment of subject matter" (1998, p. 76).

Simon (2002) suggested that good central questions address an essential element of the subject matter, are provocative to students, and can be addressed over time and explored and re-explored as students continue to learn. Therefore, "What are the unsolved mysteries of the oceans?" is a better question than "What type of life can be found in the ocean?" and "Is a democracy always democratic?" is a better question than "What elements make up a democracy?" The two former questions are clearly more interesting and open-ended. Furthermore, students with a range of skills, abilities, and needs can answer both of these questions in a multitude of ways.

One high school teacher shared how she came to view the use of a central problem as a way of differentiating instruction in her classroom:

I was very nervous at first about having all students, students with severe disabilities and all students really—they're all different, in my room. How could I pick material that they all could understand and connect with? I've found out that creating questions that all students can answer is the key. When I did a unit on slavery and the Civil War, we used the question, "Can you be free if you aren't treated equally?" Some students in my class could answer that question using information from their Civil War reading and by thinking about the progress of civil rights in the United States. One or two students in my class had to approach this question first from their own personal perspectives. Amro knew that he was treated differently from his brothers because of his disability, and he has a strong opinion about that. If we start with his personal experience, it's a little bit easier for him to make a connection with the Civil War. (Onosko & Jorgensen, 1998, pp. 77–78)

STEP 2: USE FLEXIBLE GROUPINGS

Throughout the unit, a wide range of groupings should be used. Groupings should change throughout the day and year so that students have opportunities to work with all classmates and learn from all peers regularly (Ferguson et al., 2001; Kasa-Hendrickson, 2002; Oyler, 2001). Flexible grouping means that at different times and for different lessons, students might be grouped or paired based on goals, interests, needs, or skills. During some lessons the teacher may group students with *similar* goals, interests, needs, or skills. During other lessons, the teacher may group students with *different* goals, interests, needs, or skills in order to give students a chance to share and teach each other.

One of the most important reasons to shuffle groupings is to give all learners opportunities to learn from all of their peers. In Kasa-Hendrickson's study of students with autism in inclusive classrooms, she found that the teachers mixed up groups, in part, to "work against the static labels that often came when groups were created according to perceived ability" (2002, p. 121). Consider the perspective of a teacher who does not believe ability labels are productive:

We always change the groups so no kid is stigmatized as being in the low group. Because I don't believe that any kid is low, medium, and high. Kids aren't that simple; you know they all have things they are great at and things to work on. We just group them to work on certain skills at the learning clubs, they're very diverse. There's no, "You're smarter than I am." It helps to not build that. (p. 121)

Students might work in pairs, in small groups of three or four, or in larger teams of five or six. Students with autism will profit from working with a range of peers, but for new tasks and experiences some will feel most comfortable with a trusted friend or classmate.

Some teachers allow learners to choose partners or team members. Although this practice gives students opportunities to work with familiar peers, it can also cause isolation and frustration in the classroom for those students who are not asked to be a partner or team member. Furthermore, students who choose partners and team members for every activity may constantly select from the same peer group. When this happens, students fail to become acquainted with and learn from all class members, and the community of the classroom is threatened.

One way to honor student preferences while engineering groupings that benefit all learners is to ask students to give input on group formation. Teachers might ask students to provide this information informally through a short interview or by listing a few names on a sheet of paper. Or students might be asked to fill out a worksheet that provides more detailed information about grouping preferences. Of course, this tool should be used to give students opportunities to learn about their learning, so instead of asking students to name those that they want in their group, ask them to list "a few students with whom you feel you can do your *best* work." Even if the teacher does not ask every student for input in forming the groups, the learner with autism should be given this opportunity as unexpected changes or unfamiliar situations can cause undue—and in some cases—extreme—stress and frustration.

Finally, the teacher should always let the student with autism know in advance when groups will be changing. If the student will be working in different groups throughout the day, he or she might be given a schedule with this information included. One of my former students needed not only a schedule of which groups she would work with and when but also photographs of each group so she could study the images and prepare herself to be with each different team.

STEP 3: USE A WIDE RANGE OF MATERIALS

One of my colleagues teaches longitude and latitude by slicing up an orange in front of her students (sections are longitude, slices show latitude). A high school science teacher tosses a rubber chicken around his classroom to keep students interested and alert. Students in a middle school math class read newspapers to learn about the stock market.

Using a range of materials can sometimes make the difference between students merely being present and students actually participating (Onosko & Jorgensen, 1998; Udvari-Solner, 1996). Students who are studying United States geography and culture might be introduced to maps, globes, brochures from different state landmarks, tour books, and travel literature. This wide range of materials is important because it offers every student a chance to be successful and learn in a way that best suits him or her. One student may be unable to effectively interact with an atlas or globe, but may be able to learn concepts easily by creating and studying a salt and flour map of the continents.

Some students with autism find that traditional teaching materials are not appealing or easy to use. For instance, many students with autism find writing with pencils and pens difficult and prefer to use a typewriter or computer instead. Likewise, a student I know has a hard time manipulating books (i.e., turning pages) so his teacher adapted his reading material by copying the text and placing as much of it as possible on small laminated poster boards. She also purchased several different poetry posters for the classroom so her student could read the text that was on the walls. (See Table 10.2.)

STEP 4: MIX UP LESSON FORMATS

Sometimes I hear teachers say that they do not have time for "bells and whistles" in the classroom. Some tell me that they cannot fit simulations, role plays,

Table 10.2. Materials and ideas for working with students with autism

In addition to using	Try
Books	Adapted books (laminating favorite pages for easy gripping, rewriting text to make vocabulary more or less complex, replacing illustrations with personal photos), other reading materials (magazines, pamphlets, technical manuals, comic books, advertisements, flipbooks), electronic books/computer, audio books, posters, movies, filmstrips
Pencils/pens	Computer (word processing programs), communication devices, typewriters, rubber stamps (pictures, letters, or words), magnetic letters or words, pencil grips, letter guide
Calculators	Adapted calculators (large buttons, large display), adding machine, keyboard/computer, manipulatives (unifex cubes, seeds, pick-up sticks, number tiles), number line/ruler, abacus, multiplication table, money, dominoes, number cubes, math games, flash cards
Paint/crayons	Colored pencils, paint pens, drawing/painting software programs, "sensory" art supplies (shaving cream, pudding), markers, stickers, charcoal, tools for printmaking (potatoes, blocks)
Papers/worksheets	Adapted worksheets (important information highlighted or written in bold letters), laminated sheets and grease pencil, mini chalkboard or wipe board, overhead projector, colored overlays

skits, group work, debates, cooperative learning, project-based instruction, games, drama, workshops, station teaching, centers, or labs into the school day. In reality, teachers cannot afford to *not* use a range of formats across subject areas and throughout the day. Students with and without disabilities will be more engaged, retain more, learn in a deeper way, and use higher-order thinking skills when they can learn in a variety of ways (Patterson, 1997; Silberman, 1996). According to Holt (1967b), learning is enhanced when students can state information in their own words, make use of it in various ways, and recognize it in various guises and circumstances. Furthermore, using different types of lesson formats, like using different materials, allows every student in the classroom to learn in a way that best suits him or her.

When teachers use a wide variety of formats and decrease their reliance on whole-class discussions and lecture formats, many students, but perhaps especially those with autism, will benefit. Many students with autism report that they need "hands-on" opportunities to learn. Temple Grandin (1995), a woman with autism who eventually earned a doctorate in animal science, recalled that she learned most when teachers allowed her to actively participate in her own learning:

I vividly remember learning about the solar system by drawing it on the bulletin board and taking field trips to the science museum. Going to the science museum and doing experiments in my third- and fourth-grade classrooms made science real to me. The concept of barometric pressure was easy to understand after we made barometers out of milk bottles, rubber sheeting, and drinking straws. (p. 97)

Udvari-Solner (1996) defined *lesson format* as the "infrastructure of architecture upon which the learning experience is built." She explained that "the organizational framework, methods to impart information to the students, and ways in which students interact with that information are all elements of lesson format" (p. 248). In this section, I outline several lesson formats that can be used to meet the needs and bring out the talents of every learner in the inclusive classroom.

Cooperative Learning

With cooperative learning, students interact with each other and work together to achieve optimal learning. Typically, this work is done in small groups, with students sharing information, working toward common goals, and individually participating for the good of the team, product, or learning outcome (Kagan, 1992; Putnam, 1997).

Cooperative learning is advocated by those invested in inclusive schooling due to the demands of cooperative structures. These demands include sharing, learning about differences, working together, and achieving common goals. Cooperative learning also provides opportunities for students to work outside of the "rows and columns," listening-and-taking-notes formation of traditional classrooms. It, therefore, addresses a broader range of learning styles and individual performance characteristics of students. Cooperative learning also gives students the power to organize and operate groups, to give each other feedback, and to collaborate on solutions to problems (Dyson & Grineski, 2001; Putnam, 1997).

Cooperative learning is a powerful teaching and learning tool (Johnson & Johnson, 1989; Sapon-Shevin, 1999; Slavin, 1990), especially for students with autism, because it encourages students to learn new and improve existing social and communication skills. Because many students with autism (and shy students, students using English as a second language, and students with speech and language difficulties) need practice to enhance these types of skills, lessons involving cooperative structures can both challenge students with autism and provide natural opportunities to learn new language, initiate conversations, respond to verbal directions and requests, practice turn taking, and possibly develop social relationships. Specific goals can even be targeted during cooperative learning. For instance, a student learning a new augmentative and alternative communication (AAC) device might practice saying MY TURN or GOOD IDEA during a lesson.

Cooperative learning also seems to benefit students with autism academically. One study conducted in a fourth-grade classroom showed that when students worked in cooperative groups, learners with autism *and* their peers without disabilities demonstrated learning gains (Dugan et al., 1995). Furthermore, the researchers documented that more learning occurred during cooperative groups than during traditional teacher-led, whole-class instruction.

Many teachers realize intuitively that this type of active, student-centered instruction boosts student learning and understanding, but few may realize how helpful this type of interaction can be for learners with autism who may have an increased need to move, manipulate materials, and interact with others in order to learn. Three cooperative learning structures that I have found particularly helpful in inclusive classrooms are outlined in the following sections.

Roundtable Recording   Roundtable recording is a technique used for brainstorming or reviewing. Groups are seated around a table with one pencil and one piece of paper. A question is posed, and students take turns recording answers on the paper as it is passed around the table. The question should be carefully chosen. It should have multiple answers and all students should be capable of answering it in some way.

When time is called, teams count the responses they have written on the paper. The entire class then shares answers. Variations of this technique include asking groups to read and evaluate their lists for the most creative or "on target" responses or asking groups to summarize lists in a few sentences. This technique can also be used during a movie or lecture. As students are watching a documentary on endangered species, a roundtable page entitled, "What I know about endangered species" could be passed from student to student. As they are listening to a lecture on the human body they can record responses to the prompt: One question I still have about the circulatory system is ———."

Roundtable recording is especially effective when a teacher has one or more students who tend to "drift off" during lectures, movies, or whole-class lessons. Gunilla Gerland, a woman with autism, reported that she often needs to doodle or write something in order to maintain attention to a lesson:

At [my] junior high school the teacher had let me sit and draw on rough paper during lesson and this had helped me stop sinking in to myself. With paper and pen, I could keep my nervous system awake. I didn't know that advantages of this kind were suddenly to be withdrawn, and that now that we had a new teacher...all special treatment had come to an end. I had to understand that it was not permitted to sit drawing during lesson times.

But as the teacher was talking, a monotonous heaving ocean would well up in my ears, a sea with surging waves of rustling and coughing. It would make me slowly sink into myself and stay there. (1996, p. 122)

Roundtable recording is one way to give students teacher-sanctioned opportunities to move and interact during even the most traditional of classroom situations (e.g., listening to a lecture, watching a movie).

Adaptations that can be made to roundtable recording include

- Allowing a student who cannot write or talk, to point to an existing response with which he agrees. A tally mark can then be placed by that response.
- Giving students stickers containing two or three possible responses to question; when they get the page, they are responsible for attaching one of the stickers to the roundtable paper to answer the questions.
- Giving students the option of either adding graphics *or* writing a phrase.
- Having students work in pairs to produce a single response.

Numbered Heads Together   In the strategy Numbered Heads Together (Kagan, 1992), students are arranged in teams of three or four, and each individual is assigned a number (e.g., Dave is a 1, Greg is a 2, Ashanti is a 3, Allison is a 4). Groups are assigned a question to answer, an idea to brainstorm, or a task to complete. For example, a teacher might ask students to name everything they know about the Mexican government or to generate a list of simple machines. Everyone is encouraged to participate and contribute, and groups are given a set time to answer the question and *to make sure that everyone in the group* can answer the question. Therefore, Dave is not only responsible for providing an answer to the question, but he also needs to make sure that Greg, Ashanti, and Allison can answer the question because one group member will be randomly called on later to answer for the group. Depending on the task, students are given a few minutes or even an entire class period to work.

The teacher then poses the question to the group of students represented by a particular number (e.g., "Tell me what you already know about Mexican government. I want to hear answers from the 4s in each group"). The student with that particular number in each group is responsible for reporting to peers and the teacher.

When teachers use a structure like Numbered Heads Together, all students have an opportunity to participate and students get input and ideas from several classmates, not just one or two. Contrast this structure with a traditional whole-class lesson in which only one person at a time may talk and students need to "wait their turn" to share. During this wait time, many students become bored and restless. Often, students mentally "check out" of the lesson at this point.

This structure also gives students opportunities to support each other. If a student is struggling to understand a concept, listening to his or her peers explain it in several different ways can boost understanding. Students can also receive social support when they engage in this structure. Students can ask and answer one another's questions related to content or the lesson structure. For instance, Luke Jackson, a young man with Asperger's syndrome, reported that he is often confused when engaged in individual work at his desk:

Everything is so busy at school and everyone else, all the kids and all the teachers, seems to have a purpose and I never have quite fathomed out what that purpose is. I know we are there to learn, but there seems to be so much more going on than that. It is like beginning a game without knowing any of the rules or passwords. (2002, p. 114)

Allowing learners to work together in structures such as Numbered Heads Together can help students like Luke Jackson learn the "rules and passwords" of each lesson.

Adaptations that can be made to Numbered Heads Together include

- Asking all students who are called on to give an answer without using words; students can use sign language or gestures or they can act out an answer.
- Calling on two students to answer together ("I want 2s and 4s to collaboratively give a response").
- Having students write a collective response or responses on paper and give it to the student whose number has been called to hold up or hand to the teacher.

Jigsaw   To begin Jigsaw (Aronson & Patnoe, 1997; Hertz-Lazarowitz, Kagan, Sharan, Slavin, & Webb, 1985) students in small base groups are assigned material or a multifaceted problem. Each member of the group selects or is assigned some piece of the material or aspect of the problem on which to focus. So in a classroom in which students are studying the 20th century in America, one base group of five students might split responsibilities this way: Tom is responsible for learning about transportation advances; Mike wants to learn about wars and conflict; Evie opts to study human and civil rights issues; Scott chooses politics and leaders; and Lisa examines entertainment and leisure (Barb Saxon-Schaffer, personal communication, June 2, 1995). In all of the other base groups in the classroom, students will split responsibilities in the same way. That is, every group of five would have one student responsible for transportation, one responsible for wars and conflict, one responsible for human and civil rights, one responsible for politics and leaders, and one responsible for entertainment and leisure.

At this point, every student is responsible for learning enough about his or her topic to be able to teach that content to the rest of the base group. Students do not need to do this work alone, however. Students engage in research with their expert groups. The expert group consists of a team of students who have the identical assignment. For example, all students assigned to transportation advances meet, engage in research, gather information, become experts on the topic, and rehearse their presentations together. This expert group is particularly useful for students who have problems gathering or organizing information on their own.

When students in the expert groups feel that they have thoroughly learned their portion of the material, they plan a few strategies and perhaps even create materials for teaching it to their original base group. Students then regroup into their original base groups and each student teaches his or her material to the others. In this way, all students in the classroom learn all of the material.

Adaptations that can be made to Jigsaw include the following:

- Having students break out into expert groups with a partner. Be sure to adjust the number of expert groups accordingly.
- Instead of having students create their own materials, giving all or some students the materials necessary to present their ideas to the base group.
- Encouraging students to present their learnings in a variety of ways. Talking isn't the only way to teach; students might be encouraged to use role plays, drawings, or gestures to teach their part of the content.

Games

Using games is another way teachers can involve all learners, teach new skills, and give students opportunities to participate in a variety of ways. Games tend to be fun and nonthreatening. When teachers use games, they provide students with "opportunities to treat each other in prosocial, desirable ways"; to learn to touch each other nicely, say nice things to each other, or work actively to include each other (Sapon-Shevin, 1999, p. 27).

Although teachers in the elementary classroom often use games to interest students, educators in the secondary school often abandon these approaches in place of more didactic and traditional strategies. Secondary teachers may be apprehensive about using games because they believe that this type of activity will squander important classroom time and diminish curriculum and instruction. In contrast, the creative and effective use of games can boost the participation and interest of students, help teachers make curriculum relevant and more comprehensible, and make abstract concepts concrete. All of the games outlined here are appropriate for students of any age.

Walk It to Know It   Walk It to Know It is a useful tool for enhancing understanding for learners who are visual and kinesthetic. To prepare for this game, teachers or students design flow charts on paper and then transfer each square to a separate piece of poster board or butcher paper. Then the squares are laid out on the classroom floor and all students walk through the sequence. Teachers might have students explain each step as they walk over it or simply have them read the information on the board or paper aloud. Students might trod over the charts one time or move through them several times over the period of a week or month. Teachers might make charts to teach any number of concepts including the scientific method, steps to solving a binomial equation, or the parts of a business plan. Students can also walk through a timeline or a sequence of events chain (see Figure 10.1 for an example).

Students tend to enjoy Walk It to Know It because it gives them a welcome opportunity to get out of their seats. A lack of movement during the school day can cause some learners to be restless or anxious. It can also be detrimental to learning. Patterson (1997) pointed out that many kinesthetic activities allow

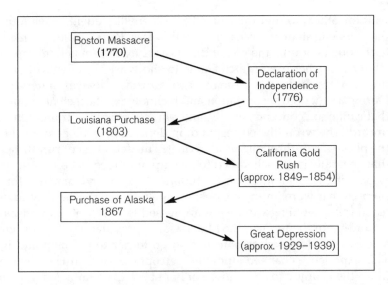

Figure 10.1. Walk It to Know It: Some major events in U.S. history.

students to see a more complete picture of the subject matter and free them from learning inhibitions. These activities also often produce long-term rather than short-term recall (Patterson, 1997). Students with autism who need a lot of movement, especially those who need occasional "walking breaks," may be especially attracted to this game.

In my own college classroom I have used this game to teach students the steps of the special education referral process; its effectiveness always amazes me. Students tend to remember the process weeks and months after they have "walked it."

Adaptations to Walk It to Know It include

- Asking students to chant the words on each square as they step on them. This will help some learners retain the information more effectively.
- Letting students hop or skip through the sequence. Adding this extra bit of movement can give some students an opportunity to release energy in a constructive way.

Match Game The Match Game allows students to teach material to each other. To play the match game, the teacher distributes a card to every student in the class. The teacher needs two groups of cards (A and B); each card in one group (A) must have a matching card in the other group (B). For instance, the teacher might create one group of questions (A) and one group of answers (B); one group of words (A) and one group of definitions (B); and one group of incomplete sentences (A) and one group of words that complete the sentences (B).

Every student is given one index card and told to walk around the room, talking to other students and comparing cards. Students are directed to help each other find their matches. Once students have found the card and the individual who matches their card, they should sit down next to that person and wait for others to find their matches. When all students have found matches, the pairs will share their match with the class. Pairs can simply read their cards to the others or quiz the rest of the class using the "match information."

One teacher used Match Game to showcase the talents of one of her students, Marn, a young woman with autism who was interested in trains. During a unit on transportation and technology, Marn created one set of cards that contained concepts, words, and phrases related to trains. On the other set of cards she wrote the corresponding definitions. One card, for instance, had the phrase "run-through" written on it. The definition of run-through, "a train that generally is not scheduled to pick up or reduce (set out) railcars en route," was written on another card. Students had to find matches for terms and phrases that were, in most cases, completely new to them. Students had fun leaning the new lingo and were impressed with Marn's expertise in this area. According to the teacher, the Match Game provided the first opportunity that students in Marn's classroom had to go to her to get help and information. This experience changed students' perceptions of their classmate and it gave Marn the courage to share more of her specialized knowledge with others. In addition, all students became interested in the Match Game activity and were anxious to take a turn designing their own set of cards for the group.

Adaptations to Match Game include

- Having some students participate in creating the cards; this will be especially rewarding for a student who has particular expertise on a subject
- Encouraging students to support each other during the game; remind them that they can help classmates find matches
- Adding pictures or icons to the cards if some students learn better this way

The Company You Keep   The Company You Keep, a face-paced and entertaining game created by Mel Silberman (1996), is appropriate as an icebreaker, an introduction to new material, or a review. To prepare for this game, the teacher makes a list of categories helpful for teaching or reviewing certain content. Each category should include at least two "sides," opinions, or items so that in choosing to affiliate themselves with certain choices, students can form themselves in subgroups. Content areas and categories might include

- Social studies: Agree or disagree with capital punishment
- Math: Do or do not understand how to measure angles
- English: Favorite character from Alice Walker's 1982 novel, *The Color Purple*
- Geography: Spanish-speaking nation you would most like to visit
- Science: Chemistry experiment from which you have learned the most

The teacher clears some space in the classroom or moves students to a hallway. Then the teacher or a student leader calls out a category and students mill around the classroom looking for others in their same category. Therefore, in the first example, students who agree with capital punishment would cluster together and those who disagree would do the same. If the prompt contains multiple responses, the teacher should tell students to cluster together with their small group and make sure they move away from other groups so all discrete groups can be identified.

When students have formed their groups, instruct them to shake hands with the "company they keep." Then do some debriefing with the class. Students can be asked to teach each other about the category they chose, to defend their choice, or to explain why they chose what they did. For example, if students were asked to choose their favorite character from a book, call upon them to defend their choice and ask students in other groups to interrogate this choice and ask clarifying questions. This discussion among participants can last for as much as 30 minutes if used to teach a lesson, or during the last 5 minutes of a class period as a recap.

The Company You Keep activity is ideal for the diverse classroom in that it offers movement and action for students who need to get out of their desks. It gives quiet students structured opportunities to interact and social students time to talk with their classmates. New social skills can be taught during this activity. Students with autism might be able to practice shaking hands and greeting people or asking or answering verbal questions.

Adaptations to The Company You Keep include

- Giving students different roles during the activity; some might lead the activity while others walk around facilitating the forming of groups.
- Writing the prompts on the board or overhead so that students can hear and see choices.
- Asking students to sit down together or to link arms once groups have formed, so all students can clearly see where the different groups are. Groups might even be asked to hold up a sign indicating the name of their group.

What Is It?   The What Is It? game is perfect for injecting laughter into a lesson and for encouraging students to take small risks in front of the group. This game begins with the teacher placing an object in front of the room, asking the group, "What is it?" He or she then encourages students to come forward and transform the object into something related to class content. One student can approach at a time and act out a short scene. He or she can tell the others what they are doing and how they are using the object or students can yell out guesses. For example, a high school history teacher might present a roll of paper towels to the class. One student might unroll part of it and pretend to read the constitution, while another puts it on her head to transform it into Abe Lincoln's tall, black stovepipe hat. The only rule is that students must wait for one student to set the object down before standing up to take a turn. You can have students get up to participate on their own; you can have them raise hands to take turns; or you can have learners pass the object to each other randomly, giving individuals an opportunity to pass if they do not have an idea.

To follow up on the content, teachers might give additional information about the scenes performed or they might ask students to identify problems with the scenes. The teacher might also use the opportunity to make additional points about content. For instance, a history teacher might follow the humorous portrayal of Lincoln with a summary of some of the former president's political beliefs.

Students with a flair for the dramatic will really enjoy What Is It? Many students with autism do enjoy performing (Fling, 2000), especially if their favorite movies or books can be integrated into the skit. This activity can also be helpful for students with autism who need help understanding different types of humor, especially if the teacher or a peer takes a moment after each transformation to explain "what is funny" about each of the transformations.

Adaptations to What Is It? include

- Giving some students time to rehearse their "transformations"
- Inviting students to come to act out their scenes in pairs or in small groups
- Showing the object and having students brainstorm ideas for transforming the object with a partner

Human Treasure Hunt   Many camp counselors, Girl Scout leaders, and church group organizers have used the Human Treasure Hunt activity to break the ice at a meeting or social gathering. It is a game that helps teachers build community and involves all students in teaching and learning.

The Human Treasure Hunt game requires every student to gather information by talking to and interacting with several different members of the classroom. Each student receives a worksheet with a list of prompts (e.g., "Find a person who knows how to multiply binomials and ask him or her to demonstrate this skill for you"). The objective is for students to find an answer to every prompt on their treasure hunt form (see Figure 10.2 for a sample Human Treasure Hunt). Those who finish early should circulate and offer support to those who are still working or go back to their desks and design new prompts to be answered.

There are only two rules for the treasure hunt game: 1) Teachers can only get one answer from each student in the classroom; and 2) If a student gets an answer from another student, he or she needs to give an answer to that other student. Teachers may also want to insist that students answer each question only a certain number of times.

Human Treasure Hunts can include simple (e.g., label, list) and complex (e.g., compare/contrast) questions, personal questions, questions related to content, or questions that are *both* personal and content-related (e.g., 'Find a person who will write you a Haiku about his or her family"). It is fairly easy to create treasure hunts that allow students to discuss curriculum while sharing something about themselves at the same time.

Sapon-Shevin (1999) suggested that teachers include items that many students will find relevant and be able to answer. This activity is a wonderful opportunity to highlight the expertise, specific gifts, or strengths of individual learners. If a student has just moved from Saudi Arabia, the teacher might include an item related to the geography of the Middle East. If a student with autism has a particular interest in *Alice in Wonderland* (Carroll, 1865), the treasure hunt might include an item asking students to act out or draw the mad tea party.

Adaptations to the Human Treasure Hunt include

- Having a few students serve as "hunt helpers"—their job is to walk around and offer assistance to students who are struggling to complete their forms.
- Letting students generate their own items as they wander around the room. If a peer cannot answer a question verbally, his or her classmate should invent a question that can be answered with body language.

Human Treasure Hunt

The goal of this activity is to learn as much as you can from the experts in this classroom. You may only get one answer from each person you approach and that person may only get one answer from you.

1. Find a person who can draw a picture of "a force acting through a distance" (work).

Have this artist sign here _____

2. Find someone who can name a use of radioactivity.

_____

Have this science expert sign here _____

3. Find someone who can explain a type of pulley you use in everyday life.

_____

_____

Have this observant classmate sign here _____

4. Find someone who will act out, explain, or draw the Doppler effect.

Have this creative individual sign here _____

5. Find someone who can name the primary colors of light?

_____

Have this knowledgeable person sign here _____

Figure 10.2.   Human Treasure Hunt: physical science example.

Figure 10.2. *(continued)*

6. Find someone who can create a concept map starting with the word, "matter."

Have the artist sign here _____

7. Find someone who can give you three examples of how he/she is energy conscious.

    •

    •

    •

Have this conscientious individual sign here _____

8. Find someone who can explain the sinking of the Titanic in terms of density.

After the short lesson, have your instructor sign here _____

After you are finished, walk around the room and help your classmates finish their treasure hunts.

Service Learning

Service learning blends meaningful and thoughtfully planned service or volunteer work with critical reflection and opportunities to meet educational goals. Having students pick up trash around the school is not service learning, it is a nice deed. If students study environmental problems and pollution, however, examine the problem locally by talking to people in the neighborhood about the litter and beautification, draft plans to keep the school and surrounding area litter-free, clean up the school and surrounding area, and then reflect on the process and discuss how grass-roots work can affect a community—that *would* be service learning. Service learning is valuable because it allows students to participate in projects with tangible outcomes, make real decisions, speak and be heard, make a difference in the lives of others, and achieve recognition for their accomplishments (Schine & Halsted, 1997).

Martin claimed that students are not acquainted with society because "…it is too easy for schools to instruct children *about* it without ever teaching them to be active and constructive participants in living—let alone how to make the world a better place for themselves and their progeny" (1995, p. 358). Many educators are responding to these claims. In the 1990s, the Detroit school system passed a high school graduation requirement of 200 community service hours and in Maryland, students must volunteer 75 hours between their eighth- and twelfth-grade years in order to get their diplomas (Markus, Howard, & King, 1993).

Yoder, Retish, and Wade (1996) found that students with disabilities who participated in service learning acquired increased self-knowledge and improved communication, problem solving, and social skills. Because students with disabilities, linguistically diverse backgrounds, and "at-risk" labels often receive services within schools and communities (Morris, 1992), some educators are especially interested in introducing service learning to these populations. Some believe these students will thrive given opportunities to *provide* services. Many students who have been singled out in the past because they are perceived as different have low self-esteem and peer status (LaGreca & Stone, 1990). Placing these students in helping or service roles provides them with a valuable opportunity to give back and connect with their community. Table 10.3 provides a list of service learning ideas.

Service projects may also motivate students to learn new skills and become more responsible for their own learning. Krystal (1998/1999) reported on how she saw students develop stronger community ties, enhance feelings of self-worth, and challenge themselves to learn more and do better in order to help others:

> When I accompanied 14-year-old Justin. . .and a group of his fellow students to a nearby public school where they tutored 5th graders in reading, I witnessed the spiritual effects of service learning. Justin, a special education youngster [sic], gawky and uncomfortable with his body, was involved in a Learning Helper Model, in which older youth read to young children. He and his peers had prepared diligently for the week's tutoring lesson because, as his teacher explained, "They don't want the 5th graders to know a word that they don't." With their guided reading books and exercises in hand, Justin and the noisy group of adolescents entered the cafeteria of the public school and metamorphosed into young adults. Suddenly, they became thoughtful and caring, smiling gently as the 5th graders ran into the cafeteria.
>
> Little Colin jumped into Justin's arms, exclaiming, "I couldn't wait to see you!" Another tutor, Shawanna, was having a different experience. "Lucinda isn't here, and this is the only reason I came to school today," she announced, hands on hips, upset that her young tutee was not among the 5th graders. (p. 60)

Krystal (1998/1999) pointed out that these students moved from being "unruly adolescents" to serious, caring, thoughtful young adults by simply being needed, engaging in a meaningful curriculum, and uncovering talents they didn't know they had.

When I was working as a second-grade teacher, I planned several service learning units with my colleagues that successfully met the needs of all of our students—including two learners with the label of autism, Luis and Katie. One such unit we implemented was designed with the needs of all students in mind. We knew that Luis and Katie would need lessons that incorporated movement. We also wanted both students to have a lot of opportunities to interact with peers because both seemed to learn best in social situations. We were also cognizant of the students' individual goals when planning this unit; both students were learning new communication systems and needed opportunities to practice using these systems.

We combined two traditional second-grade units (animals and communities) and designed a new unit titled "How can we support wildlife in our community?" We talked to students about the unit and asked them to think about what we might do to better support wildlife in our community. Together, the group de-

Table 10.3.   Ideas for service learning

Initiate and implement a public service campaign.

Plant trees.

Create a public service announcement and ask radio stations to play it.

Build a playground.

Make improvements to your school (e.g., paint a mural on a wall, repair the playground, plant tulips around the doorways, create a sculpture for the entryway, grow plants to place around the school).

Write stories and read them to others.

Organize a reading fair.

Clean a park.

Teach other students about something (e.g., safety, environment, caring for animals, study skills).

Engineer a tutoring program.

Get involved in an existing community organizations & programs (e.g., soup kitchen, library, museum).

Create art for the airport, a library, a town square, the courthouse, or for a homeless shelter.

Hold a bike safety demonstration and clinic.

Start a club to help other students (e.g., gay/straight alliance, suicide prevention club).

Make a movie or produce a play about an important social issue (e.g., racism, sexual harassment, bullying, the abuse of drugs and alcohol).

Start a recycling program.

Start a partnership between your school and local senior citizens.

Initiate a law.

cided we would build birdhouses and donate them to places in our neighborhood. The birdhouse building was the highlight and culminating activity of the unit. In the weeks leading up to the building, students also had opportunities to

- Create "facts about birds" pamphlets using a new software program; these pamphlets also became a service project and were distributed to libraries and animal supply stores in our area
- Write letters to local businesses asking for materials or funding for bird house building
- Engage in authentic mathematics exercises related to the bird houses (e.g., how many nails would we need, how much would it cost to make each bird feeder)
- Listen to bird calls and create paintings inspired by this music

Students also received a visit from a bird expert from a local specialty shop. She treated the students to a slide show and introduced them to the wildlife that lived in their backyards.

On the building day, we invited parents, teachers (e.g., the art teacher who used her planning hour to work with us) and other community members (e.g., local college students, women from the community senior center) to contribute to the bird feeder project. The response was wonderful. We had so much support that students were able to work in pairs with one adult assisting each pair!

Students needed assistance with tools, but were able to do a lot of the work independently. For many learners, this building experience was their first time using a hammer or screwdriver. They learned new skills and gained confidence, as well.

After the feeders were built and painted, students voted as a class on where we would deliver our gifts. After a long discussion about helping our community and what types of businesses and services exist in our area, students decided to donate the feeders to a father of one of the students in our class who had helped our class get supplies, an area hospital, a senior center, the specialty shop that had helped us learn about birds, a local library, the town's domestic violence center, the YMCA, and a community center. Then my colleagues and I took turns bringing small groups of students into the community to deliver the bird feeders. Students were required to use community maps to find buildings and were asked to give a short dedication speech when presenting the feeders to the organizations.

Both students with autism were able to participate fully in this unit with a few adaptations, including the following:

- Whereas every student with a signed permission slip got to visit at least one community site, Luis and Katie each went on several trips. The outings gave both learners opportunities to practice communication and social skills and to learn new skills related to the community (e.g., using a map, riding the bus).
- For the bird feeder building, Luis and Katie were paired with familiar and trusted peers.
- Katie was allowed to work on a cooperative art project while others did individual pictures of birds. Instead of spending class time listening to the bird calls and developing a picture, Katie drew a small bird (with the help of a friend) and then wandered around the room, handing her picture to classmates and getting them to add something to her collective picture.
- Luis's occupational therapist worked with his group during the building of the bird feeders and showed many students the best (and most comfortable) way to use the screwdriver.
- When students wrote letters to local businesses, Katie worked on the computer with a friend to compose a letter and Luis participated by stamping the school's address on the top left-hand corner of every envelope.

Project-Based Instruction

Project-based instruction is especially appropriate for students with diverse learning profiles because many student needs and learning styles can be addressed; increased opportunities exist for peer support and the development of relationships; students can work in a range of environments including community settings, the school library, and outdoors; students can work at their own pace; and a number of skills and disciplines can be incorporated into any project (Wheelock, 1992; Winebrenner, 1996; Wisconsin School Inclusion Project, 1997).

Projects are an ideal learning activity for those students with autism who need some time alone to work independently and those who thrive when given opportunities to immerse themselves in one topic. Donna Williams (1992), a woman with autism, found that she could be academically successful when a favorite teacher believed in her abilities and let her pursue a topic of special interest in-depth:

> While the other teachers found me a devil, this teacher found me to be bright, amusing, and a pleasure to teach. At the end of the term, I handed her the most important piece of schoolwork any of my high school teachers had received.
>
> The students had all been given a set date and topic on which to write. I had been intrigued by the way black people had been treated in America in the sixties.
>
> I told my teacher that what I wanted to do was a secret, and she agreed to extend my due date as I enthusiastically informed her of the growing length of my project. I had gone through every book I could find on the topic, cutting out pictures and drawing illustrations over my written pages, as I had always done, to capture the feel of what I wanted to write about. The other students had given her projects spanning an average of about three pages in length. I proudly gave her my special project of twenty-six pages, illustrations, and drawings. She gave me an A. (p. 81)

Teachers working in diverse classrooms often turn to project-based instruction in order to provide interesting and appropriate instruction for all and to make sure that students have opportunities to address individual objectives. Any individual student can work on reading and writing and can improve computer, videography, or interviewing skills while tackling challenging content. Students with autism might be able to practice using a new communication device or develop new social skills (e.g., asking for help, giving clear directions) while working on their project. Table 10.4 includes a list of project ideas for individuals, small groups, or the whole class. One inventive teacher allowed her student to do a project on his communication device. He got course credit for studying the different uses of the device and for gaining skills and competencies related to his system.

In managing projects, teachers should set clear timelines and teach students how to chart their own progress, develop progress reports, and produce

Table 10.4. Project ideas for individuals, small groups, or the whole class

Write and produce a movie—whole class or individual projects.

Collect oral histories.

Develop a business plan and/or start a small business.

Design a pamphlet, develop a newspaper or magazine, write a book.

Propose and launch a new school club.

Plan and create a permanent mural or sculpture for the school.

Study a community or school problem and write a proposal with possible solutions.

Design and implement a school or community survey.

Create a mini-museum for your school or neighborhood library.

Develop a manual for your school (e.g., "What every new student should know").

Create a computer program.

Make your own CD complete with songs created by class members.

Create board games related to content, complete with illustrations and rules (e.g., "Fun with Fractions").

a final product or products. Harmin (1995) suggested that teachers steer students away from projects that involve copy work and passive learning and point them toward those activities that will inspire higher order thinking and meaningful engagement. In order to prevent students from engaging in excessive pencil and paper work, teachers could ask them to design a model, compare ideas, or produce a mural (Harmin, 1995). Instead of asking them to do a report on school discipline policies, teachers could ask them to summarize the opinions of two experts, interview four local school administrators, and invent a model policy to present to the school board.

In one middle school classroom, students study pollution through independent projects. The class reviews some readings as a group and engages in a short series of discussions; then students move into small groups and select a specific topic of study (e.g., pollution and politics, asthma and the air, "Cleaning our lake: Corporate responsibility?"). Groups work on these projects daily for 2 weeks. They interview community experts, conduct surveys, read books and articles on their topic, explore Internet sources, and in some cases, visit sites in the community related to their topic (e.g., go to a local lake and take notes on how water pollution has affected the animal life). Students then present findings to each other in an end-of-unit class symposium.

Desktop Teaching

Desktop teaching is another active learning strategy designed to give students the opportunity to act as both teachers and learners (Draper, 1997; Parker, 1990). Desktop teaching involves giving students individual topics and having them prepare mini-lessons based on those topics. Students prepare a short lesson lasting from 5 to 10 minutes based on a topic or objective that is assigned to them or that they have chosen.

The students teach one another in a fair-like atmosphere; approximately ten students have materials set up on their desks for desktop teaching, while the remaining students move from "teacher" to "teacher," participating in the lessons. The students who are teaching rotate with the students who are learning so as to have the opportunity to participate in the lessons prepared by their peers. The students continue rotating around the room until each member of the class has attended the lessons prepared by all of the other members of the class.

Students can include visual aids, hands-on materials, short activities, and examples in their lessons. A student in one classroom taught her classmates about the coordinate grid and graphing lines using an "under the sea" theme. She made a large blue coordinate grid to represent the sea and she had students plot points to represent the fish and lines to represent the seaweed. Another student in the group taught how to graph inequalities and intervals using string and M&Ms (Draper, 1997).

If a student has a special skill, he or she may be able to incorporate it into the presentation. For instance, Richard, a student with autism, was very gifted in mathematics and was especially good at working out his own algorithms. Instead of presenting typical class content at his desktop, Richard asked students to suggest math problems. He then solved each problem while showing his peers at least two different ways to tackle every one.

Community Research Teams

Still another way to challenge all students in inclusive classrooms is to have them work in heterogeneously grouped research teams (Brown et al., 2000; Kluth, 2000; Sharan & Sharan, 1992; Tomlinson, 1999). Instead of using the school library as the primary base of information, students can go "straight to the source" and pursue their questions through interviews, observations, and collection of community artifacts.

Group research offers "something for everybody" in that students have choices in which topics they want to pursue and which group roles they want to adopt. This structure also enhances student collaboration and learning. Sharan and Sharan (1992) found that group research and investigation promotes cooperation and mutual assistance among students with diverse learning profiles. They also found that students engaged in group research demonstrated higher levels of academic achievement than did their peers taught in a more traditional whole-class method.

Because library research requires fairly sophisticated reading and writing skills, some students, including those with disabilities, may not be able to perform the task acceptably. Therefore, many students stand to learn very little, if nothing, from this type of research alone. Investigative research in the community, conversely, allows students to take in information visually, kinesthetically, auditorially, and otherwise experientially. Using the entire community as a resource base gives students with diverse learning profiles opportunities to pursue topics and explore environments in which they are most interested; the range of topics can be as diverse as the students themselves.

This type of research is ideal for groups of students with a range of abilities and interests; every student can easily find his or her niche. One research project alone involves a wide range of skills and competencies, including generating provocative questions; designing plans; securing information about important community environments and activities; making contacts (e.g., calling potential research sites); developing interviewing skills; and learning to use cameras (e.g., video, digital), computers (e.g., word processing, PowerPoint), and slide projectors.

Such opportunities to interact in the community also provide communication and social opportunities for all students. In fact, Miller, Shambaugh, Robinson, and Wimberly (1995) found that students gained confidence in communications skills by interviewing experts and fielding questions from community members. These opportunities may be especially important for students with autism who need practice in these areas (see Chapter 7 for more ideas on enhancing communication skills). Although interacting with peers is a useful way to practice taking turns and making small talk, having an opportunity to interview a local politician or college sports star can provide special motivation to learn new greetings or try a new joke.

An example of a meaningful research project comes from an elementary school in Ferndale, Wisconsin, where students put their investigative skills together to study airplanes. They sought the expertise of many community members including a local flying club, a pilot, and a building supply store. Part of their community-referenced experience allowed them to spend a $500 voucher in the Boeing Company's warehouse. Students built their own replica of an airplane based on their research experience and exhibited their knowledge at the Paine Field Air Fair in Everett, Washington. They also attended the show as exhibitors and shared their knowledge of airplanes, aviation, and related topics with the audience members (Morehouse, 1995). Thus, students not only honed their research skills but also were able to share their work in an authentic way.

Centers/Stations

Using centers or stations (Cook & Friend, 1995) involves setting up different spots in the classroom where students work on various tasks simultaneously. These stations invite flexible groupings because not all students need to go to all stations all the time. This format is appropriate for any class and any age and is ideal for co-teaching (one teacher can support groups, one can assess or work with individual students).

According to Cook and Friend, "In station teaching, teachers divide instructional content into two, three, or more segments and present the content at separate locations within the classroom" (1995, p. 6). By using this model, teachers are able to offer activities that engage all students in challenging content while freeing themselves to pause at different stations to listen and assess learning, provide more information about a topic, prompt a more complex discussion, ask a question, or reinforce information from lecture or readings.

Stations or centers should focus on important learning goals, contain materials that promote individual students' growth toward those goals; use materials and activities addressing a wide range of reading levels, learning profiles, and student interests; provide clear directions (if some students do not read, this will mean including auditory or pictorial instructions); include instructions about what a student should do when he or she completes the work at the center; and include a record-keeping system to monitor what students do at the center.

Stations or centers might be student or teacher led. Students can engage in a number of different activities during centers (e.g., making a project, working on a skill, participating in a mini-lesson with a teacher). For instance, students in a third-grade classroom might rotate systematically to four different centers—each representing one part of the writing process. In a secondary classroom, learners in a math class might rotate through five stations:

- Working with the teacher to learn about probability
- Solving probability problems from the textbook
- Generating a list of real-world applications for probability
- Working on new computer program with a small group
- Completing a review worksheet from the last unit

A teacher could also allow students to move fluidly between stations. In such a classroom, students might be able to work at any of the following activity centers for as much time as they choose:

- Listening to a book on tape
- Writing in a personal journal
- Writing a short play with a collaborative group
- Working with a teacher on a grammar exercise

Center or station teaching is ideal for use in the inclusive classroom because it allows teachers to work with individual students or small groups of learners without having to use a more restrictive "pull-out" model. A special or general education teacher can be teaching new vocabulary to the student with autism while a general educator can be circulating around the room making sure other students are engaged. Or a general educator can work with a student with autism and a peer without identified needs on a collaborative writing project while the special educator works at another center with a small group of students who are editing their work using a computer program. The adults and students in both scenarios are engaged in meaningful ways and all learners are getting what they need.

STEP 5: USE MULTIPLE ASSESSMENTS

Testing Adaptations

Traditionally, student learning has been assessed by a collection of tests and quizzes. Although tests are sometimes appropriate for learning about student progress, it is only one tool among many that should be used to understand the needs, learning, and academic growth of all students.

As Wendy Lawson (1998), a woman with autism spectrum disorder, explained, testing can be a very confusing and stressful experience when the proper supports are not offered. In the following passage she recounts the frustration she felt when directed to take a placement exam for secondary school:

I was accompanied into a small room not far from Sister's office. It had only one desk and one chair in it, plus a loud ticking clock on the wall directly opposite where I sat. I was given a pencil and several sheets of paper and told it was important to my education that I concentrate and work to the best of my ability. Whatever "important to my education" meant, being in that office with those bits of paper did not feel very important to me.

I drew on paper, played "noughts and crosses" and felt very anxious—I had told one of the nurses earlier that I would roll some bandages for her and I felt that really was important. (p. 42)

Not surprisingly, Lawson did not pass the exam. In reflecting on this negative experience, she offered suggestions for how the situation might have been more supportive:

Maybe if the exam had been explained to me and I had been told to read the information sheet accompanying the writing paper, I might have attempted to answer the questions. It would have been very helpful if the exam had been broken down into smaller chunks of information so that I could have worked without being overwhelmed by so many words all lumped together. This did not happen and neither did the "eleven plus" exam for me! (pp. 42–43)

As Lawson illustrated, tests can be real obstacles for students with unique learning profiles. Tests are a reality of schooling today, however, and nearly every teacher gives one at some point during the school year. For this reason, all teachers should have some strategies for adapting tests and creating comfortable testing conditions for all students (see Table 10.5).

In a fifth-grade classroom, the students were learning about United States geography. After studying the content for 3 weeks, students took a unit test, and three students, including one young man with autism, failed. The teacher felt strongly that the students knew more content than they were able to express through the test. She asked the three students to create a test as a group, to study for it, and to set a time to re-take the test. The three boys, eager to be charged with such an important task, worked on the test after school for an entire week. All three passed the new test and were able to give the teacher indirect feedback about what kind of preparation they needed and what types of test items they could best answer. Some of their changes included removing multiple-choice items and replacing them with short essay questions (all of the students claimed the choices overwhelmed and confused them); creating a test in which they were to list any 10 facts about the Western United States (instead of having to answer specific fill-in-the-blank questions about the region) and adding a word bank with pictures that helped them to decipher difficult vocabulary.

Table 10.5. Testing adaptation ideas

Allow students to retake tests.

Provide study guides.

Reduce test size for some students by eliminating items or allowing students to eliminate items.

Read the test to the student.

Prepare the student for the test; tell him or her about the content and the setting and time of the test

Let the student take two similar tests and average the scores or take the best score.

Use the "Who wants to be a millionaire?" strategy. Let some learners use a 50/50 or an "ask the class" option.

Use large print when creating the test or enlarge the original test on the copier.

Give an open book test, allow students to use highlighters and Post-it notes to mark important passages.

Read the directions aloud and make sure every student understands them. Have students repeat the directions to a peer.

Provide examples for every type of item.

Let students write the test items.

Give students the option of bringing a "cheat sheet" to the exam.

Ask students how they want to be tested.

Let students bring aids to the test (e.g., scrap paper, lucky charm).

Tell students they can skip any one item.

Provide breaks during the testing session.

Give students opportunities to ask questions during the test.

Give students opportunities to answer one question on the test orally.

Allow students to answer questions in a variety of ways (e.g., drawing diagrams, short answer).

Create a test with 75 points; students need to complete items that total 50 points.

Have students take cooperative tests with a peer.

Having students help with the creation of tests is just one way to make testing less stressful and difficult for learners in a diverse classroom. Teachers might experiment with a variety of testing adaptations throughout the year while seeking feedback from students about the effectiveness of each.

Testing adaptations need not be reserved for the learner with autism or other disabilities. All students may benefit from expressing knowledge and skills in different ways. For example, a good student who is an anxious test-taker might find that working with a group on a cooperative exam reduces his anxiety, gives him an opportunity to show more of what he knows, and helps him to learn while being assessed.

Authentic Assessments

Even with several good adaptations in place, some students with autism will never be able to demonstrate understanding by taking a pencil and paper test. The most effective way to gather information about what students know and can do is to use a wide range of authentic assessment strategies.

Darling-Hammond suggested that assessments be based on "meaningful performances in real-world contexts," and that these performances should be so "closely entwined as to be often inseparable" from the curriculum itself (1997, p. 115).

This proposal is a far stretch from the teach-test-teach-test model so often used in schools today. Despite the prevalence of the testing culture, however, many teachers are moving toward these more meaningful ways of assessing students. In one middle-school classroom, a teacher who wanted to move to more authentic ways of assessing student learning eliminated her unit test on the important topic of drugs and alcohol. Instead, she had students develop a PowerPoint presentation and create a brochure related to content learned. Students then worked with peers to edit these materials and enhanced content by talking to community professionals (e.g., nurses, doctors, police officers). At the unit's end, students gave their presentation to fellow students in the school and elicited feedback and questions about the content presented and their presentation skills. Table 10.6 includes some examples of authentic classroom assessments.

Authentic assessments offer a fuller picture of student learning in that they are linked directly to what students are learning, are continuous and cumulative, occur during real learning experiences, are collaborative, and are easily communicated to all stakeholders (Pike, Compain, & Mumper, 1994; Pike & Salend, 1995; Valencia, 1990). Perhaps most important, authentic assessments are student-centered. That is, students engaged in authentic assessments often evaluate themselves, have choices in how to be evaluated, and participate in designing criteria. A reliable, meaningful, and carefully constructed assessment system can provide all students access to academic opportunities.

Using authentic assessments may be especially crucial when teaching students with autism because of the difficulties some of these individuals experience in reading, writing, or communicating. These difficulties might prevent them from adequately completing a traditional assessment (e.g., worksheet, quiz) and may lead a teacher to believe that these students are less knowledgeable or capable than they are. For instance, one of my former students, Gail,

Table 10.6. Assessments for the inclusive classroom

Portfolios	Essays
Exhibitions	Reflective papers
Written tests	Debates
Presentations	Score sheets
Student-created tests/quizzes/exams	Puzzles and games
Formal papers	Surveys
Self-assessments	Models
Learning logs	Photographic essays
Anecdotal reports	Collages
Observations	Art work
Collaborative exams	Questionnaires
Take-home exams	Interviews
Labs	Focus groups
Journals	Daily work/selected work samples
Miscue analysis/records	Drama/performance

hated to write. When the first-grade teacher asked students to get out their notebooks or workbooks, she visibly cringed and sometimes cried. She seemed especially distressed when it was time for math instruction. She did not or could not complete the easiest math worksheets and she appeared confused when the teacher asked her to write down answers to simple math problems (e.g., "What is 2+2?").When I had my first yearly meeting with the teacher, she reported that she was enjoying having Gail in class, but that her young student "lacked any skill or ability in mathematics."

A different picture of this learner emerged when I visited Gail's home 2 weeks later. When I arrived, Gail's mother asked her to get three coffee cups out of the cupboard and two spoons from the drawer. She then asked Gail to go and play in the basement and "come back upstairs in a half hour." Gail followed these directions with ease and I went back to school with news for the classroom teacher; we would need to assess Gail in context and pay more attention to her actions and the real work she performed in the classroom.

SUMMARY

When I began teaching in a large high school, I felt my job as a special educator was to get lesson plans from general educators and create adaptations that would ensure the participation of students with disabilities in the classroom. Of course, this approach had many flaws. Because I did not work with the teachers very closely, I didn't know the curriculum well enough to make meaningful adaptations. And once lessons were planned it was difficult to make changes to them or to invent creative assignments or strategies that might facilitate the involvement of students with unique learning characteristics.

As teachers move toward using more collaborative teaching models and developing pedagogy that is inclusive and supports and responds to all learners, it is less likely that they will need to engage in impromptu adaptation-creation and lesson planning and more likely that students will be able to gain access to curriculum, instruction, and assessment that is carefully planned and thoughtfully implemented. It is also more likely that students will see each other as learners and that they will view teaching and learning as something that all students experience and need.

A popular teaching mantra in diverse classrooms is "If they can't learn the way we teach them, let's teach them the way they learn." This philosophy is especially important for today's inclusive classrooms. By choosing content that matters, using flexible groupings, offering a wide range of materials, mixing up lesson formats, and designing a variety of assessments, teachers invite all students into learning and give those with and without autism opportunities to be successful in the inclusive classroom.

For More Answers and Ideas

Christensen, L. (2001). *Reading, writing, and rising up: Teaching about social justice and the power of the written word.* Milwaukee, WI: Rethinking Schools.

Ferguson, D., Ralph, G., Meyer, G., Lester, J., Droege, C., Guoôjônsdôttir, H., Sampson, N., & Williams, J. (2001). *Designing personalized learning for every student.* Alexandria, VA: Association for Supervision and Curriculum Development.

Lewis, B. (1995). *The kid's guide to service projects.* Minneapolis, MN: Free Spirit Publishing.

Oakes, J., & Lipton, M. (1998). *Teaching to change the world.* New York: McGraw-Hill.

Putnam, J. (1998). *Cooperative learning and strategies for inclusion: Celebrating diversity in the classroom* (2nd ed.). Baltimore: Paul H. Brookes Publishing Co.

Rethinking Schools. (1994). *Rethinking our classrooms: Teaching for equity and justice* (Vol. 1). Milwaukee, WI: Author.

Rethinking Schools. (2001). *Rethinking our classrooms: Teaching for equity and justice* (Vol. 2). Milwaukee, WI: Author.

Silberman, M. (1996). *Active learning: 101 strategies to teach any subject.* Needham Heights, MA: Allyn & Bacon.

Tomlinson, C. (1999). *The differentiated classroom: Responding to the needs of all learners.* Alexandria, VA: Association for Supervision and Curriculum Development.

Weber, E. (1997). *Roundtable learning: Building understanding through enhanced MI strategies.* Tucson, AZ: Zephyr Press.

CHAPTER 11

Teaching Strategies

IDEAS FOR INSPIRING,
HELPING, AND ENGAGING ALL LEARNERS

WITH CHRISTI KASA-HENDRICKSON

For some people, [school] is like fitting a square peg into a round hole.
For me at the moment, the hole (the school) has changed its shape slightly to accommodate
me and the square peg (me) has tried to soften its edges, so a better description would be a
rounded square trying to fit itself into a circle with sticky-out bits! (Jackson, 2002, p. 134)

In a study conducted by the second author of this chapter, a teacher, Lisa Tyler,
shared the process in which she engaged in order to ensure participation of all
in the classroom:

Here are some questions I ask myself when I am thinking of how all kids can
participate: Is this student able to share his opinions and thoughts about the activity? Can the student ask a question when they need help? Does the student
have peers around to work on the subject with? Is the relationship equal, do the
[students] seek each other out? Is the work area and environment supporting the
students' attention? These are just some but I think there are many more. But this
is what I do. I have to answer these questions because it is not ok for the student
to just sit there. I want the students to participate, to interact with their own
learning. (Kasa-Hendrickson, 2002, p. 57)

Lisa and the other teachers who participated in this study, which focused
on the participation of students with autism in inclusive classrooms, used a
range of strategies to meet the needs of students with and without disabilities.
As Tyler pointed out, they were reflective about their practice and constantly
thought about how students would use the classroom space, communicate and
interact, access curriculum and instruction, and work with each other.

Teachers who participated in the study also shared that they felt comfortable trying different strategies for different students and taking risks with new

strategies when one particular teaching approach or method was not effective. As another teacher in the study commented, "If you get hit with a problem there's always a way to make it work. Nothing is insurmountable...but that's what I love, the problem-solving piece of teaching" (p. 117).

This chapter is divided into three sections. In the first section, we offer strategies that can be used to prepare for the arrival of a student with autism. The second section details strategies that can be used in the general education classroom to benefit all students; and the third includes strategies that individual students with autism may find helpful.

Because teaching is a dynamic process, the strategies that may work for one student may or may not work for another. Having expressed that, it is also true that certain strategies are often successful with some students with autism as well as many students without identified disabilities. Many of these strategies, in fact, are simply suggestions for good teaching that can support students with a range of needs, strengths, and abilities in inclusive classrooms.

GETTING READY FOR INCLUSIVE SCHOOLING: STRATEGIES TO SUPPORT STUDENTS AND TEACHERS

This section offers several suggestions for helping teachers and students prepare for inclusive schooling. These strategies are designed to prepare the learner with autism for a new school or a new schooling experience (e.g., an inclusive classroom) and can be used days or months before the student arrives in the inclusive school or classroom. These strategies can also be used throughout the school year. Although teachers can use these ideas for just one or two students, each is appropriate for use with any or all learners in the inclusive classroom.

Survey Family and Student

Consider the way a teacher might feel after reading this excerpt from a report:

> Michael's behavior has continued to escalate this year and now is directed towards almost everyone...His whole program is in jeopardy. As his aggression has increased less positives can be implemented and there is general frustration about him. Peers avoid him.

Contrast this report with an account of how Michael understood those same behaviors:

> I never got to learn in a classroom that taught academics but I was all ready to learn. The classroom was called self-contained because they wouldn't let us out. It made me feel so sad and angry and I was doing a lot of kicking.

This perspective can be incredibly helpful and can give teachers a point from which to start teaching. When educators have only test scores and clinical reports to inform their teaching, they may be puzzled by how to translate that information into practice. A teacher reading Michael's school record might feel anxious about having him in the classroom. After reading Micahel's own account, however, a teacher would have a more meaningful understanding of the behavior and she might have some ideas on how to support him. She might, for instance, engineer opportunities for him to receive more challenging instruction and talk to him about his frustration and sadness. Personal surveys can help to fill in gaps left by formal school reports.

Before the school year begins or during the first couple of weeks, some teachers ask students and their families to complete a survey. This tool can help the teacher become more personally acquainted with learners and their families. Some teachers may choose to administer different surveys to students and parents, while other teachers may design a survey that families and students complete together. Although a survey would undoubtedly help a teacher learn more about his or her student with autism, many teachers choose to use surveys with every student in the class.

Surveys are a nice way to begin the school year for a student with autism, especially because so many with this label have been diagnosed, assessed, and otherwise evaluated by dozens of professionals during their schooling career. In many cases, teachers who meet a learner with autism for the first time are introduced to him or her through these records. In some cases, these records include descriptions of and data suggesting what students *cannot* do. A survey can give a student and her family an opportunity to provide information about what the student *can* do; it elicits information that is positive and personal and can give the teacher a unique first-hand account of the individual's life.

When considering what to include on a survey, teachers should focus on learning styles, interests, needs, strengths, and even the student's ideas for the classroom. Although questions will vary by age group, possible questions include the following:

- How do you learn best?
- Think about your favorite teacher. What did you like about his or her teaching?
- What do you need in order to be comfortable in my classroom?
- What hobbies do you have?
- What do you want to learn this year?
- What is your favorite part of the school day?
- How can our classroom be more welcoming to you?
- What is your favorite thing to do at school?
- What would be a perfect school day for you?
- What do you like to read?
- What words describe you best?
- Tell me about you as an expert. What kind of knowledge do you have (e.g., skateboarding, karate, babysitting, collecting bugs, meeting people, drawing)?
- What else do you want me to know about you?

If one or more students cannot write, the teacher, parent, or support person can ask these learners to submit graphic or visual surveys. Students might draw pictures, create a collage, or submit photographs, a videotape, or audiotape in response to the survey questions.

Create a Personal Portfolio

Teachers may want to help students who have unique needs and abilities introduce themselves through the use of a portfolio. Portfolios may include photographs, artwork, writing or schoolwork samples, lists of favorite things, or even video or audiotapes. Although using a portfolio is a good idea for a student with autism, it can also be fun for the entire class. In one school, all students created portfolios to share with classmates and school personnel. They used these portfolios to get to know each other better and to educate teachers about their lives outside of school.

A portfolio can be an especially helpful tool for students who do not speak or use a reliable communication system. I worked with one young man, J.D., to assemble a portfolio he would use as he made the transition from middle school to high school. This young man did not speak, and those who met him for the first time often struggled to connect with him. When his teachers first accompanied him to his new school, J.D.'s peers began asking them questions about him: Did he understand them? Did he have any interests? Why did he flap his arms like that? The teachers decided that J.D. needed a way to represent himself so that they didn't need to serve as his voice and liaison. In order to facilitate this process the teachers worked with J.D. to create a portfolio that he could use to introduce himself to new people and to interact with those he already knew. J.D.'s portfolio included

- Four pages of photographs (J.D. with family and friends; J.D. playing soccer at a community park; J.D. working with peers on a biology experiment, vacation photos from the Rock and Roll Museum in Ohio)
- A short "résumé" outlining some of the classes he took in middle school
- A list of his favorite movies and compact discs
- A "Learning About Autism" pamphlet J.D. got at a conference
- A glossy picture of the Green Bay Packers, J.D.'s favorite football team

Although it took a few weeks for J.D. to initiate conversations with the portfolio, he soon became comfortable with approaching his classmates to share the book. Individuals who saw J.D.'s portfolio now had a way to interact with him and learn more about his life. Two of J.D.'s classmates even developed their own portfolios to share with him.

All of J.D's new teachers had opportunities to review his book before he started their classes; this helped the instructors become acquainted with J.D. and to understand something about his needs and strengths. One of J.D.'s teachers even used one of J.D's favorite movies in her English class as a result of reviewing his portfolio, and another teacher helped him to create some watercolor landscape paintings to include in his growing album.

Portfolios can be in paper, audio, or video form; formal or informal; and composed of a few pages or dozens of pages. They can include only current information and artifacts or serve as a cumulative record of the student's life. One student I know keeps his formal portfolio at home and carries a four-page condensed copy with him at all times. Another student, a young woman with Asperger's syndrome, developed a creative videotape portfolio complete with interviews of her sisters reading poetry that she wrote.

Gather Information

Teachers can learn about autism in many different ways. Several autobiographies of people with autism have been published in the last two decades (see the Bibliography). These books, without question, serve as the best soure of information on autism. Several helpful books on inclusive education are also available that can guide teachers as they prepare their classrooms for all students (see For More Answers and Ideas at the end of the chapters).

Teachers might also look for support and information from parent groups, local and national conferences, and other teachers who have successfully educated students with diverse needs and abilities in an inclusive classroom. If a student has previously been educated in a general education class, it might be helpful to talk to the teachers who supported the student in that situation. Teachers who have specific teaching roles might find it helpful to talk to others who share their responsibilities. For instance, a science teacher might find it very helpful to talk to the student's previous science teacher and the student's speech therapist might want to talk to the student's previous therapists.

Observing the student in his or her current classroom setting can also be useful. If the teacher knows that he or she will have a certain student in the classroom for the next school year, he or she should take time to observe that student. In particular, these observations should focus on the student's successes: What can this student do well? Where is she strong? What has worked to create success for the student? The observing teacher might also record questions for the student's current teacher that can be answered in a short meeting or via e-mail.

Making Action Plans Strategy

Making Action Plans (MAPS) is a strategy developed by Marsha Forest, Jack Pearpoint, Judith Snow, Evelyn Lusthaus, and the staff at the Center for Integrated Education in Canada. The key issue addressed throughout the process is this: What does the child and family want? The MAPS process is especially useful for those students who are new to inclusive education (Pearpoint, Forest, & O' Brien, 1996). This is true for many reasons, including MAPS' usefulness in helping teams create effective individualized education programs (IEPs).

MAPS is a collaborative planning process that brings together key individuals in a student's life:

> The student, his or her family and teachers, and other significant persons in the child's life gather to discuss the student and family's personal dreams and goals and to brainstorm ways of making them a reality. In the spirit of cooperation this team creates a plan of action to be implemented in a general education classroom setting. (Pearpoint, Forest, & O'Brien, 1996, p. 68)

MAPS is different from some other assessment or planning tools because the process is centered on the strengths, potential, and uniqueness of the learner, instead of focusing on his or her weaknesses or on what he or she "can't do." MAPS is based on the following core beliefs:

- All students belong in general classrooms—no ifs, ands, or buts.
- General education teachers can teach all students.
- Necessary supports will be provided when necessary.
- Quality education is a right, not a privilege.
- Outcomes must be success, literacy, and graduation for all.
- Creative alternatives will be available for populations who do not succeed in typical ways. (Pearrpoint, Forest, & O'Brien, 1996)

To use the MAPS process, stakeholders in the student's life assemble and generate ideas for including the individual in schooling and in community life. Participants typically include the student, his parents, other family members of the student (e.g., a grandmother, a sister), classroom teachers (both general and special education), an administrator, and other school professionals such as a social worker, a favorite coach, or even a playground assistant. The student's peers are also invited to the meeting and are central to the process.

A MAPS session also requires two facilitators to guide the team through questions and ensure the comfort and participation of all. One facilitator, the process facilitator, should be explaining the collaborative planning process and asking the questions. The other facilitator functions as a recorder; he or she makes a record of the process using colored markers and many sheets of chart paper.

Hospitality is also a part of the MAPS process. The MAPS sessions should take place in a comfortable room. The atmosphere should be personal and informal. To achieve such an atmosphere, the facilitator might put motivational posters on the wall, provide beanbag chairs for the younger participants, tack up favorite photos of the participant, or ask members of the group to bring a treat to share.

To begin the process, the family members answer the question "What is the individual's history and story?" Then, each of the individuals present at the MAPS session will focus on the remaining five questions and the plan that make up the MAPS process. These questions include the following:

- *What are your dreams for* _____? The facilitator should encourage the participants to think big. She might remind them that this is an opportunity to share their wishes without thinking about the constraints of money or time. Participants should share what they truly dream for the student of focus, not what they think they can get or what they think is reasonable.
- *What are your nightmares for* _____? This can be a hard question to ask and an emotional question to answer. This question is used to generate a profile of what to avoid.
- *Who is* _____? Or, *What are some words that describe* _____ *best?*
- *What are* _____*'s gifts, strengths, and talents?* This is usually an enjoyable and easy part of the process. Some team members find they view the student differently after seeing the extensive list of strengths, gifts, and talents forming on the chart paper.
- *What is* _____ *good at doing? What are his or her needs?* The latter part of this question is when the team considers the person's struggles. The team also considers the different types of supports the individual receives or needs. Needs listed can range from concrete resources such as money or a

new augmentative and alternative communication (AAC) device to abstract ideas and wishes such as friendship or happiness.

In order for the meeting to qualify as MAPS, the team must make a decision to meet again and the meeting must end with the formation of a concrete plan of action. Participants should leave the meeting with actual tasks to address immediately. For instance, a parent may need to contact the drama teacher about getting the student involved in the school play. A school principal might work on a student's course schedule, making sure he or she can take classes with some friends. A general educator might go back to her classroom and move the student's desk to the front of the room. A friend might make a date with the student to go shopping for posters of rap stars for his locker.

After the process is over, the MAPS facilitator may also ask participants to think of ways in which the student has been described on other assessments. For instance, when I conducted a MAPS with a young woman named Crystal, she was described by the team as "a good listener," "a true friend," "always ready with a smile," "loves art class," "huge fan of the Beach Boys," "can move her wheelchair by herself," "a big sister," "beautiful hair," "a dancer," and "has trendy clothes." Then the group brainstormed labels she had been given in her records. That list included the following descriptors: "mentally retarded," "physically disabled," "slow," "manipulative," "autistic," and "aggressive." As a group, we then contrasted these two groups of descriptions. Contrasting descriptions can be posted separately, but the facilitators should point out the drastic differences between the two to show that a student's reputation and the "discourse" of special education often overshadows the individual's strengths and uniqueness. Figure 11.1 includes a MAPS form for Crystal.

Study the Worst Possible Day

Although using the MAPS process to construct the student's best possible day can make it happen, studying the worst possible day can be illuminating, as well. Consider Figure 11.2, the scenario constructed by an educational team supporting Meleah, a second grader.

Once the profile of a terrible day for Meleah was complete, the team used the information gleaned on her likes and dislikes to discuss how they could prevent these types of things from happening. Examining her fears and struggles helped the team plan for Meleah; specifically it helped them plan supports, create teaching strategies, and individualize instruction for her. Viewing Meleah's education from such a unique vantage point brought out the creativity in her teachers. At first they surveyed the list and felt they could do little to avoid some of the situations. As Meleah's classroom teacher remarked, "Fire drills are part of being in school! She is going to experience fire drills every year until she graduates. There is nothing we can do about that one." After a few more minutes of conversation, however, the teachers decided they might be able to teach Meleah some coping strategies to deal with the drills. Eventually, they taught her to put her hands on her ears and repeat, "It's almost over, it's almost over." Although this did not take away all of the pain and anxiety she felt during a fire drill, it did seem to give her a sense of power and control and she stopped screaming during the drills. The teachers then continued down the list and came up with these ideas:

What are your dreams for Crystal?

- Traveling to South Padre Island
- Winning the lottery and having all the money she will need
- Falling in love
- Driving a car
- Going to chef school
- Being able to talk

What are your nightmares for Crystal?

- She will never have a boyfriend.
- She won't be able to live in her own house.
- She won't finish high school.

Crystal is . . . (What are some words that describe Crystal best?)

- Jolly
- A sister
- A daughter
- Animal lover

- Animated
- A night owl
- Family-oriented
- Funny
- Shy

What are Crystal's gifts?

- Loving
- Good listener
- Great smile
- Sensitive
- Graceful
- Active and a fast runner

What are some of Crystal's needs?

- Daily quiet time
- Soft clothes
- Access to her baseball cards at all times
- Friends
- Time to read her favorite books

IDEAS FOR A PLAN: What would an ideal day look like for Crystal?

- She would get to watch a few minutes of "CNN" before school.
- She would walk to school with a friend and go to the cafeteria to hang out before classes begin.
- She would go to general education classes with her peers.
- She would get to take two art classes including one course related to sculpture (her friend Robby would be in the class with her).
- She would have lunch with a group of friends and she would get to eat hamburgers at least once a week.
- She would get to take a 10-minute walk with one of these friends before heading back to classes;
- She would get to take a physical education class in the afternoon—preferably with Mr. Dyson, her favorite teacher. She would get to help to manage the equipment during class.
- She would get to see her friend Robby sometime in the afternoon.
- She would get to spend some quiet time in the library reading magazines during the afternoon.
- She would get to have some trail mix as a snack in the afternoon.
- She would stay after school and attend track practice.

Figure 11.1.   A MAPS form for Crystal that her team can use to help her reach her personal dreams and goals.

- Although Meleah will probably always feel a little distressed when Charles is sick, her teachers believed she might feel better if she had more friends in the class. The teachers decided they would need to work harder to facilitate social relationships for Meleah. The art teacher decided she would use more cooperative groupings in her classroom and the music teacher thought she might be able to change Meleah's seat so she could be closer to Jackie, a young woman with whom she seemed to be forming a friendship.

> **The worst-possible day for Meleah:**
>
> The school conducts a fire drill.
>
> Charles (her best friend) is absent.
>
> Ms. Hicks (her teacher) is absent.
>
> The substitute teacher forgets to put the "Our Day" schedule on the chalkboard.
>
> She forgets to bring her favorite handkerchief to school.
>
> Music class is cancelled because we have an assembly.

Figure 11.2. An example of a "worst possible day" for Meleah, a student with autism. Teachers could use this information in planning curriculum and supports for students.

- Teachers also agreed that Meleah would always be a little upset when Ms. Hicks was absent but felt that they might be able to minimize her discomfort by encouraging her to seek help and support from her peers and teaching assistants.
- The teachers knew that Meleah would be distressed about missing the calendar activity because such a situation had already occurred when Ms. Hicks had been absent and the substitute skipped the routine. The teachers felt that the calendar activity was an important organizational tool for all students and they all agreed that they should create a way to conduct the activities every morning—with or without Ms. Hicks. After talking to the students in the class, the teachers, decided that the students would be responsible for the calendar every day. Students rotated responsibilities: Every day one child announced and posted the date, another made an announcement about the phase of the moon, and still another shared an "on this day in history" fun fact. If one of the students assigned to a task was absent, any other student could step in and take his or her place. The teachers not only felt this change in process would benefit Meleah but they also felt that shifting responsibilities to students made the task more authentic and meaningful for all.
- Many students with autism (and many without) have items they carry with them for comfort. I have known students who carry toys, favorite books, lucky string, and bottle caps with them. Meleah had a favorite handkerchief she carried in her pocket daily. Although she didn't often take it out of her pocket, she needed to know it was there. On one occasion, Meleah left her handkerchief on the school bus and was distressed throughout the day. She was unable to engage in her schoolwork and asked several times if she could go home to find a handkerchief. In order to prevent such a crisis from happening again, the teachers decided that they would ask Meleah to bring in a handkerchief that she could keep at school. Meleah got two new handkerchiefs for school, and, inspired by the teachers inventiveness, Meleah's mother created handkerchief seat cushions for the desks of all 20 students in Meleah's class.

After learning about the efforts of Meleah, her family, and her teachers, Meleah's principal offered to work on the scheduling concern on the list. The principal promised to avoid morning assemblies if she could. Although she wasn't able to avoid all morning assemblies during the year, Meleah had to miss music class only one time during the year.

Plan Backward

Planning backward is most useful when working with students who need the most unique supports. Planning backward means looking first at "what works" and building from there, instead of looking at a typical school day and asking "How will he fit in to the day or schedule as it exists?" The process begins with a teacher or teachers brainstorming about all of the student's strengths, preferences, and abilities and generating ways to include the student using these ideas. Teachers beginning the process of planning backward should first ask themselves:

- In what contexts, school situations, or environments is the student successful?
- When does the student perform well?
- What opportunities does the student have to present his or her knowledge or understanding of age-appropriate curricular materials?
- When does the student successfully interact with peers in natural, meaningful, ways?

The following are examples of planning backward.

Andee: An Elementary School Example   I first used the planning backward strategy with Andee. Andee was in first grade when he came to be my student. He had never been in a general education classroom before. The adjustment to a new school seemed challenging for Andee. He didn't seem to feel comfortable sitting in his desk and needed a lot of movement throughout the day. On several occasions, he bolted from his classroom, opened the outside door, ran to the swing set on the playground, and rocked himself back and forth on his favorite swing. Although we attempted to gently introduce him to the other students, the interesting materials his classmates were using, and the exciting games and activities in his classroom, he was not able to remain at his desk or even in the room for more than 8 or 9 minutes at a time. Instead of forcing Andee to sit in his desk and manipulate materials like the other students, we sat down with his daily schedule and considered how we could plan his day in a way that would make him feel secure and help him to learn. Instead of starting with the schedule of the first graders, we started planning with Andee's strengths and preferences in mind. We knew he needed movement and, therefore, was delighted every Monday when his class went to physical education class. We also knew that he loved music and the music teacher and that he had experienced success with her. Clearly, Andee also needed playground time; it seemed that the swing offered him comfort or a "release" and relaxation."

With all of this information in mind, we started planning for Andee. We consulted with the physical education teacher and he agreed that Andee could come to physical education with all three of the first-grade classes. Then we contacted the music teacher and she agreed that Andee could come to music with all of the first-grade classes. Although Andee had to miss some first-grade content in order to attend these extra classes, his team agreed that because Andee was still being included with peers, this adaptation to his schedule was acceptable. He was still receiving instruction appropriate for a first grader and getting more opportunities to practice skills needed in music education. We also agreed that Andee should get some extended recess time, so he was allowed to leave lunch early with a few friends to join the kindergarten classes for their recess. Andee and his friends served as "play leaders" for the younger students, introducing them to new games and helping students play cooperatively with each other.

Although it was our goal to slowly increase the time Andee was in the traditional first-grade schedule, we realized that this would take time and our goal was to find a routine in which Andee would be most successful. The increased movement he experienced in physical education (PE) as well as the extra time in music allowed Andee to develop routine success throughout his school day. As a team we decided that over the course of the school year we would work to make sure Andee spent an increased amount of time in his first-grade class, but that this would be done carefully so that Andee would struggle little and shine often in his new school. Andee no longer needed extra PE and music education by the second semester of school, but giving him opportunities to be comfortable and successful immediately seemed to give him confidence to participate in some activities that were less familiar and more challenging for him.

Preshanth: A High School Example   Preshanth, a bright and curious freshman, loved to learn but had a difficult time with the seatwork and quiet study time that dominated many of the high school classes. His speech was limited, but he could interact with others by using his communication board. Preshanth was able to sit for approximately 10 minutes at a time and needed a lot of engagement to stay connected to a task. He also responded to teachers who treated him with respect; in middle school he had been most successful in classes where the teacher believed he was smart. Preshanth also loved to swim. He felt comfortable in the water and was an accomplished and independent swimmer.

Planning backward for Preshanth involved capitalizing on his strength in swimming. Preshanth's team arranged for him to swim twice a day. His high school had a swimming pool, so this adaptation to the day was fairly easy. The pool was often occupied with PE classes, however, so involving Preshanth in swimming meant getting permission from the PE teacher and arranging a way for Preshanth to participate in the classes. The teacher agreed to give Preshanth room to swim independently while working to incorporate him into classroom drills and activities when possible.

Then, the team examined Preshanth's need for active learning and targeted classes where he could be successful and active. We gave him a list of possible classes and he chose biology, family and consumer education, and English (with a teacher who often asked students to act out stories and plays). Teachers of these classes agreed to let Preshanth stand or pace in the back of the classroom during lectures. They also built errands into their lessons so Preshanth had a constructive and purposeful reason to leave the classroom for a break each day. One day, for example, the biology teacher asked Preshanth and a friend to go outside and get a soil sample. During another lesson, he asked Preshanth and a classmate to go to the office and phone a local fish hatchery to ask a question.

In Preshanth's English class, students were typically given long periods of time to do silent reading and writing. Although we did implement several different adaptations that allowed Preshanth to read and write at his desk, he struggled to participate in this activity for more than 15 minutes. The teacher, using the planning backward strategy, began thinking about Preshanth's strengths and abilities; she considered what he *could* do instead of dwelling on what he couldn't do and decided to offer him the chance to use the classroom computers at any time during the reading and writing time. She found some literacy-based computer programs he could work on during this time and eventually allowed some other students in the classroom to work on literacy-based software programs during the independent reading and writing time.

Give a Preview of the School

Many students with autism will profit from seeing, experiencing, and learning about the school before they show up on the first day. This is an effective strategy for students who are changing schools or for those who will be going to a certain classroom for the first time. A student can preview the school using many different tools. Some learners might appreciate a videotape of the school and its rooms, complete with short interviews with their new teachers (e.g., "Hi, I'm Ms. Thiel and I'm going to be your fifth-grade teacher. This classroom is really sunny but it gets a little warm in here in spring afternoons. In this room, we begin every day by telling jokes"). Other students like to tour the school themselves and meet teachers face to face before school officially starts. Still others may want to hear siblings, parents, or friends tell them about the school. Here are a few other ways students can experience a preview:

- Send them brochures of the school
- Send them school newsletters from the previous year
- Show them the school's website (if one exists)
- Have them construct questions about the school and/or new classes and ask teachers to answer those questions in writing or on audiotape
- Have a pot luck dinner before the school year begins

Some students need more than a video or brochure to introduce them to a new school. One of our former students visited his new school once a week during the summer before his arrival. On every visit, he met a different staff member and saw a different room. By September, when the school year began, he was able to make the transition with ease.

SUPPORTING TEACHING AND LEARNING: STRATEGIES TO USE WITH THE WHOLE CLASS

Many strategies that seem effective for students with autism are also useful to use with all students in the inclusive classroom. In this section, we will highlight several strategies that teachers can use to support students with autism and their peers as they plan lessons and organize instruction.

Use Routines and Schedules

As illustrated earlier in the story of Meleah, many students benefit from the development and implementation of written schedules, picture calendars, or daily planners. As one of our former students with autism explained to us: "School is very stimulating and a lot of noises and disorganization for me. So I need to get used to new places and have a schedule." Teachers should talk often to students with autism about how time will be used in the classroom. They should also try to give them as much warning as possible when they are going to alter the class schedule or when a substitute will be teaching the class.

In fact, all students in a given classroom may benefit from knowing more about the schedule. Having information about what content will be taught and what activities will take place in any given day or week can help any student become a better planner and time manager. Teachers can make going over the daily schedule a regular part of the routine in any classroom; even taking a few seconds to review this information can make a difference in the learning of some students. A high school teacher might keep a "Schedule for the Day" posted on the chalkboard for all students to see. Some students may even want to copy the agenda or schedule into an individual notebook so they can peek at it throughout the day or class period and be reminded of the day's events or the teacher may want to provide the student with a written copy of the schedule at the beginning of the day or week.

Martha Kaufeldt (1999) writes her daily agenda on a tablet of chart paper that she places on a stand. She flips the chart over daily, but the old schedules are handy at any time. This system ensures that students who are absent can independently learn about work they need to start or finish. Kaufeldt pointed out that this system also serves as a planning tool for the teacher. At any time, a teacher can see how much time has been dedicated to certain activities and when projects or units of study were started or finished.

It is sometimes surprising to discover how many students seem to appreciate knowing "what comes next." In our current roles as college professors, we often observe students highlighting their syllabi, carefully crossing off each topic as it is covered in class. We also occasionally have students approaching us at the beginning of a class to ask, "Can you tell me what we will do today?" And we have been asked by at least three different students in different semesters if we could post an agenda every day before class. Although some students may want to know what activities and transitions are happening at what specific times, others may be satisfied with even a simple description of events, such as the example given in Figure 11.3.

Whenever possible, students can be responsible for creating the schedule or presenting it to the class. The teacher might use this opportunity to teach all students about the different types of planning tools people use. Students can be introduced to linear agendas with hour-by-hour information and/or picture/word schedules. When students are more actively involved in the schedule activities, the schedule itself becomes a literacy activity. Students can enhance reading, writing, speaking, and listening skills while learning how to plan time and follow an agenda. A teacher might even ask individual students to come up and cross the items off the list as they are accomplished.

```
┌─────────────────────────────────────────────┐
│                                               │
│   Class agenda for _____           │
│                                               │
│   1. Collect homework                         │
│   2. Notebook exercises                       │
│   3. Class discussion on Napoleon             │
│   4. Cooperative group presentations          │
│                                               │
└─────────────────────────────────────────────┘
```

Figure 11.3.   An example of a class agenda.

Younger learners may want to keep a Velcro schedule at their desk. Students or teachers can draw pictures and write phrases (e.g., lunch, math class, recess) on small squares of paper to represent the day's schedule. Then small pieces of Velcro can be placed on the back of each square and the student can move the events as things are completed. This type of schedule can also be posted at the front of the room; the student with autism or any other student can be responsible for adjusting the squares as the day passes.

Support Transitions

Students with autism struggle with transitions. Some students are uncomfortable changing from environment to environment, whereas others have problems moving from activity to activity. Individuals with autism report that changes can be extremely difficult, causing stress and feelings of disorientation. Teachers can minimize the discomfort students may feel when making transitions by

- Giving first 5- and then 1-minute reminders to the whole class before any transition
- Providing the student or entire class with a transitional activity such as writing in a homework notebook or, for younger students, singing a short song about cleaning up
- Using a timer to show students how much time they have until the next activity
- Asking peers to help in supporting transition time. In elementary classrooms, teachers can ask all students to move from place to place with a partner. In middle and high school classrooms, students with autism might choose a peer to walk with during passing time
- Creating transition rituals (e.g., always begin English class with a poem, always end the day by having students write in journals)
- Giving the student a transition aid. Some students need to carry a toy, object, picture, or other aid to facilitate their movement from one place to the next. One student we know carries a rabbit's foot from class to class. He leaves it at the door and picks it up again when he needs to move to a new room. Some students need an object that helps them specifically focus on the next environment or activity. A student might, for instance, carry a tennis ball when he goes to the playground.

Using simple strategies can limit challenges during transitions throughout the school day. Helping students—those with and without identified disabilities—to recognize a change in events may result in them feeling more relaxed and comfortable. In addition, cueing students to a shift in activities can help classroom management; when students know it is almost time to leave the room or switch classes, they may find more time to clean their work space, organize materials, and otherwise prepare to finish their work.

Help Students Improve Organization Skills

Although some students with autism are ultra-organized, others need support to find materials, keep their locker and desk areas neat, and remember to bring their assignments home at the end of the day. Wendy Lawson, a woman with the autism spectrum label, remembered her schooling experience as a mess of papers, schedules, and expectations:

Secondary school posed many problems for me...I would get class timetables and rooms muddled and was often unprepared for lessons. Homework was usually forgotten or badly done. School was a confusing place to be and I dreaded having to go. (1998, p. 55)

For students who need help with organization, the most simple and natural ways to provide support should be used. A teacher might attach a small "going home" checklist to the inside of a student's locker or suggest that she keep a pencil in every classroom instead of having to carry one around all day. Teachers can also

- Ask all students to do 5-minute clean-up and organization sessions throughout the week.
- As a class, have students copy down assignments, pack book bags, put materials away, and clean work spaces. Specific skills can even be taught during this time (e.g., creating to-do lists, setting priorities for tasks). All students of all ages can profit from this strategy.
- Use the IRS method of organization (Goodman, 1995). The flap on tax envelopes prompts the taxpayer to review materials and reminds them of certain elements of their forms that should be double-checked (e.g., Did you sign your name? Did you include a copy of your state and federal taxes?). This type of checklist can be placed near a classroom assignment "in box" (e.g., Is your name on the paper? Did you check your work?) or on the door for all to read (e.g., Do you have a pencil? Notebook? Homework?).

Students with autism who depend on order and seem to have no problems keeping materials together and work areas neat might be called upon to help others and even to lead the class in organizing activities. For instance, a student might share tips for managing paperwork with the entire class.

Give Choices

Every day and throughout the year, all students should be given choices about the type of work they do, their activities, and the ways in which they spend their time. Choice can be built into almost any part of the school day. Students can choose which assessments to complete, which role to take in a cooperative group, which books to read or which problems to solve, and how to receive personal assistance and supports. Choice may not only give students a feeling of control in their lives but also an opportunity to learn about themselves as workers. Students themselves usually know best when during the day they are most creative, productive, and energetic; what materials and supports they need; and in what ways they can best express what they have learned.

Choice can be integrated into almost any activity. One teacher gives her students a choice of shaking hands or giving a high-five as they walk out of the classroom each day. Another teacher gives her second-graders a choice of seven different ways to practice spelling words, including writing them in shaving cream, tracing them on a friend's back using a finger, or "writing" them out using rubber stamps. A high school biology teacher lets students choose some of the labs they will conduct. Table 11.1 includes some ways teachers can offer choices to students.

Offer "Staying Put" Supports

Often, learners with autism struggle to stay seated or to remain in the classroom for extended periods of time. Although allowing learners to move frequently is one way to approach this need, some students can be equally comforted if they have an object to manipulate or a favorite texture to feel during lessons.

In one elementary school classroom, students visited a box with "staying put" resources at any time during the day. The box contained Koosh balls, small rubber and stuffed toys, drinking straws, stress balls, unifix cubes, and other similar items. Students borrowed the objects when they need them and returned them when they are finished. None of these interactions with objects

Table 11.1.   Choices that can be offered to any student

Work alone or with a peer.

Read quietly, listen to a book on tape, or read an electronic book on the computer.

Take a seat anywhere in the room.

Use a pencil, pen, or marker.

Conduct your research in the library or stay in the room and work.

Type on the computer, write in your notebook, or use a typewriter.

Use a calculator, count on your fingers, use manipulatives, or solve problems in your head.

Choose any topic for your research paper.

If you know the answer, raise your hand, give me the thumbs up sign, or sit on your desk.

Start your homework or find an educational game to play.

Of the ten problems on the sheet, complete any five.

Take "regular" notes on the lecture or take notes by drawing pictures of the concepts I present.

Stand or sit in your chair.

Choose any two ways to be assessed in this unit.

Pick your favorite piece of work for the bulletin board.

Let me check your paper or have a friend do it.

Write the problem down or solve it in your head.

bothered the teachers or created a stir in the class and the teachers found that allowing students to use the box gave them insight into their individual learning needs and helped them remain focused and "on task."

As one teacher explained, having this simple support can make the difference between a student's presence in the classroom and his or her engagement in an activity:

At the beginning of the year Sam could not stay seated through morning meeting and his mom suggested that we give him something to hold. She sent in the Koosh ball. Ever since then he has sat through meeting just fine. We started the box because some of the other kids said that they would like to try holding something too. (Kasa-Hendrickson, 2002, p. 134)

Allowing students to doodle or draw can be another effective "staying put" strategy. Many learners with and without identified needs appear better able to concentrate on a lecture or activity when they are given the opportunity to doodle on a notepad, draw on their folders, or sketch in a notebook. One of our student teachers reported that a student without an identified disability in her high school U.S. history class often filled in the pictures of a coloring book during lectures. Although the student teacher was initially skeptical of the young man's behavior, by the end of the semester she was convinced that he not only was able to sit and listen longer when he used the coloring books but also that he seemed to process the lectures and learn the content better when he used the crayons. As a way to honor the student's need, the teacher brought a "Heroines of the Civil War" coloring book into the classroom and offered it to the young man to use as a resource for an upcoming unit.

HELPING STUDENTS WITH AUTISM: INDIVIDUAL STRATEGIES

Although many strategies offered in this chapter will be appropriate for all students, some may be necessary only for the learner with autism or for other students with similar characteristics. To determine the need for any one of these strategies, it is typically best to follow the lead of the student or to consult with the student's family.

Teach About Autism

Helping students to be self-aware and to learn about their own label and disability communicates respect for the learner and potentially empowers them. This type of awareness is often incredibly helpful, even for younger students. Those who know about autism often feel relieved to know that others experience what they do. Furthermore, if a student is given information about others with autism, he or she might glean information about coping with practical issues such as sensory sensitivity or communication differences.

When the teacher and the student share a language about the disability, the teacher may have another tool for communicating and informing the student and the student becomes better able to understand his or her own body and experiences. For example, I was once waiting for a school bus with Jay, a

student with autism, when the bus company called to say that they were behind schedule. The bus didn't come and didn't come and didn't come. Jay became increasingly agitated and began to whimper as if in pain. Every time the
bus was late, Jay had the same reaction, but this time I was able to talk to him
about how his autism was affecting his reaction because I had been reading
him small excerpts from the autobiographies of people with autism.
"Remember that book we read about the guy who hated to wait for the bus?
He sure hated waiting too. His autism made it hard for him to wait. This is
your autism acting up again, huh? It must be hard to handle, but you are doing
a great job. How do you manage?" I said. Although the wait was still notice-
ably uncomfortable for Jay, he was able to have a short conversation with me
about how he was handling the situation. Later, we put this conversation on
paper and made it into a story about autism and waiting and how to cope with
a "misbehaving bus."

Teachers might read autobiographies of people with autism to their older
students whereas younger students might enjoy picture books on the topic.
Teachers might also take students to local conferences on autism and help them
to understand political implications of having a disability label. One of my students attended a disability rights conference over a long weekend and came
back to school with renewed self-confidence, wearing an "Autistic and Proud"
button on his jacket. This student later presented his life story at a local teachers' meeting, getting a real confidence boost from serving as an expert on his
disability and, for once, on his own life.

In a study I conducted with high school students (Kluth, 1998), a paraprofessional used autobiography as a way of supporting a young woman with
significant disabilities. The pair often read books written by Donna Williams, an
author with autism who writes about living with her disability. The two would
go to a quiet space and Ms. Colton, the paraprofessional, would read aloud. They
would also have long, serious conversations (via Candy's typed communication)
about Candy's disabilities. These experiences were very different from the types
of conversations that had filled Candy's school career. She had never before been
informed about her disability and had not previously been told by teachers that
autism could be hard sometimes or that she was doing a good job navigating her
disability or that others were experiencing some of the same things she was.

Older students might even be asked to write about their experiences and
share their stories with peers or professionals through student magazines,
school newspapers, or even through national publications. Writing can be a
cathartic experience, serving as a way for students to learn about themselves
and educate others. I know one young man who likes to "write back" to comments made on his formal education reports, often refuting the ways professionals have interpreted his dis/abilities.

Help with Movement Problems

As stated in Chapter 1, many individuals with autism experience significant
difficulties with movement. People with autism and other disabilities often report that they cannot get their bodies to do what they want them to (Donnellan
& Leary, 1995). The problems can be exacerbated when people supporting the
individual with autism believe that the student could control or change his

Table 11.2. Examples of accommodations: Ideas for students and classrooms

Individual challenge	Accommodation idea
Jason struggled to sit at his table in his classroom. He often left the table or pushes back on his chair and tips over.	Jason's teacher found that if she sat him near the wall he could lean against it. She also gave him (and a few other students) a choice to sit in a beanbag chair or in his seat for certain activities. Jason was also allowed to take 5-minute walking breaks around the room whenever he asked for them. Finally, this teacher noticed that music helped Jason sit longer, so she allowed him to use a portable walkman during seat work.
Walking down the carpeted hall-way became hard for Trey, who seemed unable to leave strings and fuzz on the floor—he had to pick up these things when he noticed them.	Trey and his classmates made key chains out of sturdy string. Trey carried this with him at all times so he could feel this texture all day, whenever he wanted to. Trey also walked in be-tween two favorite peers when transitioning from class to class. The peers gave him gentle input on each arm (leaned on him a bit) as they walked. This pressure seemed to dis-tract him from staring at the floor and helped him to keep his head up.
Barb had a hard time moving through the cafeteria line. She would sometimes run through the line without picking up her lunch. Other times she would sit down on the floor when she was halfway through the line.	Barb's teacher videotaped her walking through the lunch line for four consecutive days. She then edited the tape, taking out all "scenes" in which Barb ran, sat down, or otherwise strug-gled. She then put the footage together until the tape showed Barb successfully walking all the way through the line, getting her lunch, and sitting down. Seeing this "model day" was exactly what Barb needed. She was able to imitate the video perfectly within days.
Vang had problems going up and down stairs. He often got "stuck" halfway up the staircase and would not (or could not) come down.	A paraprofessional in Vang's classroom told the young man to imagine that he was climbing a mountain when he was on the stairs. The two wrote a story about "Vang the Mountain Climber," and Vang read the story on Thursday mornings be-fore he had to climb the stairs to get to his music lesson.
Bob often chewed on (or ate) his materials during stressful situations.	Bob's friends started rubbing his shoulders or simply resting a hand on his back when he seemed stressed out; this seemed to help him relax. The teacher also gave Bob gum or candy when he started to chew on his notebooks or papers.

Source: Donnellan & Leary (1995).

movement or behavior "if he really wanted to." For instance, we know a student who can move over the monkey bars and the rest of the jungle gym with ease, but he often finds it difficult to cross a room on his own. His teachers are sometimes confused by this contrast and find it hard to understand how some actions are so easy for him while others remain so challenging.

Students with movement differences may be supported in several ways. It is helpful to remember, though, that the supports that work for one person may create even more severe difficulties when applied to another person. In other words, keep in mind that when it comes to helping students with movement problems, "One man's meat is another man's poison" (Donnellan & Leary 1995).

Touch When a student seems unable to move, a touch cue might be ad-ministered to the back of the hand, on the arm, on the leg, or any part of the body that seems "stalled." For example, a teacher might tell a student that she can get a snack from the basket. If the child does not respond, the teacher might try reminding the student again while touching her on the hand.

Rhythm and Music For some, movement is facilitated by certain music, chants, or rhymes. One student with autism we know performed sluggishly at his hotel laundry work site until his boss began playing Billy Joel CDs at the start of the day. The music had such an impact on him that his teacher bought him a CD Walkman so he could use different types of music to help him through the day.

Modeling   Some students need to see a task performed before they can actually do it. One former student would watch peers play basketball for half of the recess period and then would join in for the second half. It can also be helpful to move *with* a student. A teaching assistant we know told us a story about Molly, a young woman, who dropped to the floor one day and seemed unable to get up. The teaching assistant dropped to the floor with Molly and then said, "Maybe this will help. I'll get up with you." Molly immediately stood up with the assistant.

Imagery/Visualization   Reed (1996) shared a fascinating example of how a man with autism, Mac, uses imagery to become "unstuck." Mac, who often becomes paralyzed or unable to move when he walks from room to room, devised a mental image to break his "feeling of confusion and disorientation." In order to get his body to move during transitions, Mac imagines that he is playing for the Minnesota Twins. In this visualization, it is a big game, the bottom of the ninth inning, two outs and Mac is up to bat. He cracks a home run, runs the bases, and is met at home plate by his excited teammates.

Provide Opportunities for Breaks

Some students work best when they can pause between tasks and take a break of some kind (e.g., walk around, stretch, simply stop working). Some learners will need walking breaks—these breaks can last anywhere from a few seconds to 15–20 minutes. Some students will need to walk up and down a hallway once or twice; others will be fine if allowed to move around a bit in the classroom.

One student needed to stand and pace constantly during classroom lessons. His teacher was warned that this student was likely to crouch at his desk (both feet on the seat), stand up during teacher lectures, and pace for a minute or more every half hour. The teacher's response was to give the student a seat in the back row and to surround him with other students who indicated on a learner profile questionnaire that they wouldn't be distracted by movement.

Another student, Mike, needed time to unwind when he arrived at school. Because Mike's school was a quarter mile from the district's middle school, he started each day by walking down to the school and back with a peer. As part of the walk, Mike started taking "kid mail" (students from the elementary school could write notes to siblings or peers in the middle school) from one school to the next. Classmates from his second-grade class took turns working with Mike to deliver the mail.

Teach to Students' Strengths and Areas of Expertise

Many individuals with autism have interests or preferences that are important to them. Many teachers say they have a student who loves trains, light switches, or horses (three very common interests); we have also worked with students interested in Korea, vacuum cleaners, screwdrivers, fences, chickens, stop signs, churches, weathervanes, triangles, *The Wizard of Oz*, Scooby Doo, and basketball. Any of these interests can be used as part of the curriculum. A student who loves trains might be asked to write a story about riding on a caboose, research different railroads on the Internet, or do an independent research project on ground transportation in America.

One student, Freddie, loved to study the calendar and answer questions about the holidays and special events throughout the year (e.g., Independence Day, Christmas, first day of spring). Although this interest in the calendar wasn't hurting Freddie's education, it also wasn't helping him to grow as a learner. To enhance Freddie's learning and to challenge all learners in his sixth-grade classroom, we developed a calendar activity appropriate for older students. Although all of the students in the classroom knew the days of the week and the months of the year, none of them knew that December 7th was the anniversary of the bombing of Pearl Harbor or that President Kennedy was assassinated on November 22nd in Dallas, Texas. The teachers had all of the students work in small groups to find important dates in American and world history. Freddie was responsible for presenting the "event of the day" each morning. All students—including Freddie—learned something new and Freddie was thrilled to have a calendar activity incorporated into the daily classroom routine.

Matt, a middle school student, loved maps; he loved to draw them, to read them, and to interpret them. When we visited him in his home, we saw some of his creations and were amazed at the detail and creativity in each. We were surprised, then, when we visited Matt's school and his teachers did not know much about his incredible abilities in mapmaking. We suggested that he be allowed to use his expertise in the classroom and his teachers were only too happy to comply. They decided that Matt would be allowed to display his maps in the classroom or school and teach peers a few new map skills. During the first week, Matt led a whole class review of latitude and longitude and gave a short lecture on how geography is used to interpret the past.

Provide Safe Space

Teachers should make quiet study or relaxation areas available for any student who seems to need a safe haven. The library might be used or a few chairs might be set up in the hallway (depending on fire codes of the school) for any student who needs a break from the chaos of the classroom.

Donna Williams stated, "Allowing me privacy and space was the most beneficial thing I ever got" (1992, p. 218). Many individuals with autism reported a need to retreat into a safe space at times. Liane Holliday Willey, a woman with Asperger's syndrome, suggested that even college students will need to find a place to "relax and re-group" somewhere on campus (1999, p. 132).

The most important part of creating a safe space is ensuring that the area will not be used or viewed as a place of punishment. Consider the example of Becky, an 11-year-old. She often needed to take a break from her fourth-grade classroom, but teachers were unsure of how to give her a private space without stigmatizing Becky and making her feel like she had done something wrong. Teachers worked closely with Becky to give her both a dignified place to unwind and a natural way to learn relaxation skills:

We first found another small room that was used for testing; there was a desk and chair in the room. The next day when she started getting loud and throwing her crayons, we walked with her to the new room. We brought a book with us that we planned to read to her while she calmed down, and then we would return to the classroom. Becky flipped the chair over and tried to stand on the desk. She then turned the two light switches in the room on and off, over and over again. The entire time she was in the room, she continued to be loud and active. Clearly, Becky did not like this room, and it would not function as a "calming down" location.

We looked for an alternative. Outside the special education resource room, a smaller room served as an entryway for students to get to the resource room. We (the special educator, the teaching assistant, and the consultant) decided that Becky might like working in this little room because other students came into this room to work each day. Because Becky also liked music and books about kittens and ballerinas, we placed these items in the room. Whenever Becky left the classroom, it was not viewed as a punishment, but as a way for Becky to "take a break" and then return when she was ready. The next day when Becky became loud, we walked her to the room that we called "Becky's room." She sat down at the desk, and we read books and listened to some music. Becky seemed to like this place, and she was able to relax and then return to her classroom without protest.

Traditional learning theory assumptions might lead us to interpret what we had done as a reward for Becky's negative behavior and we might have expected Becky's "loud-in-the-classroom" behavior to escalate in order to obtain this reward. We might have also expected her to refuse to leave "Becky's room." Neither of these things happened. We believe that, to borrow a phrase from [a teacher], Becky had given us the "best behavior she could" under the present circumstances—she wasn't trying to manipulate us directly, although she was telling us that she needed a break. When we responded to her needs by giving her a break rather than a punishment, she was apparently able to recoup and return to work. It seemed to us that this is the same kind of strategy that many of us follow when we are frustrated with something and cannot take another minute! When we treated Becky as we would want to be treated, her behavior improved. (Heeden, Ayres, Meyer, & Waite, 1996, p. 154–155)

Provide Nonverbal Supports and Cues

Some students feel overwhelmed by verbal interactions. One friend of ours, a man with autism, has told us that he cannot understand our words when we "talk them." He finds conversations especially challenging when the speaker is too loud or speaks too quickly.

Tito Rajarshi Mukhopadhyay, a young man with autism, also has problems with verbal interactions but has been strategic in coping with these problems:

Any new voice is frightening to me and it takes time for me to adjust to it. Usually people get frustrated and give up. However, if the person is persistent and maintains the same pitch, I can slowly get used to the voice. (2000, p. 72)

Tito's revelations are helpful in stressing how important it is to respect the ways in which students support themselves. Teachers need to give learners time and understanding when they converse with them or provide verbal directions or instruction. Tito's words should also serve as a reminder to interpret student behaviors and reactions with caution. Tito, and undoubtedly other students with autism, need teachers to be patient and work to understand their specific communication needs and preferences.

Because spoken words are hard for some students to process, teachers should experiment with other ways to supplement their speech. For instance, the use of sign language and gestures can be integrated into classroom instruction and routines. Sign language and speech can be used when giving simple directions (e.g., asking students to stand, sit, or stop talking). Gestures can also be incorporated throughout the day. A teacher can use his or her fingers when giving directions: [Hold up one finger] "First, you need to _____," [hold up two fingers.] "Second, you should _____," and so forth. Thumbs up can be used to communicate a job well done.

Teachers might also experiment with the written word. If students are given verbal directions, the same directions can be written on the chalkboard. PowerPoint slides or an overhead projector during lectures can also be used so that students can listen *and* see words and pictures related to the presentation.

Some students also respond remarkably well to conversations on paper; this is often effective for those learners who seem to ignore verbal directions or remarks. A teacher might approach the student before lunch and write, "Five minutes before we go to the cafeteria" in order to prepare him for the transition. Writing can also be a useful tool for calming a student. When a student is upset or confused, writing can be a way to communicate when other types of interaction seem too overwhelming.

One of us used to work with a fifth-grade student named Mickey. Mickey would get very nervous when changes occurred during the day (e.g., the announcements were late, a favorite peer was absent). He could often be calmed through writing. A teacher or peer would simply sit down next to Mickey, ask him for a notebook, take out a pen and begin writing a calming message to him. For example, if a friend of his was out sick, a teacher might sit down and write, "Hi Mickey, it seems like you are upset this morning—I'm sorry to see you so upset. I wonder if you are upset because Maggie is out sick today. Don't worry about her, though. I heard that she is doing fine but needs to rest for one more day. Maybe later you could write an e-mail note to her when we go to computer class."

Give Options for Expression

Although writing is helpful to many students, it can be a major source of tension and struggle for students with autism. Some students cannot write at all and others who can write have a difficult time doing so. Handwriting may be sloppy or even illegible. Students who struggle with writing may become frustrated with the process and become turned off to tasks employing paper and pencil. As Temple Grandin reported, an overemphasis on handwriting can cause the learner stress and take the focus away from real learning:

I was the last person in my fourth grade to get the penmanship award. This was a big deal to the children because when the penmanship was good enough, the teacher designated you as "scribe" and you were given a set of colored pencils. I didn't care so much about the "title," but I coveted the colored pencils. I tried very hard and still I was last to qualify.

Learning math was even more difficult because I had a British teacher, Mr. Brown. He was a very proper Englishman and made the class do the math problems with a fountain pen. We had to rule the plus and minus signs and be ever so neat. It was bad enough trying to understand math but having to be neat besides was impossible. No matter how hard I tried, my papers were splattered with ink. (p. 37)

Similarly, Donna Williams reported that her handwriting kept her from completing work and making gains in the classroom: "My handwriting was poor and, despite practice, always remained behind the progress of the others year after year" (1992, p. 26).

In order to support a student with difficulties in writing, a teacher may try to give the child gentle encouragement as he or she attempts to do *some* written work—a word, a sentence, or a few lines. Teachers might also allow the student to use a computer, word processor, or even a typewriter for some lessons. In addition, peers, classroom volunteers, teachers, and paraprofessionals can serve as scribes for a student who struggles with movement and motor problems, dictating as the student with autism speaks ideas and thoughts. Stephen Shore illustrated how much an alternative form of expression helped him:

The computer serves as a wonderful assistive device for me. My fine-motor skills for writing and drawing are somewhat impaired. As a result, creating a neat handwritten document is labor-intensive and time-consuming for me. Given that I have some ability to communicate with the computer via the keyboard, I can create documents that look much better in much less time. The relative ease of creating a good-looking document may determine whether the document is produced at all rather than being considered as something that will be too arduous to create. (2001, p. 131)

It seems that typed communication can do more that give students easier ways to complete assignments, however. Donna Williams (1996) who became an accomplished author and poet, shared that access to a typewriter at a young age, boosted her interest in writing:

When I was ten a typewriter was left in my room. I smelled it, licked it and tapped at the buttons. I felt its texture and the sound it made when touched, its shiny surfaces and its rough ones. I explored its mechanisms and its systems, fragment by fragment. I typed onto the roller, strings of letters and patterns of letters. The roller became indented and covered with overlays of letters. I worked out how to put the paper into it and typed strings of letters and then patterns of letters (p. 241)

Williams goes on share that over time, the typewriter unleashed the poet in her:

By the time I was eleven, I had typed lists of words running down the page and the words jumped back at me with imagery and feel to them in a way written words that had come from other people, never had. These had come from my own context from somewhere within me, beyond my conscious mind. The typed lists had pattern to them. The words written had a relationship between them. There was an inherent humour in some of the lists as the words shifted from one to the next. There was hurt and anger and beauty in those lists. There was an understanding of categories; things in nature, animals, feelings, describing words, advertised products.

By the time I was twelve, those lists had begun to look like poems. By thirteen, those poems were waterfalls falling out of my fingers. (p. 242)

SUMMARY

In a teacher workshop we gave, a teacher described how a young man in her classroom, Kelly, coped with his need for movement by scooting around on the floor occasionally. One day, the teacher was teaching about the oceans when a school administrator walked into the room. The teacher asked the students to name the oceans surrounding the United States. Kelly popped up from his spot between two rows of desks and shouted "the Pacific." The teacher asked for other answers and after a brief pause, Kelly popped up again, this time from another area in the classroom, and shouted, "the Atlantic." The principal, disapproving of this unconventional teaching and learning behavior, frowned and left the room. Later, when the teacher was confronted by the principal, she explained that Kelly did some of his best work on the floor and that while she was doing her best to give him a wide range of more conventional ways to participate in class, right now this was the most effective way to engage him in learning.

Teachers like those featured in this chapter realize that working in an inclusive classroom involves employing a huge variety of strategies—some of which may be very unique and unconventional. As Sylvia Ashton-Warner (1963), a teacher who brought unconventional methods to Maori children in rural New Zealand, found, a teacher may need to "walk alone" in finding and using strategies that work. Even Ashton-Warner often worried about how her administrators would view her unique, student-centered, culturally rich strategies, but she implemented them anyway in order to give students every opportunity to learn and succeed:

> If only I kept workbooks and made schemes and taught like other teachers I should have the confidence of numbers. It's the payment, the price of walking alone. If you saw the reading scheme I have been making the last few days you'd know why I speak of walking alone. Yet I must present it. I've got to do what I believe. And I believe in all I do. It's this price one continually pays for stepping out of line. I'm feeling too old to pay it. But I must do what I believe in or nothing at all. Life's so short. What other people call their timetables...In mine, the children, might get up and dance in the middle of their sums. (p. 198)

Surely, it is the teacher's job to respond to student needs in the classroom and to adjust his or her personal style to fit the classroom population each year. In other words, we need educators like Kelly's teacher and Aston-Warner who will meet students "where they are" instead of expecting learners to adjust to the instructional approaches used in the classroom. Although students with autism need a welcoming school and great curriculum to be successful, nothing may be more important to a student's success than the willingness of a teacher to take some risks, treat students as individuals, and implement a range of strategies that allow all learners to emerge as skilled and able.

For More Answers and Ideas

Campbell, L., Campbell, B., & Dickinson, D. (1999). *Teaching and learning through the multiple intelligences* (2nd ed.). Needham Heights, MA: Allyn & Bacon.

Feldman, J. (1995). *Transition time: Let's do something different.* Beltsville, MD: Gryphon House.

Goodman, G. (1995). *I can learn!: Strategies & activities for gray-area children, grades K–4.* Peterborough, NH: Crystal Springs Books.

Winebrenner, S. (1996). *Teaching kids with learning difficulties in the regular classroom.* Minneapolis, MN: Free Spirit Publishing.

CHAPTER 12

Collaboration and Cooperation in the Inclusive School

"They need to work together. Each one—the home and school—knows
that if they don't work together then we can't learn together. We have to learn to treat
each other with respect. We really need to trust each other." (Wilson, cited in Kluth, 1999, p. 1)

When I started teaching in an inclusive school, I felt it was enough for me to facilitate the involvement of my students in their general education classrooms and coach the teachers on how best to support these learners. After a few weeks, however, my vision of my job and my secure position behind the scenes were shattered when Peg, a sixth-grade teacher, asked for my input about her science lesson. She had one student with an identified disability in her classroom, one with significant emotional needs, two students needing speech and language support, and three others who were learning English as a second language. On top of all of this, Peg had 36 students in her classroom that year—an all-time high number. She needed help.

During a team meeting, I reviewed Peg's lessons with her and suggested that she try a cooperative learning structure to teach the concept of the food chain. "Okay," she agreed, "when can you come in and teach it with me?" I was stunned and silently tried to figure out Peg's request. I wondered: "Why doesn't this veteran teacher understand the system? Doesn't she know that I give the suggestions and she implements them?" After staring at her blankly for a few moments and stuttering something about not knowing much about food *or* chains, she told me to come to her room the next day to start planning.

I met Peg in her classroom, and we planned a cooperative lesson on the functions of the food chain. We divided students into groups and assigned them an animal to study. Groups were then provided with materials to research their animal's place and function in the food chain. The students were charged with creating a poster to illustrate how their animal fit into the cycle of life. Students then had to defend their position and their drawing to the rest of the class in the form of a short, informal class presentation. Peg and I served as judges in "Survival Court" and determined whether the groups had proved that their animal was a necessary part of the ecosystem.

Peg and I decided that I would begin the lesson by giving a mini-lecture on ecology, and she would assist by passing out materials and giving directions

241

for the activity. I was nervous in my debut as a general educator but eager to earn my stripes at the front of the classroom. Although I made a lot of rookie mistakes (e.g., talking too fast, failing to assess whether students were understanding the information as I was providing it), Peg and I were pleased with the lesson. I had a chance to experience the difficulties and pleasures of presenting a lesson I had crafted. Peg finally had a chance to talk to individual students, work with small groups of learners, and observe her classroom without having to be at the helm.

The students seemed to love the busy, active lesson and participated enthusiastically. Most important, we felt confident that students understood the content; through informal assessments (e.g., observations, short interviews), we deemed that learners were grasping the vocabulary and concepts we had introduced through the activity.

The food chain lesson was the end of my special education isolation and the beginning of my life as a collaborative team member. This does not mean that I started co-teaching full time in Peg's classroom and that I never played a behind-the-scenes consulting role again. Because I was responsible for supporting six students in six different classrooms in five different grade levels, I was not actually able to engage in a lot of cooperative teaching, but my participation in the science lesson communicated to my colleague that I was willing to take on new and unfamiliar roles in my job as inclusion facilitator. And Peg communicated that she trusted me to do more than make observations and suggestions.

THE IMPORTANCE OF COLLABORATION

In the past decade, considerable attention has been given to the benefits of collaboration among K–12 classroom teachers. In particular, general education and special education teachers have been exploring ways to work together with other service providers and families to create inclusive classrooms for students with a wide range of abilities (Lipsky & Gartner, 1996; O'Brien & O'Brien, 1996). Given the tremendous diversity in U.S. classrooms—in ability, ethnicity, and culture, for example—teachers are finding that it is difficult to deliver effective instruction in isolation. Responsive and appropriate instruction, particularly in inclusive classrooms, requires cooperation, teaming, and shifts in roles and responsibilities for many school personnel. The old wisdom of two heads being better than one is truer than ever before as our schools provide a wider array of services and become more diverse. Schools committed to inclusive schooling must encourage and value the cooperation and "inclusion" of adults as well as students.

THE TEAM: ROLES AND CONTRIBUTIONS

One day I walked into the school library and saw a paraprofessional from my team quietly reading a book with a 6-year-old boy. I watched them for at least 20 minutes, completely stunned. I had never seen the student, who was nonverbal and very active, sit still for more than 6 minutes. No teacher, therapist, or administrator had been able to help him relax so completely. After school, I had only one question for my colleague, "How did you do that?" She sat me down and told me the story of how the two came to be sitting sharing *Miss Spider's Tea Party* (Kirk, 1994) on that afternoon. She told me about the soft whispering voice she used to read and the way she allowed him to look at the book even if that meant that he would tilt it sideways and page through it at breakneck speed. She also told me about the way she talked to this student: "I tell him about things. I tell him stories when we are walking around the building. Sometimes I tell him about my kids."

This talented woman did not have much experience working in education, in fact, she had only been working as a paraprofessional for a few weeks when this incident occurred. She did have a knowledge of and respect for children and a belief that all students were learners. This colleague not only gave me some concrete strategies to try but also demonstrated that the student could be successful if his educators taught him the way he needed to learn. She demonstrated that everyone on our team has something very valuable to offer.

As a young teacher, I learned a lot from working closely with seven paraprofessionals in my first teaching job and from all others on my team. From the physical therapist I learned how to increase a student's range of motion, from the administrators I learned how to conduct sensitive staff evaluations, and from the physical education teacher I learned how to incorporate kinesthetic activities into daily classroom lessons. Clearly, every team member is critical to the success of students and to the professional development of other team members. Every individual on the team has a different area of expertise as well as a different set of experiences to share. Some members may have more experiences working in inclusive schools whereas others may be more familiar with community resources or curriculum and instruction. Therefore, it is critical that teams take advantage of the contributions of *all* members.

In this section, I describe some of the roles and contributions typically made by different team members. It should be noted that every possible team member is not and could never be listed here. For instance, teams might also work closely with a school nurse, a physician, a student teacher, a student's mentor, a member of a community agency, and those other important educational stakeholders not mentioned here. Every team is unique in its membership, with some teams being small and including only the family, a teacher, and an administrator and other teams being larger and more complex. Teams should feel comfortable including any individual who will be able to add a unique perspective or offer support that other members cannot. I have tried to outline the roles of those who most often have membership on teams in inclusive schools.

Students with Autism and Their Families

The most important members of the collaborative team are the student with autism and his or her family. Although these members may not regularly participate in teaching lessons or delivering services, their ideas, preferences, and needs should be constantly considered. The student with autism can offer the insider perspective and can provide the team with the best information on "what works." For this reason, students should be formally and informally involved in developing their own individualized education programs (IEPs) and crafting their own supports.

Families must also be at the center of the planning process. The importance of family–school collaboration and partnership has been so consistently supported by research that it is no longer considered an option, but a professional obligation (Corrigan & Bishop, 1997). Too often, families may feel relegated to the outside of their child's education. For example, parents may be asked to attend meetings where large numbers of professionals *tell* them about *their own child* without asking for their input or soliciting advice or ideas from them. This outdated model must be replaced by one in which families are viewed as equal partners in the educational process and provided with opportunities to share their knowledge (see Chapter 4 for more information on connecting with families).

Students/Classmates of the Student with Autism

Classmates are ideal team members in that they are consumers of education in the same schools and classrooms as the student with autism. Every student certainly experiences his or her education differently; however, peers can provide a general report on the effectiveness of certain types of curriculum or instruction. In one classroom, for instance, two students were asked to help in constructing a daily schedule for a peer with autism. When the team suggested that the student take a certain art class because of the student's interest in painting, both students groaned. One piped up, "That class is so boring. The teacher talks and talks and talks. We should sign Tressa up for ceramics. I'm taking that and so are some of the other kids she knows." Because Tressa did not have a reliable way to communicate, the team decided to listen to the students and value their input over the ideas of the adults. In matters of school culture, the team assumed that the students might be more knowledgeable than any professional or member of her family.

It may not be appropriate to include a student's classmates in every discussion, decision, or meeting; however, educators should be diligent about asking for their input. Unfortunately, students are often overlooked as team members, perhaps because of their age or lack of experience. Although students may not have background knowledge of disabilities, teaching, or curriculum, they certainly do have the important experiential knowledge that their own education provides and they also have the experience of knowing and being educated with the student with autism and knowing what it is like "to be a kid." These experiences and the wisdom that grows from them are sometimes as helpful or even more helpful than the textbook knowledge and professional experiences of educators or even the lived experiences and insider wisdom possessed by families.

Students can be asked to help in several ways, including making scheduling choices, suggesting curricular supports, and crafting social opportunities or any other decision or idea. If peers are enlisted for these or other ways of helping, the individual with autism should surely be the one to select them. If the student with autism does not have a reliable way to communicate, educators should observe the student to determine with whom he or she seems most comfortable. Families can also help in selecting appropriate peer team members; parents and siblings will be able to identify those peers who the student with autism knows from the neighborhood or from church, for instance.

Administrators

Educators in leadership positions, especially principals, directors of pupil services, supervisors, and department heads, are critical members of collaborative teams (Fullan & Hargreaves, 1996; Goor, Schwenn, & Boyer, 1997; Keyes, 1996; Udvari-Solner & Keyes, 2000; Villa & Thousand, 1990). Administrators serve as the philosophical backbone of an inclusive school. It is very difficult—but not impossible—to provide all students with an education that is appropriate, challenging, engaging, motivating, and inclusive if administrators are not informed about the federal laws as they relate to inclusive education and aware of the tools and practices needed to grow an inclusive school. Dramatic changes in both teaching behavior and student learning are possible when administrators communicate support and empowerment to educators (Felner et al., 1997).

It is very important that administrators communicate their commitment to inclusive education clearly. In fact, the school may want to state its position in a mission statement or slogan to ensure that all stakeholders understand the importance of such a commitment to all members of the school community. One of the administrators in my school had a banner over his desk reading, "Special education is not a place." Everyone who visited his office understood his dedication to students and to inclusive education.

As part of this commitment to inclusion, administrators might attend team meetings, assist with staff schedules and other structures that support inclusion, monitor classroom enrollment, supervise special education processes, work with parents, encourage educators, and serve in supportive capacities with students. Principals and other leaders will also help with troubleshooting and improving inclusive programming in the school.

Teachers

General Education Teachers Although general education teachers may be new to some of the language and practices of inclusive education, most have "done inclusion" without realizing it by simply responding to the diversity that has always existed in their classrooms. General education teachers are important members of the team because they are the experts on general education curriculum and instruction. A general educator is a good resource for learning about how the school's math program might intersect with a learner's IEP goals or for suggesting ways in which the occupational therapist might be able to work with the student during art instruction.

The general educator is one of the team members (and sometimes *the* member) responsible for planning lessons for in inclusive classroom. Thus, he or she should be a primary decision maker in creating supports and adaptations for those lessons. The general education teacher can also help the team understand the rituals, routines, and traditions of a grade level. For instance, he or she knows what games their students play at recess and what field trips they will take during the year; this team member can therefore help the team plan for such events.

Because the general educator is sometimes the least experienced in implementing inclusive schooling, he or she may appreciate guidance. Teachers who are completely unfamiliar with disability may appreciate a mini-inservice on special education jargon, the IEP, or the role of related services in the student's education. Furthermore, the teacher will need to receive information about autism. This can come from the student, the student's family, the special educator, therapists, books, and/or the Internet. Some teachers want to know a lot about the label of autism before they begin teaching the student. Others prefer to get to know the student before learning about his or her disability.

Special Education Teachers   Special educators are also central members of the team; these professionals often have very different roles in inclusive schools than they do in other settings. In most cases, special education teachers in inclusive schools shift from being classroom teachers to facilitators, consulting teachers, and co-teachers. This can be a rocky transition for some teachers, especially if they have become accustomed to being "in charge" of their own classroom and students. The process is often easier when general educators welcome their colleagues and work with them to reinvent classroom space, teacher roles and responsibilities, and curriculum and instruction.

The role of the special educator in inclusive classrooms is to ensure that the students with disabilities are able to participate in and benefit from the general education curriculum and instruction, but he or she should also be attending to the learning needs of students without disabilities. Just as the general educator is expected to take responsibility for all students, so should the special educator support and serve those with and without disabilities.

Paraprofessionals

Paraprofessionals play many diverse educational roles, depending on the needs of individual teachers and the hiring guidelines and requirements of each program, school, and district. Many schools employ paraprofessionals as classroom assistants or to help individual students with personal care, academic tasks, and life skills. Those hired to support students with disabilities should have roles and responsibilities explicitly defined by the program and by his or her supervisors. Many positions occupied by paraprofessionals are not so clearly defined, however, and at times, these individuals may be pulled in different directions by those who direct and supervise them. Paraprofessionals should be informed about the educational needs (e.g., IEP goals and objectives, components of the general education curriculum) and characteristics of the students with whom they work, as well as classroom and school practices and routines.

Paraprofessionals should also have opportunities to contribute to the development of the educational programs and instructional plans, but should not be given sole responsibility for these and related activities. This point is critical. Too often, paraprofessionals are asked to design curriculum or instruction, conduct formal and informal assessments, create adaptations for students, and make a range of other critical instructional decisions on their own (Downing, Ryndak, & Clark, 2000; Giangreco, Broer, & Edelman, 1999; Marks, Schrader, & Levine, 1999).

In one classroom the paraprofessional made decisions related to the student's curriculum and instruction all day long. The general educator in this classroom told me that the student with autism, Keith, was included in lessons only when the paraprofessional decided the activity would benefit him. The paraprofessional didn't necessarily want this responsibility, but she was not given direction beyond, "Use your best judgment." This system of decision-making is problematic on many levels, but one of the most egregious mistakes made is the lack of up-front planning around Keith's education. A paraprofessional should never be in the position to make such a significant decision regarding a student's participation. Although many paraprofessionals may be quite able to engage in these activities, it is the teachers' professional and legal responsibility to do so.

Teachers, special educators, and related services providers (e.g., speech-language pathologists, physical therapists, occupational therapists, school psychologists) have the ultimate responsibility for ensuring the appropriate design, implementation, and evaluation of instruction carried out by paraprofessionals; therefore, it is critical that these professionals find time and create structures and materials that will help the paraprofessional do his or her job. For instance, if a speech-language therapist wants a paraprofessional to take data on a certain behavior or skill, then that therapist must take the time and provide the necessary training to allow the paraprofessional to do so accurately.

Paraprofessionals are important members of any team (Doyle, 1997). With appropriate supervision and staff development opportunities, they can contribute significantly to planning and delivering educational programs and provide valuable collaborative support to other team members (French, 1997; French & French, 1998; Pickett & Gerlach, 1997). Because they are such central members of the collaborative team, paraprofessionals should be given ample opportunities to voice concerns, ask questions, and share ideas. If they cannot be included in regular team meetings due to time or scheduling constraints, then other tools and structures for communicating and sharing must be designed and implemented.

When I was charged with supervising and collaborating with nine paraprofessionals, I tried to keep them informed through individual 15- or 20-minute meetings scheduled during the school day a few times each month. Our group also communicated by posting notes and suggestions on a community chalkboard in our shared office. Because everyone came into the office to store personal belongings and take coffee breaks, all members of our group had some opportunity to give and get news of the day and updates on happenings related to individual students or classrooms.

During busy days, a paraprofessional may feel quite overworked and underappreciated. They are often the busiest adults in the building and are often given too little recognition and compensation for their creativity, hard work, and extra effort. In order to pull paraprofessionals into the team and to make them feel more comfortable and valued, teachers and other team members must be sure to recognize and mine all of the talents that paraprofessionals bring to the classroom. If a paraprofessional is a history buff, teachers should look for opportunities for that person to share favorite stories or to help the teaching team design a class lesson on a history topic. If a paraprofessional is really skilled at supporting a student who often gets upset, he or she might be asked to talk to other professionals and paraprofessionals about the strategies that he or she uses. Table 12.1 includes more tips on working with paraprofessionals.

Table 12.1.   Tips for working with paraprofessionals

Keep important team information in a three-ring binder or on a bulletin board in
an easily accessible location so that paraprofessionals can check information
on adaptations, lesson plans, therapist notes, and so forth.

Try to meet weekly with your paraprofessionals. Even if the meetings are short,
having this time to connect is critical.

Never ask a paraprofessional to do anything you would not do yourself.

Provide time for idea sharing.

Give plenty of time to learn new skills; paraprofessionals should not be expected
to perform a task or engage in an activity that has not been modeled for them.

Take time to observe the work of paraprofessionals. Give feedback and support
as needed.

When possible, arrange for paraprofessionals to attend team meetings and staff
development activities.

Therapists

School therapists traditionally provided their services in private offices that
often were in the basements or back hallways of schools. This curriculum and
support was typically quite disconnected from classroom teaching and learning. Teachers found that many students receiving therapy in this model were
not able to generalize their new skills to their classroom.

Educators now understand that learning skills and competencies in isolation is often an exercise in futility; students must practice new skills and competencies in the environments in which they are most likely to use them
(Giangreco, Edelman, & Dennis, 1991; Rainforth & England, 1997; Rainforth &
York-Barr, 1997).

Today, speech-language therapists, occupational therapists, physical therapists, and vision and mobility instructors are working in the inclusive classroom alongside general and special educators. Although therapists may need
to work in a private space for some aspects of their jobs (e.g., helping students
with skills related to intimate personal care), most therapeutic work can be
done within general education environments. Therapists might provide teachers with ideas for environmental accommodations, adaptive equipment and
adaptive technology needs, and activities that would help students meet individual goals. For example, a physical therapist might give the physical education teacher ideas for including a student with limited movement in a game of
basketball. A speech-language therapist might teach a student with autism and
his peers how to use a new communication system during a social studies discussion group. An occupational therapist might walk around the classroom
during journal-writing time and give a student with autism and perhaps others help with their writing posture and pencil grip.

Therapists also serve as the teachers of teachers; every therapist must educate his or her colleagues about the language and strategies related to therapy.
Teachers, paraprofessionals, and all others expected to address therapeutic
goals in the general education classroom should be given enough information
to understand why they are supporting a certain skill or behavior. For example,
if an occupational therapist wants a student to change his posture or use a different grip on his pencil, then all of the adults in the classroom should know

why these changes are important; understand how to help the student to do those things; and learn how to talk to the student about making those changes.

Social Workers, School Counselors, and Psychologists

These professionals can offer a lot of support to the team in terms of how to meet the social and emotional needs of the student with autism while helping all students to understand appropriate ways to interact with their classmate with disabilities. Individuals in these roles may spend a lot of time evaluating students, but these professionals work with students in a variety of other capacities, as well. These professionals may provide direct services to a student with autism by offering counseling or helping the learner with transition planning. He or she might also help the student and the student's team address scheduling, course selection, social supports, learning needs, and family–school communication.

A school psychologist I know worked with a young man with Asperger's syndrome on issues of self-determination. During her time with him, they visited web sites on Asperger's syndrome, read articles written by people with Asperger's syndrome, and worked on a personal portfolio of the young man's life. Using ideas from the Internet and from the articles, the young man was able to construct an autobiographical portfolio that he then used to teach his family and friends about his label and diagnosis. The psychologist, meanwhile, used the portfolio as a way to connect with the young man and to teach him effective strategies for self-advocacy.

Social workers, counselors, and psychologists can also help teams get connected with community resources. A social worker might, for instance, encourage a student to join a community club, group, or team, or help families find outside tutoring support.

These individuals can also serve an important function in supporting staff members who are experiencing major changes in job responsibilities. Mental health professionals can offer ideas for dealing with stress, negotiating conflicts between staff members, or helping team members assess their struggles and their successes.

Professional Consultants

In some instances, schools may want to call on the services of a professional who specializes in educating students with autism. Some districts have professionals available to teachers, whereas, in other instances, schools need to find help from local nonprofit agencies, colleges and universities, or independent educational consultants.

This type of support can offer the team a fresh perspective and new ideas or, in some cases, a welcome affirmation that they are on the right track. Teams might seek input from such an individual if they need more information about autism, the family seems unable to provide the expertise they need, and/or both the team and the student feel undersupported and in need of new answers. A consultant may be able to offer new materials, strategies, or information. The support from this person, however, will be temporary in most cases so the team will want to have a plan for getting support after the consultant is gone.

One caution related to the use of consultants and outside support must be given: Teams should not assume that any individual has expertise that will be helpful to his or her particular team just because that person has a certain set of credentials or title. Team members should be sure that the consultant shares the values of the team and that he or she understands that the school has an inclusive ideology. The consultant should also be attentive and respectful to all members of the team including the student and his or her family and should consider the needs and skills of the entire group when offering suggestions.

PRINCIPLES OF COLLABORATION

Sometimes teachers are put together and told to function as a team; however, it takes more than assignment to the group to be a team member and it takes more than willingness on the part of members to make a team. Although this list is by no means comprehensive, it outlines a few principles necessary for true collaborative work.

Principle 1: Common Goals, Values, and Mission

Members of any collaborative team should share goals (Appley & Winder, 1977; Thousand & Villa, 2000) and a framework or mission of some type (Schwarz & Bettenhausen, 2000; Villa, Thousand, Nevin, & Malgeri, 1996). In one of the schools in which I served as an inclusion facilitator, an entire philosophy was drafted in order to focus team members as they made decisions and to communicate the school's beliefs and values to new staff and community members (Schwarz, Bettenhausen, & Kruse, 1994) (see Table 12.2). Goals might be centered on specific students (e.g., "Teach Kenny to read") or related to the school or staff (e.g., "We will all learn how to teach cooperative lessons").

Although team members will undoubtedly come to the group with different levels of commitment to and understanding of inclusive schooling, individuals must share some core values if inclusive schooling is to become a part of school culture. Team values in inclusive schools typically include the fundamental belief that all students can learn and that those learners have a right to be educated with their peers.

Principle 2: Parity and Role Sharing

In inclusive classrooms, the adults shift and share roles and responsibilities in order to expand their own skills, further their own knowledge, and give students access to a wider range of supports. In inclusive schools, lesson planning involves not only teachers but also, in some cases, therapists and paraprofessionals. Designing classroom rules and establishing guidelines for the school community originates from all team members as well, including students and their families, and both special and general educators are responsible for IEP development and implementation.

Educators may experience some confusion and anxiety when these roles initially shift. In such cases, up-front planning and discussion about changes can be helpful. In a study conducted by Udvari-Solner and Keyes (2000), Jennie

Table 12.2. Goals included in a sample philosophy and recommended practice statement

Students of diverse abilities and educational background need to learn from one another.

Our purpose is to find the "best way" of making education work well for students with individual differences.

We can meet the needs of all students with diverse needs by individualizing the curriculum for the range of students' abilities.

Modeling for students from one another is essential in learning.

Support means more than just supervision: It means preparing to make informed, educational decisions for all students.

We own all students: Boundaries are minimized in our model.

Most school- and community-based objectives for students with disabilities in primary and intermediate grades can be met in the settings of same age peers without disabilities.

We need to empower students to be in general education settings whenever possible based on their individual needs and the degree they can tolerate the expectations or adapted expectations in the classroom.

The focus of related service support is to provide expertise within their area to successfully integrate and enhance the general education curriculum.

Every student is an "individual." Individual goals and objectives come first.

The focus of learning is to make students more independent and empower everyone to be an effective learner and citizen.

Source: Schwarz, Bettenhausen, & Kruse Education Center staff, 1994.

Allen, a principal of an elementary school, shared how she helped teachers prepare for their shifts in roles and responsibilities:

> Before team-taught classrooms came about we had some very lengthy discussions. [Discussions] about simple things like, "How do you feel about having a roommate? Essentially, you are getting a roommate. So, how do you feel about sharing a room, having somebody else's desk in that room, and their stuff and their mess? What are you going to do the first time there is a behavior problem in the classroom? Who is going to do the disciplining? Who is going to make the telephone call home? How are you going to decide that? During planning time, do you co-plan? How many weekdays a week are you going to co-plan? How many days are you going to go separately and plan? Who will teach which learning groups?" Those are the kinds of discussions that we need to take place. The message [behind those questions] was that I was not going to allow [one person] to act as an educational assistant in this classroom and the other person as the teacher. (p. 443)

As Allen pointed out, collaboration also requires parity between participants; this means that team members demonstrate their willingness to work together as classroom equals. Cook and Friend suggested that adults working together in schools send parity signals in order to communicate their cooperation to students, families, and other staff members. Parity signals are "visual, verbal, and instructional signals" that convey equality (1995, p. 11). For example, two co-teachers might host an open house night together by giving a short presentation to families and introducing themselves as a teaching team. Table 12.3 presents some signals that will communicate to educators that parity is being attempted and/or achieved.

Table 12.3.   Signals that indicate parity between teachers and
paraprofessionals

Put both/all teachers' names on the board.

Put both/all teachers' names on letters home to families.

Have both/all teachers lead open house or other classroom events.

Have both/all teachers deliver instruction, design curriculum, and assess
     students.

Have both/all participate in family/teacher conferences.

Try to give all adults the same type of workspace in the classroom (e.g., same
     size desk).

Principle 3: Structures for Planning and Communication

Effective collaboration is neither easily nor quickly achieved. Initially, collaboration is labor intensive. Effective and productive collaborative relationships
develop from time spent together exchanging ideas and information and solving problems. Time and practice are necessary to build trust and develop the informal and formal structures and procedures that enable teams to work together effectively (Larson & LaFasto, 1989).

Successful inclusive education demands that teachers have opportunities
to meet face-to-face and plan for individual students and to develop whole-
class lessons for all students. Ideally, teachers should meet weekly with all team
members to plan instruction and develop curriculum. For those groups who
cannot find time to meet weekly, longer monthly sessions can be used to engage in long-term planning while other types of tools and structures are used
for daily and weekly communication (see Table 12.4 for ideas for structures for
planning and collaboration).

Principle 4: Leadership Is Shared

Effective teams use a *distributed functions theory of leadership* (Johnson &
Johnson, 1999; Thousand & Villa, 2000) in which "task and relationship functions of the traditional lone leader are distributed among all members of the
group" (Thousand & Villa, 2000, p. 257). This means that the different team
members take turns completing certain tasks (e.g., leading meetings, calling the
family, completing paperwork related to a student's IEP) and that all participate in discussion and decision making. It may be initially challenging to move
away from traditional roles, especially if an administrator or a certain teacher
has done a lot of preliminary work to initiate collaborative work. In order to facilitate the transition to shared leadership, teams might delegate specific roles
for members and then systematically switch those roles. For instance, a teacher
may serve as the team facilitator (e.g., responsible for running meetings and
following up on agenda items) one month and then move to being the team
trouble-shooter (e.g., responsible for checking in with members, gauging the
team's progress, and clearing up communication problems) the next month.

Principle 5: Shared Responsibility for Students

A student shoves a student with autism and the student with autism shoves
back. Does the teacher speak to both students and help them to negotiate their

Table 12.4. Structures for planning and collaboration

Team meetings	Teachers can meet every week, every other week, or work together for several hours at the end or beginning of each month
Mini team meetings	Teachers typically plan to cover only one or two issues at these meetings. One team meets 15 minutes before school every week. The topic is usually shared beforehand and participants come to the meeting with ideas. A facilitator can keep members on task.
Lunch meetings	One or two team members or a whole team might plan to share a meal together a few times a month. Some teams use this time the same way they would any other meeting. Other teams engage in these meeting just to socialize and share stories of success.
"Stolen" meetings	Some team members can meet in the back of the classroom or in an adjacent room when students are watching a movie, listening to a guest speaker, or engaging in independent work.
Dialogue notebook	Some teams communicate by dialoging on paper. One team member shares ideas, thoughts, or concerns on a piece of paper and passes it to their colleague. This individual responds, adds his or her own ideas, thoughts, and concerns, and passes it back. This format can be used between two or more educators.
E-mail	E-mail can be used to ask simple questions (e.g., Did Emi hand in her field-trip permission slip?) or to plan lessons. One teacher can make notes on an upcoming lesson and mail it to another; the recipient can then make adjustments and suggestions and send it back to her colleague.
Lesson binder	Some teams keep all plans in one big binder that can be accessed by all. Teachers, therapists, paraprofessionals, and others who have ideas to add or materials to contribute can do so by adding to the binder.
Communication forms	In some schools (especially in secondary schools where team members may not see each other every day), teams communicate by filling out a communication form. The best forms have checklists, scales, or short-answer options that make the form easy to use. For instance, in one school, general education teachers filled in a form every other week that asked them to answer a number of questions, including the following:
	On a scale of 1–10, how well do you feel student IEP goals being addressed in the general education classroom?
	On a scale of 1–10, how well do you think you are meeting the needs of all students?
	How do you feel about the amount of paraprofessional support students are receiving: Not enough? Just right? Too much?
	Explain any gains individual students have made recently.
	What topics do you think we should discuss at our next meeting?

shared problem or does she speak to the student without an identified disability and tell the young man with autism that he needs to talk to "his teacher" about the incident?

Some teachers new to inclusive schooling may feel responsible for those without disabilities, but think that those with disabilities "belong" to someone else. This longstanding and deeply entrenched practice of seeing some students as "other" occurs in many ways in our schools every day. In inclusive schools, however, all adults are responsible for all students and demonstrate this responsibility actively. They show care and concern for all learners, they work hard to get to know students, and they take part in providing instruction. A speech-language therapist might teach a small reading group including students with and without identified disabilities, for example; a special educator might work on an independent project with a student without disabilities; a

general educator might work one-to-one with a student with autism; and a social worker might teach socialization skills to an entire second-grade class.

In classrooms where responsibilities for students are shared, language may
also change. For instance, when all educators teach and support all students,
the language of "yours" and "mine" is eradicated. This language can be transforming; as teachers begin to use words such as "us" and "ours," separating responsibilities and seeing students as belonging to a program or teacher often
feels awkward and unnatural.

WHAT DO YOU DO WITH ALL OF THOSE ADULTS?

Many teachers are thrilled to have help in the classroom and relieved to have
colleagues with whom to share successes and frustration, yet some are puzzled
about how to handle all of the support. I have even heard teachers lament that
they have too much support and too many adults in the classroom.

In actuality, there is seldom, if ever, a situation in which a classroom or a
school has too much support. In almost every case, students actually benefit
from lower student–teacher ratios; therefore, it is beneficial to have access to as
much adult power as possible. It is critical, however, that these supports are
used in the most efficient and effective ways. If team members are not used in
smart ways, valuable human resources are wasted and students may suffer. By
assessing proximity, using a range of co-teaching structures, and carefully planning the roles and responsibilities of everyone working in the classroom, all
students can benefit from all of the adults and all educators can participate
meaningfully in classroom life.

Consider Proximity

One day, a friend called and asked me to visit her classroom. For the first time
in her career as a seventh-grade teacher, she was going to have a student with
autism in her class and was looking for ideas. I walked into the middle school
classroom as students were conducting a science experiment and was able to
spot her new student immediately; he was sitting at a table in the back of the
room surrounded by three adults. I learned later that two of the women were
therapists and the other was a paraprofessional. Although his educators were
likely engaged in what they considered to be an important teaching and learning moment, the exchange looked more like a summit than a seventh-grade science lesson.

I use this vignette to illustrate how critical it is to consider the impact that
adult proximity has on student learning. In one study, researchers identified
eight significant problems that resulted from paraprofessional's proximity to
students (Giangreco, Edelman, Luiselli, & MacFarland, 1997). Although study
participants indicated that some level of close proximity between students with
disabilities and paraprofessionals was desirable and sometimes quite necessary
(e.g., tactile signing, personal care), they also recognized that adult support and
proximity was not always needed and could, in fact, be detrimental to students.
As one special educator in the study shared:

> Sometimes I think it inhibits her relationship with her peers because a lot is
> done for Holly and Holly doesn't have the opportunity to interact with her peers
> because there is always somebody hovering over her, showing her what to do
> or doing things for her. I'd like to get the instructional assistant away from Holly
> a little bit more so that peers will have a chance to get in there and work more
> with Holly. (Giangreco et al., 1997, p. 217)

Specifically, the findings of the study suggest that too much adult proximity results in interference with general education teacher ownership and responsibility, separation from classmates, dependence on adults, decreased peer interactions, limitations on receiving competent instruction, loss of personal control, loss of gender identity, and interference with the instruction of others. It should be noted that although these researchers specifically focused on the behaviors of paraprofessionals, this study and its results offer an important message for any adult who works with students with disabilities including administrators, teachers, therapists, and classroom volunteers. This research is not so much about the work of paraprofessionals as it is a critique of how all adult time, energy, and talent might be used or misused in inclusive classrooms.

Too much adult support and the wrong type of adult support can rob students of a typical education. For instance, one of my former students, Thomas, needed a lot of support. Thomas had a hard time sitting for any period of time. He would leap out of his chair every minute or so unless someone sat near him with a hand on his shoulder. Furthermore, he couldn't examine materials very effectively unless they were held for him. For these reasons, Thomas always had a teacher or paraprofessional sitting at his side. Although this arrangement enhanced his participation in some ways, it also robbed him of social opportunities and forced him to be completely and unfailingly "on task" at all times. That is, students who are watched, helped, and instructed by a one-to-one support person for large amounts of time often miss out on the social and cultural experiences that make schooling memorable and enjoyable. For instance, if Thomas giggled at a friend's "inappropriate" joke, his support person would immediately reprimand him. Students such as Thomas, who get a lot of personal support, are always being watched and attended to, therefore, they do not have the same opportunities as others to pass notes, exchange secrets, doodle, daydream, or even nod off! I do not mean to suggest that it is good educational practice to let students sleep in class, but I *do* feel that is very important to allow students to experience normalcy in their education.

Fading Adult Support: Two Stories of Success Fading adult proximity prompts teachers to consider ways in which students can be provided with supports that are more natural and unobtrusive. For example, one of my former students, Tim, seemed to need a lot of reassurance to stay with a large group. For this reason, his teacher put him in the back of the classroom so a paraprofessional could sit next to him and so the two could leave the room easily if the student needed a break. When we noticed that this arrangement was isolating Tim from his peers, we put his desk in the middle of the room and put his seat in between two students he knew and liked. Both of the students were able to offer the supportive comments Tim needed and the student immediately responded to the arrangement. Over time, he needed fewer breaks and ultimately, very few encouraging comments to stay with the group and participate in lessons. Meanwhile, the paraprofessional who had previously supported Tim was freed to create new adaptations for him, to float around the classroom and give support to all, and to co-teach pieces of whole-class lessons with the general educator.

Another student, Garren, was fairly independent during the school day but was always supported by a paraprofessional or teacher during lunchtime. This bothered Garren's mother because lunch was a time for socializing and the presence of a paraprofessional seemed to block Garren's engagement in typical lunchtime activities such as telling jokes, sharing news, and reporting on the school day. When Garren's mother asked if he could go to the lunchroom alone, his teachers pointed out that he needed help getting ready for lunch. He often dropped his heavy tray if he had to balance it on his own. He was also unable to open his food containers; he couldn't get his milk carton opened and he struggled to even pull the aluminum foil away from his hot lunch. Furthermore, the staff pointed out, he scarcely made efforts to interact with other students. Having an adult there, they reasoned, would help him make connections with his peers. When Garren's mother persisted, the team agreed to try new supports.

The team decided that Garren understood how to go through the lunch line and retrieve his lunch but that he didn't have the strength or coordination to do so. The team, therefore, decided that Garren could choose between having a cafeteria worker put his tray out on the table for him or that he could come a little early to the lunch room to get all of his items one at a time. The staff then taught Garren how to punch his straw into the top of his milk carton instead of opening the spout and to ask a peer to open his hot lunch. Peers were happy to help and some of them even asked Garren to open their milk in the cool new "straw-punch" way. After only a few days of the new routine, Garren was independently enjoying his lunch experience and getting to know peers without the support of an adult. Interestingly, Garren no longer needed an adult to "facilitate social interactions" when one was not sitting next to him separating him from his classmates!

Better Proximity, Better Support   The various ways in which students are supported in the classroom should be evaluated constantly. In most cases, physical supports and proximity should be faded as students gain skills and become more able to work independently. When I encourage student teachers to think about proximity and, in some cases, to fade support and their physical presence from learners with disabilities, they sometimes tell me that a particular student "can't do anything" independently or that a learner "needs full support." It is certainly true that many students with autism have significant needs and that some of these students need intensive support, but it is also true that students with such needs can get support in many ways, not just through the presence of an adult. In fact, adult support should be one of the last ways in which an individual student is supported—especially students with disabilities who have had so few opportunities to function as part of a group and do things for themselves.

Teams who engage in creative problem solving will be able to generate ideas for giving students what they need while giving them opportunities to learn new skills and develop new competencies, as well. A student who relies on an adult to organize his or her materials for each class can be taught to use a checklist and a written course schedule. A student who needs help dressing for recess can be given boots without complicated snaps and buttons and can ask peers to help, if needed. A student who relies on adult support to communicate with peers might be taught to use sign language or a communication device, and students in the classroom might be taught to communicate in ways beyond words.

Of course, some students will need adult support and it is often quite appropriate for students to receive direct instruction, one-to-one tutoring, or physical support, but educators should carefully evaluate when students need such supports. In many instances, an adult pulls a chair up to the side of a student's desk and fails to leave this position for most of the school day. Even when students do need a lot of personal support, all educators should problem solve how to minimize the use of that stigmatizing chair. Even if a learner needs individual support to get started on an assignment, the adult can offer the support and then step back from the student's desk. In other instances, an adult might pull up a chair and focus on a small group of students, providing assistance to all students in the area. Both of these options give the student with autism the support he or she needs while providing opportunities for the learner to be independent.

One of the most important reasons to change the ways in which we support students is related to cost–benefit analyses. Teachers are charged with doing the impossible on a daily basis; increasingly they are being asked to take on new responsibilities and to change their roles. Educators need all of the help and support they can get. Thinking critically about how adults will work in the classroom can prompt better instruction for all students and can make the work of all adults more manageable and enjoyable. When teachers and other adults who are working in the classroom fade back from giving intensive, one-to-one support they are free to work with small groups of students, teach lessons, plan, create materials, and communicate with families and other educators.

Use a Range of Co-teaching Structures

When I started co-teaching in an inclusive classroom, my colleague claimed to know "nothing" about autism. She seemed very apprehensive about having students with disabilities in her classroom and encouraged me to plan curriculum and design assessments for "my kids." In only a matter of weeks, however, she was creating and teaching lessons with me, questioning my decisions, and demanding to be a part of the IEP planning for students with disabilities. Through our partnership, she learned about autism, reading and implementing IEPs, and teaching diverse learners. As the special education teacher, I learned about general education curriculum and gained confidence teaching whole-class lessons. My colleague also taught me how to design thematic instruction and performance assessments and how to plan challenging science and math lessons.

Co-teaching typically involves a specialist and a classroom teacher jointly planning, instructing, and evaluating heterogeneous groups of students in general education classrooms (Bauwens, Hourcade, & Friend, 1989; Walther-Thomas, 1997; Walther-Thomas et al., 2000). By intentionally varying their roles, the co-teachers share responsibility for their classes more fully. Studies conducted since 1990 have applauded the use of co-teaching between special education and general education professionals in pre-school through high school settings

(Meyers, Gelzheiser, & Yelich, 1991; Pugach & Wesson, 1995; Walther-Thomas, 1997). In a study by Meyers and colleagues (1991), for instance, general education teachers reported that they preferred in-class support models to pull-out models because the more collaborative model seemed to inspire a greater focus on instructional issues for students with unique learning needs and resulted in more-frequent team meetings with colleagues. In another related study, educators in co-taught classrooms described themselves as confident about meeting the needs of all students in the classroom (Pugach & Wesson, 1995). In addition, Walther-Thomas (1997) evaluated 23 co-teaching teams and found that both special and general education teachers reported that professional growth and enhanced teaching motivation resulted from their collaboration. In this same study, students claimed that they received more teacher time and attention in their co-taught classrooms.

Teachers can implement various teaming structures that optimize expertise, increase interactions with students, and give adults opportunities to build skills and learn from each other. In this section, I outline five different structures that can be used by two or more teachers or other adults.

One Teach/One Assist   When teachers use this model, they typically share lesson delivery responsibilities; one leads the lesson while the other supports in some way (Cook & Friend, 1995). The lead person is usually in charge of the content while the assisting teacher adds examples; shares humor or anecdotes; or takes notes on a chart, chalkboard, or easel. Or one instructor can act as lead teacher while the other floats throughout the classroom, providing individual assistance and facilitating small-group activities. For example, one instructor provides instruction on geography while the other instructor writes important points on the chalkboard and points out different features on the classroom map.

One teach/one assist is easy to implement and can be arranged "on the spot," which is important. Because of this ease of implementation, teachers can naturally shift into one teach/one assist when one drifts into the classroom for unplanned co-teaching or stays in the classroom past a planned co-taught lesson. In using one teach/one assist, teachers should, as much as possible, trade roles so that both or all teachers have opportunities to lead instruction and to provide the assistance.

One Teach/One Observe   In some instances, teachers and paraprofessionals may want to take turns acting as a classroom observer. An observer might study whole-class dynamics (e.g., how students solve problems in collaborative groups) or individual student behaviors (e.g., how a student reacts to classroom noises, how a student communicates). Teachers can use this observational data to improve their planning and teaching and to learn about students in meaningful ways. For example, it might be difficult to assess how a non-verbal student initiates social interactions until you have an hour to watch him work with a small group of peers.

Furthermore, teachers can learn a lot about each other through the one teach/ one observe structure. One of my colleagues observed me several times when I was learning to teach whole-class lessons; she helped me to improve my teaching in countless ways and she claimed that she learned about differentiating instruction and positive behavior support from watching me.

Colleagues might even ask each other to observe specific teaching behaviors during an observation. For instance, a paraprofessional who is unaccustomed to teaching a small group of students might ask a teacher to observe the lesson and give feedback on the pace or organization of her instruction.

One teach/one observe can also be used to evaluate how much and what types of support a learner needs. In one classroom, the general education teacher was convinced that her student, a young man with Asperger's syndrome, was receiving too much personal support from a paraprofessional. The teacher believed the student could do more of his classroom work on his own and felt he would take more initiative if allowed to work independently at times.

In response to these concerns, the team decided that they should observe the student and collect information on what type of assistance he needed throughout the day. The paraprofessional agreed to collect the data. She spent an entire day observing the classroom, making notes every time the student needed help or struggled with a task or activity. The team found that the student actually needed very little direct support. Although he was confused a few times (especially when the students learned a new math game), students were able to coach him during these rough spots.

After the team was presented with the information from the observation, they asked the paraprofessional to begin supporting the student in new ways. Instead of giving him direct support and sitting near his desk at all times, she spent the day making adaptations for the young man, floating through the classroom and doing spot-checks on him and others, and helping the classroom teacher present lessons in ways that would reach a wider range of learners (e.g., writing notes on the board while the teacher gave a lecture).

Duet Teaching   Duet teaching simply involves two adults working together to provide instruction. These "duet" presentations (Greene & Isaacs, 1999) typically involve both adults engaging in primary teaching roles in the class; instructors take turns leading class discussion, answering student questions, and facilitating the lectures and activities, for example.

Station Teaching   "In station teaching, teachers divide instructional content into two, three, or more segments and present the content at separate locations within the classroom" (Cook & Friend, 1995, p. 6). For instance, teachers might create four stations; one for listening to recordings of African drum music, one for collaboratively composing a few lines of music (e.g., eight measures per group), one for learning a new drumming skill, and one for researching African dance drumming on the Internet.

Station teaching is a wonderful way to use the expertise and energy of all of the adults in the classroom, especially in those classrooms that are served by several adults at certain points in the day. One way to engage those adults efficiently is to have them float around the classroom and offer support and instruction for students at all stations. (See Chapter 11 for more on station teaching.) Although this model can be very effective, many teaching teams find that lessons are richer when adults have specific roles. For instance, one teacher may be anchored at a station in order to provide small-group instruction to five or six students at a time while a paraprofessional floats around the classroom interviewing individual students about their knowledge of key concepts. At the same time, a special educator might teach mini-lessons to a few learners who need enrichment for that particular lesson.

Parallel Teaching   Parallel teaching (Cook & Friend, 1995) involves splitting the class into equal sections and providing each group with the same lesson or activity. This structure lowers the student–teacher ratio and, therefore, "is useful when students need opportunities to respond aloud, to engage in hands-on activities, or to interact with one another" (Cook & Friend, 1995, p. 7). Parallel teaching can also be used when teachers want to introduce smaller groups to two different activities, concepts, or ideas; the two instructors teach different content for some part of the class and then switch groups and repeat the lesson with the other half of the class. This structure can be used, in particular, when students are working on experiential projects; in these situations, teachers can more carefully observe and assess student performance. The following are some examples of parallel teaching:

- A fifth-grade class is split into two groups of equal size. A special educator teaches one group about the Democratic Party while a general educator teaches the other group about the Republican Party. The students can then come back into a whole-class format and teach the content to each other.
- A general educator and a speech-language therapist each work with half of a first-grade class; both educators give students a mini-lesson on phonics.
- A paraprofessional reviews for a test with half of the class while the classroom general educator teaches all the students new study and test-taking skills (e.g., skimming text, reading questions carefully, organizing materials). Halfway through the class period, students switch groups.
- Students in a high school science class are divided into two heterogeneous groups. Twenty students work on a biology experiment under the direction of the science teacher while five learners tour the classroom with the special educator, observing the different lab stations and recording observations on how different groups are conducting the experiment.

Assign Specific Roles and Responsibilities

During visits to classrooms, I often see professionals and paraprofessionals underused and misused. In one classroom, the general education teacher was reading a story to the class and 18 kindergarten students, 1 paraprofessional, and 1 special educator sat on the floor watching her. While the paraprofessional and the special educator were undoubtedly trying to serve as role models and offering support to the three students with autism in the classroom, I wondered whether this was the best type of support for the students and use of human resources. At times, this may, in fact, be the very best model to use. Without question, having all students and all adults meeting together as a group can build a sense of community in the classroom. In many other instances, however, students can get more effective and individualized supports when teachers evaluate the lesson or activity, assess student needs and lesson demands, and creatively design the most appropriate and meaningful ways to use the skills and talents of available professionals and paraprofessionals. Table 12.5 includes some of the roles and responsibilities shared by educators.

Table 12.5.   Roles and responsibilities shared by educators

Conduct performance assessments (observations).

Observe individual students or whole-class behaviors (e.g., turn-taking, giving feedback).

Make phone calls to families.

Connect with other team members.

Create adaptations.

Complete administrative tasks (e.g., making copies, setting up a meeting).

Plan a lesson or setting up for a lesson.

Engage in a short team meeting with a team member.

Program a communication device.

Gather materials.

Ask students enrichment questions.

Collect data on individualized education plan (IEP) objectives.

Videotape or audiotape classroom interactions for future observation and reflection.

Interview individual students to assess understanding of key concepts.

In some instances, educators may purposely choose to keep their roles ambiguous. For instance, a teacher and a paraprofessional may float around the classroom as students conduct lab experiments; both may be responsible for giving support to students when they need it. This structure and these roles may be appropriate in some instances, but at other times teachers may want to take on specific roles in order to make the most of their individual skills and talents. Another way the educators could split responsibilities would be to have the paraprofessional circulate and answer general questions while the general educator focuses specifically on giving mini lessons to small groups of students and offering enrichment questions to those learners who need it. Or the general educator could circulate and manage the lesson while the paraprofessional carries a clipboard, rotates to each group, and takes notes on students' understanding of "the lab."

When educators find themselves in a slump, when they have been doing business in the same ways for years without trying different ways, or when they have wanted to do something differently but have not yet worked up the courage to do so, it is especially important to consider these different roles and responsibilities. It is also a signal to switch roles and responsibilities when educators feel overworked or underchallenged. A teacher is probably in need of a new approach if

- The only role of the paraprofessionals in the classroom is to offer one-to-one support to a student with a disability.
- The general educator never has a chance to work individually with any student.
- The special educator has never taught a lesson or worked with students without disabilities.
- Therapists are not invited to develop curriculum or teach in the classroom.
- Students do not have leadership roles and are never asked to present lessons with each other or with their teachers.

Certainly, I do not mean to suggest that teachers must change every role and responsibility they have adopted. It is important, however, that the roles and responsibilities of all team members be reviewed and assessed continuously. A model that works during one semester may not work the next, and a team member who takes on certain responsibilities one year may want to try new ones the next year.

SUMMARY

Teachers truly committed to an inclusive schooling agenda will seek the expertise and support of others, including students with autism and their families. They will be reflective and open to new ideas. They will take risks and be willing to share ideas with others. Collaborative educators will question their own practices, attitudes, and knowledge and constantly consider how they might learn from the practices, attitudes, and knowledge of others. In inclusive schools, educators also continuously question and evaluate collaborative structures. When a model of service delivery doesn't seem to work, stakeholders think about how they are supporting students, design ways to team teach more effectively, or consider shifts in roles and responsibilities. Opportunities will flourish if teams are inventive and flexible when designing and implementing collaborative models and if they are willing to craft new models when the existing ones do not work.

Since the 1980s, the business world has moved toward models that are more collaborative and team-oriented (Armstrong, 1997; Edwards, Edwards, & Benzel, 1997; Stieber, 1999). Why? Because big business realizes that teaming increases productivity and creativity; the quality of the work is better when it is done through teams. This is an important point and those in the education world should take note. Teaming is not something that is done because it is trendy or because educators have not yet learned enough about inclusive education to make it on their own. Educators collaborate because it forces them to grow and learn and because it ultimately will result in better outcomes for students.

For More Answers and Ideas

Doyle, M.B. (2002). *The paraprofessional's guide to the inclusive classroom: Working as a team (2nd ed.).* Baltimore: Paul H. Brookes Publishing Co.

Feigelson, S. (1998). *Energize your meetings with laughter.* Alexandria, VA: Association for Supervision and Curriculum Development.

Fishbaugh, M.S.E. (2000). *The collaboration guide for early career educators.* Baltimore: Paul H. Brookes Publishing Co.

Kinney, J., & Fischer, D. (2001). *Co-teaching students with autism.* Verona, WI: IEP Resources.

(continued)

(continued)

Morgan, J., & Ashbaker, B. Y. (2001). *A teacher's guide to working with paraeducators and other classroom aides.* Alexandria, VA: Association for Supervision and Curriculum Development.

Snell, M., & Janney, R. (2000). *Teachers' Guides to Inclusive Classrooms: Collaborative teaming.* Baltimore: Paul H. Brookes Publishing Co.

Walther-Thomas, C., Korinek, L., McLaughlin, V., & Williams, B.T. (2000). *Collaboration for inclusive education: Developing successful programs.* Needham Heights, MA: Allyn & Bacon.

Bibliography

REFERENCES

American Psychiatric Association (2000). *Diagnostic and statistical manual of mental disorders* (4th ed., text rev.). Washington, DC: Author.

Appley, D.G., & Winder, A.E. (1977). An evolving definition of collaboration and some implications for the world of work. *Journal of Applied Behavioral Science, 13,* 279–291.

Armstrong, R.V. (1997). *Teaming up for excellence.* Hardy, VA: Armstrong Publishing.

Armstrong, T. (1987). *In their own way.* Los Angeles: Tarcher.

Armstrong, T. (1994). *Multiple intelligences in the classroom.* Alexandria, VA: American Association of Supervision and Curriculum Development.

Aronson, E., & Patnoe, S. (1997). *The jigsaw classroom: Building cooperation in the classroom* (2nd ed.). New York: Addison-Wesley Longman.

Ashton-Warner, S. (1963). *Teacher.* New York: Simon & Schuster.

Attfield, R. (1993, February). Letter *Facilitated Communication Digest, 1*(2), p. 11.

Attwood, T. (1998). *Asperger's syndrome: A guide for parents and professionals.* London: Jessica Kingsley Publishers.

Ault, M.J., Gast, D.L., & Wolery, M. (1988). Comparison of progressive and constant time delay procedures in teaching community sign word reading. *American Journal of Special Education, 24*(1), 27–30.

Ayres, W. (2001). *To teach: The journey of a teacher.* New York: Teachers College Press.

Baggs, A. (2000). *The validity of autistic opinions.* Retrieved from http://www.autistics.org/library/.html

Baggs, A. (2002, July 3). *Autism, speech, & assistive technology.* Retrieved from http://www.autistics.org/library/spchasst.html

Barron, J., & Barron, S. (1992). *There's a boy in here.* New York: Simon & Schuster.

Bauby, J-D. (1997). *The diving bell and the butterfly.* New York: Vintage.

Bauwens, J., Hourcade, J.J., & Friend, M. (1989). Cooperative teaching: A model for general and special education integration. *Remedial and Special Education, 10,* 17–22.

Bennett, B., Rolheiser, C., & Stevahn (1991). *Cooperative learning: Where heart meets mind.* Ajax, Ontario Canada: Bookation.

Bigelow, B. (1994). Getting off the track: Stories from an untracked classroom. From *Rethinking our classrooms: Teaching for equity and justice* (pp. 58–65). Milwaukee, WI: Rethinking Schools.

Biklen, D. (1990). Communication unbound: Autism and praxis. *Harvard Education Review, 60,* 291–314.

Biklen, D. (1992). *Schooling without labels: Parents, educators, and inclusive education.* Philadelphia: Temple University Press.

Biklen, D. (1993). *Communication unbound: How facilitated communication is challenging traditional views of autism and dis/ability.* New York: Teachers College Press.

Biklen, D. (1993, November). Questions and answers about facilitated communication. *Facilitated Communication Digest 1*(2), 10–14.

Biklen, D., & Cardinal, D. (1997). *Contested words, contested science.* New York: Teachers College Press.

Biklen, D., Saha, S., & Kliewer, C. (1995). How teachers confirm the authorship of facilitated communication: A portfolio approach. *Journal of The Association for Persons with Severe Handicaps, 20,* 45–56.

Biklen, D., & Shubert, A. (1991). New words: The communication of students with autism. *Remedial and Special Education, 12,* 46–57.

Bishop, K.D., Jubala, K.A., Stainback, W., & Stainback, S. (1996). Facilitating friendships. In S. Stainback & W. Stainback (Eds.), *Inclusion: A guide for educators* (pp. 155–169). Baltimore: Paul H. Brookes Publishing Co.

Blackburn, J. (1997). *Autism? What is it?* Retrieved from http://www.autistics.org/library/whatis.html

Blackman, L. (2001). *Lucy's story: Autism and other adventures.* London: Jessica Kingsley Publishers.

Blatt, B., & Kaplan, F. (1974). *Christmas in purgatory: A photographic essay on mental retardation.* Syracuse, NY: Human Policy Press.

Blau, L. (2001). 5 surefire strategies for developing reading fluency. *Instructor, 110,* 28–30.

Bober, S. (1995). Nicholas. In A. Stehli (Ed.), *Dancing in the rain: Stories of exceptional children by parents of children with special needs.* (pp. 114–115). Westport, CT: The Georgiana Organization.

Bondy, A., & Frost, L. (2002). *A picture's worth: PECS and other visual communication strategies in autism.* Bethesda, MD: Woodbine House.

Bordin, J., & Lytle, R.K. (2000). The IEP meeting: All together now... *The Exceptional Parent, 30,(9),* 74–77.

Bracey, G.W. (1994). Reward and punishment. *Phi Delta Kappan, 75*(6), 494–497.

Brady, J. (1995). *Schooling young children: A feminist pedagogy for liberatory learning.* Albany: State University of New York Press.

Brady, J., & Dentith, A.M. (2000, April). *A critical feminist postmodern pedagogy: Linking theory with practice.* Paper presented at the meeting of the American Education Research Association, New Orleans, LA.

Brendtro, L.K., Brokenleg, M., & Van Bockern, S. (1990). *Reclaiming youth at risk: Our hope for the future.* Bloomington, IN: National Education Service.

Broderick, A., & Kasa-Hendrickson, C. (2001). "SAY JUST ONE WORD AT FIRST": The emergence of reliable speech in a student labeled with autism. *The Journal of The Association for Persons with Severe Handicaps, 26,* 13–24.

Brophy, J., & Evertson, C. (1981). *Student characteristics and teaching.* New York: Addison-Wesley Longman.

Browder, D.M., Hines, C., McCarthy, L.J., & Fees, J. (1984). A treatment package for increasing sight word recognition for use in daily living skills. *Education and Training of the Mentally Retarded, 19,* 191–200.

Brown, L., Kluth, P., Suomi, J., Causton-Theoharis, Houghton, L., & Jorgensen, J. (2000). *Research team experiences for students with and without disabilities.* Durham:University of New Hampshire, Institute on Disability.

Burke, J. (1999, December). The school of my dreams. *Facilitated Communication Digest, 8*(1), 4.

Burke, J. (2002, December). TASH: Our quest: Opportunity, equality, justice. Keynote presentation at the meeting of The Association for Persons with Severe Handicaps, Boston.

Burns, N. (1998, October). Equality. *TASH Newsletter, 24*(10).

Calculator, S., & Singer, K. (1992). Letter to the editor: Preliminary validation information on facilitated communication. *Topics in Language Disorders, 13,* ix–xvi.

Campbell, P.H., McInerney, W.F., & Cooper, M.A. (1984). Therapeutic programming for students with severe handicaps. *The American Journal of Occupational Therapy, 38,* 594–602.

Cardinal, D., & Biklen, D. (1997a). Suggested procedures for confirming authorship through research: An initial investigation. In D. Biklen & D. Cardinal (Eds.), *Contested words, contested science: Unraveling the facilitated communication controversy* (pp. 173–186). New York: Teachers College Press.

Cardinal, D., & Biklen, D. (1997b). Summing it up: What should not and what can be said about facilitated communication. In D. Biklen & D. Cardinal (Eds.), *Contested words, contested science: Unraveling the facilitated communication controversy* (pp. 199–208). New York: Teachers College Press.

Cardinal, D., Hanson, D., & Wakeman, J. (1996). Investigation of authorship in facilitated communication. *Mental Retardation, 34*, 231–242.

Carle, E. (1969). *The very hungry caterpillar.* New York: Putnam.

Carlson, R. (1998). *The don't sweat the small stuff workbook.* New York: Hyperion.

Carroll, L. (1865). *Alice's adventures in wonderland.* London: Macmillan and Co.

Centers for Disease Control and Prevention. (2002, June). *Metropolitan Atlanta developmental disabiltities surveillance program.* Retrieved from http://www.cdc.gov/ncbddd/dd/ddsurv.htm

Chandler-Olcott, K. (in press). Seeing all students as literate. In P. Kluth, D. Straut & D. Biklen (Eds.), *Access to academics for ALL students.* Mahwah, NJ: Lawrence Erlbaum Associates.

Cisneros, S. (1991). *The house on Mango Street.* New York: Vintage Books.

Colasent, R., & Griffith, P.L. (1998). Autism and literacy: Looking into the classroom with rabbit stories. *The Reading Teacher, 51,* 414–420.

Coles, G. (1987). The learning mystique: A critical look at "learning disabilities." New York: Fawcett Columbine.

Contract Consultants, Inc. (1997). *What we are learning about autism/pervasive developmental disorder: Evolving dialogues and approaches to promoting development and adaptation.* New Cumberland, PA: Contract Consultants and Temple University Institute on Disabilities.

Cook, L., & Friend, M. (1995). Co-Teaching: Guidelines for creating effective practices. *Focus on Exceptional Children, 28,* 1–15.

Coppola, F.F. (Director). (1979). *Apocalypse now* [Motion Picture]. United States: Paramount Pictures.

Corrigan, D., & Bishop, K.K. (1997). Creating family-centered integrated service systems and interprofessional educational programs to implement them. *Social Work in Education, 19*(3), 149–163.

Crossley, R. (1997). *Speechless: Facilitating communication for individuals without voices.* New York: Dutton.

Cummins, J. (1996). *Negotiating identities: Education for empowerment in a diverse society.* Ontario: California Association for Bilingual Education.

Cunat, M. (1996). Vision, vitality, and values: Advocating the democratic classroom. In L.E. Beyer (Ed.), *Creating democratic classrooms: The struggle to integrate theory and practice.* New York: Teachers College Press.

Cutler, R. (1998). Ask Rob. *The communicator.* North Plymouth, MA: Autism National Committee.

Danforth, S., & Rhodes, W.C. (1997). Deconstructing disability: A philosophy for inclusion. *Remedial and Special Education, 18,* 357–365.

Darling-Hammond, L. (1997). *The right to learn.* San Francisco: Jossey-Bass.

Davern, L. (1996). Building partnerships with parents. In M.F. Giangreco (Ed.), *Quick guides to inclusion: Ideas for educating students with disabilities* (pp. 29–55). Baltimore: Paul H. Brookes Publishing Co.

Delpit, L. (1995). *Teaching other people's children: Cultural conflict in the classroom.* New York: New Press.

Dewey, J. (1910). *How we think.* Boston: Heath.

Donnellan, A. (1984). The criterion of the least dangerous assumption. *Behavioral Disorders, 9*, 141–150.

Donnellan, A., & Leary, M. (1995). *Movement differences and diversity in autism/mental retardation: Appreciating and accommodating people with communication and behavior challenges.* Madison, WI: DRI Press.

Downing, J. (1999). *Teaching communication skills to students with severe disabilities.* Baltimore: Paul H. Brookes Publishing Co.

Downing, J., Ryndak, D., & Clark, D. (2000). Paraeducators in inclusive classrooms: Their own perspective. *Remedial and Special Education, 21*, 171–181.

Doyle, M.B. (2002). *The paraprofessional's guide to the inclusive classroom: Working as a team (2nd ed).* Baltimore: Paul H. Brookes Publishing Co.

Draper, R. (1997). Active learning in mathematics: Desktop teaching. *Mathematics Teacher, 90*, 622–625.

Dugan, E., Kamps, D., Leonard, B., Watkins, N., Rheinberger, A., & Stackhaus, J. (1995). Effects of cooperative learning groups during social studies for students with autism and fourth-grade peers. *Journal of Applied Behavior Analysis, 28*, 175–188.

Dyson, B., & Grineski, S. (2001). Using cooperative learning structures in physical education. *Journal of Physical Education, Recreation & Dance, 72*, 28–31.

Education for All Handicapped Children Act of 1975, PL 94-142, 20 U.S.C. §§ 1400 *et seq.*

Edwards, P., Edwards, S., & Benzel, R. (1997). *Teaming up.* Los Angeles: J.P. Tarcher.

Edwards, E., Heron, A., & Francis, M. (2000). *Toward an ideological definition of literacy: How critical pedagogy shaped the literacy development of students in a fifth-grade social studies class.* Paper presented at the meeting of the American Education Research Association, New Orleans.

Egel, A.L. (1989). Finding the right educational program. In M.D. Powers (Ed.), *Children with autism: A parent's guide* (pp. 169–202). Bethesda, MD: Woodbine House.

Erickson, K. A., Koppenhaver, D. A., & Yoder, D. E. (1994). *Literacy and adults with developmental disabilities* (NCAL Technical Report TR 94-15). The Center for Literacy and Disability Studies, University of North Carolina at Chapel Hill. (ERIC Document Number ED 377 340).

Faber, A., & Mazlish, E. (1995). *How to talk so kids can learn—at home and at school.* New York: Avon Books.

Falvey, M., Givner, C., & Kimm, C. (1995). What is an inclusive school? In R. Villa & J. Thousand (Eds.), *Creating an inclusive school* (pp. 1–12). Alexandria, VA: Association for Supervision and Curriculum Development.

Farlow, L. (1996). A quartet of success stories: How to make inclusion work. *Educational Leadership, 53*, 51–55.

Felner, R.D., Kasak, D., Mulhall, P., & Flowers, N. (1997). The Project on High Performance Learning Communities: Applying the Land-Grant Model to School Reform. *Phi Delta Kappan, 78*(7), 520–527.

Ferguson, D., Ralph, G., Meyer, G., Lester, J., Droege, C., Guoôjônsdôttir, H., Sampson, N., & Williams, J. (2001). *Designing personalized learning for every student.* Alexandria, VA: Association for Supervision and Curriculum Development.

Fihe, T. (2000, November). *Speech in an Abnormal Psychology class.* Paper presented at University of California in Santa Cruz.

Fisher, D., & Roach, V. (1999). *Opening doors: Connecting students to curriculum, classmates, and learning.* Colorado Springs, CO: PEAK Parent Center.

Fling, E. (2000). *Eating an artichoke: A mother's perspective on Asperger syndrome.* London: Jessica Kingsley Publishers.

Fling, F.M. (1994). One use of sources in the teaching of history. *Social Studies, 85*, 206–210.

Fombonne, E. (1999). The epidemiology of autism: A review. *Psychological Medicine, 29*, 769–786.

Freedom Writers, & Gruwell, E. (1999). *The freedom writers diary.* New York: Doubleday.

Freire, P. (1970). *Pedagogy of the oppressed.* New York: Continuum.

Fullan, M., & Hargreaves, A. (1996). What's worth fighting for in your school? New York: Teachers College Press.

Gallagher, P. A. (1997). Promoting dignity: Taking the destructive D's out of behavior disorders. *Focus on Exceptional Children, 29,* 1–19.

Gambel, J. (Director), Kasa-Hendrickson, C., Broderick, A, Biklen, D, & Burke, J. (Producers). (2002). *Inside the edge: A journey to using speech through typing* [Motion Picture]. (Available from the Facilitated Communication Institute, Syracuse University, 370 Huntington Hall, Syracuse, NY 13244.)

Gardner, H. (1983). *Frames of Mind.* New York: Basic Books.

Gardner, H. (1993) *Multiple intelligences.* New York: Basic Books.

Garmston, R. (1997). Can collaboration be taught? *Journal of Staff Development, 18,* 44–46.

Gerland, G. (1996). *A real person.* London: Souvenir Press.

Giangreco, M.E., Broer, S.M., & Edelman, S.W. (1999). The tip of the iceberg: Determining whether paraprofessional support is needed for students with disabilities in general education settings. *The Journal of The Association for Persons with Severe Handicaps, 24,* 280–290.

Giangreco, M.E., Cichoski, K.E., Backus, L., Edelman, S., Tucker, P., Broer, S., Cichoski, K.C., & Spinney, P. (1999, March). Developing a shared understanding: Paraeducator supports for students with disabilities in general education. *TASH Newsletter, 25*(1), 21–23.

Giangreco, M.E., Edelman, S., Luiselli, T.E., & MacFarland, S.Z.C. (1997). Helping or hovering? Effects of instructional assistant proximity on students with disabilities. *Exceptional Children, 64,* 7–18.

Giangreco, M.F., Edelman, S.W., & Dennis, R. (1991). Common professional practices that interfere with the integrated delivery of related services. *Remedial and Special Education, 12*(2), 16–24.

Gibbs, J. (1995). *Tribes: A new way of learning and being together.* Sausalito, CA: Center Source Systems, LLC.

Gillingham, G. (1995). *Autism: Handle with care.* Edmonton, Alberta, Canada: Tacit Publishing.

Gillingham, G. (2000). *Autism: A new understanding.* Edmonton, Alberta, Canada: Tacit Publishing.

Gilroy, D.E., & Miles, T.R. (1996). *Dyslexia at college.* New York: Routledge.

Ginott, H. (1972). *Teacher and child: A book for parents and teachers.* New York: Macmillan.

Gomez, M.L. (1996). Prospective teachers' perspectives on teaching "other people's" children. In K. Zeichner, S. Melnick, & M.L. Gomez (Eds.), *Current reforms in preservice teacher education* (pp. 109–132). New York: Teachers College Press.

Goodman, G. (1995). *I can learn!: Strategies & activities for gray-area children, grades K–4.* Peterborough, NH: Crystal Springs Books.

Goor, M.B., Schwenn, J.O., & Boyer, L. (1997). Preparing principals for leadership in special education. *Intervention in School and Clinic, 32,* 133–141.

Gould, S. J. (1981). *The Mismeasure of Man.* New York: Norton.

Grandin, T. (1988). Frequently asked questions about autism. Retrieved January 2003 from http://www.autism.rg/temple/faq.html.

Grandin, T. (1995). *Thinking in pictures and other reports from my life with autism.* New York: Vintage Books.

Grandin, T. (1996a). *Emergence: Labeled autistic.* Boston: Warner Books.

Grandin, T. (1996b). *Interview with Temple Grandin.* Retrieved from http://www.autism. org/interview/temp_int.html

Graves, M., Graves, B., & Braaten, S. (1996). Scaffolding reading experiences for inclusive classes. *Educational Leadership, 53,* 14–16.

Gray, C. (1994). *Comic strip conversations.* Arlington, TX: Future Horizons Inc.

Gray, C. (2000). *The new social story book: Illustrated edition.* Arlington, TX: Future Horizons Inc.

Green, G., & Shane, H. (1994). Science, reason and facilitated communication. *Journal of The Association for Persons with Severe Handicaps, 19,* 173–184.

Greene, M., & Isaacs, M. (1999). The responsibility of modeling collaboration in the university education classroom. *Action in Teacher Education, 20,* 98–106.

Hall, K. (2001). *Asperger syndrome, the universe and everything.* London: Jessica Kingsley Publishers.

Hamrick, D. (2001, May 4). *Living with the challenges of autism.* Keynote presentation handout from the meeting of the Autism Society of Wisconsin, Green Bay.

Harrison, L. (2000, May 2). *Breaking away. Crossing dis/ABILITY borders: Beyond the myth of normal.* Paper presented at the meeting of the Facilitated Communication Institute, Syracuse University, Syracuse, NY.

Harry, B. (1992). Restructuring the participation of African American parents in special education. *Exceptional Children, 59*(2), 123–131.

Harry, B. (1995). Communication versus compliance: African American parents' involvement in special education. *Exceptional Children, 64* (4), 364–377.

Hart, C. (1993). *A parent's guide to autism.* New York: Pocket Books.

Harvey, S., & Goudvis, A. (2000). *Strategies that work: Teaching comprehension to enhance understanding.* York, ME: Stenhouse.

Harwood, A.M. 1992. Classroom climate and civic education in secondary social studies research: Antecedents and findings. *Theory and Research in Social Education 20,* 47–86.

Heeden, D.L., Ayres, B.J., Meyer, L.H., & Waite, J. (1996). Quality inclusive schooling for students with severe behavioral challenges. In D. Lehr & F. Brown (Eds.), *People with disabilities who challenge the system.* (pp.127–171). Baltimore: Paul H. Brookes Publishing Co.

Henderson, J. (1992). *Reflective teaching: Becoming an inquiring educator.* New York: Macmillan.

Hernandez, H. (1989). *Multicultural education.* Columbus, OH: Charles E. Merrill.

Hertz-Lazarowitz, R., Kagan, S., Sharan, S., Slavin, R., & Webb, C. (Eds.). (1985). *Learning to cooperate: Cooperating to learn.* New York: Plenum.

Hirshorn, A., & James, G. (1995). Further negative findings on facilitated communications. *Psychology in the Schools, 32,* 109–113.

Hitzing, W. (1994, November). Facilitated communication: Communication and black box psychology. *Facilitated Communication Digest, 3*(1), 2–3.

Hodgkinson, H.L. (1985). *All one system: Demographics of education and service delivery system.* Washington, DC: Institute of Educational Leadership, Center for Demographic Leadership.

Holt, J. (1967a). *How children fail.* New York: Pitman.

Holt, J. (1967b). *How children learn.* New York: Pitman.

Hornby, G., Atkinson, M., Howard, J. (1997). Controversial issues in special eduation.

Howlin, P. (1998). *Children with autism and Asperger syndrome: A guide for practitioners and carers.* New York: John Wiley & Sons.

Hundley, J. (1971). *The small outsider.* New York: Ballantine Books.

Hutchinson, J.N. (1999). *Students on the margins: Education, stories, dignity.* Albany: State University of New York Press.

Individuals with Disabilities Education Act (IDEA) of 1990, PL 101-476, 20 U.S.C. §§ 1400 *et seq.*

Individuals with Disabilities Education Act (IDEA) of 1997, PL 105-17, 20 U.S.C. §§ 1400 *et seq.*

Institute for the Study of the Neurologically Typical. (2002, March). http://isnt/autistics.org/

Irvin, J. (Director). (1987). *Hamburger hill* [Motion Picture]. United States: Avid Home Entertainment.

Jackson, L. (2002). *Freaks, geeks, and Asperger syndrome: A user guide to adolescence.* London: Jessica Kingsley Publishers.

Jacobson, J. W., Mulick, J.A., & Schwartz, A. A. (1995). A history of facilitated communication: Science, pseudoscience, and antiscience. *American Psychologist, 50,* 750–765.

Janzen-Wilde, M., Duchan, J., & Higginbotham, D. (1995). Successful use of facilitated communication with an oral child. *Journal of Speech and Hearing Research, 38,* 658–673.

Johnson, D.W., & Johnson, R.T. (1989). *Cooperation and competition: Theory and research.* Edina, MN: Interaction Book Company.

Johnson, M. (Producer), & Levinson, B. (Director). (1988). *Rain Man* [Motion Picture]. United States: United Artists.

Jorgensen, C. (1998). *Restructuring high schools for all students: Taking inclusion to the next level.* Baltimore: Paul H. Brookes Publishing Co.

Kagan, S. (1992). *Cooperative learning: Resources for teachers.* San Juan Capistrano, CA: Kagan Cooperative Learning.

Kallem, M., Hoernicke, P.A., & Coser, P.G. (1994). Native Americans and behavioral disorders. In R.L. Peterson, & S. Ishii-Jordan (Eds.), *Multicultural issues in the education of students with behavioral disorders* (pp. 126–137). Boston: Brookline Press.

Kanner, L. (1943). Autistic disturbances of affective control. *Nervous Child, 2,* 217–250.

Karagiannis, A., Stainback, S., & Stainback, W. (1996). Historical view of inclusion. In S. Stainback & W. Stainback (Eds.), Inclusion: A guide for educators (pp. 17-28). Baltimore: Paul H. Brookes Publishing Co.

Kasa-Hendrickson, C. (2002). *Participation in the inclusive classroom: Successful teachers for non-verbal students with autism.* Unpublished manuscript, Syracuse University, New York.

Kauefelt, M. (1999). *Begin with the brain: Orchestrating the learner-centered classroom.* Tucson, AZ: Zephyr Press.

Keefe, C.H. (1996). *Label-free learning: Supporting learners with disabilities.* York, ME: Stenhouse.

Keller, H. (1954). *The story of my life.* Garden City, NJ: Doubleday.

Kennedy, M. (2002). Creating ideal facilities. *American School & University,* 74(5) 30–33.

Kephart, B. (1998). *A slant of sun.* New York: Norton.

Keyes, M.W. (1996). *Intersections of vision and practice in an inclusive elementary school: An ethnography of a principal.* Unpublished doctoral dissertation, University of Wisconsin-Madison.

Kim, Retrieved Feb. 2003 from ani.autistics.org/kim.html

King-Sears, M.K. (1996). *Curriculum-based assessment in special education.* Baltimore: The Johns Hopkins University.

Kingsley, J., & Levitz, M. (1994). *Count us in.* New York: Harcourt Brace & Co.

Kinney, J., & Fischer, D. (2001). *Co-teaching students with autism K–5.* Verona, WI: IEP Resources.

Kirk, D. (1994). *Miss Spider's tea party.* Danbury, CT: Scholastic.

Kliebard, H. (1987). *The struggle for the American curriculum.* New York: Routledge.

Kliewer, C. (1998). *Schooling children with Down syndrome.* New York: Teachers College Press.

Kliewer, C., & Biklen, D. (2000). Democratizing disability inquiry. *Journal of Disability Policy Studies, 10,* 186–206.

Kliewer, C., & Biklen, D. (2001). School's not really a place for reading: A research synthesis of the literate lives of students with severe disabilities. *The Journal of The Association for Persons with Severe Handicaps, 26,* 1–12.

Kliewer, C., & Landis, D. (1999). Individualizing literacy instruction for young children with moderate to severe disabilities. *Exceptional Children, 66,* 85–100.

Kluth, P. (1998). *The impact of facilitated communication of the educational lives of students: Three case studies.* Doctoral dissertation, University of Wisconsin-Madison, Special Education Department.

Kluth, P. (1999, December). Developing successful schooling experiences for FC users: An interview with Franklin and Pat Wilson.*Facilitated Communication Digest.* (8)1, 7–11.

Kluth, P. (2000). Community-referenced instruction and the inclusive school. *Remedial and Special Education, 21,* 19–26.

Kluth, P., Biklen, D., & Straut, D. (in press). *Access to academics: Critical approaches to inclusive curriculum, instruction, and policy.* Mahwah, NJ: Lawrence Erlbaum Associates.

Kluth, P., Diaz-Greenberg, R., Thousand, J.S., & Nevin, A.I. (2002). Teaching for liberation: Promising practices from critical pedagogy. In J.S. Thousand, R.A. Villa, and A.I. Nevin (Eds.), *Creativity and collaborative learning: The practical guide to empowering students, teachers, and families* (pp. 71–84). Baltimore: Paul H. Brookes Publishing Co.

Kluth, P., Villa, R., & Thousand, J. (2001, December/January). "Our school doesn't offer inclusion" and other legal blunders. *Educational Leadership, 59,* 24–27.

Knight, T. (in press). Academic access and the family. In P. Kluth, D. Straut, & D. Biklen (Eds.), *Access to academics: Critical approaches to inclusive curriculum, instruction, and policy.* Mahwah, NJ: Lawrence Erlbaum Associates.

Kochmeister, S.J. (1997). Excerpts from SHATTERING WALLS. *Facilitated Communication Digest, 5*(3).

Kohl, H. (1967). *36 children.* New York: New American Library.

Koppenhaver, D., Coleman, P., Kalman, S., & Yoder, D. (1991). The implications of emergent literacy research for children with developmental disabilities. *American Journal of Speech and Language Pathology, 1,* 38–44.

Koppenhaver, D., Evans, D., & Yoder, D. (1991). Childhood reading and writing experiences of literate adults with severe speech and physical impairments. *Augmentative and Alternative Communication, 7,* 20–33.

Kozol, J. (1967). *Death at an early age.* Boston: Houghton-Mifflin.

Krystal, S. (1998/1999). The nurturing potential of service learning. *Educational Leadership,* January, 58–61.

Kumashiro, K. (2000). Toward a theory of anti-oppressive education. *Review of Educational Research, 70,* 25–53.

Ladson-Billings, G. (1994). *The dreamkeepers.* San Francisco: Jossey-Bass.

LaGreca, A.M., & Stone, W.L. (1990). LD status and achievement: Confounding variables in the study of children's social status, self-esteem, and behavioral functioning. *Journal of Learning Disabilities, 23,* 483–490.

Lalli, J.S., & Browder, D.M. (1993). Comparison of sight word training procedures with validation of the most practical procedure for teaching reading for daily living. *Research in Developmental Disabilities, 14,* 107–127.

Larson, C.E., & LaFasto, F.M.J. (1989). *Teamwork: What must go right, what can go wrong.* Newberry Park, CA: Sage.

Lasley, T.J., Matczynski, T.J., & Rowley, J.B. (2002). *Instructional models: Strategies for teaching in a diverse society.* Belmont, CA: Wadsworth.

Lawson, W. (1998). *Life behind glass: A personal account of autism spectrum disorder.* London: Jessica Kingsley Publishers.

Leary, M.R., & Hill, D.A. (1996). Moving on: Autism and movement disturbance. *Mental Retardation, 34,* 39–53.

Lemann, N. (2000, July 31). Gore without a script.*The New Yorker,* pp. 44–63.

Linton, S. (1998). *Claiming disability.* New York: New York University Press.

Lipsky, D., & Gartner, A. (1996). Inclusion, school restructuring, and the remaking of American society. *Harvard Educational Review, 66,* 762–796.

Loomans, D., & Kohlberg, K. (1993). *The laughing classroom: Everyone's guide to teaching with humor and play.* Tiburon, CA: H J Kramer.

Lopez, C. (1999). What food from the 'hood has done. In J.C. McDermott & L.B. Bird (Eds.), *Beyond silence: Listening for democracy* (pp. 37–38). Portsmouth, NH: Heinemann.

Lovett, H. (1985). Cognitive counseling & persons with special needs. Westport, CT: Praeger.

Lovett, H. (1996). *Learning to listen: Positive approaches and people with difficult behavior.* Baltimore: Paul H. Brookes Publishing Co.

Mairs, N. (1996) *Waist-high in the world.* Boston: Beacon.

Marcus, E. (1998, June). On almost becoming a person. *Facilitated Communication Digest, 6(3),* 2–4.

Marcus, E. (2002, Spring). Compulsion and yes, freedom too. *Facilitated Communication Digest, 10(1),* 7–10.

Marcus, E., & Shevin, M. (1997). Sorting it out under fire: Our journey. In D. Biklen & D. Cardinal (Eds.), *Contested words, contested science: Unraveling the facilitated communication controversy* (pp. 115–134). New York: Teachers College Press.

Marks, S.U., Schrader, C., & Levine, M. (1999). Paraeducator experiences in inclusive settings: Helping, hovering, or holding their own? *Exceptional Children, 65,* 315–328.

Markus, G.B., Howard, J.P., & King, D.C. (1993). Integrating community service and classroom instruction enhances learning: Results from an experiment. *Educational Evaluation and Policy Analysis, 15,* 410–419.

Martin, R. (1994). *Out of silence: An autistic boy's journey into language and communication.* New York: Penguin.

Martin, R. (2001). Disability rights are "civil rights" too. Retrieved 2/03 from www.reedmartin.com/specialeducationarticles.htm

Matthews, J. (1988). *Escalante: The best teacher in America.* New York: Holt and Company.

Maxwell, J. (1996). *Qualitative research design: An interactive approach.* Beverly Hills: Sage Publications.

McBee, R. (1998). Readying teachers for real classrooms. *Educational Leadership, 55,* 56–58.

McDaniel, E., & Colarulli, G. (1997). Collaborative teaching in the face of productivity concerns: The dispersed team model. *Innovative Higher Education 22,* 19–36.

McIntyre, T. (2002). Are behaviorist interventions inappropriate for culturally different youngsters with learning and behavior disorders? Retrieved from http://maxweber.hunter.cuny.edu/pub/eres/html

McKean, T.A. (1994). *Soon will come the light.* Arlington, TX: Future Education.

McMaster, K.L., Fuchs, D., & Fuchs, L.S. (2002). Using peer tutoring to prevent early reading failure. In J. Thousand, R. Villa, & A. Nevin (Eds.), *Creativity and collaborative learning: The practical guide to empowering students, teachers, and families* (2nd ed., pp. 235–246). Baltimore: Brookes.

McNabb, J. (2001). *I don't want to be a pioneer.* Retreived from http://www.autistics.org/library/nopioneer.html

Meier, D. (1996). *The power of their ideas: Lessons from a small school in Harlem.* Boston: Beacon Press.

Melnick, C., Capella-Santana, N., & Sentell, C. (2000, April). *Co-teaching in a pre-service program: Collaboration between special and elementary education professors.* Paper presented at the meeting of the American Education Research Association, New Orleans.

Meyer, L., Mager, G., Yarger-Kane, G., Sarno, M., Hext-Contreras, G. (1997). Syracuse University's inclusive elementary and special education program. In L. Blanton, C. Griffin, J. Winn, & M. Pugach (Eds.), *Teacher education in transition* (pp. 18–38). Denver, CO: Love Publishing Company.

Meyers, C., & Jones, T.B. (1993). *Promoting active learning: Strategies for the college classroom.* San Francisco: Jossey-Bass Publishers.

Meyers, J., Gelzheiser, L.M., & Yelich, G. (1991). Do pull-in programs foster teacher collaboration? *Remedial and Special Education, 12,* 7–15.

Michie, G. (1999). *Holler if you hear me.* New York: Teachers College Press.

Miller, L., & Opland-Dobs, D. (2001). Students blow the whistle on toxic oil contamination. In *Rethinking our classrooms: Teaching for equity and justice* (Vol. 2, pp. 144–147). Milwaukee, WI: Rethinking Schools.

Miller, P., Shambaugh, K., Robinson, C., & Wimberly, J. (1995). Applied learning for middle schoolers. *Educational Leadership, 52,* 22–25.

Mirenda, P. (1999). Augmentative and alternative communication techniques. In J.E. Downing (Ed.). *Teaching communication skills to students with severe disabilities* (pp. 119–138). Baltimore: Paul H. Brookes Publishing Co.

Molton, K. (2000). Paper presented at the Annual General Meeting of the National Autistic Society (UK), Cheshire, England.

Morehouse, P. (1995). The building of an airplane (with a little help from friends). *Educational Leadership, 52,* 56–57.

Morris, R. (Ed.). (1992). *Solving the problems of youth at-risk: Involving parents and community resources.* Lancaster, PA: Technomic.

Morrow, L., Tracey, D., Woo, D., & Pressley, M. (1999). Characteristics of exemplary first-grade literacy instruction. *The Reading Teacher, 52,* 462–476.

Moses, R.P., & Cobb, C.E. (2001). *Radical equations: Math literacy and civil rights.* Boston: Beacon.

Mukhopadhyay, T. (2000). *Beyond the silence.* London: National Autism Society.

Myles, B., & Simpson, R. (1994). Facilitated communication with children diagnosed as autistic in public school settings. *Psychology in the Schools, 31,* 208–220.

National Education Association. (1992). *Status of the American public school teacher.* New Haven, CT: Author.

Nieto, S. (2000). *Affirming diversity: The sociopolitical context of multicultural education.* New York: Longman.

Noddings, N. (1984). *Caring: A feminine approach to ethics and moral education.* Berkeley: University of California Press.

Oberti v. Clementon, 995 F. 2d 1204 (3rd Cir. 1993).

O'Brien, J., & O'Brien, C. (1996). Inclusion as a force for school renewal. In S. Stainback, & W. Stainback (Eds.), *Inclusion: A guide for educators* (pp. 29–48). Baltimore: Paul H. Brookes Publishing Co.

Olmedo, I. M. (1997). Challenging old assumptions: Preparing teachers for inner city schools. *Teaching & Teacher Education, 13,* 245–258.

Olney, M. (1995). Reading between the lines: A case study on facilitated communication. *Journal of the Association for People with Severe Handicaps, 32,* 109–113.

O'Neill, J. (1997, Spring). A place for all. *The Pennsylvania Journal on Positive Approaches, 1* (2). Retrieved from http://www.quuxuum.org/~greg/journal/o_neill.html

O'Neill, J. (1999). *Through the eyes of aliens: A book about autistic people.* London: Jessica Kingsley Publishers.

Onosko, J., & Jorgensen, C. (1998). Unit and lesson planning in the inclusive classroom: Maximizing learning opportunities for all students. In C. Jorgensen (Ed.), *Restructuring high schools for all students* (pp. 71–105). Baltimore: Paul H. Brookes Publishing Co.

Oyler, C. (2001). Democratic classrooms and accessible instruction. *Democracy & Education, 14,* 28–31.

Paley, V. (1979). *White teacher.* Cambridge, MA: Havard University Press.

Paley, V. (1990). *The boy who would be a helicopter.* Cambridge, MA: Harvard University Press.

Paley, V. (1992). *You can't say you can't play.* Cambridge: Harvard University Press.

Palinscar, A.S., & Brown, A.L. (1984). Reciprocal teaching of comprehension-fostering and comprehension-monitoring activities. *Cognition and Instruction, 1,* 117–175.

Parker, J. (1990). *Workshops for active learning.* Vancouver, British Columbia, Canada: JFP Productions.

Patterson, M. (1997). *Every body can learn.* Tucson, AZ: Zephyr.

Peterson, K. (2002). Positive or negative? *Journal of Staff Development, 23* (3). (Retrieved from http://www.nsdc.org/library/jsd/peterson233.html).

Peterson, M. (1996). Community learning in inclusive schools. In S. Stainback & W. Stainback (Eds.), *Inclusion: A guide for educators* (pp. 271–293). Baltimore: Paul H. Brookes Publishing Co.

Pearpoint, J., Forest, M., & O'Brien, J. (1996). MAPs, Circles of friends, and PATH: Powerful tools to help build caring communities. In S. Stainback, & W. Stainback (Eds.), *Inclusion: A guide for educators* (pp. 67–86). Baltimore: Paul H. Brookes Publishing Co.

Peek, F. (1996). *The real rain man: Kim Peek.* Salt Lake City, UT: Harkness.

Pickett, A.L., & Gerlach, K. (1997). Paraeducators in school settings: The future. In A.L. Pickett & K. Gerlach (Eds.), *Supervising paraeducators in school settings: A team approach* (pp. 263–267). Austin, TX: PRO-ED.

Pike, K., Compain, R., & Mumper, J. (1994). *New connections: An integrated approach to literacy.* New York: HarperCollins.

Pike, K., & Salend, S. J. (1995). *Authentic assessment strategies: Alternatives to norm-reference testing, 28,* 15–20.

Powers, M.D. (Ed.). (1989). *Children with autism: A parents' guide.* Bethesda, MD: Woodbine House.

Pritchett, P. (1993). Try something different. In J. Canfield & M.V. Hansen, *Chicken soup for the soul: 101 stories to open the heart and rekindle the spirit.* Deerfield Beach, FL: Health Communications Inc.

Prizant, B.M., & Duchan, J.F. (1981). The functions of immediate echolalia in autistic children. *Journal of Speech and Hearing Disorders, 46,* 241–249.

Pugach, M.C., & Wesson, C. (1995). Teachers' and students' views of team teaching of general education and learning-disabled students in two fifth-grade classes. *The Elementary School Journal, 95,* 279–295.

Putnam, J. (1997). *Cooperative learning in diverse classrooms.* Upper Saddle River, NJ: Prentice Hall.

Rainforth, B., & England, J. (1997). Collaboration for inclusion. *Education and Treatment of Children, 20*(1), 85–104.

Rainforth, B., & York-Barr, J. (1997). *Collaborative teamwork for students with severe disabilities: Integrating therapy and educational services* (2nd ed.). Baltimore: Paul H. Brookes Publishing Co.

Rajapatirana, C. (1998). On being mute. *Faciliated Communication Newsletter, 7*(1), 6.

Reed, D. (1996). *Paid for the privilege: Hearing the voices of autism.* Madison, WI: DRI Press.

Regal, R., Rooney, J., & Wandas, T. (1994). Facilitated communication: An experimental evaluation. *Journal of Autism and Developmental Disorders, 24,* 345–355.

Reid, R., & Maag, J. (1998). Functional assessment: A method for developing classroom-based accommodations for children with ADHD. *Reading and Writing Quarterly, 14,* 9–42.

Renzuli, J. (1995). Teachers as talent scouts. *Educational Leadership, 52,* 75–81.

Rethinking Schools. (2000). *Failing our kids: Why the testing craze won't fix our schools.* Milwaukee, WI: Author.

Robillard, A.R. (1997). Communication problems in the intensive care unit. In R. Hertz (Ed.), *Reflexivity and voice* (pp. 229–251). Beverly Hills, CA: Sage Publications.

Robinson, W. (1999). *Gentle giant.* Boston: Element.

Robinson, M. (1995). Todd. In A. Stehli (Ed.), *Dancing in the rain* (pp. 183–189). Westport, CT: The Georgiana Organization, Inc.

Rocco, S. (1996). Toward shared committment and shared responsiblity. In S.J. Meisels and E. Fenichel (Eds.), *New visions for the developmental assessment of infants and children.* Washington DC: Zero to Three/The National Center for Infants, Toddlers, and Families.

Roncker v. Walter, 700 Fd. 1058 (6th Cir. 1993).

Rosinski, D. (2002, June). Literacy on the autism spectrum. *The Spectrum.* Available from the Autism Society of Wisconsin.

Rossman, G.B. (1992). *State policy for integrating all students.* Thousand Oaks, CA: Corwin Press.

Rubin, S. (1998, December). *Castigating assumptions about mental retardation and low functioning autism.* Paper presented at The Association for Persons with Sever Handicaps National Conference, Seattle, WA.

Rubin, S. (1999, December). Independent typing. *Facilitated Communication Digest, (8)*1, 5–6.

Rubin, S., Biklen, D., Kasa-Hendrickson, C., Kluth, P., Cardinal, D.N., & Broderick, A. (2001). Independence, participation, and the meaning of intellectual ability. In *Disability & Society, 16*(3), 415–429. (http://www.tandf.co.uk)

Sabin, L., & Donnellan, A. (1993). A qualitative study of the process of facilitated communication. *The Journal of The Association for People with Severe Handicaps, 18,* 200–211.

Sacks, O. (1973) *Awakenings.* New York:Vintage Books.

Sacramento City School District v. Rachel H., 14 F.3D 1398 (9th Cir. 1994).

Sandler, L., Vandegrift, J.A., & VerBrugghen, C. (1995). From desert to garden: Reconnecting disconnected youth. *Educational Leadership, 52,* 14–16.

Sapon-Shevin, M. (1999). *Because we can change the world: A practical guide to building cooperative, inclusive classroom communities.* Needham Heights, MA: Allyn & Bacon.

Sapon-Shevin, M. (2001). Making inclusion visible: Honoring the process and the struggle. *Democracy & Education, 14,* 24–27.

Schine, J., & Halsted, A. (1997). Alienation or engagement? Service learning may be an answer. In S. Totten, & J. Pederson (Eds.), *Social issues and service at the middle level.* Needham Heights, MA: Allyn & Bacon.

Schmidt, J. (1998). Where there's a will there's a way: The successful inclusion of a child with autism. *B.C. Journal of Special Education, 21,* 45–63.

Schwarz, P., & Bettenhausen, D. (2000). You *can* teach an old dog new tricks. In R. Villa, & J. Thousand (Eds.). *Restructuring for caring and effective education: Piecing the puzzle together* (2nd ed., pp. 469–483). Baltimore: Paul H. Brookes Publishing Co.

Scott, J., Clark, C., & Brady, M. (2000). *Students with autism: Characteristics and instruction programming.* San Diego: Singular Publishing Group.

Selden, S. (1999). Inheriting Shame: The Story of Eugenics and Racism in America. New York: Teachers College Press.

Sellin, B. (1995). *I don't want to be inside me anymore: Messages from an autistic mind.* New York: Basic Books.

Shapiro-Barnard, S. (1998). Preparing the ground for what is to come: A rationale for inclusive high schools. In C. Jorgenson (Ed.), *Restructuring high schools for all students: Taking inclusion to the next level* (p. 12). Baltimore: Paul H. Brookes Publishing Co.

Sharan, Y., & Sharan, S. (1992). *Expanding cooperative learning through group investigation.* New York: Teachers College Press.

Shevin, M. (1987). *The language of us and them* [poem]. Unpublished manurscript.

Shevin, M. (1999, September). On being a communication ally. *Facilitated Communication Digest, 7(4),* 2–13.

Shevin, M., & Chadwick (Eds.) (2000). *Facilitated communication training standards.* Syracuse, NY: Facilitated Communication Institute.

Shevin, M., & Kalina, N. (1997, December). *On being a communication ally.* Presentation at the annual conference of The Association for Persons with Severe Handicaps, Boston.

Shore, S. (2001). *Beyond the wall: Personal experiences with autism and Asperger syndrome.* Shawnee Mission, KS: Autism Asperger Publishing Company.

Silberman, M. (1996). *Active learning: 101 strategies to teach any subject.* Needham Heights, MA: Allyn & Bacon.

Simon, K.G. (2002). The blue blood is bad, right? *Educational Leadership, 60*(1), 24–28.

Simon, E., Toll, D., & Whitehair, P. (1994). A naturalistic approach to the validation of facilitated communication. *Journal of Autism and Developmental Disabilities, 24,* 647–657.

Sinclair, J. (1992). Personal essays. In E. Schopler & F. Mesibov (Eds.), *High functioning individuals with autism.* New York: Plenum Press.

Sinclair, J. (1993). Don't mourn for us. *Our Voice, 1* (3), Autism Network International. Retrieved from http://ani.autistics.org/don't_mourn.html

Skinner, B.F. (1976). *About behaviorism.* New York: Random House.

Slavin, R. (1990). Cooperative learning: Theory, research, and practice. Englewood Cliffs, NJ: Prentice Hall.

Sleeter, C. E. (1986). Learning disabilities: The social construction of a special education category. *Exceptional Children, 53,* 46–54.

Smith, C., & Strick, L. (1997). *Learning disabilities: A to Z.* New York: Fireside.

Smith, H. (1999). To teachers and their students: The question is "How can we learn?," not "what are we going to do today?." In J.C. McDermott & L.B. Bird (Ed.), *Beyond silence: Listening for democracy* (pp. 37–38). Portsmouth, NH: Heineman.

Snow, K. (1998, October). To achieve inclusion, community, and freedom for people with disabilities, we must use person first language. *TASH Newsletter, 24*(10).

Stainback, S. (2000). If I could dream: Reflections on the future of education. In R.A. Villa & J. S. Thousand (Eds.), *Restructuring for caring and effective education: Piecing the puzzle together* (2nd ed., pp. 503–512). Baltimore: Paul H. Brookes Publishing Co.

Stallworth, B.J. (1998). Practicing what we teach. *Educational Leadership 55,* 77–79.

Staub, D. (1998). *Delicate threads: Friendships between children with and without special needs in incluisve schools.* Bethesda, MD: Woodbine House.

Stehli, A. (1991). *The sound of a miracle.* New York: Avon Books.

Stieber, W. (1999). *Teaming for improvement: Building business profits.* Bookpartners.

Stokes, S. *Increasing expressive skills for verbal children with autism.* Written by Susan Stokes under a contract with CESA 7 and funded by a discretionary grant from the Wisconsin Department of Public Instruction. Retrieved 1/31/03 from http://www.cesa7.k12.wi. us/sped/autism/verbal/verbal11.html.

Stone, O. (Director). *Platoon* [Motion Picture]. (1986). United States: MGM Studios.

Strully, J., & Strully, C. (1996). Friendships as an educational goal: What have we learned and where are we headed? In S. Stainback & W. Stainback (Eds.), *Inclusion: A guide for educators* (pp. 141–154). Baltimore: Paul H. Brookes Publishing Co.

Szempruch, J., & Jacobson, J. (1993). Evaluating facilitated communication of people with developmental disabilities. *Research in Developmental Disabilities, 14,* 253–264.

Tavalaro, J., & Tayson, R. (1997). *Look up for yes.* New York: Kondansha International.

Taylor, D., & Dorsey-Gaines, C. (1988). *Growing up literate: Learning from inner-city families.* Portsmouth, NH: Heinemann.

Thousand, J., Nevin, A., & McNeil, M. (2000). Achieving social justice through education for responsibility. In R.A. Villa & J.S. Thousand (Eds.), *Restructuring for caring and effective education: Piecing the puzzle together* (2nd ed., pp. 137–165). Baltimore: Paul H. Brookes Publishing Co.

Thousand, J., & Villa, R. (2000). Collaborative teaming: A powerful tool in school restructuring. In R. Villa, & J. Thousand (Eds.), *Restructuring for caring and effective education: Piecing the puzzle together* (2nd ed., pp. 254–291). Baltimore: Paul H. Brookes Publishing Co.

Tomlinson, C. (1995). *How to differentiate instruction in a mixed-ability classroom.* Alexandria, VA: Association for Supervision and Curriculum Development.

Tomlinson, C. (1999). *The differentiated classroom: Responding to the needs of all learners.* Alexandria, VA: Association for Supervision and Curriculum Development.

Treacy, D. (1996, Spring). A meditation. *The Communicator, newsletter for the Autism National Committee, 7*(1).

Trump, G., & Hange, J. (1996). *Teacher perceptions of and strategies for inclusion: A regional summary of focus group interview findings.* Charleston, WV: Appalachia Education Laboratory (ERIC Document Reproduction Service No. ED 397 576)

Udvari-Solner, A. (1995). A process for adapting curriculum in inclusive classrooms. In R. Villa, & J. Thousand (Eds.), *Creating an Inclusive School* (pp. 110–124). Baltimore: Paul H. Brookes Publishing Co.

Udvari-Solner, A. (1996). Examining teacher thinking: Constructing a process to design curricular adaptations. *Remedial and Special Education, 17,* 245–254.

Udvari-Solner, A. (1997). Inclusive education. In C.A. Grant, & G. Ladson-Billings (Eds.), *Dictionary of multicultural education* (pp. 141–144). Phoenix, AZ: Oryx Press.

Udvari-Solner, A., & Keyes, M. (2000). Chronicles of administrative leadership toward inclusive reform. In R. Villa, & J. Thousand (Eds.), *Restructuring for caring and effective edu-*

cation: Piecing the puzzle together (pp. 428–452). Baltimore: Paul H. Brookes Publishing Co.

Valencia, S. (1990). A portfolio approach to classroom reading assessment: The why, whats, and hows. *The Reading Teacher, 43,* 338–340.

Van der Klift, E., & Kunc, N. (1994). Beyond benevolence: Friendship and the politics of help. In J.S. Thousand, R.A. Villa, & A.I. Nevin (Eds.), *Creativity and collaborative learning: A practical guide to empowering students and teachers* (2nd ed., pp. 391–401). Baltimore: Paul H. Brookes Publishing Co.

van Dyke, R., Stallings, M. A., & Colley, K. (1995).How to build an inclusive school community: A success story.*Phi Delta Kappan, 76* (6), 475–479.

Vargo, R., & Vargo, J. (2000). In the mainstream: A confirmation experience. In R. Villa, & J. Thousand (Eds.), *Restructuring for caring and effective education* (pp. 242–248) Baltimore: Paul H. Brookes Publishing Co.

Vasquez, C. (1995). Failure to confirm the word-retrieval problem hypothesis in facilitated communication. *Journal of Autism and Developmental Disorders, 25,* 597–610.

Villa, R.A., & Thousand, J.S. (1990). Administrative supports to promote inclusive schooling. In W.C. Stainback, & S.B. Stainback (Eds.), *Support networks for inclusive schooling: Interdependent integated education* (pp. 210–218). Baltimore: Paul H. Brookes Publishing Co.

Villa, R.A., & Thousand, J. (Eds.). (2000). *Restructuring for caring and effective education: Piecing the puzzle together* (2nd ed.). Baltimore: Paul H. Brookes Publishing Co.

Villa, R. Thousand, J., Nevin, A., & Malgeri, C. (1996). Instilling collaboration to inclusive schooling as a way of doing business in public schools. *Remedial and Special Education, 17,* 169–181.

Waites, J., & Swinbourne, H. (2002). *Smiling at shadows: A mother's journey raising an autistic child.* Berkeley, CA: Ulysses.

Walker, A. (1982). *The color purple.* New York: Pocketbooks.

Walther-Thomas, C.S. (1997). Co-teaching experiences: The benefits and problems that teachers and principals report over time. *Journal of Learning Disabilities, 30,* 395–407.

Walther-Thomas, C., Korinek, L., McLaughlin, V., & Williams, B.T. (2000). *Collaboration for inclusive education: Developing successful programs.* Needham Heights, MA: Allyn & Bacon.

Waterhouse, S. (2000). *A positive approach to autism.* London: Jessica Kingsley Publishers.

Weatherbee, I. (1999, March). The view from Huntington College. *Facilitated Communication Digest, 7*(2), 2–6.

Webb, T. (Director). (1995). *A is for autism* [Film]. (Available from National Autistic Society, 393 City Road, London EC1V 1NE, 44 Tel:44–171–833–2299.)

Weiss, N. (1999). It may be non-aversive, but is it non-coercive?: The ethics of behavior change. *TASH Newsletter, 25*(11), 20–22, 27.

Weiss, M., Wagner, S., & Bauman, M. (1996). A validated case study of facilitated communication. *Mental Retardation, 34,* 220–229.

Weiss, M., & Wagner, S. (1997). Emerging validation of facilitated communication: New findings about old assumptions. In D. Biklen & D. Cardinal (Eds.), *Contested words, contested science: Unraveling the facilitated communication controversy* (pp. 135–156). New York: Teachers College Press.

Wheelock, A. (1992). Crossing the tracks: How "untracking" can save America's schools. New York: The New Press.

Wilhelm, J.D. (2001). *Improving comprehension with think-aloud strategies.* New York: Scholastic.

Willey, L.H. (1999). *Pretending to be normal: Living with Asperger's syndrome.* London: Jessica Kingsley Publishers.

Willey, L.H. (2001). *Asperger syndrome in the family: Redefining normal.* London: Jessica Kingsley Publishers.

Williams, D. (1992). *Nobody nowhere: The extraordinary biography of an autistic.* New York: Avon Books.

Williams, D. (1996). *Autism: An inside-out approach.* London: Jessica Kingsley Publishers.

Wheelock, A. (1992). *Crossing the tracks: How "untracking" can save America's schools.* New York: The New Press.

Winn, J., & Blanton, L. (1997). The call for collaboration in teacher education. In L. Blanton, C. Griffin, J. Winn, & M. Pugach (Eds.), *Teacher education in transition* (pp. 1–17). Denver, CO: Love Publishing Company.

Williams, D. (1998). *Autism and sensing: The unlost instinct.* London: Jessica Kingsley Publishers.

Winebrenner, S., & Espleland, P. (1996). *Teaching kids with learning difficulties in the regular classroom: Strategies and techniques every teacher can use to challenge and motivate struggling students.* Minneapolis, MN: Free Spirit Publishing.

Winner, E. (1996). *Gifted children: Myths and realities.* New York: Basic Books.

Yell, M. (1995). The law and inclusion: Analysis and commentary. *Preventing School Failure, 39*(2), 45–49.

Yoder, D. I., Retish, E., & Wade, R. (1996). Service learning: Meeting student and community needs. *Teaching Exceptional Children, 28*, 14–18.

BOOKS ON AUTISM WRITTEN BY PEOPLE WITH AUTISM AND ASPERGER'S SYNDROME

Barron, J. & Barron, S. (1992). *There's a boy in here.* New York: Simon & Schuster.

Blackman, L. (1999). *Lucy's story: Autism and other adventures.* Brisbane, Australia: Book in Hand.

Gerland, G. (1997). *Finding out about Asperger syndrome, high functioning autism and PDD.* London: Jessica Kingsley Publishers.

Gerland, G. (1997). *A real person: Life on the outside.* Souvenir Press, London, UK.

Grandin, T. (1995). *Thinking in pictures.* New York: Vintage Books.

Grandin, T. & Scariano, M. (1986). *Emergence: Labeled autistic.* Navato, CA: Arena Press.

Hall, K. (2001). *Asperger syndrome, the universe and everything.* London, PA: Jessica Kingsley.

Jackson, L. (2002). *Freaks, geeks, and Asperger syndrome: A user guide to adolescence.* London, PA: Jessica Kingsley.

Lawson, W. (1998). *Life behind glass.* London, PA: Jessica Kingsley.

Mukhopadhyay, T. R. (2000). *Beyond the silence.* London: National Autistic Society.

O'Neill, J.L. (1999). *Through the eyes of aliens: A book about autistic people.* London: Jessica Kingsley Publishers.

Sellin, B. (1995). *I don't want to be inside me anymore.* New York: Basic Books.

Shore, S. (2001). *Beyond the wall.* Shawnee Mission, KS: Autism Asperger Publishing.

Willey, L.H. (1999). *Pretending to be normal.* London: Jessica Kingsley Publishers.

Willey, L.H. (2001). *Asperger syndrome in the family: Redefining normal.* London: Jessica Kingsley Publishers.

Williams, D. (1992). *Nobody nowhere: The extraordinary biography of an autistic.* New York: Avon.

Williams, D. (1994). *Somebody, somewhere: Breaking free from the world of autism.* New York: Times Books.

Williams, D. (1996). *Like color to the blind: Soul searching & soul finding.* New York: Times Books.

Williams, D. (1998). *Autism and sensing: The unlost instinct.* London: Jessica Kingsley Publishers.

Index